# The Flying Years

Richard Boult

Merlin Massara Publishing

First published in Great Britain by Merlin Massara Publishing in 2005

ISBN 0954390008

Typeset by Hope Services (Abingdon) Ltd.,
Printed on acid-free paper in Malta at Progress Press Ltd.

Published By:
Merlin Massara Publishing
17 Tovey Close
London Colney
Hertfordshire
AL2 1LF

## Dedication

This book is dedicated to the memory of:–

Jimmy Aitken
David Blucke
Jeremy Hall
Terry McGrath
Norman Savory
Neil Thornton
Mike Withey

—and some of the others who did not come back.

\*   \*   \*

# Contents

# Contents

# Contents

# *Foreword*

*by* Air Vice-Marshal P A Latham CB AFC RAF

Richard Boult, known from his earliest days in the RAF as Bill, began his career in 1950, and ended it, like many other very able Squadron Leaders, with compulsory redundancy during the rank restructuring in the mid 1970s. His service was divided almost equally between flying and administration.

He flew fast jets in both No 63 and No 26 Day Fighter Squadrons and later became a test pilot at Boscombe Down where he was amongst the first RAF pilots to fly the English Electric Lightning. Following a year at Staff College he completed twelve years in various ground appointments the earliest of which brought him face to face with the need to improve leadership skills within the RAF.

As the Station Administration Officer and Deputy Station Commander of RAF Gan in the Maldive Islands he served in a senior position in one of the few remaining remote outposts of the RAF. Later, as the Assistant Defence Adviser to the British High Commission in Singapore, he took part in organising the withdrawal of the British military presence from South East Asia.

A year or so after returning to Britain in 1970 he commanded a squadron at the Officer Cadet Training Unit at RAF Henlow. It was here that he found himself in a position to influence the leadership training which he believed the RAF needed to improve. The insight into the techniques of such training which he acquired and his skill in using them led to a very successful civilian career.

His passion for skiing enabled him to take a leading part in the promotion of this adventurous sport within the RAF. It is through fostering such activities that the Services maintain the spirit of endeavour and excitement so necessary during times of peace.

The book contains a detailed and very readable account of what post war RAF training and service was really like. There is a fascinating description of life on the remote island of Gan just before we left South East Asia and, while it contains several descriptions of insensitive leadership throughout its narrative, it finishes with a constructive criticism of leadership training in the RAF and the author's views on how it could be improved.

For those readers with a desire to know more about the detail of day to day life for a young fighter pilot it is invaluable. For those who know it intimately from their own experience it is a happy reminder of their own young days and will resurrect memories for so long dormant. It is book with a tale to tell and a source of sound opinions and shared memories.

Peter Latham                                                    October 2005

# *Preface*

This is the story of my time in the Royal Air Force and during a shorter second career. The story is in two parts. During the first part of the story, which is mainly about flying, I joined the RAF, trained as an officer and as a pilot at the Royal Air Force College, Cranwell, and then learned to fly jets. I served two tours on front-line fighter squadrons before reaching the high point of my flying career. This was my three years as a development test pilot at the Aeroplane and Armament Experimental Establishment, Boscombe Down.

During the second part, my years on the ground, there were two high points. The first was my tour as a Squadron Commander at the Officer Cadet Training Unit, the second, after I had left the service, was as a Management Adviser with The Industrial Society.

My first two years on a front line fighter squadron fell into what has become in many ways a forgotten era. The allied fighter aeroplanes of the Second World War have passed into history and into legend. These were firstly the Hurricanes and Spitfires of the Battle of Britain and then the Tempests, Typhoons and Mustangs which defeated the Luftwaffe and established air supremacy over the ground battles. Equally the first aeroplanes capable of passing the speed of sound and depositing sonic booms—initially Yeager's rocket powered Bell X1 and then the jet-propelled, swept-wing fighters, the Hunters, Swifts and the North American Sabres also caught the popular imagination and are still well remembered. We flew Meteors. Although they were one of the first jet-propelled aeroplanes in the world to enter squadron service, and the Meteor was for a time holder of the World Air Speed Record, they were not supersonic and so have been eclipsed by their successors. However to us who flew them they remain memorable and an account of the techniques and drills of those days may be of some interest. Similarly, the work of the Officer Cadet Training Unit had, I believe, relevance far wider than just to the RAF or to the military and so may be of interest too.

Strictly my flying years were from the start of my Initial Flying Training on the Percival Prentice in 1951 until the end of my tour at

Boscombe Down, mainly on the English Electric Lightning in 1963, just thirteen years. But from my arrival at Cranwell to my final retirement all the years seem to have flown by, so for that reason too they are all included in this account.

Richard Boult                                                    September 2005
Beech Cottage
Denham

# *Acknowledgements*

My thanks are due to Eric Jenkins, Chris Phillips, Peter Rose and Peter Terrell for reading the manuscript and making many helpful suggestions, but in particular to Gil Massara for his constant encouragement and support as we prepared this book for publication. Without his help it would never have seen the light of day.

Richard Boult

The publishers are grateful to Alison Renshaw for editorial and proof-reading help. Also to Blackstar Studios and Amanda Massara for diagram and photograph restoration work.

# The Royal Air Force College

## R A F Cranwell

### PROLOGUE

IT IS NO longer quite dark as the grey, still dawn creeps over the sleeping meadows and villages of Cambridgeshire. But even at this hour six Meteor single-seat jet fighters stand parked on the Operational Readiness Platform beside the runway threshold. I can just see the other pilots' helmets inside their closed cockpit canopies but our groundcrew are invisible, huddled together for warmth inside the nearby Landrover. A telephone wire, the telebrief, is plugged into the back of each aeroplane and we are listening to the well known voice of Bill Elton in the Waterbeach Station Operations Room trying to discover from Sector if they have any indication of when they might have some trade for us. "Trade" for us as interceptors is one of the many brief jargon words and phrases we used on the R/T, the radio telephone, which linked us in the air to each other and to our ground controllers. We slip into its use without thinking, and sometimes still do, to the puzzlement of our non-aircrew friends.

The year is 1954, just nine years after the end of the Second World War, and it is only a NATO exercise that we are engaged in. But one day the Cold War might suddenly warm up and then we would be waiting for real to be scrambled, to climb up over the east coast and to be

1

vectored on to bombers coming in from the continent of Europe, over the Dutch Islands and across the North Sea. If we do get any trade today it will be Canberra bombers from various RAF bases in Germany—and they will not have red stars painted on their sides—but all the same we want to prove to ourselves that the whole interception system works as intended.

Suddenly the tone of Bill's voice changes and he says, "OK Sector, I got that," and then, "Red and Blue sections—scramble!" John and I are the first pair, Red Section, and before Bill has finished speaking we have pressed our engine start buttons. One of the joys of jet engines is that there is no warming up, you press the tits, open the throttles and you're off. As our engines light and wind up Bill is passing us a vector, a course, to steer after take off and saying, "Make angels three-five." I look across at John, he gives me a thumbs up and as one we push forward the throttles and move on to the runway. It is a bit lighter now and the runway lights look quite dim as they go flashing past and I raise the nose.

We're airborne, wheels up, start a slow turn to port and almost before I've done so John's Meteor is in formation, perched just eight feet from my starboard wing tip. Before we have levelled the wings and rolled out on to a compass heading of east we are into the low stratus cloud and I am on instruments. It seems even darker than it was on the ground and we hold our heading and best airspeed for climbing as the altimeter winds up past ten, fifteen and twenty thousand feet. It is only a few minutes since we got airborne and we are already two-thirds of the way to being level with the top of Mount Everest. We change radio channels, I check in with the Sector controller and he gives us a small heading change.

Twenty-four thousand feet on the clock and the cloud suddenly lightens. A moment later and we are in the clear and the cloud blanket below us stretches away in all directions, grey and tinged with blue and darker streaks as at this height the sun is still well below the horizon. There, forty miles to the east, is our trade. At about 40,000 ft the Canberras are already catching the first rays from the rising sun and they are trailing, creating dense gleaming contrails, condensation trails, which because we are below them seem to spread out across the blue sky like the Prince of Wales' feathers or an open fan. And they are not white but vivid crimson pink. It is a quite unforgettable sight of great beauty but it only lasts a few minutes. As the sun climbs the approaching trails change to a more pastel shade of pink and then to cream and to white. We make our interception, call for a course to steer to base and start our recovery. Back on the ground I can see that John is grinning even before he takes off his helmet and oxygen mask. We are both almost speechless, "Did you ever see anything like that!" we both say. It was a sight that we will never forget. It seems incredible that it is part of a job that I actually get paid to do, the job I have arrived at after a journey which I embarked on while I was still at school.

*   *   *

My father came from an old Norfolk family who had for many generations farmed near North Walsham, north of Norwich. His first marriage had been to Nell Waller, whose family was in fact mentioned in Burke's Irish Peerage, and who traced their descent to Earl de Warrenne. There were two sons, my half-brothers Teddy and Norman, and all my father's stories of his earlier life were of living with the boys in a caravan on the edge of Loch Dearg, near Nenagh in County Tipperary. Throughout my early life, wherever we lived, he was always liable to refer to the nearest town as Norwich, or perhaps Nenagh.

My mother came from a south London family, the Huntleys. She was the eldest of four children. There was my Auntie Vi and uncles Tony and Dick. Auntie Vi married Harry French, a career civil servant, who rose high in the service to become Sir Henry French and Auntie Vi, to her great amusement, became Lady French. She was probably my favourite relation, a kind and gracious person.

During my childhood we had lived in various parts of the home counties but my education had been disrupted by the war. When my parents saw that the south coast was not a good place to be living with young children, we had evacuated from Eastbourne back to the Thames Valley and then the second prep. school I joined was itself forced to move when its temporary home was commandeered by the RAF. However, I had enjoyed five years at Shrewsbury, where I had learned to appreciate the Shropshire Hills and, during a summer camp, the mountains of Scotland. Five foot eleven tall and rather thin, I was not a natural games player although I managed to gain my House Rowing Colours and, except in science for which I had a natural

3

aptitude, was not academically distinguished. I progressed as far as the Maths Lower Sixth and in my last year I was a House Monitor.

Ever since I can remember it had been assumed, especially by my father, that I would follow my half-brother, Norman, into the Royal Air Force. Norman, eighteen years older than me, had belonged to the old pre-war era flying biplanes around Iraq and the Canal Zone and had had one or two dicey moments. He used to say that they spoilt half the fun of flying when they put radios in aeroplanes. He had spent most of the Second World War in the Rhodesian Air Training Group, but had come home and got on to operational flying in time for the second front in Normandy and had won a DFC for bringing home a badly damaged Mitchell B25 from a bombing raid over Caen. However he was not a communicative person and sadly we were never close.

The only other career I had considered was engineering. On a number of occasions when Dad and I had been in London he had said, "Let's go and drop in on my old friend Jim Waller, he's an engineer, you'll find him very interesting." But his old friend never happened to be in his office when we called and so in fact I never did meet him. I am not sure anyway that it would have changed my mind. During my time at Shrewsbury School I had come to look upon a future in the RAF as a natural progression. At Shrewsbury everyone joined the "corps" and for 90% this meant the army section. There was a regular weekly parade, everyone took Cert. A, and on Field Days had hugely enjoyable and very muddy days clambering over the Shropshire hills and firing off blank ammunition. To want to drop out of such normal macho activities was to invite derision. However, I took the plunge and joined the Air Training Corps.

The Section was commanded by Mr Hagger, an able and effective maths master. Arnold Hagger had enjoyed a distinguished career in the RAF as a navigator, culminating in being one of the navigators chosen to take part in a series of long range flights over the North Polar regions, pioneering navigation techniques in the high latitudes where the magnetic compass cannot be relied on.

Brilliant navigator and excellent maths teacher which he was, he was not really cut out to command a school Air Section. One day the section parade was to be inspected by a visiting Group Captain. Mr Hagger had come into morning lessons wearing a normal pale blue RAF shirt with black shoes, grey flannels and sports jacket. Hence to change into uniform for the parade Mr Hagger only had to change from his jacket and trousers into uniform ones, and collect his hat. Unfortunately, having failed to look in a mirror, he forgot to change his tie. He brought us smartly to attention and advanced smiling confidently to meet the Group Captain, his RAF uniform immaculate in every respect except for a bright blue and white chequered tie which rather spoilt the effect.

We spent our Field Days at Shawbury, the local RAF station, and it was from there that I had my first flight—in an Anson. It was a very hazy day and although I took photographs of the Wrekin they were a failure and the flight was in no way memorable. However, during the spring term of 1950 I went down to London to sit the Civil Service exams in a dusty, anonymous office building behind the Methodist Central Hall.

Having passed the first hurdle it was on to Hornchurch. The RAF station which had played its part in the Battle of Britain now housed the Aircrew Selection Centre where one went to 'put square pegs in round holes' or more precisely to carry out the battery of tests devised to weed out those without the necessary hand-eye co-ordination needed to be a pilot. I am sure that since those days everything has been computerised, but then the most memorable test was to be seated before a large opaque glass screen on which a light spot was projected from behind. Some device caused this spot to wander and in addition you could control it by moving a control column or 'joystick.' The test was to counteract the random movements of the light spot to keep it within the small circle in the centre of the screen. At the same time a red or green light periodically flashed on beside the screen and these could be cancelled by moving fore or aft a small lever similar to an aeroplane throttle control at your left hand. I have heard that for all its simplicity this was a very effective indicator of pilot ability. It was extraordinary what a quantity of adrenalin this simple gadget could generate. Within a few minutes one was sweating freely.

As I left the train at Hornchurch station, there on the platform heading for the exit was obviously another candidate. Ian Brettell from Cheltenham College and I went through the aircrew selection process together and met up again at Ramridge House near Andover for the officer selection week. Ramridge House was the RAF's equivalent of the WOSB, the army War Office Selection Board. Here we all wore denim overalls to conceal any differences of background and were identified in our working groups by just a number. By the end of the week I was used to being addressed as "Two." We took part in practical outdoor exercises with planks and empty oil-drums to assess how well we could organise a team and in discussion groups to see if we could state a sensible view and defend it against criticism. Which view you held was of no great importance, what mattered was whether you became flustered or abusive or simply caved in when challenged. I often found myself arguing with Ian, who happened to be in the same group, about whatever topic the Directing Staff had put to us. Later we became good friends and we have agreed that at Ramridge House we each found the other acutely irritating and would promptly contradict whatever they had said to the extent that no-one else in the group could get a word in edgeways. I went back to school and before the end of term a telegram arrived from my father to say that I had been accepted.

Thus, a few weeks later I found myself gazing out of the window of a little rural train as it puffed its way across the open Lincolnshire landscape towards the sleepy market town of Sleaford. It was a grey, early spring day, of April showers and the occasional rumble of thunder. I was one of the four young men in the carriage all bound for the Royal Air Force College, visible for miles around among the fields and woods of the Lincolnshire wolds. We left the train at Sleaford, as our joining instructions had told us to do, and were shepherded into a 3-ton truck for the five mile drive, through Cranwell village and into the RAF station. The truck did not turn in to the formal gates which opened on to the wide sweep of grass and the twin drives leading up to the imposing main college building. Three hundred yards further on the truck turned left, by a row of small conifers, down past some undistinguished single storey brick and pre-fab huts and pulled up outside a two storey brick-built barrack block. The building was surrounded by not very neat grass and narrow concrete paths. This was Block 77, and was to be our home for the next eight months. Sergeant Ward had lists of our names and I was allocated to C Squadron. Our barrack room was on the right at the top of the stairs. I dumped my suitcase on the iron bed. I had arrived.

Forty of us arrived at Cranwell on 26th April 1950 as No 57 Entry. We soon found that our loyalties and circle of friends extended in two directions. We, the April intake, were 57 Entry but we were also

6

members of A, B or C Squadrons. We were distinguished by coloured tapes on our cadets' white shoulder epaulettes, red for A Squadron, yellow for B and blue for us. In each squadron the Senior Entry, who when we arrived were No 50 Entry, provided the Under Officer and three Flight Cadet Sergeants. To us ex-public schoolboys they were the Head of House and the House Prefects. The two Junior Entries, 56 and ourselves, were housed in Block 77; later for one term we would occupy Daedelus House and only at the start of our fourth term would we move up to the main college building. At present we were Cadets; when we got to the college itself we would become Flight Cadets. To those of us who came from boarding schools I suspect that living in a large dormitory and to a strict time-table was much less of a shock than to those who had never lived way from home. Our lives were controlled almost to the minute by Sergeant Ward. Tom Ward was meant to be a terror and his job was to lick us into shape in the way of the traditional drill sergeant portrayed in so many films, but although he looked the part he was really far too nice a man for the job. One could almost see him gearing himself up to be fierce, but his natural humour and kindness constantly let him down.

He was assisted by a Corporal Tiny, an unfortunate name, as he was a little, short man and hence the butt of every joke around. But Tom Ward at least sounded the part. An exchange down the corridor in the block one evening went as follows,

"Corporal Tiny!"

"Yes, Sergeant."

"Where's the photies?"

"Wot photos, Sergeant?"

"The photies wot was took!"

Three members of No 57 Entry were Cadets 'ives, 'arris and 'arper. We also had two Pakistanis, actually Cadets Sadruddin and Sahibzada. For Tom Ward they became "Strubid-zaydi" and "the other one"!

We took an oath of allegiance to the sovereign, to "King George, his heirs and successors." We got issued with uniforms, but for some of us these needed tailoring and so we marched around for a few days in a curious mixture of some items of uniform and perhaps a civilian sports jacket. This seemed particularly to infuriate one of the other drill instructors, a Flight Sergeant Masters, and I discovered the disadvantage of a surname which lent itself to startling and explosive delivery. I lost count of the number of times my wandering attention was recalled by "Mr BOULT, sir!" We attended lectures, we drilled on the parade ground and we spent time in the workshops getting a very brief insight into the world of engineering.

We were given military haircuts, we learned to polish our boots and to march. We went on the range and shot with rifles and Bren guns. We learned to arrange our kit layouts in the lockers beside our beds and to make up our beds neatly with blanket-sticks to ensure the stack of blanket, sheet, blanket, sheet, and blanket were exactly upright and square. These were the areas where the ex-airmen excelled. We turned to them for advice and for the many old soldiers' tricks which make life so much simpler. We never walked about the barrack-room without using floor-pads, folded squares of blanket, one for each foot, which one stood on and skated about on to preserve the glossy shine of the wooden floor.

If it all sounds unbelievable, it didn't at the time seem any more irksome or outrageous than these days having to buy a ticket for a car-park or to queue for a bus. It was just the way of life and we realised, even if we could not easily have put it into words, that if we were going to live in and contribute to a disciplined fighting force we all had to learn to conform, to obey, to be self-disciplined and to be punctual. We were learning to live according to laid down standards. What the standards were was not really the point; learning to live by them, eventually without effort, almost without conscious thought, that was the point. Also, we quickly discovered that making the effort to be punctual oneself was a small price to pay when you found that you could rely on everyone else around turning up on time too.

We very quickly got to know each other, our fellow cadets, our foibles and quirks, those who had a sense of humour and those who did not. Where we could not remember names we invented nick-names. Everyone came in for their turn of leg-pulling. One soon learned to cope. George Coatesworth, a Yorkshireman, had his name repeatedly mispronounced by Sergeant Ward as Coatesworthy. George would loudly complain which always led to much leg-pulling, in mock Yorkshire, by the rest of us. Many years later, after he had left the RAF, George told us that he had at one time started a company and had called it Worthy Engineering, so in fact he had the last laugh. Chris Doggett became our resident humorist and leg-puller. A particular friend of Chris' became at the same time another of his favourite victims. Ray Martin was a large, amiable, rugby-playing Ulster-man, for whom Chris invented the extraordinary name of Roots Mulloy, the Great Gilhooley. Later, when we moved up into the main College and dined at long tables, Chris would seat himself opposite Ray and throughout dinner, with his thumb and forefinger would simulate a bow-legged man walking across the table, to a running commentary in undertone, interrupting whatever Ray was saying, of "Ah, 'tis the Great Gilhooley himself, he's a broth of a bhoy from the bogs, isn't he now!" and so on. A sudden crash and the cutlery leaping a foot in the air would signal that Ray had finally lost patience and lashed out with his boot at his tormentor, and missed. It was Roots Mulloy, or rather Ray Martin, who invented the name which stuck with me for the rest of my time in the RAF. On some occasion he greeted me with, "Hey you, Boult, Boult, what's your name, Billy Boult." I had never been too keen on my own first name, and certainly not Dicky, which seemed to be the only available alternative, so I was happy to settle for Billy Boult and it stuck.

We were allotted our bed-spaces in alphabetical order and so mine was between "Babe" Birchall and Nobby Clarke. Birchall was not cut out for the life and was soon withdrawn from training. Nobby was an ex-airman, 6ft 3ins, and a master of all the labour-saving tricks which he was cheerfully eager to share with a clueless ex-schoolboy. Les Davis, an ex-PTI Sergeant had initially a marked Geordie accent—which he quickly lost. He soon emerged as one of the leading characters of the Entry. John Dunn, quietly dignified and of precise speech, was soon nicknamed The Vicar or The Brethren. He would have sounded exactly right in some cathedral pulpit. Below Ray Martin in alphabetical order came Gerry Muncaster, "Gunga Din" Sahibzada and Mike Withey, but they were across the corridor in ABC Room with the end-of-the-alphabet men of 56 Entry.

On the other side of our C Squadron room were the bed spaces for No 56 Entry. At our end of the room were Dennis Atherley, Colin Benson, Derek Birley, David Blucke, Ron Dick, Roger Forrest and John Heard. Probably destined in due course to have reached very senior rank was David Blucke, a most attractive, quietly spoken character, but later, as a very young Group Captain, he was sadly to kill himself in a Phantom. Johnny Heard was to have an amazing escape in a Meteor while a member of No 64 Squadron aerobatic team. They were practising their display which concluded with a downward "bomb burst." They came over the top of the loop, down into the vertical and the leader left the "Break" call a fraction late. John, as No 5 in the formation, had to roll through almost 180° before pulling out of his dive. He only just made it, hitting the ground a glancing blow but miraculously the aeroplane stayed in one piece and there, a mile straight ahead of him, was the runway of a disused airfield. He dumped his wheels and put the aeroplane safely onto the ground, uninjured—but slightly breathless.

D G "Charlie" Slade was the character and humorist of 56 Entry. In due course when 56 became the Senior Entry I happened to be at some meeting of the current Junior Entries on the evening when up in the main college building the cadet promotions had been announced. Some Junior Entries approached me and asked if I had heard who was to be our C Squadron Under Officer. "Yes," I said, "It's Flight Cadet Slade." Blank looks all round. I repeated it, "Flight Cadet Slade, Charlie Slade." "Oh, Charlie! Well that's marvellous!" It summed him up exactly, that his popular nick-name was much better know around the College than his surname.

During our time in Junior Entries our only introduction to flying was a weekly ride in an Anson. We did some superficial map reading and navigation but to ex-Boy Scouts it was very basic. We were introduced again to the Dalton Computer which some of us had met in the ATC. There was nothing electronic about it, it was a circular tin slide rule on which one plotted with a wax pencil the desired track and the forecast wind to discover the heading to fly. In a navigation test one question was "What is the Circle of Uncertainty?" Someone wrote down—"The Dalton Computer."

Cranwell lies fifteen miles south of Lincoln, five miles from the town of Sleaford on the Lincolnshire wolds. Sir Hugh Trenchard, founder of the Royal Air Force, is said to have had strong views that such a remote site was the best for his fledgeling service. Beyond the station perimeter pastoral farmland stretched to the horizon. The surrounding countryside certainly offered no big-city distractions, but there was a sprinkling of pleasant village pubs. One of the favourites was the Red Lion at Caythorpe. I acquired an old hand-change 250cc BSA motorcycle to get around them.

In January 1951 we moved up from Junior Entries to the main College and started to learn to fly. Our leaving Junior Entries coincided with Sergeant Ward's retirement from the RAF. We held a whip round and presented him with a silver cigarette lighter. He was very fierce and said it was completely against regulations but was clearly very pleased and appreciative.

The main college building, a landmark for miles around, is an elegant red brick and stone building. It has a domed clock tower and below the porch and main doors a flight of stone steps runs down to the wide gravel parade ground and the Orange, an almost circular area of grass, flanked by the twin drives sweeping down to the main gate. The central block of the college is flanked by symmetrical wings accommodating to the west A and B Squadrons and to the east C Squadron. The C Squadron wing was to be my home for the next two years as No 57 Entry moved up through the college to our planned graduation in December 1952. We now attended lectures on a more interesting range of subjects; among them were those on navigation by Squadron Leader "Crystal" Fountain, of meticulous pronunciation and droll sense of humour. "Navigation for long flights needs to be very accurate, you know. For example, the Atlantic is a big place and you may, say, have to navigate a Coastal Shackleton round a route that goes—from Base to Rockall, C*** all, F*** all, Base."

We spent considerable periods in the gymnasium. Less, I suspect, to improve our fitness than to develop our moral fibre, we were required to do backward somersaults into the swimming pool from the top board. Once you got the knack it was not difficult but poor Jack Hodgson of B Squadron never did and could always be relied on for a most spectacular splash. Each term there was an Inter-Squadron Gymnasium Competition. At once your particular friends in the Entry, who happened to be on other squadrons, became your deadly rivals.

There was also First Term Boxing. A vigorous argument raged over whether it was sensible to make potential pilots indulge in boxing, where one unlucky blow to the eye or ear could have ended a career. However, as long as Air Commodore George Beamish, ex-Ireland Rugby Inter-national and boxing enthusiast, remained Commandant, First Term Boxing remained on the curriculum. I was tall for my weight with a correspondingly long reach, so that when matched against the rather shorter Brian Huxley of A Squadron I was able to keep him out of range.

11

Each term there was also the Ferris Drill Competition. Not only were we assessed on our actual drill but the turnout of each cadet on parade was scrutinised in minute detail. The judges checked us from our gleaming white hat bands to our equally gleaming toe caps. Once the inspection was over the actual drill sequence seemed comparatively relaxed. The judges were from the staff of the RMA, the Royal Military Academy, at Sandhurst and in contrast to our simple blue uniforms, which apart from badges of rank would stay the same throughout our careers regardless of what part of the RAF we served in, those of the army officers looked to have come out of some Ruritanian Opera. Quite apart from officers wearing the kilts of the Highlander regiments and the tartan trews of the Lowlands others were others wearing dark blue frock coats, khaki or scarlet tunics or the dark green of the Rifles, and all with an amazing selection of hats. We had learned a bit about the history and customs of the RAF and of the other services and the different policies of the RAF and the army on uniforms was interesting.

The RAF had always rejected variations of uniforms or any official recognition of corps elites. Perhaps we reckoned we were all elite. The only exception was that during the Second World War the Pathfinders of Bomber Command wore a small golden eagle on their left breast pockets, and unofficially the fighter boys kept the top button of their tunics undone. In contrast the army thrived on variety. Every regiment had its own distinctive cap badge. Thus, for example, any young soldier who wore on his cap the red and white cockade of the Lancashire Fusiliers or a second badge on the back of his cap as a member of the Gloucestershire Regiment soon saw himself as a member of a family, his regiment, a family with its own traditions and history stretching back over many campaigns and many years. This was because the army, who would claim to specialise in understanding men and in how to help them to perform at the highest level, believed that when a young man found himself alone on the battlefield in a dangerous foxhole, cold, hungry and frightened, a feeling of belonging to his unique regiment, of being someone special, was helpful to him.

In a later lecture, an officer of the Brigade of Guards reminded us that the reason for the Glosters' second cap badge was that the regiment had twice in its history fought its way out of encirclement, of having been surrounded. He then added dryly, "You will no doubt observe, gentlemen, that this actually says rather more for their bravery than it does for their tactics." The Guards, of course, had always regarded themselves as the elite—their officers referred to themselves simply as "The Brigade."

However, where the army specialised in managing men and in leadership, we were on our way to becoming professional aviators. This difference in the priorities which the two services attached to the different roles of their officers was to be impressed on me strongly some years later.

Now that we had come up to the main college as Flight Cadets, flying was soon to become our daily occupation. The most interesting lectures of all were those by Squadron Leader "Flash" Button on aerodynamics. Here we studied the actual physics and the mechanics of flight, how the air flows over the wings in various configurations, how the wings generate lift, what happens at the stall, how the ailerons and elevators and the flaps and the rudder work Frieze ailerons, Fowler flaps, horn and mass balances, Handley Page slats. We were reminded of what Newton had said about moving bodies. The wags insisted that this was "What goes up must come down—except undercarriages." We learned of what Bernoulli said about air flowing through convergent/divergent nozzles, what Ernst Mach (hence Mach Number) said about the importance of the speed of sound, what causes wing flutter and auto-rotation (spinning) and the relative merits of thick or thin, swept or unswept wings. We learned about thickness/chord ratios, aspect ratios and dihedral, static and dynamic stability.

We learned, basically that aeroplanes are completely logical, that if they behave in some way there is a reason, that gremlins are just excuses for someone having forgotten to do something that they ought to have done or done something else that they ought not to have done! It is seldom with any other subject that a lecturer, explaining a bit of theory, can say, "Now when you next get airborne get your instructor to show you..." One of the problems with studying aerodynamics is that, unlike the waves created by ship, the air flowing past the aeroplane is invisible. Various means can be used to show how the air is behaving; wool tufts attached to the surface will stream in the direction of the airflow right next to the surface but the most striking demonstration is the smoke tunnel. In this thin filaments of smoke are created and allowed to flow past the wings or over a model aeroplane to reveal sometimes spectacular and most surprising patterns. I had been keen on physics at school but this was far better. Flying was physics come to life in a vivid and striking way. Flash Button had an attractive way of teaching, offering a proposition, allowing the class to start arguing about it, and only interjecting occasional comments until the logic of the situation crystallised out of our discussions.

Along with lectures and the daily drill parade we joined the Initial Flying Training Wing to learn to fly the simple Percival Prentice. Derived from the Proctor two-seater, the Prentice had a variable-pitch propeller but a fixed undercarriage, side by side seating for student and instructor and a third seat behind for a passenger. To relieve the numbers in the circuit at Cranwell itself, much of our early training, especially during the circuits and bumps stage, took place at Barkston Heath, five miles south of Cranwell or at Spitalgate, a grass airfield on top of the hill behind Grantham. This is where the Prentice's third seat proved its value. Two students would set off with their instructor, one flying dual and the other as passenger. The latter would be dumped at the runway controller's caravan at the satellite airfield until it was his turn. The Prentice was a good aeroplane as an initial trainer but it lacked personality. With its large fin and rudder and small engine cowling it looked under-powered. It was unkindly known as the clockwork mouse.

Much that is of interest in flying takes place in or near "the circuit." The circuit is an imaginary rectangle, the long side of which is the runway and its extensions at each end. We normally flew round this rectangle anti-clockwise. The long side opposite the runway is the Downwind Leg. As we will be planning to land against the wind, on the Downwind Leg we will be flying with the wind or—downwind. At the start of the downwind leg we call on the radio to the Local Air Traffic Controller "Downwind." It is their job to keep a check on who is in the circuit and where they are in order to warn others if necessary. As we pass opposite the threshold of the runway and approach the end of the downwind leg, we call "Finals," turn left on to the Base Leg, close the throttle and start our final descent towards our landing.

My instructor was Flight Lieutenant "Tug" Wilson and my co-student was Mike Withey. Together Mike and I learned straight and level flight, taxi-ing, the effects of the controls, climbing, descending, medium turns, taking off into wind, the approach and landing, and steep turns. We learned that the secret of smooth flying is the constant use of the trimmers. These are little tabs attached to the back, the

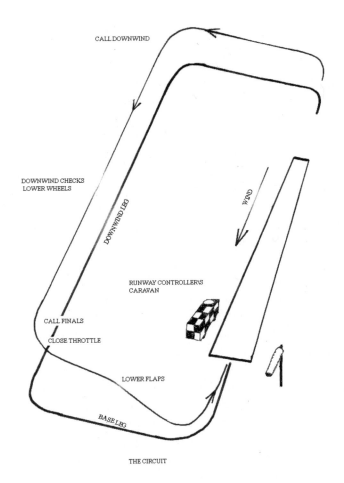

CALL DOWNWIND

DOWNWIND CHECKS
LOWER WHEELS

DOWNWIND LEG

WIND

RUNWAY CONTROLLER\S
CARAVAN

CALL FINALS

CLOSE THROTTLE

LOWER FLAPS

BASE LEG

THE CIRCUIT

trailing edge, of each flying control. They can be wound up or down and when properly adjusted hold the main control surface in the right position and so allow the aeroplane to be flown hands off. Greatly daring, we moved on to stalling and recovery, spinning and re- starting the engine in flight.

We learned the value of memorising lists of Vital Actions, one for Before Take Off, one for use on the downwind leg Before Landing. Later, when we would move on to fly aeroplanes with retractable undercarriages, the most important of the downwind checks would be "Undercarriage Down And Locked," so to get us into the right habit immediately we included in our downwind checks in the Prentice "Undercarriage Down And Riveted."

15

We flew more circuits and bumps. It had already become apparent to us that the landing is the critical stage of any flight and it was now impressed upon us that a good landing cannot be made from a badly judged approach. We learned to judge when the wind was not exactly down the line of the runway, so that we could adjust our heading on the downwind leg and so fly parallel to the runway. We learned to judge the point on Finals to close the throttle and the point on the Base Leg to lower the flaps and the point to start our turn into wind so that we straightened out exactly in line with the runway without needing an awkward s-turn at the last moment. We learned, most vital of all, as we came over the hedge, to judge where "the green turns to grass," to start the round-out so that we neither arrived on the ground with an undignified crunch before we expected, nor ballooned up again into the air to hang in suspended animation ten feet above the ground before our instructor either said resignedly, "Alright, go round again," or more urgently, "Oh, God, I've got it!" We learned, more subtly, just what a hash we could make of a manoeuvre before our instructor would grab the controls. He had, if possible, to let us handle our own minor mistakes or we wouldn't learn from them. He had to let the fault develop far enough for us to realise it was a fault. On the other hand he had a vested interest in not letting us break the aeroplane or both our necks. It was not surprising that instructors occasionally gave vent to outbursts of colourful language. Great competition developed as to who would be the first of the Entry to be sent solo.

There are a small number of experiences in life which can only be tasted once and one's first solo flight in an aeroplane ranks high among them. We signed our log books to the effect that we understood the fuel, brake and pneumatic systems of the Prentice and had successfully completed a Blindfold Cockpit Check. We certified that we had been instructed in the Action To Be Taken In The Event Of Fire In The Aircraft and on How To Abandon The Prentice In The Event Of An Emergency. Without wishing to be macabre the instructors well knew how important such bits of paper would be if there ever had to be a subsequent Court of Enquiry.

On 22nd February Mike Withey and I climbed into a Prentice with Tug and flew over to Spitalgate to start the now familiar routine of circuits and bumps. After my second circuit as we taxied back to the threshold Tug said casually, "Stop by the caravan, will you." He opened the hood, got out, hauled out his parachute and re-fastened the straps across his seat. "OK," he said, "Off you go, just one circuit and don't break the bloody thing." He shut the hood and ambled away. I did my pre-flight checks and moved toward the take-off point. It was all quite familiar and yet it was all so utterly different. The magic moment was over before I had time to appreciate it, which of course was exactly what was intended. I undershot slightly on the approach and had to use a dribble of power to maintain speed coming over the hedge. I had gone solo in just about the average number of hours.

We moved on to navigational cross-countries, learning to plot a course, allow for the wind, recognise turning points and get back to Cranwell at the time planned. We started low flying, started to learn aerobatics, my favourite, and to fly on instruments, not my favourite. We did a mid-course check with the Squadron Commander.

As the end of each term approached the morning parade took on a higher profile as we geared ourselves up to take part in the graduation parade of the senior entry. Warrant Officer Millis, encouraging diminutive Under Officer Alan Merriman, who as commanding the parade, to make his words of command better heard, told him, "Come along, sir, shout at them, sir, spit all over 'em, sir!" Flight Sergeant Longhurst of C Squadron more enigmatically told a cadet, "You're not idle, sir, you're just lazy." At the climax of the parade the senior entry, who were graduating as Pilot Officers, would march off the parade ground in slow time, up the steps, in through the main doors. As they passed into the college they had become officers, shortly to receive the King's Commission.

Some inspecting VIPs made little impression, others became part of the folk-lore. Admiral of the Fleet, Lord Fraser of North Cape endeared himself to us by saying that as in his experience nothing that was said on such occasions was ever remembered he did not propose to make a speech at all. "Instead," he said, "let me just pass on to you the advice I was given by a wise old petty officer when I joined the Navy. I arrived late for some lecture of his and when I apologised he said, 'That's all right, sir, but remember, them wot's keen gets fell in previous.' Perhaps you will remember that, so good luck to you all." After the formal luncheon the Admiral was to leave in his car from the front of the College. We cadets were ranged around the parade ground ready to deliver three cheers. The Admiral, accompanied by the new

Commandant, Air Commodore Sinclair, came out of the College and walked down the steps. As the Admiral got into his car one of the Under Officers called out, "Three cheers for Admiral Fraser." The admiral was so impressed that he slid across the rear seat, hopped out of the other door of the car and stood, waving his thanks. The driver, not having noticed this, drove off without him. The cheers faltered into chaos as we watched the Commandant, his medals jangling, sprinting after the car and banging on the back window shouting "Stop, Stop" and the Admiral doubled up with laughter.

The holiday breaks between the college terms were opportunities to have a go at sports that we had never had the chance to try before. For one break I joined a group at the RAF Parachute School at Abingdon. Quite apart from the excitement and momentary terror of the actual parachuting it was interesting to see the way the course was designed as a series of very gradual increments up to the real thing. The first jump from the basket of a static balloon was unforgettable. The week was a disappointment only because too much wind prevented more than a couple of jumps apiece.

For another break over Christmas 1951 we went skiing at Meribel in the French Alps. There was an English family also in the village, an army colonel with his wife and children. He later became famous as Lord Hunt, leader of the first successful Everest Expedition.

I joined the College Amateur Dramatic Society. The Christmas play was some murder thriller where I played a hard-bitten business man. As a non-smoker my attempts to act hard-bitten taking a long, calculated draw on a cigarette only produced a fit of coughing and hilarity in the rest of the cast. The part was re-written. I was acting opposite "Topsy" Button, actually the wife of Squadron Leader "Flash" Button, the producer. At a moment of high drama at the end of one scene, Topsy turns to her villainous accomplice, me, and says with great emphasis, "Go home, and stay there!"—Curtain. For some reason we both started to find this particular line intensely amusing. Try as we might to suppress it, both Topsy and I would start to shake with uncontrollable laughter. The angrier Flash got in rehearsals the more helplessly we giggled. I cannot remember how we eventually resolved the problem.

At the start of 1952, our second year at the college, we moved on to the Harvard, a more advanced and much more interesting aeroplane. It had a squat, purposeful appearance, a big, round, radial engine, a retractable undercarriage and fore and aft seating. This meant that as the student in the front seat, under the narrow canopy, you felt much more in command, as if you were in a real single seater, even if an instructor was lurking a few feet behind you. The Harvard was very much in the tradition of many radial-engined American fighters, or pursuit airplanes, as the Americans would have called them. One could easily imagine oneself on the way to Iwo Jima or Guadalcanal. The engine-starting procedure was a complex affair of first winding up the inertia flywheel, then engaging it with the engine while simultaneously working the fuel wobble pump and in cold weather the ki-gas primer. It was all part of the fun. The cruising technique in the Harvard was to set the engine boost and then as the speed settled down to bring the revs as far back as possible consistent with maintaining speed, for minimum fuel consumption, and engine wear. I do not recall on the Prentice the same insistence on high boost/low revs, but the notion has stuck with me and I am still sometimes accused when driving of under-revving a car engine. I am quite sure that most people over-rev.

Anyone around the college could soon see that we had moved up from the Prentice on to the Harvard—we soon acquired our Silver Spurs. While flying the Harvard the normal practice was to place just the front part of your feet on the rudder pedals, in such a way that your heels rested on the bare metal of the cockpit floor. With the constant movement of the rudder pedals the heels of your shoes soon got polished a dull silver colour. We wore them proudly.

Converting on to the Harvard threw up a number of instances which illustrated the fact that many of the details of an aeroplane, or in fact of any piece of equipment, and the techniques needed to operate them may, in the overall scheme of things, be trivial but are by no means obvious until you have been shown them. One such example on the Harvard was the drill needed to close the hood. In the normal, strapped in, seating position and with the hood fully open it was actually impossible to reach the handle until shown the knack. Having not been shown this one of our Entry started up his aeroplane, taxied out to the runway and then had to taxi all the way back in again to be shown. The incident stayed with me and later on when I was showing other people new techniques I tried not to take for granted items that needed to be demonstrated. It is too easy to dismiss things as "common sense" when they are nothing of the sort.

At the college, we heard the sad news that the king had died. We took coaches down to London, arriving in Hyde Park in the dark. We formed up into our squadrons and marched down the West Carriage Drive, parallel to Park Lane, past the statue of Achilles defying the lightning, out through the gates beside Apsley House and into Piccadilly and down St James' Street, and formed part of the guard lining the route of the funeral on the road beside St James' Palace.

One of the instructors in our Harvard Flight was Arthur Kell, veteran of the famous raid by No 617 Squadron on the Tirpitz in a Norwegian fiord, so we felt we were getting a bit closer to the real operational RAF. With hindsight I have realised that during my time at Cranwell I found the college a much bigger world than that of a sheltered public school, especially in the wide range of backgrounds that people came from. I was reasonably confident of my flying ability, but I was easily thrown by people whom I found abrasive or over critical. My first Harvard instructor was perhaps over critical, as he soon put me on the defensive and made me jumpy and careless so that I performed badly. Instrument flying again became my least favourite part of syllabus and I was finding it increasingly difficult. Presumably it was a perceptive Flight Commander who moved me to the younger and more genial Flight Lieutenant McGrath. For the rest of the Harvard year my instructor was Terry McGrath whom I liked immediately and got on with well. Towards the end of the course the brief introduction to formation flying was really exciting as was the chance to toss some very small bombs on to a very large canvas target. My scores were indifferent.

Part of the attraction of formation flying is the sheer pleasure of acquiring the skill involved in moving your flying controls less and less consciously until your aeroplane seems to become a part of the other, of reaching the point where both could be painted on a single sheet of glass and move as one. But there is another aspect. I believe that before you start flying you visualise it as an affair of this sleek, camouflaged or even silver aeroplane, glinting in the sun, its wings stretching gracefully from the fuselage, soaring and wheeling like a great bird. But when the time comes you find that you actually go flying seated and strapped tightly into a not very comfortable shabby, cramped, tin box-like compartment, full of switches, levers and dials, peering out through thick perspex, at quite a restricted view. Every type of aeroplane has its own distinctive smell; of hydraulic oil, of kerosene, of paint and of a dozen other components. A noisy radio clicks and buzzes in your ears, from a heavy helmet. With the bumping about, the smell and sometimes the heat or cold you may feel quite queasy. The sleek beauty of the aeroplane cannot be seen—until you fly in formation with another.

Then the magic returns. Any discomfort is forgotten at once, as there, a few feet away, is the aeroplane which until then you have only ever seen resting on a clumsy set of wheels on the ground, now with its wheels tucked away, suspended as if by magic apparently almost stationary in mid-air. Every aeroplane has its characteristic pose or posture in the air—the one feature least likely to be captured by any aviation artist (except Frank Wooton or David Shepherd.) Any slight venting of fuel provides the artistic "whiz" stripes so necessary for a convincing picture of speed, while at height in a jet the condensation trail forming behind the engine looks remarkably like the foaming wake of a speed-boat. When you "pull g" in a turn the wing-tip vortices stream backwards just as any artist would wish them to do. The sunlight streaming down between the clouds, or the distant dappled country-side, the whole scene makes one long to be an artist oneself. But it is mainly, when flying in formation, the other aeroplane in the foreground that completes the picture.

At Cranwell we only flew in formation with an instructor and then only straight and level or in very gentle turns. It was enough to whet the appetite for the future. However familiar formation flying became as a necessary technique and as part of the job, for many of us it never lost its special fascination.

Just before the end of the 1952 spring term we were visited by the cadets of the Swedish Air Force College. We held sporting fixtures against the Swedes and the visit concluded with a Dining In Night for the cadets of both colleges. After dinner it seemed a good idea to hold a joint moonlit parade. One thing led to another and the Swedish cadet inspecting the parade was towed around in a broken-down car and had to be escorted by four motor-cycle outriders. The next idea was that we motor- cyclists should ride into the college and down the length of the corridors and through the main hall as fast as we could.

That was a pity. We had for the moment forgotten that due to some other recent horse-play an edict had been issued that, due to there being

21

some valuable items of furniture and pictures in the college, such games were to be confined to outside the building. The previous week our Pakistani friend "Gunga Din" Sahibzada had got fed up with some mickey-taking and had been chasing his victimizer with hostile intent and a billiard cue. Together they had managed to smash a glass door and had been awarded fourteen days' Restrictions. It had also been made clear that any further infringement would get double that. We four motor-cyclists, Les Davis, Mike Withey, Pat Lewis and I, were formed up and marched into the Commandant's office next morning to be involved in a very one-sided conversation and the award of twenty- eight days apiece. The ignominy was that the sentence would be served at the start of the Summer Term when we would be the second-most senior entry. The inspections and drilling which made up the routine of Restrictions or 'Jankers' would have to be carried out by our friends on No 56 Entry.

There was nothing for it; it had been a fair cop so we decided to make the best of it. We would be the smartest 'Janker Wallers' there ever had been. We seem to have succeeded because on the nineteenth day the Commandant sent for us again and cancelled the rest of the sentence. Honour seemed to have been satisfied all round. Les Davis eventually reached the rank of Air Vice-Marshal.

For our last leave period at the College a list went up of Operational RAF stations where we were offered an opportunity to spend a week seeing something of the real air force. Most of the entry opted to go to stations flying Canberra light bombers, which were then a brand-new type just entering service. However, a friend of mine on A Squadron, Ron Humpherson, said to me, "Look, the Canberra is going to be around for years. We shall certainly catch up with it one day. But the Sunderland flying boats are just about to be retired. We shall probably never see them again." Pembroke Dock was on the list of stations on offer and Ron and I spent a memorable week there. The Sunderland was the military version of the pre-war "Empire" flying boat which had pioneered the route to the Far East via Poole Harbour, Luxor on the Nile, Trincomalee in Ceylon, and Seletar in Singapore. We learned briefly about the problems of operating an aeroplane which having not landed but alighted behaved like a boat, subject to tide as well as wind, and had to be manoeuvred up to a mooring buoy so that someone could lean out of the bow to grab it with a boat hook. Taking off from the water was an unforgettable experience as with the engines at full throttle the hull at first bumped sluggishly over the waves and then rose gently on to the "step" and gained speed leaving a long white plume of wake.

We got back from Pembroke Dock just in time to go up to RAF Shawbury, at that time the air navigation school, and to join a dozen others from the Entry on another jolly. We were taken as supernumerary crew on a flight of four Lincolns embarking on a long-range navigation exercise. The first leg took us on a long sweep out over the Atlantic to land at Gibraltar. We spent 24 hours in this old fashioned colony, going over the border for the evening to La Linea, to have a look at some of the exotic entertainment on offer and the next day across the bay in a primitive steamer to Algeceras. The next leg was along the North African shore of the Western Mediterranean to Luqa airfield on Malta. I immediately liked Malta and I still do. Everything is built of an attractive, honey-coloured stone, and as I was to find again many years later in Singapore, an island small enough to be compact but not small enough to be claustrophobic seems to develop an ideal sort of community. The weather was perfect, Valletta was an attractive city steeped in history, the beaches at St Paul's Bay, before the days of mass tourism, were not crowded, the locals, before all the agitation for independence started, most friendly.

In September we started our last term as the Senior Entry. In C Squadron we were not surprised when Les Davis was made our Under Officer, the small matter of a recent twenty-eight days being quite rightly overlooked, while on A and B Squadrons the promotions went to Robbie Robinson and Charlie Boyer. During our last couple of terms we had been required to write a thesis on a subject of our own choice. My latent interest in engineering re-surfaced and I wrote mine on Long Span Bridges getting much generous help from companies that I contacted such as Dorman Long. I got a lot of fun out of drawing a series of illustrations of various bridges and the Director of Studies wrote, "The work you have put into both the small insets and the full-page pictures is most commendable, and I find the result extremely attractive. I wish there were a prize for the most meritorious illustration of a thesis." Mine was an adequate effort but we were reminded that in a rather different class had been the Cranwell thesis on Gas Turbines submitted some years earlier by a certain Flight Cadet Frank Whittle.

Exams and the flying competitions loomed and our thoughts turned toward our pending commissioning and being awarded our pilots' "wings" badges. No 57 Entry had started our course numbering forty. A number had fallen by the wayside and been withdrawn from training and so thirty of us eventually graduated. I passed out exactly in the middle of the order of merit but a gratifying 5th in flying.

It was a college tradition that at their last Dining In Night the Senior Entry should put on a review or some sort of show. With Brian Huxley and John Dunn, I became one of the contributors in writing ours. The title wrote itself. With our Entry number the show had, of course, to be "The Fifty Seven Varieties." Someone painted us a stage backdrop of a picture of the college but with the clock-tower replaced by a huge bottle of Heinz 57. Being just before Christmas it became a sort of pantomime and although we say it ourselves it was a great success. It was the story of "Split" Whittington, played by the handsome Charlie Boyer who wins through against all the plots of the evil villains. We wrote parodies to popular songs, Mike Withey and Ian Weston sang a Cranwell version of the gendarmes' song from 'White Horse Inn'. Ron Humpherson and Brian Huxley as the Weston Brothers, sauntered elegantly through a guide to Getting On While Wearing The Old School Tie which concluded that:–

"The way to promotion's the way to the altar,
So marry an Air Vice-Marshal's daughter,
Wearing the old school tie!"

We made the audience join in a community sing-along and we impersonated members of the college staff. It just so happened that Chris Doggett bore a strong resemblance to Wing Commander Don Peveller, the Chief Flying Instructor. Chris had borrowed the Wing Commander's uniform and when he made his entrance to the cue "Look out, here comes the Demon King!" it brought the house down. We concluded with everyone on stage and a 57 Entry version of Widdecombe Fair and managed to include the names of the whole entry even if this entailed some rather dodgy rhymes.

The last week came. My parents came up and stayed in an hotel in Grantham. Ian Weston collected both the flying prizes and Les Davis the Sword of Honour. The "wings" presentation ceremony took place the afternoon before graduation day and our wings were presented to us by Mike Walmsley's dad who happened to be Air Marshal Sir Hugh Walmsley. It was a delightfully friendly family affair.

Our great moment was to be when we slow-marched off the college parade ground and up the steps of the college as we had seen so many Entries do before us. On the morning of the parade the unthinkable happened. The rain was torrential with a gusty, gale-force wind. There was no alternative but to revert to the alternative wet-weather programme and to hold the parade, cramped and awkward, in a hangar. The wind banged and rattled the hangar doors, the rain seeped across the floor, but it couldn't dampen our spirits. In slow time we marched off the parade and squeezed out of the narrow door at the back of the hanger, but all the same we were now Pilot Officers.

# No 209 Advanced Flying School

**R A F Weston Zoyland**

# No 226 Operational Conversion Unit

**R A F Stradishall**

IN OUR LAST week at Cranwell we had been awarded our "wings" badges. In one sense this meant that we had learned to fly. But only on the Harvard, a slow, simple, propeller driven aeroplane and only in the sense that we could be trusted to take off, to find our way and fly across country (so long as the weather was reasonably clear) and to land again safely. On the same simple aeroplane we had done some straightforward aerobatics, and (with an instructor looking over our shoulder) flown briefly in formation. Before we could be considered competent not just to fly this aeroplane but to cope with bigger, faster, heavier and much more complicated ones, and with jet engines, there was a great deal more to be learned. We had, in effect, just passed our initial driving test and could now discard our "L" plates. Our postings were to various Advanced Flying Training Schools. I was posted to Weston Zoyland in Somerset to learn to fly Meteor jet fighters.

Ever since we had arrived at Cranwell as cadets we had always been conscious of being members of No 57 Entry, always surrounded by friends we had got to know well over more than two years' of ups and downs. Our moves to our AFS's would set a pattern that was to be repeated roughly every two years for the rest of our careers, that of arriving at a new station, to a new job and to a new circle of colleagues. Many of these would in turn become good friends but they too would in due course be left behind, themselves to be replaced by others. Later a familiar face would occasionally reappear but this was the exception rather than the rule.

Weston Zoyland, five miles from Bridgewater and not far from the site of the Battle of Sedgemoor, was housed completely in pre-fab temporary buildings. Many of the roads and paths were constantly muddy as if the station had only recently progressed from being a building site. The course I joined was comprised of four Sergeant Pilots and eight Pilot Officers.

The names of the RAF ranks have regularly confused outsiders. We eight were in fact officers and we were pilots. But the term Pilot Officer is a rank, equivalent to Second Lieutenant in the army. The rank of Pilot Officer could equally be held by Navigators as well as by Air Traffic Controllers, Equipment and Supply officers, RAF Regiment officers and those of all the other branches such as Physical Educators and even Padres. It is said that when the RAF was in its infancy and struggling to remain independent from the other older services, the army and the Navy, Air Marshal Trenchard was determined to give it a distinct and recognisable identity of its own. We were therefore saddled with these certainly distinctive but clumsy and often inappropriate names. So we have Squadron Leaders who do not lead squadrons and Wing Commanders who do not command wings—and Pilot Officers who are not pilots. When the USAAF, the United States Army Air Force, became an independent force, the USAF, the United States Air Force, they retained their army ranks—majors, colonels and the rest.

We in the RAF persist with the unique names of our ranks but the rings on our sleeves mimic the Royal Navy minus their twirl. Thus our flight lieutenant has two rings as does the Navy lieutenant, and our squadron leader has, like their lieutenant commander, two rings with a very narrow one between them. Quite logically the Navy refer to a lieutenant commander as a "two and a half." Possibly because we see ourselves as a technical service we refer to a squadron leader as having a "scraper." I have to confess that it was many years after I had joined the RAF, in fact only after I had a scraper myself, that it dawned on me that this referred to the oil scraping ring which is located round an engine piston, between the two compression rings. To complete the picture our non-commissioned officer ranks of corporals, sergeants and flight sergeants mimic the army chevrons for their corporal, sergeant and sergeant major, but our airmen's rank badges of two or three bladed propellers are unique to us. Finally, the RAF eagle on our airmen's shoulder badge always turns its head towards the wearer's back.

Much more important to us however, the new intake of student pilots at Weston Zoyland, was the Gloster Meteor. Here we were greeted for the first time by the smell of paraffin and the high pitched scream of the jet engine, which were to form the familiar background all our flying from then on.

These days when the jet is universal, it is hard to remember how novel and exciting this new era of flying then seemed. The very first Meteors had entered service just in time for the last few months of the Second World War. They were the only fighters fast enough to overhaul the doodle-bugs, the V1 Flying Bombs. After the war a Meteor, flown by Group Captain Teddy Donaldson, had for a time held the World Air Speed Record. At Cranwell, as we had started flying the Harvard we had tried to convince ourselves that we were getting near to the leading edge of our trade. Here there was no need to play games. We were about to take a very large step up to a much faster, more powerful, more demanding aeroplane. The main question now for each of us was whether we would be able to cope. The expression, 'Mach Number' and the mystique of the Speed of Sound, as well as the phenomenon of "Hitting the Mach" were suddenly our everyday concern.

At Zoyland we had two marks of Meteor, the Mk VII (in those days we always used the Roman numerals), the dual control, two-seater and the Mk IV, the single-seat fighter, only recently replaced in front-line squadrons by the Mk VIII. In contrast to the squat, dumpy Harvard with its big, round radial engine and its nose-up attitude on the ground the silver Meteor looked sleek, streamlined and purposeful. On its low, nose-wheel undercarriage (no need for ground clearance for propellers—no propellers!), the elegant nose dropped away from the cockpit giving an excellent forward view. Two cigar shaped nacelles housing the Derwent engines nestled on the small wings and the slim fuselage tapered back to a wasp waist in front of the cruciform tail which arched up like the sting of a scorpion. The sleek, streamlined lines of the Meteor meant that a new problem was how to lose speed when you wanted to. There was a new unfamiliar flying control in the form of airbrakes. Between the engine nacelles and the fuselage were large perforated plates which could be extended into the airflow to kill the speed. They were very effective.

The Mk VIIIs were equipped with the Martin Baker Ejector Seat, and when we joined our squadrons we would, for the first time, encounter what has since become standard kit for high-performance aeroplanes. Ours would be manual seats, so if in an emergency you used one to get out of an aeroplane you had then to release the seat harness, push yourself out of the seat and make sure it had dropped clear before you could pull the rip-chord of your parachute. It was realised that at low level you might not have the height to do this and urgent work was being done by Martin Baker to develop the fully automatic seat.

The other main novelty of the Meteor over the Harvard was in the form of the two Rolls Royce Derwent jet engines. The controls were simplicity itself—fuel cocks, starter buttons and throttles. The dials were a pair of large RPM gauges, a pair of much smaller oil pressure gauges and the gauges for the critical JPT, the jet pipe temperature. On a conventional petrol engine the carburettor manages the air/fuel ratio and the throttle only controls the amount of mixture entering the engine. With the jet there is no carburettor and the throttle simply controls the amount of fuel, in this case kerosene, being fed in, which is why the JPTs were critical. Although it was the temperature in the jet pipe which was measured, what really mattered was the temperature of the gas passing through the turbine and hence the temperature of the highly stressed turbine blades. That must never exceed a certain value. On a modern jet, once you have pressed the start button, the starting sequence is all automatic. On the Meteor you had to take care not to exceed the JPT limits. Having pressed the start button you listened. You heard the electric motor start to spin the turbine and impellor up to the speed at which the engine would be self-sustaining, it sounded like an electric train pulling away from the platform. A few seconds later there was a click and, as the second stage cut in, the pitch of the whine from the starter motor rose and the revs increased. Only then was it safe to open the fuel cock very slowly and start to feed fuel into the flame tubes carefully watching the JPT as you did so.

We had already learned that the much faster speed of the Meteor demanded that the turn from the end of the downwind leg down to the runway threshold was not flown in two right angle turns with a short base leg as we had done in the Harvard. In the Meteor it had to be flown in one long, nicely judged, descending turn to bring you over the hedge on the centre-line at exactly the right height and speed. All the margins for error were much smaller. The much higher landing speed made the judgement of the right approach more critical, the margin for variation of speed was less too because even with the longer runway too fast an approach would simply be more than the brakes could cope with and would result in an undignified departure through the hedge at the far end of the runway.

The question of how well we should cope was brought home to us powerfully just a couple of days after we arrived. At the end of our Ground School lectures for the day it was already dark as we walked up the hill from the airfield towards the Officers' and Sergeants' Messes. The senior course was night flying. We paused to look back at the aircraft lights as they came down round the finals turn, over the invisible hedge and on to the runway. We reckoned that to learn this technique in daylight was going to be quite a challenge, but in the dark...

Apart from their higher speeds and the very real effort initially needed to keep up with the aeroplane mentally, there was one characteristic of the early jets that presented a genuine handling problem for the unwary, most often encountered on the final approach to the runway. As you lose the last hundred feet of altitude it is possible to encounter an unexpected wind gradient, or a sudden gust of turbulence. With the normal four-stroke piston engine, when the throttle is pushed open quickly the engine response is almost instantaneous. If the final approach has been slightly misjudged, the speed is a bit low and you are undershooting the threshold, it is an easy matter to apply a quick burst of power to hop safely over the hedge. Not perhaps regarded as neat airmanship, as you should not have misjudged the approach in the first place, but nice to have available for the day you need it. In the Meteor this comfortable option was not available. With the engines at idling power, when the throttles were suddenly opened, it took an appreciable 4-5 seconds for the power to come on. 4–5 seconds may not sound much, but it gave ample time for the aeroplane to sink ungracefully into the hedge, rather than getting over it.

Another feature of the Meteor which we were meeting for the first time was that it had twin engines. The Derwent engine was extremely reliable so the obvious advantage of having a second in case one should fail was largely academic. But, because it was possible that we might one day have to return to the airfield and land on one engine, this was a drill which had to practised. The snag was that below a certain speed the rudder, even at full travel, was unable to counteract the full power of one engine on its own. If one attempted to overshoot and go round again from a missed landing, having let the speed get too low, this could lead to real problems.

However these concerns were well in the future as we sat in Ground School absorbing details of the Meteor's flying characteristics, the flying controls, management of the fuel system, radio, hydraulic and pneumatic systems and sundry other details. We flew dual with an instructor in tandem behind us. Here at least was one similarity with the Harvard. Another feature of all jets is the very high fuel consumption at low level and on the ground. There was no time to sit in dispersal after starting the engines while carrying out the pre-take-off checks. These had to be done while taxi-ing, but here the big plus was the excellent forward view, resulting from having no engine in front of you and the tricycle undercarriage which avoided having the nose cocked up in the air as it is with a tail-wheel. A vital extra check to be added to the familiar list was Oxygen On, Connected and Flowing. Most of our flying now was well above oxygen height and we had been given a trip in the decompression chamber and shown the dangerous effects of anoxia, which are mainly due to the fact that the victim is quite unaware at the time that anything is wrong.

The time came for our first Meteor solo. It was by no means as dramatic as our original first solo, but of interest because up to now we had been flying the two-seat Mark VII Meteor and went solo in the single-seat Mark IV. This was the first time we had flown an aeroplane which, being a single-seater, had no internal inter-com system. There was no background buzz in the earpieces until one pressed the button to transmit. I had almost decided the radio was u/s (unserviceable) before I got the message.

When we had left Cranwell it was in the first flush of confidence due to having just been awarded our wings and we no doubt all privately considering ourselves to be fully competent all-round pilots. But up till then we had only experienced the slow, simple Prentice and Harvard. Having now moved up a class onto fast jets, our limitations where soon to be brought home to us. A few days after my first solo on the Meteor I was briefed to go off, again solo, to do a trip of general handling and then to come back into the circuit for three or four circuits and landings before finally staying down. When practising circuits and landings in the slower aeroplanes we had always rolled to a stop on the runway before turning off, raising the flaps, taxi-ing back to the take-off point and repeating our pre-take-off checks before lining up for the next take-off. On jets that would have consumed far too much time—and fuel. Having landed in the Meteor we now held the nose up while we continued to roll down the runway, raised the flaps, opened the throttles and went straight off into the circuit again and turned straight onto the downwind leg. We called this manoeuvre a roller, as opposed to a full stop. The whole drill had to be carried out quite smartly as even if you had touched down at the right point and at the right speed you were still using up runway quite fast while you got sorted out ready to get airborne again.

I did three rollers and came round the circuit again for my final landing. However, by now it was apparent that the aeroplane was running ahead of my brain and I was finding it all somewhat hectic. As I lined up with the runway centre line I was not fully organised or in control, I came over the hedge too fast and floated some way down the runway before getting the wheels on to the ground. With more experience I would have opened the airbrakes to kill the lift and then held the stick right back to keep the nose as high as possible and to let the aerodynamic drag slow us down, which it did most effectively. As it was I lowered the nose-wheel onto the ground, applied the brakes and hoped for the best. I was out of luck. With a stronger head-wind I might have got way with it, but today there was very little wind and the brakes couldn't cope. At least I had the sense not to try to turn off on to the taxi-way at the rate of knots I was still doing when I got there and so it was off the end of the runway on to the grass and a final stop some hundred yards further on. The Air Traffic Controllers in the tower had, of course, seen what had happened and told me calmly that a tractor was on its way. I had a vigorous de-briefing by my instructor on the need to get sharpened up a bit.

It was at about this time that I heard that a Harvard at Cranwell had got into trouble in sudden bad weather and had crashed, killing both the instructors in it. One of the instructors was Terry McGrath.

Soon after we went solo we had to take a written exam on all the information we had covered in Ground School. We had worked really hard during the previous week on revision and so on the Friday of the exam I was not to be put off by what felt like the onset of a heavy cold, possibly 'flu. Naturally I wanted to get the exam out of the way so I dosed myself up with aspirin and sat the exam with the rest of the course. Then, of course, it being Friday night and with the exams behind u, the course decided on a trip into Bridgewater to check out the pubs. A couple more aspirins and we were off. I believe it was a splendid evening and we got the last bus back to camp.

I woke up next morning sweating heavily with a bad headache and a pain in my chest. The doc took one look at me and rang urgently for an ambulance to get me down to Bridgewater Hospital. The two RAF medical orderlies were told not even to let me walk from the ambulance but that they were to carry me into the hospital on a stretcher. We arrived at the hospital, the lads manoeuvred the stretcher out of the ambulance and up the steps of the hospital, carrying me feet first. This did not seem to me a problem but in the entrance we met Matron. Apparently medical convention is that only a corpse should be carried feet first, and we were not crossing her threshold like that. I sat up and helpfully offered to get out and walk, but was quelled by a look from Matron. We completed a complicated bit of backing and filling in the constricted space of the porch until I was travelling the correct way head first. Then we got to the lift and as luck would have it the large ancient RAF stretcher was too long for the lift door to shut. Matron and medical convention was defeated, I got out and stood smirking rather unkindly as we travelled up in the lift. I was smirking rather less when a couple of days later the hospital doc told me I had double pneumonia and was quite lucky to have been brought in so promptly. The next few days were rather a blur but I do remember on one occasion telling myself, "I think I really am pretty ill. I had better not get much iller."

By the next week I felt better. Most of the other patients in the ward were elderly but then a chap about my age appeared in the bed next to mine. I don't recall what was wrong with him but he apparently didn't feel too bad and we started swapping anecdotes and laughing a good deal. It became a regular occurrence for a nurse to be sent down the ward to say, "Will Mr Smith and Mr Boult please make less noise." I had become friendly with one particularly lively and amusing nurse and one morning she announced she wanted to give my back a massage to avoid bed sores. I rolled over on to my front and pulled up my pyjama jacket and then nearly jumped out of my skin as she whacked on to my back a large handful of crushed ice. Quite soon after that I was discharged from hospital and sent on two week' sick leave.

I returned to Weston Zoyland having missed a full month and so I was transferred to a later course. This also involved moving to a new instructor and so I met Sergeant Jack Sherburn. As had happened during the previous year at Cranwell I had found my first instructor at Zoyland intimidating and he had somehow put me on the defensive. Jack Sherburn and I hit it off immediately and we became firm friends. He still insisted on proper attention to the job in hand. I had become, I suppose, rather over-confident about my flying. Jack was a stocky, no-nonsense Yorkshire man. Whenever he sent me off on a solo exercise he would end his briefing by grasping me firmly by the lapels, frowning up at me as I was much taller than him, and saying, "And be bludy careful!"

The course I had joined had all done their Initial Flying Training together out in Rhodesia or Zimbabwe as it has now become. I soon learned all their banter in broad Afrikaans accents and the stories about Heaney and Thorn Hill. I became particularly friendly with Norman Savory, but this had its disadvantages. We were physically not dissimilar, and on any shopping expedition to Bridgewater or Taunton if I saw a sports jacket I particularly liked Norman was sure to fancy it too, and vice versa. As none of us owned cars our sorties around the local area were dependent on the local buses and so pretty restricted, but I did manage to get out to the spectacular Cheddar Gorge.

Once more my instrument flying was becoming a serious problem. This time I was sent off for some dual with another instructor, Flight Lieutenant Dennis Luke. To him I owe a great deal. Again we struck up some sort of rapport and he got me to see that flying smoothly and accurately on instruments could be regarded not as an irksome chore but as a fascinating and enjoyable, mainly intellectual, challenge. The problems vanished and I became, if not an immediate enthusiast, at least a confident and competent performer. Looking back on these episodes one can see how important are the human factors in what are often regarded as purely technical and mechanical fields.

The ability to fly an aeroplane solely by reference to its "blind flying" panel is, of course, essential if one is going to fly through cloud. This is most often needed when recovering back to the airfield. We now spent much of our time virtually above the weather at altitudes of 30,000 ft or more. As any passenger in a modern airliner has seen, on occasions the view from that height is spectacular, but more often than not the ground is at least partially obscured by layers of cloud. Then one has to be able to recover down through cloud flying on instruments and be guided back to the runway. In those days our main aid was the simple directional radio at the airfield, using the principle which can be demonstrated by any portable radio, which is that the signal fades when the aerial is perpendicular to it. Two such aerials on the airfield control tower mounted at right angles were linked up to a large ground-glass screen in the Approach Control room bearing a map of the local area with the airfield at its centre and surrounded by a compass rose. The system was simplicity itself. When an aircraft transmitted on its radio a beam of light shot across the map to a point on the compass rose. The Air Traffic Controller could then pass the information to the aircraft either as its bearing from the station or as the reciprocal which was the course it should steer to be flying towards the station.

With its smooth, effortless flying controls and abundant engine power the Meteor was, for its era, a superb aeroplane for aerobatics, and these rapidly became my favourite occupation. In contrast to my mixed feelings about instrument flying I was perfectly at home in exercises involving "unusual positions" and became an enthusiast for negative "g." This is when the aeroplane is turned upside down, the wings act in reverse, and you are only held in your seat by tightly adjusted straps. For one particular solo flight I was briefed to go and practise aerobatics. I climbed up to about 15,000 ft and found a nice clear area well away from clouds. I opened the throttles, dived to gain plenty of speed and then, taking a very deep breath, rolled the aeroplane inverted and pushed the stick steadily forward, up into the vertical, on to the top of the loop, down past the vertical again and so back to inverted level flight to complete the "outside" loop before rolling the right way up. I never even told Jack about that one.

We were due for a mid-course check ride with the Squadron Commander during which we were required to demonstrate a short aerobatic sequence. The boss, Squadron Leader Franklyn, was also said to be an aerobatic enthusiast. My sequence included rolling inverted while flying straight and level and then pushing up into the vertical before completing a stall turn and pulling out. It was only that evening when I next looked in a mirror that I realised I had rather overdone the negative "g." I had ruptured a small blood vessel in one eye and now had a vivid red stain all over the white. I decided that was about enough negative "g."

As I had discovered at Cranwell on Harvards, formation flying has a special attraction, partly because of the sheer physical challenge of acquiring the skill of keeping station smoothly and accurately. The sleek lines of the Meteor enhanced the exhilaration. Our own formation flying was restricted to our following a lead aircraft flying either straight and level or carrying out gentle turns. The immediate aim was for us to be able, if the need arose, to follow a leader down through cloud, while he flew on instruments, if for example we had suffered a radio failure and so could not be guided down by the ground.

One afternoon the Flight had completed all the student training sorties planned for the day and a couple of the instructors decided to end the day with a quick formation flying refresher trip themselves. One of their aeroplanes was going to be a Mk VII—a two-seater—so I grabbed the spare seat and took my camera. We finished up with a couple of loops in close formation and I got some spectacular pictures. Most exhilarating.

Low flying was another highly enjoyable exercise. We all realised how disturbing it can be for those on the ground, especially with fast aeroplanes which cannot be heard approaching, but because it poses quite unique difficulties for navigation it must be practised. At Zoyland and also later, once I had joined a squadron, I found that low flying was always quite rightly closely controlled to try to cut down the nuisance aspect to a minimum.

The Advanced Flying School course was coming to an end. We had learned to fly the Meteor and at the same time were gaining general flying experience and improving our airmanship. We realised we had come a long way since we had got our wings, but by now were realising that we still had a long way to go. We flew a Final Handling Check with the Squadron Commander, got our log books signed up and prepared to leave. I was sorry to say goodbye to Jack Sherburn, now a Flight Sergeant. He had been an excellent instructor for me with exactly the right balance of encouragement and restraint. I thanked him for all he had done for me and we shook hands. He wished me well and added, "And be bludy careful." Some of the course were destined for night fighters, which would mean teaming up with navigators, but Norman Savory and I and a couple of others were delighted to be going on to single-seat day fighters. Our next move was to Stradishall in Suffolk, the Day Fighter Operational Conversion Unit. We had learned to fly the Meteor, now we had to learn to use it—as a weapon.

The international affairs of the early nineteen-fifties were, of course, dominated by the Cold War. I had joined the RAF less than five years after the episode of the Berlin Blockade, when it had seemed there was a distinct possibility of the Cold War turning hot. Britain's defence strategy at the time was based on the deterrent, our force of nuclear bomb carrying V-Bombers, and at the same time we needed the ability to defend this country against attack by long range Soviet bombers. This was the role of the fighter interceptor force, consisting of both day and night/all-weather fighters. The latter carried a crew of two, the day fighters were single-seaters and so naturally had a superior flying performance. For this reason we "day-boys," I suspect quite unreasonably, considered ourselves the elite.

The east coast radar network, extending out over the North Sea, would detect incoming raiders and control the defending fighters to within three or four miles of them. Then, just as during the Battle of Britain and the blitz, the actual interception depended on the navigator/radar operator of the all-weather fighter acquiring them on his airborne radar or the day fighter pilot visually sighting the "bandits." Before we could usefully join a front-line squadron there were two specific skills we budding fighter pilots had to learn: to fly in flexible, manoeuvrable formations, known as battle formation, and to use our guns. Stradishall, home of the Day Fighter Operational Conversion Unit, was set among the farms of rural Suffolk not far from the town of Haverhill. The course only lasted two months and did not attempt to do more than introduce us to the rudiments of the techniques, the detailed training would come later when we joined a front-line squadron.

Up to now we had enjoyed one-to-one relationships with our flying instructors. Thus I can still well remember Tug Wilson, Terry McGrath and Jack Sherburn, their gestures, their turn of phrase, their personalities and numerous incidents that we shared together. I find I cannot remember a single personality at Stradishall. At the OCU we were not allotted to specific instructors. Apart from that I retain the impression that there was much less of the enjoyable banter and good humoured intercourse between staff and students that we had enjoyed earlier. However, we were engrossed with our flying and this topic of relationships and morale was an aspect of organisations that only really began to attract my attention many years later. At Stradishall all our attention was directed towards the aeroplanes, we had come to learn about using the Meteor tactically, we just got on with that. My log book records that on arrival at Stradishall the only dual trips I flew were an initial general flying and aircraft handling check, an instrument flying check and an asymmetric handling check. Later in the course we had a couple of dual demonstrations on air gunnery.

Most of our flying hours at OCU were spent in learning the basics of tactical, "battle" formation flying. On the face of it what could be simpler? We would not be attempting to fly in close formation, with only a few feet between aircraft. We were aiming simply to fly in extended line abreast. By doing so each of us, by screwing our head round, could see sufficiently far behind our colleagues that we would sight an enemy, sneaking up from behind, before he was close enough to open fire. We would be flying a couple of hundred yards apart, not much closer than "Same day, same direction." The difficulty lay in the fact that jets at height, even more so than other aeroplanes, are not easily able to gain or lose speed. This presents no problem when flying in a straight line, but in a turn what is to be done about the man on the outside of the turn, who gets left behind or the man on the inside who gets ahead of the leader? The solution is for the leader to call by radio how far he plans to turn, for example, "Rancho Red Section, ninety port—go." The man on the outside, who as soon the turn starts will have dropped steadily back, after about forty five degrees, slips across the back of the formation on to the inside, where for the remainder of the turn he will move forward relative to the leader so that he is once more in line abreast when the formation rolls out on the new heading. The man originally on the inside of the turn has the additional problem that he crosses ahead of the lead aircraft, but must of course keep him in sight throughout the manoeuvre. Throughout the turn everyone must continue to scan around for possible enemies. Explained during the pre-flight briefing on a black-board it all sounds reasonably straightforward, in practice it is far from easy and many hours of practice were needed before even the minimal standards were achieved. It is one of those skills like swimming or riding a bicycle. Once you can do it, you find it incomprehensible how inept you were as a beginner. Battle Formation figures as the main exercise of a sortie in my log book for much of the OCU course and subsequently during my time on the squadron.

The Meteor was armed with four 20 mm. cannons. Just as with the Spitfires and Hurricanes of the Battle of Britain, or for that matter with the Sopwith Camels over the trenches, the guns were aimed by pointing the whole aeroplane at the target. However, while our predecessors for anything other than a straight line astern shot were like a man aiming a shot gun at a pheasant and had to estimate the deflection needed, we were aided by an ingenious gyroscopic gun sight. This greatly improved the aiming accuracy, but the technique of using it still needed concentrated practice. The gunnery exercises were done using a small movie camera incorporated in the gun-sight to record hits or misses. Later we fired live ammunition against a target towed by another aircraft. There are few more satisfying vindications of one's efforts than to see the target come back riddled with real, indisputable holes.

There was one character at Strad who impressed his personality rather frighteningly on us students. The OC Flying was a Wing Commander McKenzie. Due to some highly stressful experiences during the war he had acquired a bad stammer, but he still found plenty of occasions to express to us forcibly his poor opinion of many young, diffident pilot officers. He also had a marked Northern Irish accent and would loudly aver that he "Knew many NCO p...p...pilots who... who... who were each worth two of you on the grr...grr... on the ground and te-te-te-TEN of you in the air!" It was said that he had arrived back in the circuit one day, had turned downwind and intending to call "Finals" as he started to turn down towards the runway, had only managed, "F..ff..ffff..ffffff.................... *ck it, I'm down!"

The OCU course ended and so came the usual parting from friends. Norman Savory had emerged as something of a star and had got what was generally regarded as a plumb posting. The Fighter Reconnaissance squadrons, whose Meteors were equipped with high-performance downward and sideways looking cameras had the additional role of much very low flying, seeking out enemy installations and bringing back the photographic evidence of what they contained. Norman was to go on to Fighter Recce and after the course would join a squadron in the Canal Zone in Egypt. Mick Stabler, Pat Gardiner and I were to join No. 63 (Fighter) Squadron at Waterbeach.

# No 63 Squadron

## R A F Waterbeach

IN ANY FLYING career your first squadron tour must be a special highlight. Here is the opportunity to put into practise all that you have learned, to learn a great deal more and to become at last a professional in the job. We were in the same boat as the brick-layer who finally places his bricks in mortar and not in sand, as the teacher who stands up in front of his first class of children and not of his fellow students and the doctor with his first patient.

Waterbeach was one of a string of fighter stations covering the east and south coasts of Britain and we worked in collaboration with a network of early-warning radar units whose purpose was to detect any "bandit" approaching the coast and to vector defending fighters on to it. Our role was described as interceptor day fighters. While operating with GCI—the Ground Controlled Interception—stations who would be providing our navigation and at the end of an interception would give us a vector back to base, after which we would be recovered if necessary down through cloud by our airfield approach and final talk-down radar. For general navigation we relied on obtaining bearings and distances from a series of ground stations to estimate our position on a hand-held map. There is a limit to how much detailed plotting you can perform with one hand in an aeroplane without an automatic pilot.

In spite of the background of the Cold War it was hard to remember, in the summer of 1953, that our purpose in life was to be prepared to intercept and to shoot down enemy aircraft which in turn would be intending to inflict the most terrible devastation on this country. I do not recall that we squadron pilots studied in detail the characteristics of the opposition we would meet in the event of the Cold War becoming hot. We had an intelligence section on the station which held details of the various Soviet bombers and fighters and it was presumably reckoned that there would be an adequate warning period of time during a deteriorating political situation to get ourselves briefed. Flying had become just the job we did, and we were enormously lucky to have a job which was so much sheer fun. I cannot recall that we thought much more about it than that.

I had always enjoyed the early morning as the best part of the day and now we would get airborne at first light on a grey, drizzly morning, climb through a solid overcast of gloom and break out into glorious sunshine, with a sheet of dazzling white cloud below stretching to the horizon to find above a brilliant blue sky patterned with white contrails. We often thought, "Good heavens, I am actually getting paid to do this!" We were engaged now in learning the finer points of the job. Soon we were able almost to take for granted what our hands and feet were doing inside the cockpit and to direct our attention to the sky around us, to use the aeroplane to its best advantage, learning to slip automatically into Battle Formation, learning to avoid clumsy throttle movements which wasted fuel, to make minimum use of the radio so as to avoid cluttering up the frequency which many others might be waiting to use. We learned, with the most fleeting glimpses of the ground or with none at all, to keep an accurate mental navigation plot going so that towards the end of the sortie when you called base for a course to steer, it was no more than 20° from what you had estimated.

Waterbeach village, eight miles north of Cambridge, was a small undistinguished collection of cottages centred on a village green, with a village shop, George Nice's garage, and PC Brown's Police Station. Otherwise similar to many of the villages scattered across the fens of East Anglia, Waterbeach was a stop on the Cambridge to Ely railway. Beyond the level crossing the slow moving river Cam wound past the east side of the village and where the road crossed the river at Clayhithe, Harry Jacobs' Bridge Hotel served excellent Worthington "E" draught bitter. A couple of miles down the River Cam towards Cambridge in the village of Fen Ditton was The Plough. Run by Kerry and Eileen Pipe, this in fact was the traditional 63 Squadron pub, where Eileen's omelettes were worth going a long way for. The villages and the neighbouring farms were linked by long straight stretches of lanes running between the meadows and lines of weeping willows. But the lanes contained many a sudden right-angle turn when they met one of the numerous dykes or drainage channels. In autumn and winter the flat, low lying land was prone to heavy evening mists and in these the sudden corners were a constant hazard to those trying to get back to the station before the bar closed.

Pat Gardiner, Mick Stabler and I arrived at RAF Waterbeach on 24th August, 1953. The airfield was the home of No's 56 and 63 Squadrons. Fifty Six was one of the most famous squadrons in the Royal Air Force, mainly due to the memory from the 1914–18 war of Captain Albert Ball VC. A glass case in the Officers' Mess still proudly displayed his tunic. No 63 Squadron could claim no such distinguished history, but we reckoned that we were quite as good as any other squadron in current performance. Our squadron crest was of a hand holding aloft a battle-axe and our motto was "Pone nos ad hostem." It was Latin for something about getting at the enemy, more freely translated as "Pitch us where the s*** lies thickest." During the First World War the tradition grew up of painting distinctive markings on fighter aeroplanes. The Meteors of 56 Squadron displayed red and white chequer-board markings on each side of the fuselage, ours—63 Squadron's—were black and yellow.

Mick, who soon acquired the nick-name of Winger, joined B Flight; Pat and I, A flight. The boss of No 63 Squadron was Squadron Leader Fred Doherty and my immediate boss was Flt Lt C I "Joe" Blyth, commanding A Flight. Level-headed and imperturbable, Joe reminded me of an experienced, respected and somewhat feared school-master. Laconic, occasionally irritable, especially on the mornings after a touch too much Worthington E at the Bridge or at 63's haunt, The Plough at Fen Ditton, Joe relied much on the other experienced members of the flight to coach and guide Pat Gardiner and me, the newcomers to his Flight. Deputy Flight Commander was Dickie Wirdnam whom I had known by sight at Cranwell where he was two years ahead of me. Dickie, aged about 24, was almost bald and the butt of endless jokes and presents such as little pink combs brought from Cambridge. In the Officers' Mess I shared a bedroom with Dave Hurley, wise and thoughtful. It was from him and the endlessly energetic Bill Shepperd that I learned the most. Other members of the Flight were Terry Mulligan, Dennis Tann, and an excellent pianist, Dave Parry, who had an attractive fiancée in London and was working hard at being the debonair man-about-town. Unforgettable too was Ron Plowman, Cambridge graduate, intellectual, eccentric, occasional drunk and general comedian.

On A Flight I encountered once again two able and well-respected NCO pilots. Sergeant Jim Pearson, 'Pea-son', and Flight Sergeant 'Mac' McCausland. After Joe had given me an initial dual check it was Mac who checked out my instrument flying. This situation of an NCO occasionally being put in a position of authority over 'a superior officer' causes puzzlement in many circles not familiar with how it works. When de-briefing me on that dual check and on many subsequent occasions when Mac or Jim Pearson led training formation sorties they were unmistakably in command. Again, at the subsequent de-briefing they would pull no punches if any member of the formation had done anything even mildly stupid or unhelpful. The point was that in the air Jim and Mac were among the experienced professionals, Pat and I were novices. Rank had nothing to do with it.

But we junior officers took our turn at being Station Orderly Officer and one of the duties was to go to the Guardroom at 6pm to inspect the Defaulters' Parade. One might then find that the Orderly Sergeant, who brought the parade to attention, saluted and then courteously and respectfully conducted you around, was the very man who had that morning been calling you all sorts of an idiot for your efforts in the air. It created no problem whatever. In these situations we each, as professionals in our respective jobs, simply had a part to play.

After the boss and the Flight Commanders the most influential man on the squadron was Warrant Officer Jude. Mr Jude was a master of his craft, the servicing of our aeroplanes and also of the genial but firm management of around sixty ground crew. I realised his formidable status early on when Ron Plowman dropped a pencil in his cockpit and it disappeared somewhere under the ejector seat. Loose objects in the cockpit are a menace and to recover it meant removing the seat, an irritating and time consuming job for engineers already quite busy enough. I heard Ron confessing to Sergeant Saunders what had happened and adding, "Please, please, don't tell Mr Jude." Our airmen were the usual range of characters, from the quiet and self-effacing to the opposite, such as SAC—Senior Aircraftman—Parrott. Ginger-haired, endlessly cheerful, conscientious, hard-working, usually in trouble, only "Rocky" Parrott could bounce into the Flight Office, slap Mr Jude on the back and say, "Morning, Bob, so how are we today then!" None of the pilots would have dared anything of the sort.

There was one particular way to incur Mr Jude's wrath. We discovered that a few minutes breathing neat oxygen was an excellent way to overcome a hang-over. Even the docs—the medical officers—confirmed that there are medical reasons for this; it is not just an old wives' tale. So on mornings when one might be feeling rather delicate one might creep off to the back of the hangar, climb into an aeroplane that happened not to be flying and have a few restorative whiffs from the oxygen system. That was fine until the aeroplane was next being given a pre-flight servicing when it would be discovered that for no apparent reason the oxygen system was half empty. Mr Jude would come into our crew-room and read the riot act while we all tried to look the picture of innocence.

As very new, junior squadron pilots we had less direct contact with the more senior officers on the station and in the higher chain of command. OC Flying was Wing Commander PPC "Paddy" Barthropp, who had been a junior pilot in the Battle of Britain and the Station Commander Group Captain Arthur Donaldson, brother of the High Speed Flight's Group Captain Teddy Donaldson. The Air Officer Commanding No 12 Group of which Waterbeach was a part was the legendary Air Marshal the Earl of Bandon. I only saw "Paddy" Bandon once when he came to Waterbeach for his annual AOC's inspection. The formal luncheon turned into a hilarious and not totally sober affair and the afternoon's programme was abandoned altogether when someone suggested to the Air Marshal that to grab some twelve-bore shot-guns and a couple of Landrovers and go hare shooting on the airfield would be more fun.

There are legions of stories about Paddy Bandon. One of the best is from during the war when he and a group of friends in a posh hotel bar were holding a celebration and so causing a certain amount of annoyance to quieter people in the vicinity. They were approached by a tall, imposing figure who started to tear them off a strip, adding, "I don't know who you all are, but I am Major the Honourable ———." To which Paddy Bandon replied, "Well I happen to be Wing Commander the Earl of Bandon. And that tops you on both counts!"

Although we had learned to fly the Meteor at Zoyland and had been briefly introduced to tactical flying at Strad we still had much to learn and to practise before we could be considered properly professional squadron pilots or deemed to be operational. The basic element for air fighting was the pair of aircraft. The element leader would attack the enemy and the wing-man's job was to maintain an all round lookout and prevent the element being taken by surprise and attacked in their turn. We normally flew two pairs together and so made up a "finger four," the aeroplanes in Battle Formation making a pattern like the four fingertips of an extended hand. The overall leader and the number 3, the second element leader, occupied the positions of the second and third fingers with the two wing-men on the outsides of the formation both scanning mainly inwards to provide maximum cross cover.

One day Joe Blyth was leading a four and I was flying as No 3, leading the second element. I must have done something more than normally stupid as Joe suddenly ordered "Red 3 become Red 4" demoting me to the junior position in the formation. Even Dave Hurley said to me after the debrief, "I think that was a bit hard really!"

Joe rather liked to play the part of the hard man. During one summer exercise we had hardly paused for breath all week. Watching him work out on the blackboard who would fly on the early morning slot for the next day Ken Rumley, one of the few married men on the Flight, who had hardly seen his wife for days, said, "Joe, do you think I could miss the first slot once this week?" Joe looked round with a scowl, "What do you think this is—a flying club!" On another occasion one of the junior pilots came into dinner wearing for the first time and rather self-consciously an RAF Pilots' tie. This was also known as the "500 hours" tie, as this was the flying experience you needed to have notched up before you qualified for it. Joe gazed across the table and innocently asked, "What's the tie, John?" "It's my 500-hour tie, Joe." "Hmm, I'll have to see if I can find my dressing gown." But he was not that tough. Some years later we all went to his wedding when he married a gorgeous air hostess.

Joe left at the end of his tour and was replaced by Olaf Bergh. Olaf was a South African, a big, rugby-playing extrovert with a marked

Afrikaans accent and a wealth of amusing phrases. He had been in the Korean War, been shot down and had spent a year in a Chinese prison camp. As he explained in his clipped tones, "I got pretty cheesed off with the gooks, so I used to bang their heads together." Not surprisingly he had spent a record amount of time in solitary. He would start a briefing with, "OK. Let us snap our teeth into fine pitch and leap into the luft with a glad cry!" He was a great man for a party; on a Friday night he would say, "I think tonight we should tie a small one on!" One of the new pilots on the Flight was Ken Fuller. Ken must one morning have done something in the air to incur Olaf's displeasure because that afternoon he came into the crew-room and said, "Olaf, now that the last four is airborne there is a spare aeroplane on the line. May I take it for an individual trip and go and do some bouncing?" Bergh's immortal reply was "Ach, Foolah, you couldn't bounce a ****** rubber ball!" Poor Ken, in spite of a distinguished career as an airline pilot, has had to live with the joke for the rest of his life.

Before any sortie there was a pre-flight briefing. It seemed such an obvious necessity that I have often, since on the ground, watched incredulously as people set off on some project or job without having made the slightest effort to sort out the simple details of who is going to do what, to what standard and by when. Much later I have come to realise that in some parts of society there is a strange, irrational prejudice against the simple notion of making it clear to all concerned who is in charge. We had no such socio-political hang-ups! We needed to know who was calling the shots, what was the purpose of the trip, what was the expected weather, what we were going to do, in what order, which radio channels we were going to use, at what fuel state we would start to come home and what diversion airfield we would use if for some reason "the 'beach's'" runway had got blocked.

We now always referred to Waterbeach as "the 'beach," just as Stradishall had become Strad and the other airfields we occasionally used had become "Colt" for Coltishall, 'Tangers' for Tangmere, 'Biggin' for Biggin Hill and 'Rissi' for Little Rissington. For some reason RAF airfields often seemed to have acquired the most long-winded name of any of their neighbouring villages. Hinton-in-the-Hedges and Holme-on-Spalding-Moor (!) were long disused but Horsham St Faith was still active, but who would want to clutter up the R/T with names like those?

We signed the Authorisation Book to the effect that we accepted the task, and had been authorised to go and fly it by someone qualified to do so. In the Flight Office we checked the Form 700, the comprehensive document for our aeroplane, that it had been serviced and re-fuelled. Of particular interest were the 'red ink' entries. These recorded any aspects of the aeroplane which might be non-functional but that we could decide at our discretion would not affect this particular trip. For example, if we were getting airborne at 10 am and would certainly be out of fuel in one-and-a-half hours, it was no great problem if the cockpit night lighting was not working. We signed the 700 that we were taking responsibility for the aeroplane, and would do our best not to break it.

We invariably carried out a brief walk-round external check of the aeroplane. This in no way implied that we did not trust our ground-crews who had just refuelled and completely checked it already. But it was acknowledged that even the best technician in the world could suffer a momentary lapse. We could not, of course, check any work that had been done internally, but that would already have been checked by an NCO who had then signed the Form 700 to the effect that all was in order. In spite of all our precautions there continued to be stories from around the Air Force of aeroplanes taking off with a panel missing or some other obvious defect. Also, very occasionally a technician would leave something from his tool-bag inside the aeroplane where he had been working. To try to prevent this there was in the flight office a shadow board. All the tools were kept hung up on a large white board, the position where each tool lived being depicted by a vivid red silhouette. It was then very easy to see at once if any item had not been returned to its place. The accident prevention branch issued regular posters reminding everyone of the need for vigilance. One such poster stated that, "If all the loose objects which have been left inside aeroplanes during the last year were placed end to end on a runway—flying would be very much safer."

We climbed aboard, strapped in and completed our cockpit pre-starting checks, including having the safety pin removed from the ejector seat, and then awaited the formation leader's signal to start engines. The only time that the engines needed a really powerful electrical input was to spin them up to their self-sustaining revs on starting. To avoid the need to fly around with now unnecessary but very heavy electrical batteries this power was therefore obtained from external accumulators carried around in wheeled trolleys, the 'trolley-accs.' After start-up the ground-crew disconnected the trolley-acc, shut the panel, stood by to remove the chocks and we were ready to go. Our Meteors were not in their first flush of youth and our ground-crews had learned to cope with their little ways. Just occasionally one of the engines would fail to wind up properly because the relay controlling the electric starter motor had stuck. We all knew the sound this made and when it happened one of the lads would dash forward, duck under the engine nacelle and, lying on his back, deliver a gentle but accurately placed kick to a certain panel. Recognising the touch of a master craftsman, the relay unstuck, the revs built up and we were on our way!

The Meteor was equipped with two radios, each with just four channels. We selected the channel that had been ordered at the pre-flight briefing on one of the radios and again awaited the leader's call, "Rancho Red Section, check in." Each one of us would call in turn "Red Two," "Three," "Four." From the leader, "All strength five, Channel Bravo, go." The new channel would be on the other radio box. "Red, check in." "Two," "Three," "Four," "All fives, Waterbeach, Rancho Red Section to taxi." The tower would reply and pass us the runway in use and the appropriate pressure setting for our altimeters, and we would also in just a few seconds confirm that we all had two-way communications on both radio sets, a vital consideration for aeroplanes with limited fuel and sometimes about to take off into indifferent weather.

We taxied out to the downwind end of the runway, the leader called the tower for take-off clearance and we lined up on the runway, the leader close to the left-hand edge, his wing-man just to the right of the centre line, the second pair's leader twenty yards behind them opposite the gap between them and his wing-man on the right hand edge. In this way when we opened up the engines no-one would be in line for any dust or debris that was blown back. The leader called "Rolling now." If the weather was clear the first pair pulled straight up to 300 ft and the second pair kept low, again to avoid their jet wash. As soon as he judged the second pair was airborne the leader called a ninety-degree turn, the second pair cut the corner and by the time we rolled out on the new heading all four of us were in finger-four formation.

If the weather was not clear a "Snake Climb" would have been briefed. The second pair rolled ten seconds after the first, and then followed any turns called during the climb up through cloud with a ten second delay. In both pairs the leader flew on instruments and the wing-man kept in formation on his wing tip. In this way even if we didn't emerge in the clear until something like 30,000 ft. we would, if all went well, be immediately in visual contact and able to join up.

We usually started with a bit of Battle Formation and looking around to see if we could find another formation to attack. In those days the sky over East Anglia was full of fighter wings and it taught you to keep your wits about you. We would then do some cine gunnery, one man in the pair flying straight and level while the other practised ranging and tracking, filming while he did so in order that his aiming accuracy could be assessed back on the ground. On many sorties we did PI's or practice interceptions. This was mainly for the benefit of the Interceptor Controllers peering into their radar displays on the ground. Having established radio contact they would then split us apart, giving one pair a course to steer of, say, 045° or north-east, and the other pair 135° or south-east. After some twenty miles they would turn the northern pair on to about south-east and then attempt to vector the other pair into position to intercept them. To indicate the direction in which we should look out we all used the "Clock Code." We imagined ourselves at the centre of a clock face and would indicate straight ahead as "At 12 o'clock," out on our starboard (right-hand) beam as "At 3 o'clock" and so on. As we closed they would say, "Your target is at your 10 o'clock range eight miles .... Your target is now at your 10 o'clock range five miles..." and so on. Some controllers clearly needed the practice but others were uncannily good and could vector you to within a few hundred yards.

PIs were clearly necessary but tedious. Far more exhilarating were tail-chases. This was especially so on days of giant cumulus clouds, towering up, brilliantly white, tens of thousands of feet high with deep, steep-sided chasms between them giving tiny glimpses of the ground far below. The serious purpose of tail-chasing was to give us experience of handling the aeroplane to its limits, of becoming accustomed to looping and rolling, always keeping the aeroplane in front in sight, regardless of great changes of speed and occasional fierce bouts of "g."

The leader would call, "Long line astern"; we all spaced ourselves at some 800 yards intervals and endeavoured to maintain this as the leader dived down into one of the chasms among the clouds and then pulled up almost vertically, rocketing up an apparent cliff of white vapour. He rolled through a gap between two clouds and then down again into the next valley or hauled round one of the pinnacles, gleaming against the blue sky, rolled inverted and swept down again. When we pulled into a hard turn and the "g" loading built up, "streamers" curved back from the wing-tips adding greatly to the visual excitement of the scene. The leader would level out and call reluctantly, "OK, Red, Reform." If we could see the ground we would let down, turn towards the 'beach and arrange ourselves into echelon formation to join the circuit.

After each sortie we would de-brief. There were always lessons to be learned. Perhaps the initial start up, checking in and take-off drills had not gone properly, perhaps incidents had occurred during the PIs which needed to be discussed, perhaps we needed to ring up the controllers, to offer some comments on their interceptions or often just to thank them for an excellent session. It was a standard drill during sorties for anyone in the formation to call attention to any other aircraft which was seen. This was both for safety reasons and because as interceptors it was our job to "bounce"—to stalk and to attack—any "trade" or "bandits" we could find and we needed to get in the habit of scanning perpetually around. "Two new trails at four o'clock high." They needed watching carefully as they might have been a pair from another squadron planning to bounce us. "Airliner at eight o'clock very low." That one we watched clear but of course didn't bounce. Sometimes a new boy's enthusiasm got them a bit carried away. We once had an excited call of, "New trail, six o'clock, its turning in!" We turned hard round to meet the threat and having done so could see it more clearly. It was the new moon.

Sometimes we succeeded in bouncing a formation of F86 Sabre jets from one of the neighbouring USAF stations. But even if we did they had an infallible way of escaping us. In contrast to the Meteor's straight wings and manually-operated flying controls the Sabre had swept wings and fully powered controls. If we ever got into a firing position behind a Sabre it would just roll inverted and pull down into a vertical dive. At high altitude, if we followed him into this manoeuvre, we would suddenly find that before we could recover and pull out of the dive into level flight we would have "hit the Mach." If we exceeded our Critical Mach Number and the airflow over our wings became supersonic we would lose aileron control and just about lose elevator control too.

51

Close the throttles, pop open the airbrakes and go flicking helplessly down a few more thousand feet until the denser air brought the Mach Number down subsonic. By that time the Sabres were probably in the next county. Damn Yanks.

Learning the art of dog-fighting was not about learning drills, it was much more a matter of acquiring a general all-round awareness of what was going on in the sky around us in a rapidly changing scene and in all its three-dimensional complexity. Some of us eventually picked it up at least adequately, others somehow never did. We came to understand roughly why during the biplane battles of the First World War and then during the Battle of Britain some pilots seemed to lead charmed lives while others survived no more than few weeks—if that.

One day I had a cold and was not flying. I was spending the day in the Ops Room doing odd jobs. A four came in wearing flying kit, held their pre-flight briefing and went off to fly. An hour or so later they were back. I listened with interest to the de-briefing as it seemed to have been a good trip. They had found a couple of other formations to bounce and had an exiting ten minutes weaving their contrails into complex patterns as they got plenty of cine film shots of their opponent's. In such a fight you were frequently pulling plenty of "g" to get inside an opponents' turning circle and so washing off much of your speed. You then needed to dive to regain speed and so invariably the whole fight steadily lost altitude. There had, it seemed, been only one regrettable incident. As they had initially been attacked by the other formation the leader had called a break. This entailed everyone pulling hard round through at least 90°, or until you saw, by peering right round over your shoulder, that the attackers had been thrown out of position, when you could stop turning and start some other manoeuvre designed to bring your gun-sight to bear on them. On this occasion Peter, a Canadian and a very new member of the Squadron, had really not broken with anything like enough gusto, and had then weakly straightened up almost immediately and so had given the opposition a perfect chance to get on his tail. The de-brief concluded, "OK, Peter I know you're new to all this but if you have learned one thing today it is that if someone says break you keep breaking, keep a really tight turn on until you know for sure that you are in the clear. OK, I'm for a coffee."

I continued to potter about with my odd jobs. It so happened that the next four was for three other pilots but with Peter once more in a junior

52

position in the formation. Off they went and they seemed to have enjoyed an equally profitable trip. Except for one incident; after a highly enjoyable fight right down to quite a low altitude the leader had called off the fight and ordered the formation to reform. But where on earth was Number 4? They scanned all round the horizon to no avail and then someone looked up. There, far, far above them, but clearly visible against the dark blue of the sky, a tiny Meteor was circling round and round and round …. The debrief concluded with words to the effect of, "OK, Peter, I know all this is new to you but if you have learned one thing today it is that is if someone says break you don't just sit there in a tight turn you … ." Peter slumped back in his chair, "I goddam give up!" That is not a made-up story—I actually heard both these debriefings.

If the weather was not clear enough for a visual recovery we would need to come home under ground control and so call for a QGH/GCA. Because air-to-ground radios in those days could suffer from poor, distorted reception it could sometimes be extremely difficult to hear what was being said. To help combat this, messages were wherever possible sent in standard, well-known phrases, "I say again," "Roger, Willco," "Are your oranges sweet?"- Meaning is the weather at the airfield OK? We had recently adopted the American and NATO practice of giving each pair of aircraft a Mission Number and we used a series of "Q" codes. So QNH and QFE were altimeter settings, based on height above mean sea level or above an airfield, while QGH was a "Controlled Descent Through Cloud," usually leading into a GCA, or Ground Controlled Approach.

Where we were working as interceptors we were usually in the clear far above any cloud, but we needed radar guidance to get us back to the airfield if we were to operate when there was much low-level cloud. The QGH could recover you to within a couple of miles of the airfield, but in some weather states that was not good enough and we needed the GCA to guide us to within a couple of hundred yards of the runway threshold. It might also be necessary to recover a number of aircraft at the same time, so to increase the capacity of the system we would fly the recovery in pairs. Only the pairs' leader, flying on instruments, would communicate with the ground controller, the second aircraft in the element would fly in close formation, "glued to the wingtip" of the element leader, from high above cloud right to touch-down on the runway.

We might start the recovery as a formation of four, six or sometimes more. The formation leader would call for a QGH/GCA. Having been brought back to overhead the airfield by CR/DF as we had at Weston Zoyland, we would then turn on to the heading for the initial let-down. This would be the reciprocal of the runway heading plus 30° so that having, half way down the descent, turned inbound, one would straighten out heading towards the airfield and on the extended runway centre-line. One pair, say Mission 54, would extend airbrakes and start their descent while the rest completed another orbit. Before they entered cloud the No 2 of the leading element would have slipped into close formation and settled himself on the leader's wingtip. Just occasionally in very thick cloud the near wing-tip was all that you could see, the rest of the leader's aircraft, although only ten yards away, could be invisible. The No 2 could hear the ground controller's instructions and so would be ready for, "Commence turning inbound on to a heading of 236, I say again, 236 degrees." With the prevailing south-west wind the runway we used most was that heading 240°, or Runway 24. The controller would have estimated the strength of any crosswind component and hence the expected drift and given a heading, the direction to point the aircraft, in order that the track, the actual progress over the ground, would be as required.

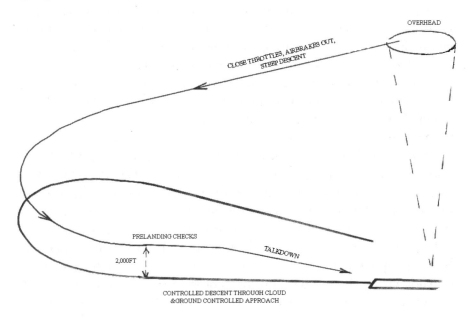

OVERHEAD

CLOSE THROTTLES, AIRBRAKES OUT, STEEP DESCENT

PRELANDING CHECKS

2,000FT

TALKDOWN

CONTROLLED DESCENT THROUGH CLOUD
&GROUND CONTROLLED APPROACH

We steadied on the inbound heading and levelled out at 2,000 ft probably still in cloud. By this time the approach controller would call, "Mission 54, your final controller has you in radar contact, change channel to Talk-down Control." It was important that the final approach was conducted on its own dedicated radio channel as the controller would eventually be transmitting continuously. Typically, the first contact would be, "Mission 54, this is your talk-down controller, I see you levelled at 2,000 ft and heading 236°, you are approaching the centre-line, I shall shortly be turning you right on to 239°." By now the pair would have slowed enough to retract airbrakes and lower their wheels. The leader would signal these items to the No 2 by hand signals, a hand raised fingers splayed for airbrakes in and a pulling-the-chain for lower undercarriage. No call was needed on the R/T and the No 2's formation keeping was made easy because the controls of both aeroplanes were being operated simultaneously. With practice it was amazing how one could sit comfortably in formation in the thickest cloud, perhaps wondering if one could find a squash partner for this evening or which local it would be pleasant to visit, while one's hands and feet flew the aeroplane almost without your conscious thought.

"Mission 54, you are now approaching the glide-path, prepare to descend, I say again, prepare to descend. Confirm three green lights." It was pretty important to check positively that everybody's undercarriages were down and locked. It has been said that even if you can make aeroplanes just about fool-proof, you still can't make them bloody-fool-proof. The leader would momentarily take his eyes off his blind-flying instruments and glance across at the No 2, who would give a slight nod of the head to indicate that he too had checked his undercarriage lights. That was all that was needed. "54, affirmative, three greens."

"Roger, 54, do not acknowledge further instructions, your heading is good, you are on the glide-path, commence standard descent, I say again, commence your descent." A duck-quacking hand signal, flaps lowered, and down we go. "Your descent is good, come port on to 237° ... your glide-path is good ... your heading is good ... you have six miles to touchdown ... you are slightly above the glide-path, increase your rate of descent ... your heading is good ... you have four miles to touchdown ... you are back on the glide-path, resume normal rate of descent ... you have been cleared to land from this approach ... come starboard on to 239°, I say again 239° ... your heading and glide-path are good ... you have two miles to touchdown ... you are approaching minimum altitude for this approach, look ahead to land, roll or overshoot. Talk-down out." The runway lights have been visible through the rain on the windshield for the last 30 seconds and Jack Jarvis, whose voice we know well, has as usual got us exactly on the centre-line. Over the hedge, cut the power, feel for the concrete and we are down. Keep the nose high to let the aerodynamic drag slow us down, saving the brakes. We turn off at the end of the runway and trundle back to dispersal. Having spent the last hour in hot, brilliant sunshine it comes as quite a surprise to see the ground-crew arriving with the chocks, the accumulator trolley and the fuel bowser huddled in parka jackets with their hoods up, splashing through the puddles on the tarmac. Stop-cock the engines, all switches off, unfasten the seat and parachute harnesses and yawn widely to un-pop your ears. Open the hood and before climbing out replace the safety pin in the ejector seat blind. The ground-crew would greet you, "Any snags, sir?" "No, none at all, thanks."

Just occasionally there might be some snag or defect to report. The most baffling were minor electrical problems. You tried to be as explicit as possible in the Form 700, and to reinforce this by talking to the technician concerned, describing to him all the actual symptoms of the malfunction. But even so the next entry in the F700 might be "Ground tested—Found serviceable." The problem, which we all understood, was that the ground test would have been made with the aeroplane on the chocks, at ambient ground level temperatures instead of the normal −70° of the tropopause and without the vibrations of the airflow over the airframe and the engines under power or the effects of "g." So the aeroplane was accepted for another trip, you climbed to height and guess what! You would have loved to have said to the Flight Sergeant or whoever, "OK, get your flying kit on, come up to 30,000ft, and I will show you what happens!" With single-seat aeroplanes this was unfortunately not an option and so teamwork, tolerance and patience would eventually cure the problem.

Normally we re-joined the circuit visually. As soon as we had finished whatever exercise we were doing, the operational priority was that we get the aeroplanes back in dispersal, on the chocks and being re-fuelled in the shortest possible time. On most four-ship training flights we flew to the east of the airfield. We were soon able, even with a brief glimpse of the ground, to pin-point ourselves anywhere over East Anglia. As Ron Plowman put it, "I always know exactly where I am—Norfolk, Suffolk or lost." A couple of miles to the east of Ely by a bend in a canal was a row of eight white cottages. The cottages were eight miles from Waterbeach airfield and happened to be exactly in line with the runway. Over the cottages we turned on to 240° calling the formation into echelon starboard. We ran in at high speed, dropping down to (nominally!) 800 ft, on the "dead" right-hand side of the circuit. The quickest way to lose speed and be ready to lower the wheels was to pull a hard 3g turn. Opposite the runway threshold the leader popped his airbrakes and pulled into a climbing turn, up on to the downwind leg. The rest of the formation followed at two second intervals and were then nicely spaced out downwind as we retracted airbrakes, lowered our wheels and flaps, swept round finals and over the hedge on to the runway. It was one of the many manoeuvres that we took pride in carrying out neatly and professionally, everyone at exactly the same height down-wind and all evenly spaced.

From the ground we never seemed to tire of watching a section of Meteors re-join the circuit. One of the reasons was the splendid noise of the Rolls Royce Derwent engines, especially when the aeroplane was approaching fairly fast. Once the aeroplane had passed, the sound from behind, from the jet-pipe, was the familiar roar of any jet, but from ahead the Derwents gave a unique and most attractive sound which we called the "blue note." Any jazz trumpeter would have been proud of it. Everyone is familiar with spine-tingling crackle of the Rolls Royce Merlins in Spitfires and Hurricanes and, most impressive of all, when multiplied by four in the Lancaster bomber. But our blue note was in its way just as distinctive and evocative.

It was when we were flying in bad or marginal weather that we were most dependent on each other, the other members of a formation, on proper drills and on everyone behaving sensibly and predictably. In the clear, away from cloud, minor misunderstandings such as someone getting on to the wrong radio channel while annoying could be sorted out reasonably easily. Rocking your wings meant come into close formation and then one signalled the appropriate letter for the channel by hand waving. But at the back of our minds was always the limited time available before we were going to be out of fuel. The formation leader would, whenever possible, get any channel changing done well before we needed to let down into cloud. But once we were on the descent this might not be possible. Also we needed to practise for the day when anyone in the formation might have a total radio failure. It was essential that the wing-man could keep in close formation and if necessary could follow the leader right down to the ground and on to the runway. This depended on the leader flying smoothly on instruments and signalling any configuration changes clearly and deliberately.

As with many other aspects of the job we didn't dwell on the more melodramatic possibilities. But the truth was that if you had lost your radio and become detached from the rest of the formation on a day when the cloud was right down on the deck it was unlikely that you would have been able to find the 'beach, or for that matter any other airfield. East Anglia might be flat but with high-tension cables strung across the countryside you would have been pushing your luck too far to try to get down below cloud, and we used to joke that anyway it would probably have been just your luck to hit Ely Cathedral. In the event you would have had to climb up and bail out. However as our aeroplanes were extremely reliable you also came to rely totally on your fellow pilots. This was what created the very close relationships.

We would have pooh-poohed the suggestion that there were occasions when we held each other's lives in our hands, but actually we did. Our relationships were therefore intense but narrow. I regret now that even for the close friends with whom I flew regularly for many months I could not tell you very much about them, except at the trivial level of whether they were any good at squash or if their car was reliable enough to get into Cambridge and back. With many of them I don't think I ever knew where they had been at school, or for example their family backgrounds, their hobbies or other interests. Nor, except for a few special friends, did we take the trouble to keep in touch after we had moved on to other postings. What interested us was how good a formation leader they were or how well we could rely on them in the air and in coping with the unexpected.

The most common cause for concern in all our flying, especially in winter, was the weather. We regularly practiced the QGH/GCA procedures but even so it was possible to miscalculate the time that the recovery was going to take and so the fuel you would have left on your final approach. Perhaps you were leading a four and coming back to overhead already cutting it a bit fine, you found that another formation had got there just in front of you, meaning you had to do a couple of extra orbits before you could start to let down. Or you had opted to recover visually and then discovered that Met had been over-optimistic about the cloud-base or visibility. Either way you might find that you were going to be critically short of fuel by the time you reached the circuit. A well-known reaction to stress is to raise one's voice and to start to talk faster. Apart from being seriously unprofessional, for a formation leader to be heard talking like this on the R/T gave away, of course, the fact that he was stressed and did nothing at all for the morale of the rest of the formation. We tried to remain, at least audibly, languid and relaxed but even so one could not fool those who knew you well. During my early days on the Squadron Bill Sheppard was a very experienced member of the flight and often led fours. But we soon got to know his stress symptoms too. The more concerned he became the more he lowered his voice—deliberately avoiding the shrill tones of panic. We soon learned that the more softly Bill whispered the more frightened the rest of us ought to be!

During my first year at the 'beach we all learned an interesting lesson on security and on how easy it is to let out information that was intended to be "classified." This being the time of the Cold War all the fighter stations around East Anglia took turns to ensure that for their week they had at all times a certain number of aeroplanes on the ground with loaded guns available to be scrambled to intercept any unidentified aircraft coming in over the North Sea. We "day-boys" covered from dawn to dusk after which the night fighters took over. This commitment also meant that for that week the pilots needed to be more or less constantly available too. We referred to this task as "the exercise" and it was impressed on us that for security reasons we did not advertise the dates of when "the exercise" came round. It therefore came as a nasty shock one evening when someone was in The Bridge and another customer turned to him and said casually, "I understand that 63 is on the exercise next week." The pilot concerned spluttered something to the effect of, "How the hell did you know that?" to be told, "Oh that's easy, you just ask George Nice when he has all your cars booked in for servicing!"

Olaf Bergh had long cherished the ambition of bringing a formation of eight aircraft, all neatly arranged in echelon starboard, back to the airfield, running into the circuit and "breaking" round onto the downwind leg in one continuous stream. The main challenge of trying to fly neatly in a long echelon, with each aeroplane to the right and behind the one in front, all in a straight line, is that the slightest movement of the first couple of aircraft next to the leader gets magnified and ripples down the line like a whiplash so that unless everyone is flying really smoothly the last few are riding a rough sea. One can often see the same problem, even for the Brigade of Guards, in the Trooping the Colour parade when they are attempting to march in line abreast. The trick is to watch not just the aeroplane next to you but the one or even two beyond it and so to try to smooth out rather than pass on any undulations coming down the line. Easier said than done. In the air the best time for this is in the dusk, the wind has probably dropped and air turbulence is at a minimum. One evening Olaf arranged to have two sections of four airborne together for the last trip of the day. He planned to make a very long straight run-in to allow time for all eight of us to get settled in formation. After all we were not the Red Arrows! It had been a clear, late autumn day and as the sun set the air temperature steadily dropped. The Met Office was warning that low stratus cloud, in effect lifted fog, would form in the dusk.

The two sections of four met up at 30,000 ft somewhere around Newmarket, turned north and started letting down. Air Traffic called us to say that they were getting worried. Low cloud had formed beyond Cambridge and was drifting north-east and towards the airfield. What was our estimated time of arrival? Bergh gave a non-committal answer and we continued to let down heading north. Way beyond the white cottages, right up in the fens a bit east of Littleport, we finally turned south-west towards base and the first four moved into echelon starboard and settled down in close formation. As we passed Ely and the white cottages numbers five and six and finally seven and eight were edging carefully into position. Air Traffic called again to say "The low cloud has reached Landbeach. We can see it from the tower, will you expedite your recovery!"

We swept over the edge of the airfield, all eight of us, beautifully in formation and Bergh broke left onto the downwind leg followed neatly by the rest. Numbers six, seven and eight were somewhat disconcerted on the break as they turned downwind to find themselves in cloud. We

60

were too surprised really to register and instinct took over. Wings level, airbrakes in, undercarriage down and we were suddenly in the clear again ready to turn finals. As the last of us taxied into dispersal the thick stratus cloud at about two hundred feet had covered the airfield. At the de-brief we took our leader in one corner and said firmly, "Look, Bergh, never do that to us again!" He had the grace to look quite sheepish, but he added, "Mr Jude says that ground crews thought it was great!"

Having found my feet on 63 I found that the 'beach owned two de Havilland Tiger Moths, used for casual local flying and to provide a short-range taxi service. Light, delicate little biplanes, they had once been the standard initial trainer for the RAF and they provided a delightful contrast to the Meteor. They were constructed of light wooden frames and covered with some plywood but mainly fabric so that if you were clumsy you could have put your foot through the surfaces almost anywhere. They could be manhandled on the ground by a couple of men hoisting the tail on to their shoulders and trundling them around on their main wheels. The two seats were in tandem, behind tiny wind-shields but open to the elements. The Tiger Moth had no radio and no starter motor. Also there was no tail-wheel, merely a metal tail skid, so that they had to operate off grass.

You dressed up warmly and found someone to swing the prop for you. You made sure that the ignition switches were 'off', the man on the ground turned the prop over a couple of times and pulled it down against the compression in one cylinder. He called, "Switches on." You pushed the throttle one inch open, held the stick right back, flipped the ignition switches up and called, "Switches on." "Contact." He pulled the prop vigorously down, swinging himself out of its arc so as to be clear of the other blade. If the engine didn't start—"Switches off"— and you went through the drill again. The engine usually started after a couple of goes, you warmed up, waved away the chocks and bumped out over the grass to the light aircraft strip parallel to the runway. Having no radio you got a green light from the runway controller's caravan and you were off. In any headwind you were airborne in a ridiculously short distance and climbed away bumping gently about in the gusts, for all the world like a miniature sailing dinghy on a choppy day. We often took for rides any of the airmen who wanted to come and trundled around the local area at between two and four thousand feet, pointing out to them the local landmarks. Navigation really was a matter of simple map reading and if necessary having a quick look at the station name boards. On one occasion I took a Tiger Moth up to West Raynham to bring back a friend of Joe's for the weekend. It was a day of a brisk south-westerly wind of about 20 knots which whisked me rapidly up to north Norfolk but the return journey took almost exactly twice as long. The Tiger Moth was my only experience of flying in an open cockpit and in the summer at any rate it was a delightful affair, fully justifying traditional fleece-lined jackets and blue and white silk scarves blowing in the breeze. We felt ourselves to be the spiritual brothers of Amy Johnson, Jean Batten, Sir Francis Chichester and Sir Alan Cobham

We offered rides to various non-aircrew people around the station both in the Tiger Moth and in our two-seat Meteors. Some jumped at the chance to get airborne, others could in no way be persuaded. One of our non-flying friends was Pilot Officer "Dickie" Bird, the junior Station Medical Officer. One day Dickie came in to lunch and joined us at our table. He was grinning broadly and kept chuckling to himself as if at some private joke. At last someone turned to him and asked, "Dickie, what on earth is the matter?" He related that at his morning surgery an airman had presented himself and asked the doc to syringe some wax out of his ears. "We were without our medical orderly this morning," he explained, "so while I got ready to operate the syringe I asked my patient if he would hold the kidney basin beneath his ear to catch the warm water and wax. I got ready to syringe his left ear, and he helpfully held up the basin—under his right ear. God knows what he was expecting to happen!"

Many of us, eager to expand our experience, took the trouble to obtain a Private Pilot's Licence, which involved an exam paper on civilian Air Traffic Control procedures and the like. My parents lived in Eastbourne on the Sussex coast and I was keen to take my father flying. In north Sussex there was at that time a small, sleepy, grass airfield, the home of a flying club equipped with Austers. One week-end I took my father up there and we had an enjoyable hour flying around the peaceful local area and admiring the Sussex countryside. Over the years the airfield has changed a bit—it was at a place called Gatwick.

Every morning at Waterbeach we attended a briefing on what weather was expected for the day. Mac the Met man (it is amazing how many meteorologists are Scottish) displayed his charts and described what we could expect, cloud amounts and heights, winds, freezing levels, probable heights for trails and so on. One of the well-used phrases was "contrails dense and persistent." Someone muttered, "Yeah, I know people like that too." The OC Admin Wing at the time was a Wing Commander Hillock, whose wife was an elegant and invariably well-dressed lady. At morning Met briefing they sometimes tried to educate us to be able to interpret the Met charts for ourselves. One morning the Met man pointed to an unusual symbol on the chart and asked Wing Commander Barthropp, OC Flying, if he knew what it was. It was actually the symbol for a cunim—a cumulo-nimbus cloud. Paddy Barthropp thought for a minute and said, "Not a clue. Perhaps one of Mrs Hillock's hats?"

In due course Wing Commander Barthropp was posted and was succeeded by Wing Commander Mike Giddings and shortly afterwards a new station Commander arrived, Group Captain Bernard Chacksfield. The new regime provided a change from the previous rather hard-drinking era. As far as I remember Group Captain Chacksfield was a teetotaller but no less sociable for that and we still had memorable parties.

The third Wing Commander, in charge of the Engineering Wing, was George Morris. He was also the PMC, President of the Mess Committee, and he had an infallible way of quelling over-talkative officers at General Mess Meetings. He wore in his breast pocket a rather prominent hearing aid, with the wire going up to his ear-piece. As some boring man warmed to his theme George would simply reach up, ostentatiously switch off his hearing aid, and sit beaming benevolently around the room until the bore gave up.

One particularly genial officer at the 'beach was the SATCO, the Senior Air Traffic Control Officer, Squadron Leader John Dickie. He was a born raconteur but his stories, whether about continental holidays, hair-raising flying incidents from the war or anything else always included exact details of the wine that had been drunk. "So after this panic we had to land in a hurry at this very bumpy temporary airstrip and so we grabbed a quick meal while they took a look at our engine, and with meal we had a very nice little bottle of '51 Chablis—or was it a '49—no, I'm pretty sure it was a '51 …" He owned an elderly, scruffy Bull Terrier, Pranger, who as the legacy of many fights in his youth now had a heavily scarred face and lacked half an ear. The stories would often get interrupted by Pranger who was then admonished with, "Down, Pranger, noble beast." Pranger was by now pretty arthritic and harmless but noble beast was not actually the description which would have most readily occurred to most of us.

Missing Met briefing could lead to serious problems. Stories of these quickly circulated around Fighter Command to the joy and delight of all those who were not personally involved. Four Meteors from a certain squadron had one morning got airborne on a training sortie from Tangmere, near Chichester on the south coast. There was no low cloud to complicate recovery but a complete cover of medium level cloud, so from high altitude the ground was not visible. When the time came to return to base the four let down confidently knowing that they would be clear below the cloud at around 10,000 ft and so easily able to pinpoint their position over the unique outlines of the Isle of Wight and the adjacent Hampshire and Sussex coasts. To their amazement they found below them utterly unfamiliar countryside stretching to the horizon. They came lower and then the horrid truth dawned. The cars were driving on the right-hand side of the roads. It emerged that they had not heard that a strong northerly jet stream covered the area and that it was in effect moving the whole sky southwards at around 100 kts. They were far too short of fuel to get back to Tangmere and landed at some disused airfield in central France. Rumour has it that the formation leader sent his boss a postcard saying, "Wish you were here."

On days when the weather was clear it was amazing how far you could see from height. One fine winter day I was airborne somewhere just north of London at around 40,000 ft. It was gin clear. To the north I could see the sun shining on the chalk cliffs of Flamborough Head in Yorkshire and to the south it was glinting on the water of the Seine estuary by Le Havre.

As we had no airborne radar in our Meteors our role was to operate as interceptors by day when we would be able to see the enemy but at the same time we did enough night flying to keep our hands in. We flew night navigation cross-country sorties, calling the "fixer services" or simply calling up for bearings from various airfields for some rudimentary pilot navigation. On clear nights at height the views of the moon or stars above was far more brilliant than ever it is from ground level. While below the clusters of lights of all the towns of southern

England glowed like so many shining clusters of jewels scattered across the black velvet of the countryside. On a clear night London from the air was magical. The River Thames showed up as a dark curving snake winding through the city, crossed by the many bridges. It was possible to pick out the dark patches of Richmond Park, Regents Park, Hyde Park and the gardens of Buckingham Palace as well as all the main streets especially in the west end, with the glow of theatre-land around Shaftesbury Avenue and the distinctive curve of Regent Street meeting the straight lines of Piccadilly and Oxford Street.

One night I had the unique experience of encountering a spectacular display of St Elmo's fire. It was a very dark night and we had been warned by met that there were thunder clouds around. I was on a cross-county navigation exercise at about 30,000ft flying through intermittent cloud when quite suddenly the windscreen lit up looking just like the sparkling "snowstorm" effect on a television screen when there is no signal coming in. Except that my windscreen was sparkling with bright pink light, presumably the flashes were showing where each individual electrically charged rain-drop was hitting the screen. At the same time each of the small dagger-blade aerials near the wing tips wore a halo of the same pink light. The display only lasted about thirty seconds and so when it faded I pulled a hard turn and tried to fly back through the same bit of cloud. However I couldn't find it again and it was the only time I ever saw this interesting phenomenon.

Sometimes, especially in winter, an anti-cyclone built up giving days of fine sunny weather, negligible cloud and very little wind. Then the whole of southern England would be laid out like a map, the coast visible from the North Foreland, past Dungeness and Beachy Head away to the Isle of Wight in the West. But London, almost directly below, would be invisible. This was before the passing of the Clear Air Act and London's smog was notorious. Even looking vertically down you simply could not see the ground at all, between about Watford and the North Downs, only a dirty yellow/brown smudge, looking rather like a sewer outfall you can sometimes see in the sea.

During my tour our Meteors were eventually fitted with a simple but helpful radar device called DME—Distance Measuring Equipment. In the cockpit we had just an on/off switch, a dial showing ranges up to about 100 miles, a beacon selector and an unlock button. When switched on and with a given ground beacon selected the DME sent out pulses, measured the time it took the selected beacon to respond, and displayed this as a distance from the beacon. We made up maps with distance circles from all the beacons in our part of the country. By getting the distances from two or more beacons you could accurately fix yourself. On days when the set was working really well—as being electrical it was, of course, temperamental—you could get it to display your distance from a nearby beacon, and it would remain locked on even while you selected the frequency for another beacon. You then pushed the unlock button and it unlocked and immediately locked onto the further beacon, giving you a nice, virtually instantaneous fix.

Without DME and unless you could see the ground, the way to get a check on your navigation was to call someone, usually the 'beach, for a steer. During training sorties we normally all stayed on the Wing Natter Frequency. This was a channel which all Waterbeach aeroplanes had but no-one else. The formation could talk to each other without disturbing others or being disturbed and Air Traffic knew where we were if they wanted to contact us. If, as formation leader, you decided you were not quite sure of your position and would like a quick check steer, the temptation was to change channel yourself onto Waterbeach Approach and call them. But on rare occasions the channel change got stuck and if that happened there you were, unable to talk to the rest of your formation and so unable to tell them what had happened. The proper drill was to swallow your pride and to tell another member of the formation to get a steer for you. Then if they got stuck on the wrong channel at least it was quite obvious what had happened and anyway you were still in contact with everyone else.

In marked contrast to our high-level work were Rat and Terrier exercises. Our interception of high-level raiders was dependent on the ground radar stations vectoring us on to them. But it was foreseen that raiders coming in at very low altitude would not be seen by the radar and that some other technique would be needed. Interceptions would have to rely on the Royal Observer Corps. The ROC manned a network of observation posts across the country and would report raiders they had seen passing overhead. Sector would co-ordinate these plots and instead of attempting to control individual elements of fighters on to the raiders would broadcast a continuous commentary of their positions. It would be up to the fighters to navigate themselves visually and to work out the headings to steer to intercept the raids. It was clearly going to be a hit-and-miss business but extremely enjoyable to practise. Someone got airborne singly and acted as Rat. Bill Shepperd often grabbed the job and became King Rat. He flew in from the coast on a pre-planned route at 500 ft and regularly transmitted a slightly out-of-date statement of his position and heading, which simulated what was the best that Sector would have been able to do. But it was the Terriers who had the real fun. The pair's leader flew at 1000 ft in order to be able to pick up the radio transmissions. The only way the fighters were going to be able to see the Rat once they were within visual range was to get him silhouetted against the sky. Thus the number two kept the leader in sight above him and could legitimately really be down among the weeds!

Night flying was one novelty but I preferred the occasions when we took off in the dawn and climbed up to meet the sunrise. All the pilots obtained certificates as being qualified to carry out pre-flight inspections on our aeroplanes and on occasions we gave the ground-crews a lie in and got the aeroplanes out ourselves. The unfamiliarity of that job was interesting. To climb into a Meteor jet fighter and climb up to 40,000 ft—that was old hat. But to cycle down in the dark, collect the squadron key from the guardroom, to winch open the massive hangar doors, start up the tractor, hitch it to the aeroplanes and tow them out onto the line—now that was really something!

Every month we signed that we had read the Flying Order Book. But this presented a problem. As aeroplanes and the procedures for operating them became ever more complicated more and more orders appeared. This was fair enough, but in addition to this every time there was an accident or even some fairly minor incident, yet another order appeared. These often added nothing whatever to the overall safety or efficiency of our air operations; they seemed to have been produced solely to cover the backs of the Flight Safety staffs. It seemed that Boards of Enquiry tended only to ask, "Is there a Flying Order covering this point and if not why not?" instead of asking, "Did this chap do something damn silly, in which case kick his arse!" The result was that our Flying Order Books were so massive that it was literally impossible to wade right through them. Also having to skip through them meant that one perhaps missed something important among all the dross.

Although the Mark VIII Meteor had been in service for some years a number of small improvements continued to be introduced as retrospective modifications. It was found that the performance of the engines could be improved by enlarging the air intakes at the front of the nacelles. These became known as big suckers. If the front end of the original nacelles said "Oooh" the later ones said "Aaah." The original cockpit canopies only allowed a restricted rear view as the last two feet were not perspex. Their replacements were perspex all the way back and greatly improved the rearward view. But the modification which made the biggest difference was the replacement of geared tabs with spring tabs on the ailerons. The Meteor's flying controls were operated by muscle power, there was no hydraulic assistance. At high speed the original ailerons became really heavy in spite of their being fitted with geared tabs. These tabs were mechanically linked to the ailerons themselves and moved in the opposite sense, so that the air streaming past them actually helped to move the control. Great care had to be taken with their design because if they were too big and powerful, at lower speeds they would have removed any feel from the controls which could have been dangerous and so they were not as powerful as we would have liked at high speed. Spring tabs were linked to the ailerons through a system of springs and these allowed the tabs to be docile at low speeds and to become progressively more effective and helpful at high speeds when one really needed them. They were a great improvement and markedly enhanced the aircraft handling.

In spite of their being nominally identical many of the aeroplanes had certain unique traits of their own. In particular "A," the boss's aeroplane had a curious characteristic in the elevator controls. Once you had been at height for about half-an-hour and the airframe had got really cold there developed a very small but noticeable amount of backlash or free movement in the fore and aft movement of the stick. At the same time every time you moved the stick there was a slight tinkling sound through your headset earpieces. It sounded like tiny, very distant sleigh-bells! It didn't seem worth mentioning and besides admitting to hearing sleigh-bells might have caused some strange sideways glances around the crew-room. At last, one night in the pub someone said after a few beers, "Do you know I was flying A-Alpha today and ..." There was a sudden silence and everyone else turned to listen, "and I must be going bonkers because strange as it seems I thought I could hear something like bells." At least half a dozen other people said, "Oh, thank goodness, you too!"

Back in the 1950s we had one routine which, with time for reflection and the benefit of hindsight, I believe is hard to defend. As with most of the early jet fighters the Meteor only carried internally the minimum fuel required for its task as a high level interceptor. To give it more flexibility it was fitted with an additional ventral fuel tank which was streamlined and shaped to hug the underside of the fuselage and contained a few hundred gallons of extra fuel. This tank was normally refuelled for each sortie at the same time as the internals. In fact to fill just the internal tanks required our ground crews to re-set various fuel cocks which isolated the ventral. As the extra fuel in the ventral, while giving us useful extra endurance had, apart from restricting our aerobatic manoeuvrability, very little effect on the aeroplane's handling, we seldom bothered to get them to do so. As a result, usually on the last trip of the day, when we planned to stay airborne for only 50 or 55 minutes, the formation leader would sometime start the briefing, "As soon as we're airborne we'll open our airbrakes and burn off the ventral." After doing so we could them start on the exercise which was the purpose of the sortie. Quite apart from the cost of the wasted fuel, with today's increased understanding of the effects on the environment of the burning of hydro-carbon fuels, this would of course be quite unacceptable but even in those days it seems amazing now that no-one took us to task.

Air gunnery was the whole purpose of our existence and needed to be regularly practised. The Meteor was armed with four 20mm Hispano cannons grouped either side of the cockpit in the aircraft nose with ammunition boxes immediately behind us. A few miles out to sea off Felixstowe was Knock Deep, an area designated as a live firing range. At Stradishall we had had the targets towed for us. Now we did this ourselves. With rather a carnival air, as everyone enjoyed the gunnery week, we used the squadron Landrover to take a supply of the 6 x 30 ft fabric targets and their long nylon towing cables to lay out beside the runway. The targets were fitted with an aluminium spreader bar with a heavy lead weight at one end to ensure that the flag flew vertically. The towing aircraft was fitted with an electrically operated clip at the back of the ventral tank and once it was lined up on the runway ready for take off the flag organiser, often Bill Sheppard, would duck under the hot exhausts of the jet engines, clamber under the aircraft and attach the cable. On one occasion I found in the crew-room an old copy of Evelyn Waugh's novel "Put Out More flags." Our humorist, Ron Plowman, had added to the title—"From an Idea by Flt Lt Sheppard."

The tug aircraft trundled up and down Knock Deep while the attackers practised "quarter attacks" on the flag, some 600 yards behind it. It was to some extent an artificial exercise but it was the best that could be devised. The target was travelling very slowly and it only presented a target to an attack perpendicular to its flight path. In any case it was most important for the safety of the tug that the attacker did not fire at less than 10° angle-off. To attack, one positioned oneself in the "perch," flying parallel to the tug, a mile inshore of it and 1,000 ft above. The skill of the game was firstly to judge the point from which to turn in, into a smooth S turn down towards the target, finally arriving in the curve of pursuit turning tightly enough to come within range, still with plenty of angle-off but not turning so tightly that one slithered past the flag in a high speed stall.

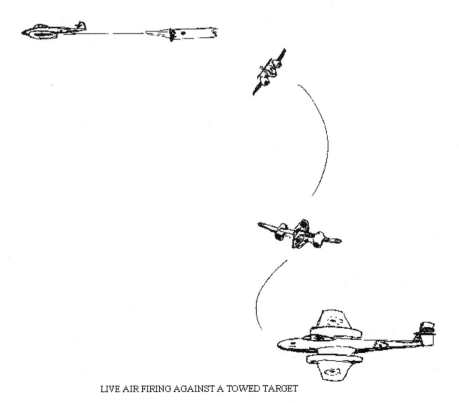

LIVE AIR FIRING AGAINST A TOWED TARGET

The guns were aimed by the use of an optical gun-sight. The sight generated an image of a spot of light on to a sloping plate of glass in front of the pilot. This glass reflected the light spot so that it appeared to the pilot to be way out in front of the aircraft indicating the point where the bullets would go. A gyro in the sight adjusted the position of the sighting mark, the "pipper," when you were flying in a turn and so automatically showing the correct deflection. The second skill was to fly the aiming mark, the "pipper," smoothly on to the flag and to hold it there for the half second available for firing before one was too close to the flag for safety.

We heard of an incident from another airfield when a Meteor had come back from a live firing sortie with the aluminium spreader bar and the lead weight embedded in the leading edge of one wing. One could in fact position the pipper on the flag by using the rudder, making the aeroplane skid to do so. This looked OK on film, the only trouble was that the bullets were no longer going where the pipper was indicating.

Back at base we waited with growing impatience for the flag to get back after the second pair. We rushed out on to the airfield in the Landrover to collect it and to lay it out on the grass in front of the hangar. Then the arguments started. The noses of bullets were coated with sticky bitumastic paint, a different colour for each aeroplane. But the paint on the bullets did not always mark clearly and everyone claimed to be able to see microscopically invisible specks of their colour to prove it was their hole. The squadron PAI, the Pilot Attack Instructor, looked like a mother gannet surrounded by yelling chicks all demanding their (un)fair share. We kept graphs of gunnery scores in the crew room. The ground crew, particularly the armourers, always enjoyed the gunnery week. There was no other event which so clearly confirmed that the whole system, the engineering and the flying, was achieving results than seeing a flag come back riddled with holes. Obviously someone was hitting it.

Fitted to the gun-sight was a miniature cine camera which filmed every time the trigger was pressed and the attacks could be analysed a frame at a time. The camera normally ran at 24 frames a second but the projector could be switched to two frames a second or even stopped if a closer scrutiny was required. The keen ones spent many hours in the dark room with dividers and charts analysing their films. It did actually pay off, revealing clearly where they were going wrong.

71

Once a year the squadron moved up to the Armament Practice Camp at RAF Acklington, near the Northumberland coast fifteen miles north of Newcastle for a concentrated month of air gunnery with the locals towing the flags for us. We enjoyed the gunnery and also the opportunity to explore the beautiful, wild Northumberland countryside. While we were at Acklington in November/December 1954 I got the opportunity to fly a new type of aeroplane. We all jumped at the chance to fly a new type. It would be nice to believe that this was just a sober wish to broaden our experience. Partly it was, but there was also the competitive element of enjoying being one up on one's friends. "Ho, Ho, I've flown more types than you have!" Waterbeach maintained an Oxford, a sedate twin piston-engine transport and communications aeroplane, useful as a cheap aerial taxi and runabout. During the first week in December the Station Commander from Waterbeach, Group Captain Chacksfield, came up in the Oxford to visit us. The Group Captain was returning to the 'beach the next day and someone was needed to go down with him and to bring the Oxford back. I had a grand total of about forty-five minutes dual on the "Oxbox" and I persuaded Olaf Bergh that I was the ideal chap to go.

I flew back with the Group Captain and stayed the night. The next morning taxi-ing out at Waterbeach for what would be my first solo on type, I actually had the Pilots' Notes for the Oxford on the seat beside me to check I didn't overlook anything important. I had drawn a line on the map from Waterbeach to Acklington and set off confidently across Cambridgeshire and Lincolnshire, below cloud so that I could map read, at about 2,000 ft. Some time after getting airborne I happened to hear a Meteor going the same way, but of course way above me, calling Dishforth, an airfield near York, for a radio bearing. However Dishforth's reply was to the effect of, "We hope you are not planning to come in here, the whole of the Vale of York is covered in thick cloud and fog, right down on the deck, visibility is zero." The Vale of York was exactly on my intended track, so a re-think was clearly needed.

Fools rush in... Today I would certainly turn back and await better weather, however at the time, with all the confidence of just a year on the squadron and a sublime trust I decided there was one easy way of avoiding the low cloud. This was to turn right a bit, reach the coast near Spurn Head and follow the coast round the bulge of Yorkshire flying over the sea. I now realise that I hadn't considered what I should do if I met fog over the sea. Nor, even more stupidly, had I called anyone to tell them of my change of flight plan. I reached the coast at Spurn Head, and turned left to follow it. The cloud base got lower and Past Scarborough and Whitby I was flying low over the sea, in not brilliant visibility, below a very low cloud base and trying to keep parallel with the cliffs whose tops were hidden in the cloud. If there had been any sort of problem I was far too low to reach anyone on the radio and had I lost an engine, unlike the Meteor the single-engine performance of the Oxford left much to be desired and no-one would have had the slightest idea where to start looking for me. With the benefit of rather more experience I believe that this was certainly the most foolhardy trip I ever did but I suppose providence looks after rash, impetuous young men. In due course I reached Coquet Island, turned inland and followed the river up to Aklington. At the time I considered it not a bad trip for a first solo on type.

Before the start of the gunnery week every aeroplane had the harmonisation of the guns and gun-sight checked, to make sure that they were both pointing at exactly the same point. Harmonisation, until one learned the drill, seemed something of a black art, presided over by the PAI. The aeroplane was set up on jacks, exactly level, and a board bearing the aiming marks for each of the four guns and the gun-sight was set up across the hangar. Special sighting telescopes were fitted into the gun muzzles and the PAI squinted through the gun-sight in the cockpit to ensure that all the guns and the gun-sight were properly aligned.

As the Meteor's guns were grouped close together in the nose we did not have the problem of deciding whether to have our guns "spot" or "spread" harmonised. Our predecessors in their Spitfires and Hurricanes, with their guns sited out in the wings could either have the guns spread harmonised, adjusted to give a cluster, or for the ace shots, to have them spot harmonised, all concentrated exactly on the same spot. Knowing this bit of technical history, someone came in to dinner one evening and finding that the salt-cellar, with its single hole, had been filled with the pepper instead of the salt remarked, "Huh. So the bloody pepper's spot harmonised again."

Some people turned out to be naturally good shots while others struggled. Brian Weaver as a new pilot had great difficulty in ever getting more than two or perhaps three bullets through the flag. The more he struggled and the more seriously he took it the more his scores declined. He slaved over analysing his films, and always went to bed early if he was on the range the next day. Bergh suddenly hit on the solution. Brushing aside Brian's earnest objections he insisted he come with the rest of us one evening to The Bridge and saw that he took on a full load of Worthington E. The next morning Brian looked, and said he felt, terrible. However, he was so fully relaxed that he scored a 20% and never looked back.

On Saturday mornings we often met the married chaps with their wives and kids around the shops in Cambridge. Bill Shepperd and I met Danny and his young family coming out of the supermarket. His kid's pram was decorated with a string of brightly coloured plastic ducks for the little one to play with. After a few minutes friendly conversation Bill suddenly asked, "Danny, why do you keep your gunnery scores on your kid's pram?" Only kick a man when he's down … .

In addition to the pubs in the local villages such as The Bridge in Clayhithe and The Plough in Fen Ditton we often visited some of those in Cambridge itself. One of the most popular was The Eagle, just off King's Parade. Here we may unknowingly have been jostled by history in the making. In his book, The Double Helix, Jim Watson relates how he and Francis Crick were also drinking at The Eagle at that time during their epic research work that led to the discovery of the structure of DNA.

In the evenings we often went into Cambridge to the cinema. Now that television is universal it is hard to remember the popularity of the "flicks" in the 1950s or the long queues that used to form outside the cinemas as we waited for the start of the evening programme. One of the cinema queues used to form all down the pavement outside The Fountain, an excellent Younger's house. We left one person in the queue and the rest of us went in and propped up the bar. After a time someone else went out and took their turn in the queue. It was not unknown that before the picture started we had decided that the Younger's beer was excellent, the film might not be, and anyway a couple more pints and then a chicken biriani would be a better way of spending the evening. In that way I believe I missed out of ever seeing some of the Hollywood greats which, for some reason, have never come round on television.

In recalling these days I have found that my memories of the social events—the cinema, parties in the mess or in peoples' houses, sailing on the Cam, visiting the pubs—are inextricably mixed up with the flying—with dramas or hilarity in the air, coping with the weather and occasionally with temperamental aeroplanes. The pilots in the Battle of Britain, writing about their memories often remark too of the extraordinary mix of facing in the mornings' combat with the Me109's and then coming back, during that glorious summer weather of September 1940, to enjoy afternoon tea in the garden under the apple trees. Our lives, mercifully, were infinitely less stressed, but the mixture was the same.

We used to take it in turns to tow the flag. Having stopped on the runway to check the electrical release switch and for the flag to be attached one did a steep climb on take-off to get the flag clear of the ground. Air Traffic would pass the message, "Your flag appears to be flying OK," and you set off for the coast. A couple of miles out to sea off Walton-on-the-Naze was an old coastal defence gunnery tower, which marked one end of the Knock Deep Live Firing Area. A characteristic of our Derwent engines was that they were much more economical at high power than at low power. Stooging along low and slow with the flag it was therefore better to turn off one engine and increase power on the other, only prudently re-lighting the dead engine to re-join the circuit and land. We cruised up and down over the sea on one, fully relaxed, with one's knee comfortably braced straight to hold on rudder against the asymmetric thrust from the single engine and often with a package of sandwiches propped on the gun-sight. Perhaps too relaxed?

One day I had been enjoying just such a laid-back lunch and the second pair of gunnery aeroplanes had just called that they had finished firing. I turned towards the coast and set course for Waterbeach. A few minutes later there was a click and I found that the radio had gone dead. Checking round the dials I found that every single electrically operated gauge or dial was registering zero, so there had been a total electrical failure. The soporifically lazy airborne lunch had clearly not sharpened my thinking processes because my first thought was, "Oh, not to worry, when I get back to the 'beach I'll just tell the tower what has happened." A few minutes later I thought, "Ah, I shan't be able to tell the tower shall I—no radio—OK, so I'll just re-start the dead engine and...Ah, Ho, Hum, without the electrics I shan't be able to re-start the engine, so I'll just fly across the airfield and drop the flag and then..." It was quite some minutes before I had woken up the fact that I was not going to be able to do any of these things! I realised I would have to drop the ventral tank (by pulling a lever) to which the flag was attached and then carry out a rather careful single-engined landing hoping that Air Traffic would guess that I had lost my radio and had not actually gone completely mad.

Flag towing was not exactly exciting but through it I got an opportunity to fly a new type. The Royal Auxiliary Air Force, which had played such an important part in the Battle of Britain, was still in existence and we had a call from No 614 (County of Glamorgan) Squadron who flew Vampires asking if we could loan them a Meteor tug and a pilot for a weekend. I took a Meteor down to Llandow in South Wales and flew four towing trips for them to do some firing and was rewarded with a trip in their single seat Vampire. It was a nice little aeroplane but one couldn't help feeling that it did rather deserve the Meteor force's unkind nickname for it of Kiddy-Kar.

As I had discovered much earlier, formation flying is very enjoyable but the most fascinating version of all is formation aerobatics. Olaf had an ambition to form a squadron aerobatic team and when the opportunity occurred, often at the end of the day, we would grab a couple of aeroplanes or a threesome and do a quick trip. Throughout training we had usually practised formation flying in echelon starboard, with the number two on the right of the leader, for no special reason except possibly that with your right and left hands respectively on the control column in the centre of the cockpit and the throttles on the left it was more natural to look to the left. I decided to take every opportunity I could to sit in echelon port. Thus if we ever got round to forming an actual team I would have some scarcity value. We would climb up and find an area away from cloud and Bergh would call us into close formation. We tightened our straps, adjusted our sun visors and got settled. The secret of formation aerobatics is smooth, predictable flying by the leader. In a Meteor the proper position for the formatting aircraft was to have your head opposite the red, white and blue roundel on the leader's fuselage and to be able to see his head bracketed between the two short aerials on the top surface of his wing.

Bergh would fly a couple of gentle turns and then wing-overs, climbing up and rolling to about 60° of bank, letting the nose drop, diving out and rolling level again. He would glance back for each of us to give him thumbs up. We were comfortable and ready for something more interesting. "OK. We'll do a Barrel Roll." Here the trick was to keep your aeroplane in the same plane as the leader's. If he was rolling towards you the tendency was to let the formation become saucer-shaped, with your aeroplane tilted towards his and using your rudder to keep flying parallel. Although you were pulling a bit of "g" you had consciously to edge down below him as the roll progressed. Although you were concentrating totally on holding your position you had too to stay detached enough to say to yourself, "Don't tense up, sit comfortably, stay relaxed, don't hold your breath!" On whatever heading you were flying, at some stage during the manoeuvre the leader's aircraft was going to be into sun. You had to be prepared to ignore the dazzle and keep on watching him and holding your position. A loop was more difficult. As the "g" came on during the pull up you tended to over-control, oscillating up and down like a yo-yo. Over the top as the "g" relaxed it was easier and then the "g" came on again as you dived out. Bergh waved us out into loose formation to take a breather. We would do a couple more manoeuvres and then it was time to come home and anyway by that time we were bushed. I found formation aerobatics totally fascinating. They almost became a sort of drug. We never managed to form an official team before I left the Squadron, but I had seen enough of formation aerobatics to have the greatest respect and envy for the Black Arrows, and the Fighting Cocks—the 111 Squadron and 43 Squadron Hunter teams—and of course the Red Arrows.

I was once airborne at around 20,000ft on an individual sortie, practising some aerobatics and about to head back to the circuit for a couple of rollers before the final landing when I spotted approaching and a bit below me a solitary American F86 Sabre. He was flying straight and level, presumably on a cross-country. Instead of bouncing him I decided to join him in formation. I let down and closed gently until I was flying alongside him, about 200 yards away. The pilot saw me and waved a salute. I moved in a bit closer, and as he didn't seem to object moved into close formation alongside him. He looked across and waved again. It was at the time when I had formation aerobatics on the brain and as it seemed too good a chance to miss I signalled to him "Do a loop!" He gave me a thumbs up, dropped his nose to gain speed and then led us up, over a loop and back to level flight. I waved my thanks and moved away. I wonder who he was. Obviously a nice guy with a healthily sceptical attitude to rules and regulations. He probably went home and started telling people about meeting some "goddam crazy limey in a funny old Meteor."

Fred Doherty was succeeded as Squadron Commander by Squadron Leader John "Simmy" Simpson. Simmy was a genial, relaxed individual who usually started a conversation with "Ah, me boy ... ." He was never at a loss for a quiet money-saving ploy. His car was a Ford van which he had converted into a comfortable saloon by replacing the metal side panels with windows. Typically he had completed his conversion just before the law was changed to prevent the tax avoidance which this allowed. The Simpsons had two young children. John, aged about six, had one leg encased in irons helping him to overcome the effects of polio. However this never seemed in the slightest to faze him, and he took his frequent tumbles off his tricycle with complete equanimity. He was soon a familiar figure around the squadron. On one occasion Olaf Bergh greeted him with some rude, teasing comment. Little John turned to him and in his high baby voice responded coolly, "Watch it, Bergh."

Olaf was a keen rugby player and turned out regularly for, as far as I remember, the 12 Group team. For an away match at Biggin Hill he had driven down to Kent in his dark red open MG, but during the game had broken his collar bone and had to be carted home with his arm in a sling. Hence the MG was stranded. He talked me into allowing someone to give each of us in turn a ride in a Meteor down to Biggin so that I could drive back with him. I thought that the sensible answer would have been for me to drive, but he would not hear of it. He insisted that he would drive—his right arm being the serviceable one not in a sling—while I changed gear at the appropriate moments. We came right through London and up to Cambridgeshire without any dramas so we must have got quite good at coordination.

We often had more car trouble getting back from The Bridge Hotel to catch the officers' mess bar before it closed. The pub was just beyond the level crossing over the Cambridge to Ely railway and the level crossing was an old hand-operated one. On many evenings just as we piled out of the pub and into our assorted cars, the Ely Flyer was due and the gate-keeper would come stumping down the steps from his signal box and shut the gates. By the time the train had passed we would be lined up, two abreast behind the gate, all revving our engines like on a Grand Prix starting grid. I am ashamed to recall that, disgracefully, on more than one occasion as the poor man came down the steps again to open the gates someone started a chant, which we all took up, of "Open the gates, open the gates … ." He was so angry that he turned on his heel, went up to his box again and slammed the door.

Our other old friend in the village was Police Constable Brown. Immensely long suffering, he was used to the antics of generations of Waterbeach pilots. He put up with endless leg pulling, in which Wing Commander Paddy Barthropp was the main culprit. The Wing Commander, whenever he was bringing a crowd of us back late at night from some event in his Landrover and encountering PC Brown on his bicycle, would open his window and shout, "You'll never make Sergeant, Brown, you're too bloody dim!" Years later, when someone had occasion to revisit the 'beach, now an army unit, he met Sergeant Brown in the village, who greeted him as an old friend with, "Well, as you see, sir, I made it in the end!"

Our Meteors were definitely getting old. On exercises we would climb finally out of high cloud at perhaps 42,000 ft and attempt to intercept Canberra bombers only to find that at that height they could turn more tightly and climb more steeply than we could. It often ended up, humiliatingly, with their bouncing us. An airframe is designed to achieve so many thousand flying hours in its lifetime. I have no idea how many ours were reckoned to be good for but one day Wing Commander Giddings got up at the end of met briefing and said that he simply wanted to remind us that our aeroplanes had now flown a great number of hours and that it would be as well to bear this in mind. In particular he reminded us of the fact that some of our airframes were after all this flying perhaps fractionally distorted and prone to getting into a "Mach Spiral." This was the technical term for the phenomenon where if we "hit the mach" in a steep dive we could, as we well knew, find ourselves losing many thousands of feet before we could recover full control. He suggested that this was perhaps not something to indulge in too often. Some weeks later a formation of four was airborne and got involved in an exhilarating dogfight. Such warnings were promptly forgotten until one of the four, flown by a relatively new pilot, Don Chubb, was seen to disappear out of the fight going steeply downhill. It was lost to sight and a moment later Don's voice wailed over the radio, "Oh gosh, I'm in—one of those things!" But he was evidently still in one piece and all was well.

In the early summer of 1955 it was confirmed that we at Waterbeach were to be the first Wing in Fighter Command to get the new transonic interceptor, the Supermarine Swift. 56 Squadron was to get the first of them and then within weeks we on 63 would get ours. A date was finally announced and one exciting evening we all stood outside our hangar to watch the first Swift touch down and taxi slowly round to 56.

The arrival of the Swift turned out to be a great disappointment, as much for 56 as for us. Every new type entering service can be expected to have a number of teething troubles, probably minor, but niggling, time consuming and wearing for all concerned. But 56's new Swifts were much worse than that. Because we were eager to keep in touch we would often drop in on them, but always to find their hangar full of Swifts all with their panels off, being swarmed over not just by their airmen but by an army of civilian representatives from the makers. As the work went on to try to cure the numerous defects of the Swift they were initially restricted to below about 25,000 ft or rather they were meant to be. Four of us in our Meteors were airborne at somewhere about 40,000 ft. Our scanning around could not have been too good that day because suddenly, having crept up on us unseen, a gleaming silver Swift shot past us and climbed arrogantly away doing a lazy barrel roll as it did so. But then it suddenly levelled its wings and nosed down into slow, gentle descent. We chased after it and eventually came alongside. The pilot looked up and gestured quite unmistakably, "For God's sake go away, I'm busy!" That evening Alan Harvey sidled up to me in the bar and offered me a drink. "Oh, Billy, I hear you were leading that four today at round 11 o'clock? Just in case anyone asks you were not above about 25,000 ft when I saw you were you? Just as I bounced you my engine flamed out. All most frightening! I eventually got it going again and I see now why we have this height restriction!" By mid summer it got to the stage that the 56 Squadron pilots were hardly getting any flying at all and would come down to do the odd trip on our Meteors just to get airborne.

One morning I had dropped in on 56 for a social call and a coffee when a Swift started up, taxied and took off. A moment later one of their Flight Commanders rushed out of the offices, hurled himself into a squadron Landrover and shot off towards the control tower. There had been a call to say that the Swift was in trouble and he was wanted in the tower to talk to the pilot on the RT. He was too late. The Swift, flown by a very young member of 56, Neil Thornton, had experienced some sort of trouble with the hydraulically powered flying controls, probably the ailerons, and had gone straight in. Neil was killed instantly. No 63 Squadron never did get Swifts. They soldiered on with Meteors until after I had left on posting, when they finally converted to Hunters.

A standard chore for junior pilots was to go out on the airfield to use the Hand Bearing Compass for a compass swing. On many occasions when an aeroplane had been worked on by the engineers there was a need to re-calibrate its magnetic compass. This entailed running the engines with the aeroplane on each of the cardinal headings, adjusting the compass correctors and then doing a check all round the circle to complete a chart of the residual errors. The only way to do this was to compare the aircraft compass readings with those of another compass lined up with the aircraft axis but well away from its magnetic field. With the engines running it was, of course, a noisy procedure and was usually done right away across the airfield in some secluded spot. The junior pilot tramped round the aeroplane checking its actual headings, getting bored, deafened and frozen or sunburnt as the case might be.

I had kept in touch with one or two friends from earlier stations, one of whom was Norman Savory from Weston Zoyland and Strad. Having completed the Fighter Reconnaissance Course he had been posted out to the Canal Zone in Egypt, still the base for a significant part of the RAF Near East Air Force. I didn't hear from Norman for some months and then the dreadful news came through. Norman had gone out on the airfield to help with a compass swing. At the end of it he had done what we were all tempted to do, he had scrambled up on the wing and sat there to hitch a lift back to the hangar. Somehow he had slipped off and in falling had crashed his head on the concrete. He died in hospital a week later. I went up to visit his parents in their small, smart bungalow in a village near Norwich. His parents were quite elderly and the bungalow had obviously been lovingly cherished in order for it in due course to be left to Norman. He was an only child.

An accident such as Norman's always struck us with much more impact than a straight-forward flying accident. To hear that someone had "bought it," "cashed their chips," or "speared in" in an aeroplane was not exactly par for the course but had been mentally prepared for.

At our age too we knew of various friends who had wrapped their cars or motor-bikes round trees and had not always walked away from it. It was I suppose, par for the course of being in one's early twenties. We knew all the phrases from the recent war, "you're bound to lose a few," "you can't make an omelette without breaking eggs" and so on and sadly over the years quite a few of my friends killed themselves in aeroplanes or in other high-risk activities. Except that we didn't ourselves consider flying as high risk. It was just the job we did and greatly enjoyed.

I think I personally only had one really close call. With the summer season approaching one or two pilots were needed to be trained up ready to take a Meteor around the country to perform aerobatic displays at RAF Station Open Days. Olaf agreed that I should be one of them from 63 Squadron. The form was to work out a sequence and then go and practise it well away from towns. You practised first at height where there was no risk of getting dangerously low and then as your competence and confidence improved you brought it progressively lower until you were down at the actual display height. There was a large area of pine plantations, the Thetford Forest, beyond Newmarket which was ideal and also had a long, straight fire break running through it which you could visualise as the front of the crowd and use to align yourself. At this time I must quite clearly have combined inexperience with considerable over confidence. I had not practised enough at height before I brought my practise down to just a few thousand feet above the ground.

All went well until I started what I intended to be a horizontal figure of eight. For the first part of the eight I pulled up to 45° above the horizon, rolled inverted and pulled down round the second half of a loop, swooping round the bottom of the manoeuvre at about 1,000 ft as intended. But when I started the second part of the eight I must without realising it have only pulled up to about 35° or perhaps 40°. I didn't notice this until I had rolled inverted again and pulled round to the vertical. When I looked back over my head to see the ground I suddenly found that it was very much closer than it should have been. It was frighteningly close and I hauled back franticly on the stick to pull out of the dive as the pine trees rushed up towards me.

I am still not sure by how much I missed them. It could have been 30 feet or it could have been 3 feet. Having got the nose above the

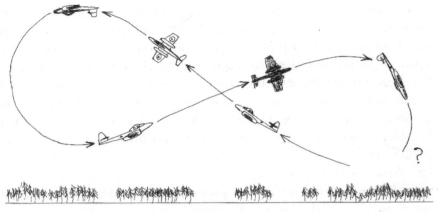

HORIZONTAL EIGHT

horizon I sat there paralysed and immobile for some minutes while my breathing and heart-beats returned to something like normal. I flew back to base in a very chastened mood and with the aeroplane on the chocks I took a furtive look underneath to see if there were any pine needles stuck to it. Thankfully there were not but I resolved to have a very careful think about pushing one's luck too far. Perhaps I was not yet exactly God's gift to air displays. I had not at that time heard the saying that there are old pilots and there are bold pilots, but that there are very few old, bold pilots. It has much truth in it.

The main Cambridge to Ely road ran right past the western side of Waterbeach airfield, so that the up-wind end of our main north-east/south-west runway was only separated by a low hedge from the road verge. A hundred yards on each side of it, up and down the road, were traffic lights, controlled from the Control Tower, so that the road traffic could be halted clear of the runway whenever an aeroplane was about to take off. The local "lads" perhaps driving delivery vans, builders' trucks or their own bangers were occasionally in the habit of jumping the lights to avoid delay. Air Traffic always spotted them and the controller would call us just as we started to roll and say, "Mission 23, someone has jumped the lights, would you hold it low over the road, please." It gave us the greatest pleasure to see a fleeting glimpse of a horrified, white face peering out of a van window as we held the aeroplane down on take-off, more or less passing our wheels either side of the van. People seldom jumped the lights more than once.

83

The airfield construction people decided that they needed to do some work on Waterbeach's runway. This would take a month to six weeks and so the squadrons had to be detached elsewhere. 63 struck lucky and were sent down to the Royal Naval Air Service station at Culdrose, near Helston on the Lizard. It was the height of the summer holiday season and we soon got to know the villages of Porthleven, Coverack, Cadgwith, Mullion Cove and the Helford River, with their old pubs and delicious fresh crab salads, and the beaches of Kinance and Gunwallow Coves. The Navy operated a squadron of Pembrokes, light twin-engine communication aeroplanes, and thanks to the Navy's typical relaxed generosity I managed to get checked out and allowed to do a short solo. One more type in the log-book. While we were at Culdrose my second ring came through, that is I got promoted to Flight Lieutenant. We had a pleasant party in the Coverack village pub to celebrate.

Culdrose was fun but there was one tragic and unfortunate incident while we were there. Taff ****, a new, inexperienced member of the Squadron, who had joined us just before the attachment, had been authorised for a singleton trip, of climbing to height, some aerobatics and a couple of circuits and landings. We discovered afterwards, however, that he was in the habit of unauthorised low flying over both his own home village and the crowded, bikini-covered holiday beaches. On this occasion he was beating up a beach and had not noticed in the heat haze that it ended in a line of high cliffs, which he flew straight into. Thank goodness no-one on the ground was hurt. In spite of the fact that it was totally his own fault and the result of gross indiscipline and disobedience the snuffing out of a young life was still tragic. Remembering some of our own antics both in aeroplanes and in sports cars I wonder which of us could have claimed to be totally innocent.

We came back to the 'beach relaxed and sunburnt. For once 56 had drawn the short straw and had spent the month at some undistinguished airfield in the smoky old midlands surrounded by slag heaps.

An interesting break from routine was when we flew as a Wing. This would consist of three fours each from both 56 and ourselves and was often to provide a ceremonial fly-past for some occasion. A "Wing Ding" demanded careful planning and a much more detailed briefing than our usual four-ship sorties. It usually developed quite a carnival air as we and 56 all assembled in the Wing Briefing Room where a series of formation diagrams, lists of call-signs, radio frequencies and diversion airfields would be displayed. Our flying suits had small white plastic panels sewn on to the front of our right thighs, except where we left-handers had had ours modified to the other leg, and with wax pencils we carefully noted down the key details. The wing leader went through the plan for the sortie and invited questions. Invariably there were questions raised, usually by Flight Commanders or other experienced types, who had foreseen some possible contingency that needed further thought. Our two squadron dispersal areas were not visible to each other and so exact timings for the initial start up and taxi-ing were briefed. Back to the squadron, across the hangar for "a quick nervous" (pee), collect your helmet and Mae West flotation jacket, to the Flight Office to sign up your aeroplane and to check if there was a spare in case yours had troubles on start up. Then out to the flight line, a walk-round check of the aeroplane and strap in.

With a few minutes in hand there was a sudden calm and a sense of suppressed excitement as the minutes ticked away and you waited for curtain up. Various ground sections, the parachute packers, photographers and the rest had probably come down to the edge of the perimeter track to watch. After start up we followed the normal drill for checking in on the radio, but with sixteen or twenty-four involved there were far more opportunities for mistakes and misunderstandings than with four. Taxi-ing down to the threshold and lining up together entailed everyone being properly on the ball, paying proper attention and taxi-ing close enough to the aircraft in front to prevent the whole thing getting strung out and delayed. With the whole Wing on the runway the air danced and shimmered with all the hot exhausts, and if you were near the back of the formation your aeroplane swayed and teetered gently about on its wheels. We took off as usual in pairs, joined up straight away into fours and then, as we climbed away, the boxes of four moved into their assigned place in the overall formation. Now we could relax somewhat and take a quick look around at the novel sight of the rest of the Wing all airborne together.

Often the purpose of the sortie was to take part in a fly-past over Buckingham Palace for some state occasion. We would head east and then south-east coming up to the Essex coast and turning west up the Thames Estuary. The timing now was critical and we would have been keeping an especially sharp look out for the other wings we were probably joining up with. Soon we would be in company with wings from Wattisham, Duxford, and Horsham St. Faith. Together we would come up the Thames, past Tilbury and docklands, over the City of London, the Strand, Admiralty Arch and finally straight up the line of the Mall to Buck House. As a junior member of the formation, however, one had no time now for sightseeing, you were too busy holding your position and trying to fly smoothly. After over-flying the destination the wings moved apart, we headed north for the 'beach and relaxed into looser formation. We skirted Cambridge and ran in to join the circuit in echelons of four for the break and stream landing. Now everyone relaxed and the debrief consisted of much repartee and probably adverse comments on the other wings.

It just so happened that on the day of one such fly-past Jerry Price, a skiing friend of mine and a leading member of the RAF ski team, was getting married at the RAF church, St Clement Danes, at the eastern end of the Strand and thus exactly on the line of the fly past. By great good fortune, just as Jerry and his bride came out of the church, a formation of 48 Meteors swept overhead. With great presence of mind Jerry raised a nonchalant hand and murmured, "Thank you, chaps!" The civilian wedding guests were very impressed.

Navigation at high or medium altitude was a matter of map reading if the cloud allowed it or of getting a series of "steers" or bearings by radio if it did not. Flying single-seaters we prided ourselves that our pilot–nav was normally entirely adequate and that we had no need of the talking ballast—navigators. However we sometimes got it wrong, occasionally spectacularly.

One day a certain Wing Commander was leading his wing of twenty-four Meteors from Linton-on-Ouse in Yorkshire. He had started his distinguished flying career during the Battle of Britain in 1940, but was perhaps by now not quite the sharp officer he had once been. There was some misunderstanding about which radio channels were in use to call the radar fixer service or he had brought the wrong map or something of the sort and eventually it all became a bit too difficult. The story is that he finally lost patience and called on the radio, "Look, sorry chaps, it's every man for himself." The formation broke up, individual aircraft or at best pairs let down through cloud until they could see the ground and pinpoint themselves. Everyone landed safely at a variety of airfields around north-east England. The wing leader himself and his faithful No 2 found themselves over a clearly disused airfield but by now they were critically short of fuel and the only priority was to get down on the ground in the shortest possible time before the engines stopped. The wing leader turned finals. As he came over the hedge he looked up along the length of the runway. There at the other end of the runway his No 2 was just coming over the far hedge in the opposite direction. "OK," he called, "Don't panic, you keep left, I'll keep right." His No 2 had, however, already cannily sussed out the situation and they passed each other rather breathlessly, in the middle of the runway going in opposite directions.

Normally, at height, we coped well enough but navigation at low level was a different ball-game and so needed to be regularly practised. As with so many advanced skills the secret was careful pre-flight planning. The first move was to select the route you intended to follow and to find turning points that had positive lead-in features—converging railway lines, a river estuary, power station cooling towers or the like. Generally railway lines were a more useful navigation aid than roads. Their smooth, flowing curves made them much easier to follow by eye even from quite long distances or in hazy weather. From height almost any hill in the English countryside was so low as to be more or less invisible and so irrelevant. But from low level the slightest rise or river valley became a major feature. Overhead power cables were a menace and we made sure that they were clearly marked on our maps.

To keep any sums in nice round figures we normally planned to fly at 360 kts. (6 miles a minute) or in the Hunter at 420 kts. (7 miles a minute). At those speeds you could not ignore the size of your turning circle when you reached a turning point and altered course. Depending on which scale of map you were using you used a coin, perhaps an old half-penny, and traced round it until you got to your new heading. You then noted the heading and length of each leg, including the distance round the turn, and thus the time it would take to cover. All the details were noted for easy reference in the air and after that it was a mainly a matter of flying accurate headings and air-speeds and using a stop-watch. If care was taken it was striking how well it worked out. Being at low level there was even less time than usual to be looking at maps inside the cockpit and so you could find yourself temporarily quite unsure of your actual position. However you eventually acquired the confidence to say to yourself, "Well, in one minute and 30 seconds we should be over that bridge over the canal," or whatever it was, "And then we turn onto 232°." Sure enough a minute and 25 seconds later the canal appeared and there within 10° of the nose was the bridge.

One particular landmark in the middle of Norfolk became especially well known. Away in the middle of open heath-land, beside the Thetford to Norwich road, is a miniature Nelson's Column but with a sort of stone flower vase on the top. You could film this with your gun-sight cine camera and the game was to see how big a picture of the flower vase you could get—that is how big without collecting the vase itself through the front of the aeroplane.

On a Squadron, each pilot is allotted an aspect of the job on which they can concentrate and make their contribution to helping to raise standards. In August 1954 I had been on 63 Squadron a year and Olaf Bergh sent me to attend the course at the Instrument Training Squadron at West Raynham. On return I became one of the Squadron's Instrument Rating Examiners, charged with flying dual with other Squadron pilots to check their instrument flying standards and if necessary with demonstrating to them the proper techniques. Clearly my own instrument flying had improved quite a bit since the troubles I had encountered a couple of years previously. Thank you, Dennis Luke.

In November we anticipated, with decidedly mixed feeling, the annual Escape and Evasion Exercise. The objective was to give us some experience of what it would be like if, having had to bale out over enemy territory, we had to try to evade capture and get back to safety. One Friday afternoon we were taken by coach to RAF Wattisham, near Ipswich. Two or three hundred aircrew from all the surrounding airfields were crowded into the Briefing Room. We would be given dinner and then taken out, this time in a blacked out coach, and dropped off in pairs over a wide area of the surrounding countryside. The local population, the military and the police had been told that the exercise was taking place and had been asked to keep a lookout for "escapers." Our job was to evade capture. If we could do this and get to within 10 miles of the coast by mid-day on Sunday we could regard ourselves as having won. We could then ring up Wattisham and ask to be picked up.

Buster Skinner and I were duly dropped off in some anonymous country lane and the coach drove off into the night. We had managed to retain a map and compass and set off hopefully in a generally easterly direction. A long night of wet fields, muddy ditches, heavy clinging plough, brambles, nettles and other joys followed. Eventually as the dawn started to break we decided to go to earth. In the dim light we found a barn full of straw bales, climbed on to the top of the straw and, confident that we had not been seen, stretched out thankfully under the roof. It seemed that we had hardly dropped off to sleep when the police car arrived. Suffolk farm folk evidently got up and were alert rather earlier than we had anticipated.

We were driven to the local police station, where the police contacted the RAF and were presumably asked to deliver us to Wattisham where a large hangar was being used as the cage. The police collected us from our cell to take us out to the car. In order to avoid unnecessary incidents the rules of the exercise were that if someone was in physical contact with you, say holding you by the arm, it was reckoned you were being covered by a gun and had to behave accordingly. Although it seemed that the game was up I decided to try some amateur psychology. The senior policeman led the way, holding Buster firmly by the arm, but as we walked out of the police station and across the yard, I turned casually to my captor and made some remark about how tiresome it must be for important people to have to spend their time on these military exercises. I could hardly believe my luck as he agreed—and released his grip.

My sudden dash through the gate and down the lane took him completely by surprise and I opened up a vital ten-yard lead. I turned onto a cinder path beside bushes and between fields. Luckily he was a large, rather fat man and I soon had a lead of some thirty yards. The path turned a corner and the moment I was out of his sight I took a flying dive into the brambles and lay still. I heard his heavy breathing as he clumped past. Luck was still on my side and he soon gave up searching. Having hidden for the rest of the day I went on at dusk. Being alone instead of with company made a great difference and weariness soon slowed me right down. Some time during the night I came to a village. A handy lamp-post let me look at the map and I saw that the village was bisected by a small river. Should I attempt to wade or swim the river or go into the village and over the bridge? I chose the latter and very carefully walked down the village street. I was ready for a challenge and reckoned I could make another dash if necessary. I tiptoed over the bridge and just as I did so I heard in the distance the unmistakeable whine of an army 3-ton truck. It was clearly coming this way and I only had a moment to find a hiding place. Just beyond the bridge was a familiar red telephone box, with its three glass sides and a solid back.

My best chance seemed to be to get behind the telephone box and to flatten myself against its back. In my haste to get there, I nearly tripped over an old bundle of sacking lying on the path. The army truck came slowly down the hill and stopped right opposite the telephone box. A voice called out, "Come on, Nobby, we've had orders we can pack it in and get back to barracks." The bundle of sacking which I had just tripped over got unsteadily to its feet and started to climb into the truck. He suddenly stopped and said, "Hang on I've left my haversack, lend me a torch will you." Nobby came back flashing his torch around and so of course found me, I was bundled into the truck and finished the exercise with many others in the cage at Wattisham.

My tour with 63 was coming to an end. Had I been give the choice I would certainly have chosen a second flying tour. However the boss, 'Simmy' Simpson would have none of it. Firmly he pointed out that, especially as a Cranwell cadet, I should be thinking of career development and that I should try to get a tour as an ADC. The post of aide de camp, or as the Royal Navy calls it Flag Lieutenant, is that of being a general dogsbody for a senior officer, looking after the trivia of his everyday life in order that he may use his time more productively and concentrate his attention on his wide, strategic responsibilities. The payoff for the dogsbody is that he becomes privy to the higher management of the service and the routines of senior people in a way that will greatly advance his own understanding and allow him to gain a wider perspective of the service.

I was happy to take Simmy's advice, and with his help and many contacts started checking around for any ADC posts which were on offer. I went for one interview at West Raynham where the Commandant of the Central Fighter Establishment was about to go on promotion to Air Vice-Marshal to the Ministry of Defence, but I was not selected. We then heard that the post of ADC to the Air Officer Commanding, Transport Command was soon to become vacant. I contacted his office, arranged an appointment and flew down to Upavon on Salisbury Plain to be interviewed. It only took about ten minutes, at the end of which the Air Marshal evidently decided that I was acceptable. We agreed a date for me to succeed Freddie Yetman, his current ADC, and I flew back to the 'beach and started packing.

I had enjoyed a splendid flying tour on 63. Our ground crews knew the servicing of the aeroplanes with their eyes shut and we got masses of hours each month. In those days East Anglia was full of aeroplanes, bouncing and dog-fighting were available in abundance and I had turned out to be, if certainly not an ace, quite a fair performer at air gunnery. I was still probably somewhat over–confident but at least some of it was now justified. During the week in which I left the 'beach I did a couple of individual trips in a very new Mk VIII, with big suckers, aileron spring tabs and no ventral tank. That really did seem to be flying at its best. The Meteor did not have anything like the performance of later, swept-wing, powered-control fighters but equally it seemed to have no vices. Although I was destined later to fly much more advanced and exciting aeroplanes, the Meteor, and in particular the Mk VIII, has always remained my first love.

I was rather regretting that I was about to spend the next year or so on the ground, but Simmy promised that if I could get back for the odd weekend when the Squadron was flying I could always count on a couple of trips to keep my hand in. I started the familiar process of saying goodbye to old friends, loaded my kit into the Oxford, and with Hector Munro of 56 Squadron coming with me to bring the aeroplane back, set off from fens of Cambridgeshire to Upavon and the wide open pasturelands of Wiltshire and Salisbury Plain.

# Headquarters
# Transport Command

## R A F Upavon

U PAVON IS ONE of the oldest stations in the RAF. Its small grass airfield commands sweeping views across the wide horizons of Salisbury Plain, its gallops, its pastoral acres and wild flowers and in those days its spring and summer skies filled with skylarks. Many of the building still in 1956 retained an air of the 1920s. The Offices' Mess in particular, with its spacious, glass-roofed ante-room seemed to need potted palms and a small string orchestra to complete the scene.

My boss, a New Zealander, was the Air Officer Commanding, Transport Command, Air Vice-Marshal Andrew McKee, responsible for the smooth running of the whole outfit. My own job concentrated on more mundane affairs. My office was next door to the Air Marshal's and I shared it with the AOC's typist, Sergeant Don Winterbottom.

I had quickly to brush up my awareness of the ranks, abbreviations and other nomenclatures of the various senior officers with whom I was now working. Air Vice-Marshals are known colloquially as air marshals, in the same way that rear- and vice- admirals are referred to as admirals and lieutenant colonels as colonels, (or more specifically as half-colonels as opposed to full colonels). RAF officers of the rank of air commodore and above are referred to as holding Air Rank. Their equivalents in the army and navy as having respectively Field Rank or Flag Rank. Falling in line with the Americans all the British services now also designated these very senior officers by stars as worn on the Americans' shoulders. Air Commodores and their equivalents were one-star officers, AVMs two-star and so on. This was a nice simple system and avoided the problem of trying to remember which sort of Air Marshal was the equivalent of a Rear Admiral (two-star) or a Lieutenant General (three-star).

My boss was also referred to as the AOC—The Air Officer Commanding or sometimes just as the AVM. Later in my tour he was promoted and his post became Commander-in-Chief or C-in-C. We seemed to live in a world of initials and abbreviations. He told an amusing story of a visit he and a certain Air Chief Marshal (a four-star officer) had made some years previously to a secret facility in Australia. They arrived, in civilian clothes, at a security gate and the laconic Australian soldier on guard wanted to note down their details. It came to the Air Chief Marshal's turn, the soldier turned to him and the exchange went "Rank" "ACM" "Nah, sport, not initials, Rank." "Air Chief Marshal." "Yeah, my life, that'll be the day won't it!"

Across the corridor from my office was that of the Air Marshal's Personal Staff Officer, the PSO, Squadron Leader Harry King who was to have an influence on my work second only to the AVM's. He had been with him for many years, and had made himself indispensable. He worked like a demon, had a heart of gold but was maddeningly untidy and a chain smoker. I quickly lost count of the times he told me about some job which should have been mine in the first place but which he had started "just to save time" but had only half finished. He would tell me all about it without taking the cigarette out of his mouth, the story constantly interrupted with "Oh, sorry, Bill, sorry" as he brushed cigarette ash, his ash, off my tunic.

The whole of Transport Command Headquarters had the pleasant air of a club. The transport force aircrews and engineers tended to stay within the Command and the staff officers had mainly all known one another for many years. The three branches mimicked those of a normal station organisation—Air Operations, Technical and Administration. The heads of the three branches were Air Commodore Carter, Senior Air Staff Officer, Air Commodore Hartley, Senior Technical Staff Officer and Air Commodore Kippenberger, AOA, Air

Officer in charge of Administration. "Kip" was one of the many New Zealanders in the Headquarters. Immaculate, imperturbable and courteous, he would arrive quietly in my office and enquire, "Good morning, Bill. Is master able to spare me a few minutes, please." One of his hobby-horses was the existence of the many different sets of attire which passed in the RAF for uniform, which he referred to, he maintained more accurately, as "multiform." For the new ADC trying to find his way around the Air Commodores and their staffs were invariably friendly and helpful.

The most interesting place in the whole Headquarters was the Command Operations Room. On a map of the world were displayed the positions of the Command's aircraft as they flew out from UK to Malta, Cyprus and the Near East, on down the main route to Singapore and Australia or as the occasional Western Ranger going west-about across the Atlantic, the USA and the Pacific. A smaller map showed the locations of the Command's bases in the UK from Lyneham, near Chippenham, the main base of the Hastings force to Dishforth, the training base in Yorkshire, Abingdon, housing among other things the Parachute School, Aston Down in Hampshire, home of a Ferry Squadron and of which more later, and finally the quaint rural backwater of Cliffe Pipard, basically a simple set of sleeping huts providing B&B for passengers about to set off down the route from nearby Lyneham.

The main workhorse of the Command was the Handley Page Hastings, stately, bulbous, with four Bristol Pegasus piston engines and a tail-wheel undercarriage. Somebody said it reminded them of a clipper ship under full sail. It was just being joined by the Blackburn Beverley for short range, heavy lifting jobs, and with outstanding short landing capabilities, and for long range trooping by probably the most beautiful aeroplane the RAF has ever flown—the de Havilland Comet. Clearly I had joined a very different air force from that of the single-seat Meteors and familiar flat fields and estuaries of East Anglia.

It only took me a short time to learn the basic outlines of the job, much longer to try to become an integrated member of a smoothly running team. The idea was that Harry King, Don Winterbotham and I as well as Sergeant Jock Wise, the AOC's driver and Flight Lieutenant Jim Gresham, the pilot of his Devon light transport aeroplane, operated behind the scenes and automatically so that the Air Marshal could take for granted his briefing papers, his personal transport arrangements and a host of other details in order to concentrate his attention on running Transport Command.

My job was difficult to define but consisted of attending to all the details—except his working papers, the concern of the PSO—of the Air Marshal's travel arrangements, accommodation when away from base, kit and similar items. It included the supervision of the staff in his residence, Littlecott House, and as I got to know him and Mrs McKee well, there became not much distinction between his official and private affairs. The clear purpose was to allow the boss to concentrate his attention on running Transport Command, the introduction of new aircraft, the appointments of the Station Commanders and other senior staff at all the Command's stations, a host of questions concerning the Transport Command stations and staging posts down the route to the Far East and to Australia. In order to do that I spent much of my time on the telephone, checking the movements of other Air Marshals whom the boss needed to contact, checking train times, passing details to our airfields and their Station Commanders, checking with Met on the likelihood of air travel being disrupted, talking to MOD to find out who had some information we needed, going down to the residence to ensure that the carpenters and painters had cleared up after some repair job, taking a uniform into Salisbury to the cleaners, going over to the NAAFI to buy his cigarettes, meeting his weekend house guests from Salisbury station or helping Harry King collate his papers for a forthcoming lecture. If something needed doing to smooth the running of the boss' office then that was all part of my job.

Perhaps I would start Monday morning alerting Jim Gresham, pilot of the Devon, that the AOC was summoned to a meeting at the Ministry of Defence later in the week and wanted to be flown to RAF Northolt. I might then be at my desk talking to Northolt by telephone, to arrange for a car to take the AOC in to the MOD Main Building, when he would buzz for me. "Bill, get me ACAS Ops will you." Soon I knew that the Assistant Chief of the Air Staff, Operations was Air Marshal Sir Ronnie Lees and what his phone number was. When ACAS Ops' staff officer answered I said, "AOC Transport to speak to your master, please." "OK, put him through." Buzz my master. "ACAS Ops, sir," flip the switch, confident that ACAS Ops' staff officer had also done so and that the two Air Marshals were now talking to each other.

It sounds mundane, but it did not take long to realise the intense pressure that these senior people were under and how time was always at a premium. To rid them of all the minor irritations that we lesser mortals have to put up with clearly made a definite contribution to their work and gave us on the staff a real sense of satisfaction.

One of the insights I came to realise was that for senior management, either in the services or in civil organisations, to be surrounded by staff to deal with all these day-to-day affairs was not, as those on the political left seem to think, a matter of arrogance or their insisting on the cushy life. If someone is expected to use their energy, experience and intellectual ability to tackle wide, complex, abstract questions it is the grossest inefficiency for them to have to spend time getting their car refuelled, queuing to buy a ticket or lugging their own suitcases about. The misconception seems to arise, apart from sheer envy, from the fact that a senior executive is paid mainly to think. To the onlooker they appear to be "doing nothing" as their driver conveys them smoothly through the traffic congestion through which the rest of us have to struggle. I started to acquire some idea of the notion of different time horizons. It was my and Sergeant Winterbotham's jobs to be thinking in terms of the rest of today and to the end of the week, Harry King in terms of the next couple of weeks, his senior staff in terms of the next six months to a year and the Air Marshal in terms of the next five or more years.

I still managed to get some flying, quickly getting myself checked out on the Anson and the Balliol. The latter was an excitingly powerful advanced trainer, with a Merlin engine, in fact down-rated, but still a Merlin like in a Spitfire! Whenever the Air Marshal was away Harry King would generously look after the office for me while I went flying. It is churlish to say so but it was a mixed blessing. I would come back to find my desk knee deep in Harry's papers and files, hidden in a thick haze of tobacco smoke and with his current cigarette not in an ashtray but balanced and standing upright on the desk like a miniature rocket waiting to be launched.

One or both of us always accompanied the boss on his visits to our stations. In No 1 uniform we both wore ornate gold epaulettes. The purpose of these was for us to be easily visible in a crowd in case the boss wanted us for some errand. Having checked the time that the function was planned to end and having briefed the driver accordingly, the job at official functions was discreetly to circulate. There would invariably be a large number of people wanting to talk to the AVM so our job was to keep an eye on him and at the same time allow ourselves to be button-holed by anyone who tactfully didn't want to take up his time but who wanted to leave a message for us to pass on at some appropriate moment later. We also tried to judge when someone really did need to have a few words with him and should be enabled to get to the front of the queue, or was who was already being a bore and should be tactfully moved away. One quickly got to learn who fitted into the various categories. As the function began to look like ending, you slipped out and checked that the driver, usually Sergeant Jock Wise, was standing by. Sometimes he had some interesting gossip to pass on that he had heard from other drivers. They ran a very efficient and useful bush telegraph.

A subtler aspect of being on the personal staff was brought home to me by a rude shock that I got when I had been in the job about a month. Harry King and I had accompanied the AOC one evening to a cocktail party at RAF Lyneham, the main UK base for the Hastings force. I listened to the conversation of a number of senior officers on the subject of a political row that was currently going on in a Middle Eastern country where there was a large RAF base. I ventured the remark that it seemed possible that we, Britain, might be tempted to take rather strong-arm action unless the matter was soon resolved. The conversation moved on.

First thing next morning I was sent for by Air Commodore Bob Carter, SASO, who had also been at Lyneham the night before. His warning was blunt. "I want to warn you," he said, "about security. Probably all those taking part in that conversation about the Middle East crisis know about our contingency plans, but it was still unwise to talk about it. You can only have known about it from what you have seen in a Secret file in the AOC's office. Please realise that you are in a privileged position and you must be very careful." I was horrified. I was quite sure I had never seen such a file. If I had I would have known very well not to talk about it, but how could I convince SASO of this and clear my own conscience.

At the end of work I went grimly back to the Officers' Mess and collected all the newspapers of the previous week. I was prepared, if necessary, for a long search of the papers of the previous month if need be. In fact I found the item quite quickly. It was on the back page of one of the less highly regarded tabloids, but still there it was in cold print and that was where I had seen it. I was greatly relieved to be able to take it round to the Air Commodore's house to show him. However his warning was well taken. As a member of the personal staff it would invariably be assumed by others that you were privy to all sorts of top level information, of both operational and personal matters. It was much better to keep one's mouth shut and to be thought stupid than to open it and remove all doubt.

Over the next fifteen months I got to know Air Vice-Marshal McKee pretty well. He treated his staff with pleasant casualness. Only very seldom did he ever express irritation at some thoughtless or unhelpful action one had taken. The occasional raspberry was invariably well deserved. Also I came to realise that if he was able occasionally to snap at his staff this acted as a valuable safety valve. He was a short, tubby man with untidy silver hair. He had the engaging habit when something really funny struck him of actually laughing till real tears streamed down his face. His nick-name among his peers was Square McKee. When Harry King was away I would open his mail and take his letters in to him. One tried to keep a straight face when many of them were addressed to "My Dear ☐ ?." In correspondence from the other services, from admirals and generals, it was surprising how many were addressed to "Air Marsha<u>ll</u> McKee. When he noticed it the AOC sometimes said to me, "You tell the typist to make sure we write back to Genera<u>ll</u> …." RAF Benson, near Oxford, was one of our stations and as with many military units the roads around the camp were named after various distinguished officers, so that one found Slessor Avenue, Tedder Road and so on. In the middle of the officers' married quarters there was, and I think still is, a McKee Square.

Local flying in the Anson or Balliol was pleasant enough but as our Headquarters controlled the whole of the RAF's transport fleet worldwide it seemed to me that I should set my sights higher. Slightly tongue in cheek I suggested to the AOC that it was difficult for me to grasp the significance of some of the concerns of HQ Transport Command or to do my job properly unless I had been "down the route" and had seen the overseas staging posts and bases for myself. He rightly dismissed that argument as highly dubious, but nevertheless agreed that it was only fair that I should indeed see something of the

Transport Force in operation. I happily spent two days at Lyneham getting checked out as a second pilot on the Hastings. I was thus qualified to do odd jobs, to relieve the captain while we flew straight and level and to raise or lower the flaps and undercarriage when told to do so. I joined a crew of No 511 Squadron and we set off for the round trip down the route to Edinburgh Field near Adelaide in Australia.

The cargo bay of the Hastings was filled with a load of crates, mainly equipment for Woomera, the Rocket Testing Facility in South Australia. Wedged in as well were seats for half a dozen civilian passengers, scientists and others. After a very early breakfast and a visit to Met and the self-briefing room for the latest details of the Air Traffic facilities down the route, we climbed into a crew coach for the short trip down to 511 Squadron's aircraft dispersal area. We all climbed aboard and walked up the steeply sloping fuselage. The steps were removed, Pilot Officer Bill Monk, Pilot and Captain, and I as Second Pilot settled ourselves in the cockpit with the Flight Engineer, Navigator and Signaller in their own seats just behind. Brakes on, Fuel on, engines ready for starting, Bill leant out of his side window and pointed to the Port Outer. He engaged the starter motor and the port outer propeller motored slowly over. A couple of coughs, clouds of blue smoke and the engine kicked into life. The Port Inner and the two starboard engines were started and all set at idling revs to warm up. We strapped in to our seats, the Engineer switched on the radio and intercom and we could all talk to each other. Once they were up to operating temperatures Bill ran up each engine in turn, exercising the Constant Speed Units and checking the magnetos and the idling revs.

He waved away the chocks, we trundled out to the marshalling point beside the runway threshold and parked to complete the very comprehensive pre-take-off checks. This was my first experience of the challenge and response means of ensuring that nothing was overlooked. Sergeant Grace, the Flight Engineer, got out a long printed list of items and went steadily through them while the Captain responded. "Oil cooler shutters tested and open." Bill tested them, set them to open and confirmed, "Shutters tested and open." "Flaps 15° for take off." Bill selected 15° of flap and confirmed, "Flaps set at 15° for take off." And so on, through the list concluding with, "Flying controls checked for full and free movement." Bill heaved the heavy spectacle grip of the control column back and forward, wound the ailerons fully from side to side and responded, "Controls checked for full and free." Sergeant Grace tossed the list back into its stowage and announced, "Take off checks complete, Captain." It was a far cry from the fighter-boy's reputed pre-flight checks of, "Fuel, noise, we're off!" or as the Americans have it "Kick the tyres, light the fires and into the wide blue yonder!"

"Thank you, Eng." Bill released the parking brakes and applied a dribble of power to taxi us on to the runway, moving forward in a straight line just far enough to ensure that the tail-wheel was straight. "Right everyone, here we go." He released the brakes and slowly inched forward the four throttle levers, alert to catch any tendency of the aeroplane to swing away from a straight line. As soon as the throttles were fully open he transferred his right hand back on to the flying controls and the Engineer leant forward and placed his hand on the throttles to ensure that they stayed fully open. As soon as we were airborne "Undercarriage up." That was a job for me, I flipped the lever up and watched the indicator lights turn from green (locked down), to red (unlocked), and then go out (undercarriage retracted). We climbed steadily away over the patch-work fields of Wiltshire, brought the revs back to the cruising setting and turned south. The Navigator gave Bill a course to steer and we were on our way.

In no time it seemed we had levelled out at 8,000 ft, had left the English coast, crossed the Channel and were cruising over Northern France, covered with broken cloud. The cockpit was most comfortable, the forward view excellent, the seats with their adjustable arm-rests wide and padded. Regular cups of coffee appeared from the galley followed by a cold lunch. Bill Monk and I flew alternate two-hour watches. There was a rudimentary form of auto-pilot which maintained the selected heading and flying the Hastings consisted of occasionally re-trimming the attitude hold to adjust the trim for level flight. We didn't see Paris but by the early afternoon were skirting the western edge of the Alps and coasting out over the Riviera and across the brilliant blue of the Mediterranean. Our first re-fuelling stop would be Idris, once the Italian airfield of Castel Benito in Libya. We let gently down over the last thirty miles or so, arrived over Idris at 2,000 ft. The downwind pre-landing checks were almost as extensive as those for take-off, and Bill brought us round in a long slow turn, lining up with the runway a good two miles from the threshold. The Hastings had simple manual controls, one of the biggest aeroplanes to have them, and required quite a lot of muscle power especially if the air was at all bumpy, so for the final approach Bill kept both hands on the flying controls. The Engineer looked after the power, moving the throttles progressively back to "minus two pounds boost," "minus four" and "slow cut" as Bill ordered. We floated over the hedge, actually just the dusty edge of the desert, for an immaculate wheeler landing. You don't try a three pointer with a big heavy aeroplane like a Hastings.

This close co-operation between pilot and engineer is only achieved with practise and is, of course, very essential. The tale is told about another Hastings in which the pilot, having ordered "minus four boost" then realised he was badly under-shooting his approach, that is descending too steeply. He asked progressively for "minus two," then "zero boost" and finding he was still undershooting, eventually for "take-off power" meaning the full power normally used for take off. The engineer completely misunderstood and took the power off, closing the throttles completely. They eventually sorted out the misunderstanding from their adjacent hospital beds.

We arrived at Idris in time for a swim, a drink under the palm trees watching the sun sink over the desert, and dinner. After breakfast we set off along the North African coast, across the eastern Mediterranean and Lebanon and out over the desert to Habbaniya in Iraq where the evening programme was repeated. I began to think that perhaps flying these long range transport aeroplanes had something going for it after all. At Waterbeach we had always kidded the transport aviators that their after take-off checks consisted of "Wheels up, flaps up, coffee up, auto-pilot on." They reposted that the fighter boys after take-off call was "Wheels up, I'm clearing the airfield circuit, Mayday Mayday, I'm lost!"

From Habbaniya the next leg was down the Tigris to the top of the Persian Gulf and then to follow the east coast of the Gulf to Mauripur in Pakistan. Here I encountered for the first time that excellent "east of Suez" institution the dhobi wallah. You gave them your soiled shirt, slacks or shorts, socks and everything else and forgot all about them. Next morning there they all were, washed, neatly pressed and with new buttons sewn on if needed.

The next day took us down the west coast of India to Negombo in Ceylon. Here I saw for the first time a true tropical landscape of endless palm trees, white shining sandy beaches and blue, blue sea. So many of the images we first meet in the nursery we find later in real life are a disappointment. But the tropical cocoanut palm with its graceful, sinuous trunk and starburst of gently trembling green fronds of the crown lived right up to my expectations. Then it was on, due east, across the Bay of Bengal and down the Straits of Malacca between Sumatra and Malaya to land at Changi in Singapore.

From that day Singapore has always been a place of special magic and attraction. Just outside the camp entrance was the village of Changi, a dusty street overhung with palms and casuarinas, with young Chinese dashing past on noisy scooters and hordes of younger children running in and out of the shops lining each side of the street. And the shops, or Emporiums as their signs had it … . It was an Aladdin's cave of silks and batik, shirts made to measure within twenty-four hours, carvings of native heads or elephants, cameras, HI-FIs, tape recorders, camphor wood furniture, mah-jong sets, fans, coolie hats, flip-flops, sun cream and films. From the cafes drifted the enticing smells of curries and the rest and pervading all the gentle scent of joss sticks. Each shop would try to entice you in by the offer of an iced Coca-Cola and seat you while displaying for you their wares. Haggling was part of the system. They started by quoting the "laughing price." You countered by offering a pittance and the game went on from there.

Reaching Singapore had taken us five days from UK and so we had a rest day before setting off again early across the islands of Indonesia and the Timor Sea and so to Darwin in the Northern Territory of Australia. One of the attractions of the piston-engine Hastings, if one was not in a special hurry, was that we flew at a modest 6,000 to 8,000 ft altitude where we could enjoy a grandstand view of the land passing slowly below. Some of the Indonesian islands contained spectacular mountain scenery of cliffs, gorges and even volcanoes. It was a long flight to Darwin and as we taxied in and stopped the engines, tired and parched we were looking forward to Australian hospitality. As we swung open the door a rugged Australian Air Force Sergeant pushed the steps into position and greeted us with "Welcome to the arse-hole of Australia."

The last leg to Adelaide seemed interminable. Soon we left the north coast behind us and were flying over a barren red desert with stony ridges stretching to the horizon. In the afternoon as Bill Monk was flying the aeroplane I left the cockpit and lay in the perspex nose, watching the empty landscape with its occasional homestead and water pumping windmill slipping slowly past below. So this was the outback. I was warm and comfortable, the muffled roar of the engines never varied and I slept for over an hour. I woke up and looked down and we needn't have moved. The red desert and the stony ridges seemed identical. Australia is a big, empty place.

At Edinburgh Field we handed the aeroplane over to the local freight handlers who would unload the gear we had brought out for Woomera and reload with the cargo for UK. We said goodbye to our passengers and went into town for the evening. The next morning we set off on the journey back. Having come half way across the globe it seemed rather an anti-climax. Two days to Singapore, a day off for a spot of shopping and after five more uneventful days we were letting down over Wiltshire and trundling down the runway at Lyneham. I thanked 511 for their hospitality. It had been a novel and interesting experience but a touch monotonous. Maybe I would try to stay with single-seat fighters after all.

Some of my duties as ADC were concerned with the McKee's residence, Littlecot House. This was a pleasant, sprawling, rather undistinguished Victorian house overlooking the meadows beside the River Avon. As I have said Harry King could sometimes become more than a little irritating and on more than one occasion I invented plausible reasons to go down to the residence. Mrs McKee soon guessed this. She took a minor interest in horse racing, and I would find her with the newspaper on the sofa beside her open at the racing pages and the television tuned in to Newmarket, Kempton Park or wherever. "Good afternoon, Bill, Harry in one of his tiresome moods is he? Ring for a cup of tea and then come and tell me what you fancy for the 3.30 will you!" Mrs McKee was a very talented violinist and under the name of Cecilia Keating gave regular concert recitals. Being myself almost tone deaf I never took the trouble to go to one. I wish I had.

During the summer months the AOC carried out his annual formal inspections of our stations around the country. Except for Dishforth in Yorkshire we travelled by car. On our arrival we would find the whole station formed up on parade ready for inspection. The day came when it was the turn of RAF Abingdon. We arrived, were greeted by the Station Commander and moved out on to the parade ground.

The form was that the AOC, now followed by the Station Commander, his ADC (me), and the Station Warrant Officer, was greeted as we arrived at each Wing by the Officer Commanding, who saluted and reported for example "No 2 Wing, 14 officers and 82 other ranks on parade and ready for your inspection, Sir." We arrived at the Engineering Wing and the Wing Commander drew himself up, saluted and reported "No 3 Wing on parade and about as ready for inspection as they'll ever be, Sir." For just a moment I thought I had dreamed it, and could not possibly have heard what I thought I had. I caught sight of the Station Commander's face and realised from his expression that he too had heard this novel greeting.

As luck would have it the Wing Commander was a very tall man and this unusual greeting had gone right over the AOC's head. He had at the crucial moment caught sight of the familiar face of a short, elderly Flight Sergeant and was already advancing on him, grinning and saying "Morning, Flight, where have we served together?" He had simply not heard. Somehow we got to the end of the parade, the Wing Commander, who of course was as the Irish say away with the fairies, was taken quietly on one side. He had only a couple of months to serve until his retirement date. He was persuaded that after his long and distinguished career it would be the best thing if he retired early, such as today, such as actually right now. A black coffee and a car were found and he passed into honourable retirement.

The more formal and dignified an occasion is meant to be, the more glaring and hilarious, for those not involved, a cock-up becomes. We on the personal staffs lived in constant fear that we ourselves would put up some memorable "black." The best story that emerged about this time involved Tony Chambers, from whom I heard it later when we were both on the same squadron in Germany.

Tony was also ADC to an Air Marshal, and they went off to a similar station parade. The added interest however was that on this parade the Air Marshal was to present to another Flight Sergeant his Long Service and Good Conduct medal. The medal duly arrived, suitably engraved, and was put for safe keeping in the office safe until the day. They set off, arrived on the parade and the Air Marshal mounted the dais. Flight Sergeant X was ordered to approach the dais for the presentation and marched smartly forward. The citation was read out and the Station Commander turned to the Air Marshal to make the presentation. The

Air Marshal turned to Tony for the medal—and Tony thought, "Oh God, its still in the office safe!" With only the briefest pause the Air Marshal rose imperturbably to the occasion. He stepped down off the dais, grasped the Flight Sergeant firmly by the hand and kept hold of him while he said something to the effect of "Chiefy, you're not going to believe this but my wretched ADC has forgotten to bring the damn thing. I promise you we'll make it up to you at a future date." The now broadly grinning Flight Sergeant saluted, said, "Very good, Sir." marched back to his place and the parade proceeded. Tony waited for the skies to descend on him but as they got back into the car the Air Marshal simply turned to him and said, "Oh, Tony …!"

I had a near miss with a disaster when the AOC visited RAF Colerne, not far north of the A4 in the Cotswolds. It was just after the Suez crisis and Britain was subject to strict petrol rationing, and the use of fuel coupons. Thinking that we ought to economise I had arranged for Corporal Sims, the stand-in driver, to bring the small Humber staff car to the office instead of the Austin Princess. As usual I had to interrupt a meeting the AOC was holding in his office a couple of times to say, "Excuse me, Sir, we ought to be leaving for Colerne." "What, already? No need, Bill, there's plenty of time." By now Corporal Sims was making faces at me through the window and pointing to his watch. I finally got the AOC to move, he collected his hat and came out of the office. "What's that for?" Pointing to the Humber. "I'm not going in that! Go on, Corporal, go and get the proper car." As we set off Sims whispered to me "I haven't re-fuelled this car, sir, I just hope we make it." Half way to Colerne he pushed back the glass screen between the front and rear seats and announced, "Sir, I really don't think we have enough fuel to get to Colerne." I had visions of our stopping at some village filling station and trying to persuade them to sell us a gallon or so without coupons. The boss wouldn't hear of it. The last couple of miles were up narrow country lanes through which I tried to map-read with the boss looking over my shoulder at the map and disagreeing. We arrived at Colerne with about thirty seconds to spare. I gratefully handed the boss over to the Station Commander and said to Corporal Sims, "Before you do anything else take the car down to the MT Section and get re-fuelled." Later in the day he told me that before he had reached the MT Section he had run out of fuel. What the Duke of Wellington would have called a damned close run thing.

My great day came when the AOC was summoned to an Air Council reception at the Ministry of Defence. For Air Council receptions, even Air Marshals were not invited, they were summoned, and required to wear No 1 uniforms, or "Best Blue." By an unfortunate series of co-incidences I failed properly to brief the batman down in the residence. We despatched the AOC in the Devon to Northolt in the usual way and it was only when he got to the Northolt VIP flat to change and opened his suitcase that he discovered that his No 1 uniform had not accompanied him. We had a short, rather one-sided conversation on the telephone, but it was too late for me to do anything about it. He never made the Air Council reception but had to spend the evening at Northolt, no doubt nursing his wrath to keep it warm. This happened on a Friday evening and he had planned to spend the weekend away, not returning to Upavon until the Monday evening. I had plenty of time to reflect on my inefficiency and the probable contents of our forthcoming interview. It promised to be another rather one-sided conversation.

Late on Monday afternoon the Devon touched down and Sergeant Jock Wise met him with the car and brought him up to the office. I offered up a final silent prayer. He stumped up the steps on to the verandah, stopped, put his hands on his hips and barked, "All right, where is he!" In spite of the seriousness of the occasion I couldn't suppress a weak grin. There was a terrible moment of silence and then to my great relief he started to laugh too. In his office I apologised, I cringed, I grovelled. We had about ten minutes of "Bloody, hell, Bill … How the blazes can I do my job if I can't rely on you to … You know you have to tell that damned batman every last detail … How the hell do you expect me to … etc. etc." It was so painful because it was all so eminently fair and well deserved. Finally he slapped his hat on and went home. He never referred to the incident again except that in the charming and generous letter of thanks which he sent me when I finally left the job on posting there was a remark about the fact that "both our memories sometimes need attention."

I had one other near miss. I wanted one Monday morning to go into Salisbury on some private job of my own and so, looking for a pretext, I asked the AOC hopefully if there was any errand in town that I could do for him. Over the weekend he had been writing some private letters to friends. "Yes, Bill, you can get some stamps for these and post them for me." I collected some cash from the petty cash box for the stamps and drove into Salisbury. I posted the letters and went off to deal with my own affairs. Walking back to the car I suddenly thought to myself, "now why did I bring this cash?" I suddenly realise that I had posted the letters without stamps. What fun it was going to be when all his friends had to stump up for the postage due, and no doubt to ring up and tell him about it. Luck was on my side. I was of course in uniform, the collection from the post box was due in ten minutes and the AOC had happened to have been using up some old air-mail envelopes with their distinctive red and blue edges. Also the postman to whom I poured out my troubles had a sense of humour. We spent minutes on our hands and knees sorting through his bag for the stamp less letters. I will never hear a single hostile word said about the old GPO.

On one occasion I was in the car with the Air Marshal on our way to some function when, simply to make conversation, I mentioned a recent staff meeting of his which I had attended. I commented that I was impressed by a certain Group Captain. I said it appeared to me that whereas other people seemed to blurt out the first thing that occurred to them, this Group Captain always waited, sucking thoughtfully at his pipe, until he had sorted out his opinions. The Air Marshal gazed out of the car window for a bit and then turned to me. He laid a friendly hand on my arm and said, "Bill, let me give you a word of advice. Don't always let yourself be too impressed by people who suck their pipe and say bugger all. It may just be that they have bugger all to say!" However the real punch line of the story was that many years later I noted in the press that this silent Group Captain eventually retired as Air Marshal Sir—. Perhaps after all silence sometimes is golden.

The Air Marshal had one characteristic that I have since found to be shared by a number of senior people who are much concerned with broad policy and other highly conceptual matters. He found it difficult to remember peoples' names. Having discovered this I would, whenever I went off with the boss to one of our stations, take with me a small card with the names of the locals. As the Devon taxied in I would be handing the boss his gloves and hat, trying to pick silver hairs off his shoulders and saying, "May I remind you, sir, that the Station Commander's name is Hobbs, Group Captain John Hobbs, and his wife's name is Mary." "Yes, alright, Bill, alright." The door opened, the steps were pushed into position, the Air Marshal descended and returned their salute, "Hullo, old … hullo, hullo, how are you?" A station commander once said to me "Bill, why don't you remind him of our names? It's quite embarrassing you know." I disloyally retorted, "Sir, what the hell do you think I've been doing all the time we were taxi-ing in!"

During my previous tours I had owned a couple of old bangers but at Upavon I had the chance to get a much nicer car. This was a dark green MG TC, the last of the traditional, square, angular MGs. It had a black fabric hood and wire wheels. For some years it was my pride and joy.

Unlike all us youngsters at Waterbeach many of the staff officers at Upavon had growing up families. Air Commodore Carter's wife Sally was a charming and lively American and they had three pre-teenage children. Ian Brotherton, one of the Operation Room officers, and I became supplementary uncles to the Carter children and we spent many happy summer afternoons down at The Beeches, their house in Upavon village.

For the annual inspections of the minor stations the AOC delegated the job to one of the Air Commodores. Thus Air Commodore Carter and I flew off one day in a Balliol to Aston Down. Aston Down housed among other units a Ferry Squadron, whose job as the name implies was to move aeroplanes around, particularly to and from the Maintenance Units for their Major Inspections. It was reckoned better to have the job done by pilots experienced in dealing with all the paperwork than to have it messed up by simple folk from the front line squadrons. Over a very nice VIP lunch and to make conversation, the CO of the Ferry Squadron turned to Air Commodore Carter and remarked that during the coming month they would have the unusual and exciting job of collecting and delivering a Spitfire. Why didn't he come back and have a trip in it? SASO modestly replied that these days he was probably a bit past high performance types like Spitfires.

As soon as we were back in the Balliol on our way home I said to him that even if he was past Spitfires these days I was certainly not! He promised me that he would get his PA to ring Aston Down and say that that he might change his mind and would like to know when the Spitfire was with them. A week later his PA rang me and said "SASO says its there, now it's up to you!"

I had taken the precaution of telling my master what had happened and so when I got the message I went in to his office to ask if I might possibly have the day off. He was busy with the final preparations of an important speech he had to make at RAF Manby in Lincolnshire that evening, but even so he immediately and generously interrupted me almost before I had finished asking. "Yes, of course you can! Bill, you must. Go on, off you go, don't mind me, it could be a once in a life-time opportunity." I jumped into a Chipmunk and flew over to Aston Down. There on the tarmac was that beautiful, silver, so well known shape, with its long powerful nose, its tiny, neat cockpit cover, narrow undercarriage and those graceful elliptical wings. Thank goodness I had plenty of recent hours on Balliols and so although this particular Spitfire had a Napier engine and not a Merlin I started it without trouble and watched enchanted the little puffs of black smoke spitting out of the stub exhausts just as one had so often seen in films. Sure enough the view ahead when taxi-ing was even worse than from the back seat of the Harvard, but it all seemed strangely familiar.

Run up the engine, final pre take-off checks, trimmers set to neutral, pitch selected to fully fine, flaps up, straps tight, canopy shut, compass set, fuel contents, temperatures and pressures all OK, controls for full and free, and the magic moment was here. Air Traffic cleared me for take-off, I taxied on to the runway and lined up. Open up the power very gently, doesn't it sound marvellous, be ready with rudder to correct the swing. As the tail comes up a quick look at the airspeed, gently back on the stick and we are away. Undercarriage up, bring back the revs to max. continuous power and climb away. It was a memorable hour and twenty minutes. Naturally I flew over to Upavon, and as luck would have it, Jim Gresham in the Devon was just getting airborne, to fly the boss up to Manby. I was able to fly briefly alongside them. What pity they didn't have a camera. Of course by jet standards the performance was nothing to shout about and the noise from the engine was terrific, but even in that short time the smooth, light flying controls made an impression and a few simple aerobatics were a total joy. All too soon it was time to land. In the excitement of the moment I completely forgot to make the proper turning, curved approach in order to see comfortably ahead down to the threshold, the pattern that we had so often been bawled out for making, quite un-necessarily, in Meteors because we were pretending we were flying Spitfires. I straightened out, nicely lined up with the runway 200 yards short of the threshold and as I rounded out, that long elegant nose came up and hid everything, but I was on the centre-line and all was well. I hugged myself over and over again as I flew back to Upavon in the Chipmunk. The date was June 14th, 1956 and I had flown a Spitfire!

I also managed to keep my hand in on Meteors as 63 Squadron kindly alerted me when they would be flying over a weekend. If I could escape from the office on a Friday afternoon I would take a Chipmunk or better still a Balliol up to Waterbeach and join in normal squadron flying until an early start on Monday morning back to Upavon. On one such weekend I had an individual, general handling trip on the Saturday afternoon and booked a long and most enjoyable session in the Low Flying Area. I arrived down at the Squadron on Sunday morning to be greeted by a serious looking Bill Shepperd. "Oh, Billy, weren't you in the low Flying Area yesterday afternoon?" "Yes, why?" "Where-abouts were you, because we've had a call from a fisherman who says an aeroplane came down the river he was sitting by, lower than he has ever seen an aeroplane before."

My heart sank. Thank goodness I had been properly authorised for some low flying and although minimum heights always tended to be interpreted a bit flexibly, as a mere visitor I should have been on my best behaviour. The last thing I needed was an awkward enquiry into whether I had broken the rules. The Squadron kept the joke up for most of the morning and then announced that the fisherman himself was here! It was Sergeant "Twiggy" Hazlewood, our Squadron Armourer, and they had all greatly enjoyed my discomfort. Twiggy said that I had in fact been so low that the downwash from the aeroplane had actually rippled the surface of the water.

Before any aeroplane can enter service it is necessary to carry out proving flights, in effect full dress rehearsals with costumes and orchestra. It is only when the real aeroplane actually arrives that the hundred and one tiny details that may have been overlooked will be noticed and can be sorted out. Before the Beverley arrived at Abingdon much attention was given to its large size and equally large turning circle when it was taxi-ing. What was overlooked was the height of the twin fins, too high for the hangar doors. When it arrived it was found to be necessary to jack up the nose wheel, to lower the fins enough to get it into the hangars.

Transport Command's No 216 Squadron was about to take delivery of the most beautiful aeroplane ever flown by the RAF—the de Havilland Comet. The Air Marshal decided to fly out as a passenger on the Comet proving flight to Singapore and to take just a couple of staff officers with him, the Command Principal Medical Officer and me. We flew via Aden and Ceylon, had VIP treatment all the way and enjoyed a splendid ten days.

The airfield of Upavon and the collection of buildings accommodating the Head-quarters lie on Salisbury Plain. At the bottom of the hill the village of Upavon as well as those of Pewsey to the north and Netheravon to the south lie in the valley of the Hampshire Avon. South again beyond Salisbury the river winds on past Downton, Fordingbridge and Ringwood to meet the sea in Christchurch Harbour and Mudeford Haven. Soon after the First World War four young men from around Pewsey village were challenged that they couldn't put a boat into the river at Pewsey and paddle, tow or eventually, once there was room for it, row to the sea. They used a clinker built skiff, the sort of boat used on summer afternoons to row one's girl friend down the Thames or around the Serpentine, while she steers with a couple of ropes to a rudder at the stern.

They did not hurry. The trip entailed numerous portages, places where the boat had to be lifted out of the water to negotiate various obstacles, barbed wire, low overhanging trees, or weirs. They slept in barns or friends' cottages and took about a week over the trip, eventually triumphantly rowing out of Mudeford Haven and being able lean over the side and scoop up water to taste the salt from the sea. The trip passed into village mythology and in about 1950 four sons, cousins or nephews of the original Pewsey Mariners decided to repeat the voyage and try to beat the old timers' record. They lowered the elapsed time to about four days.

Thus in the spring of 1956 as the conversation in the Greyhound Pub in Pewsey happened one evening to get round to the Pewsey Mariners, someone asked Squadron Leader Gus Thouard, wasn't it time that the RAF had a go at repeating the trip again. Gus agreed it was and came and found Ian Brotherton, and put the idea to him. Ian, a laid back Navigator, had spent many months trying unsuccessfully to get me to have a go at his favourite sport, the Cresta Run but immediately roped me in to this project. We also grabbed Sid Wilkinson, an engineering officer and as the fourth member of the crew, Graham Tunley, the representative at Upavon of the Bristol Aircraft Company. We even did a spot of training in the gymnasium with medicine balls but more to the point we tried to get a bit organised. Air Commodore Chris Hartley became the enthusiastic, overall manager of the support party and arranged walkie-talkie radios, transport and, taking advice from the medics, an endless supply of high energy food—and drink. We also researched the river to work out the best dates. It had to be late enough in the year for long light summer evenings but not so late that the river weed had grown up into its full, clogging profusion.

Ian and I carried out a series of aerial reconnaissance trip down the river. We went off in a Chipmunk armed with a large scale map and marked in anywhere where from the air it was not obvious which way to go. We then went down again by car and tramped over the meadows beside the river, working out the best ways to go so as not to waste time by having to retrace our steps on the actual trip. We went down to Christchurch, found a friendly boat yard and hired a skiff complete with oars and paddles. One of our supporters had an inspired thought. We knew we would repeatedly have to lift the boat bodily out of the water and around obstacles so we got the parachute section to make webbing slings attached to the seats which we could slip over our shoulders to make the lifting dead easy.

One Friday night just before mid-summer we took the boat up to Pewsey and left it in the field of a friendly farmer. We were there ready for the start before the dawn. It had also been the night of the Lyneham Summer Ball and we were sent on our way by a mess-kitted and evening dressed contingent of revellers. At Pewsey the Avon is just a narrow stream that one could almost jump across, the boat just floated empty and we took it in turns to wade and tow it. By breakfast time we had reached Upavon village and an eggs and bacon party on the bridge was most welcome. So it went on throughout the day, at every bridge the support party was there with Mars bars, apples, coffee or whatever took our fancy. By evening we had reached the Rose and Crown at Harnham just beyond Salisbury. Our supporters were there in force, the beer was flowing and the whole expedition could have foundered or at least been seriously delayed.

We just had the presence of mind to tear ourselves away and back into the boat. At Longford, as it finally got completely dark, our

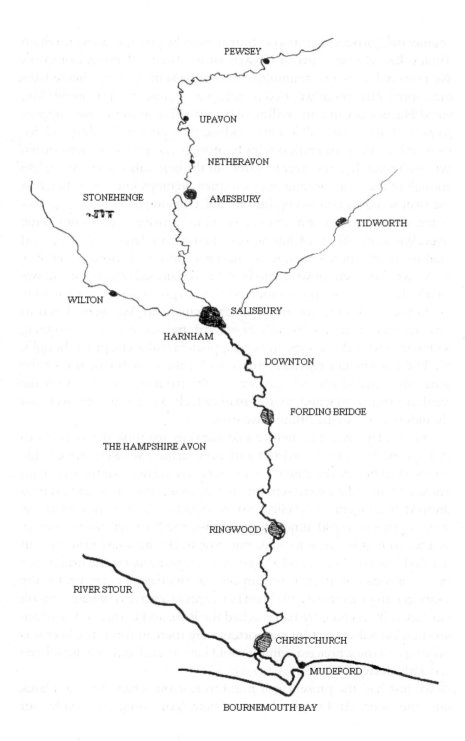

PEWSEY

UPAVON

NETHERAVON

STONEHENGE

AMESBURY

TIDWORTH

WILTON

SALISBURY

HARNHAM

DOWNTON

FORDING BRIDGE

THE HAMPSHIRE AVON

RINGWOOD

RIVER STOUR

CHRISTCHURCH

MUDEFORD

BOURNEMOUTH BAY

113

supporters produced their master-stroke. Squadron Leader Peggy Potter, one of the staff at HQTC, was a keen show jumper. Our supporters had borrowed Peggy's horse box, cleaned it out and equipped it with rugs and sleeping bags. As we came ashore we were handed steak, chips and all the trimmings and told we would be called at first light.

The second day was idyllic. The river was now wider and deeper and we could paddle and soon row. The Avon wound down through water meadows and past tiny villages, willows hung over the stream, and we disturbed swans, moorhens, herons and every variety of duck. On the Sunday evening we came finally in to Christchurch quay to disembark and were greeted by the town Mayor. If you go to Pewsey today you will find in the Public Bar of the Greyhound Hotel a framed map of the river and selected photographs of the third generation of Pewsey Mariners.

As the year drew to its end Upavon prepared to celebrate Christmas and the New Year. The New Year's Eve party was already going with a swing when hush was called for a special announcement. The New Year's Honours list included promotion and a knighthood for the Air Vice-Marshal, now to be Air Marshal Sir Andrew McKee. Squadron Leader Ted Lewis went up to him and said "Sir, I hear you are to be known as Sir June 21. You must surely be the shortest knight of the year!" The party continued with renewed vigour.

Early in the New Year I heard the exciting news that 63 Squadron had finally been able to say goodbye to their faithful Meteors and had re-equipped with the latest Mark of Hunter, the Mk 6. I arranged another few days at the 'beach and managed to get checked out. There was no two-seater at the time and it was just a matter of someone leaning over the side of the cockpit and showing you where everything was before you shut the hood, started the engine and went. Compared with the Meteor the performance was spectacular. Perhaps most striking was the incredible lightness of the powered ailerons. On the first trip most of us found it almost impossible to prevent over-controlling and so gently waggling the wings as we climbed away on take off. However such is one's adaptability that after a couple of trips the ailerons were no further trouble. The Hunter was certainly a most delightful aeroplane to fly, hence its long term and universal popularity.

Before I left the 'beach to fly back to Upavon I called in to see the

Wing Commander Flying, Ken Pugh to thank him for my Hunter trip. He then said, "You must be getting near the end of your tour as ADC. What are you hoping to do next?" I told him I was of course keen to get on to Hunters, but added the AOC had promised to see me right. When I had joined his staff the Air Marshal, as he now was, had promised me he would not keep me on his staff more than fifteen months. As the spring arrived he called me in and asked me what posting I would like. I told him I wanted to fly Hunters, and he said to leave it with him. The next day he called me in again. He had been in touch with the Air Secretary who had told him there were no Hunter Squadron vacancies at present. He suggested I opt for Canberras. I asked for time to think about it and put an urgent phone call through to Wing Commander Pugh. He called back the next day. "It's all fixed!" he said, "You can come back to 63 at the start of next month." It was rather fun then to be able to tell the Air Marshal I no longer needed his help. It's not what you know it's who you know!

It had been an interesting tour and an enjoyable one mainly as Air Marshal and Lady McKee had been delightful people to work for. In his farewell letter to me he wrote, "As you know and no doubt you found out, an Aide's life is not a bed of roses .... We both send our very best wishes .... We hope, now that we have become personal friends, you will from time to time come and see us."

# No 63 Squadron

## (Second Tour)

### R A F Waterbeach

IN JUNE '57 I returned to Waterbeach and to No 63 Squadron, almost feeling that I had never been away. Squadron Leader "Sid" Walker was now the boss. Mike Scarrott was OC A Flight and "Cosy" Cole OC B Flight. Many of the old faces were still there— among them Danny Hicks. Since I had last seen him he had actually left the RAF, decided to re-enlist, re-joined 63 and been handed back his old inventories to carry on running them. Newcomers included Don Hall from whom I had taken over as Secretary of the Climbing Club at Cranwell, Ken Petrie, Pete Jarvis, who would become an aerobatic ace, Derek Hine and Mick Davis, the best air gunnery pilot I ever met. One often hears the dictum that one should never re-visit old haunts and apart from the opportunity it provided me to get on to the Hunter force my second short tour with 63 was not as enjoyable as the first.

In spite of the presence of some excellent men this time round there was too a rowdy, exhibitionist element on the squadron which I thoroughly disliked. When I had arrived I had gone to see Wing Commander Ken Pugh to thank him for fixing my posting. After talking for a few minutes about my return to 63 he had suddenly said,

"Can you be an absolute bastard?" I cannot remember what I had replied and I did not think much more about it. But I soon came to see that some of 63 at that time needed to be grabbed by the scruff of the neck and brought back into line. I have grave doubts about whether I could have done it effectively even had I been back on the squadron longer. The situation was not helped by the fact that I had been allowed to short circuit the system and so I had never completed a proper conversion on to the Hunter. At the time I was just pleased to be flying it and back on the Squadron and I was confident I could learn all about the aeroplane as I went along, but I never became as familiar or comfortable with the Hunter as I had been with the Meteor. Conversion Units are there for a purpose and with the benefit of hindsight I can see that I should not have been allowed to miss the proper conversion course.

We were now equipped with Mark 6 Hunters, in every way a great advance on the much-loved but by then very out-dated Meteors. The two aircraft were of different generations. The Hunter had one immensely powerful axial-flow Rolls Royce Avon engine, swept wings and fully powered controls. The Avon, unlike the old Derwents, had a fully automatic starting sequence. You just hit the start button and the automatics did the rest. All the early problems with the hydraulic controls had been sorted out and once they were engaged the ailerons in particular were unbelievably light and powerful. Almost everyone on their first solo climbed away with their wings gently rocking as they kept over-controlling. At height the Hunter had a minor vice in that when you pulled "g" the wing tips stalling before the inner portions of the wings. This moved the centre of lift inboard and so forward and caused the aeroplane to pitch up. It was cured by adding a bit to the front, the leading edge of the outer part of the wing, giving the leading edge a slightly unsightly saw-tooth kink in its otherwise graceful line.

The Hunter was the latest of the line of famous fighter aeroplanes from the Hawker Company stretching back to the Harts of the 1930s through the Hurricanes of the Battle of Britain, the Typhoons and Tempests from the end of the Second World War. It was certainly a most graceful aeroplane, the shape of the swept wings matched by the top line of the slim, circular fuselage where it swept up to the tail like the fin of a cruising shark. The engine air intakes merged into the wing roots without interrupting the smooth line of the leading edges. The

Hunter was armed with four Aden 30mm cannons or could carry a wide selection of loads on its four under-wing pylons.

In contrast to the old problem of "hitting the mach" in the Meteor, with the Hunter in even a gentle dive you found you had without knowing it gone sonic and that the controls were unaffected. Should you, for any reason, lose hydraulics oil pressure, the controls reverted to straight manual control. They were certainly a bit heavy but you then flew the aeroplane as if it had been a big cumbersome transport doing wide gentle turns and there was really no trouble at all.

There was one curious omission in the design of the original Hunter in that it had no airbrakes. It had been intended that the flaps could be lowered 10°, one notch on the selector, to reduce speed but this was found at high Mach Numbers to produce a strong nose-down trim change. There was an instance of someone getting into a steep supersonic dive, forgetting that he had a notch of flap selected and bailing out. An airbrake had to be added to the Hunter underneath the rear fuselage as a rather clumsy afterthought.

It was found that another minor modification was needed on the Hunter when the guns were fired. The relatively heavy spent cartridge cases were ejected clear of the aircraft without any trouble but the sprung steel links which held the rounds together into belts, being much lighter, where whipped back by the air-stream along the underside of the fuselage scratching and gouging the skin as they went. To collect the links and to prevent this damage two streamlined fairings were added covering the link ejector openings under the aircraft nose. At the time there was on the television a certain celebrated personality, a girl with rather prominent assets, called Sabrina. The two bulbous fairings under the forward fuselage of the Hunter were always known as Sabrinas.

With the high performance of the Hunter, in combat, we were going to spend much of our time pulling lots of "g." The sensation of "g" or acceleration is seldom experienced on the ground and so it is hard to describe. Acceleration in this sense does not necessarily involve a change of speed but of direction. In a car cornering fast we have all experienced the sensation of being flung sideways. In an aeroplane you are not flung sideways because, unlike in the car, you are banked into the turn but you are pressed downwards. At 2g, quite a gentle turn, the apparent weight of every part of your body is doubled. At 3 and higher "g"s your apparent body weight increases accordingly, at 4 or more "g" it becomes quite hard for your neck muscles to hold your head up and even to hold your eyelids open! At higher "g" still the blood tends to pool in your lower limbs and trunk and so it cannot easily be pumped up to your head. You experience darkening and tunnelling of your vision and eventually you "black out" as your brain too is failing to get its proper blood supply.

In practice it was less alarming than it sounds because if you blacked out you of course relaxed your backward pull on the control column and the "g" diminished. To combat the effects of "g" we were equipped with "g"-suits. These were a sort of corset, worn under your flying overalls, with tight fitting bladders fitted over your calves, thighs and stomach. When you climbed into the Hunter you connected your "g"–suit to a compressed air supply in the aeroplane. Then when you pulled "g" compressed air was fed into the suit preventing your blood from unhelpfully pooling down below your waist and raising your "g" threshold quite a bit. I never liked "g"-suits. Especially in hot weather they were prickly and uncomfortable but they were a necessary evil.

It would clearly take me a bit of time to become even adequately familiar with the Hunter but before I could do so a further question arose. For anyone wanting eventually to become a Flight Commander it was more or less essential for them to attend DFLS, the Day Fighter Leaders' School, part of The Central Fighter Establishment at West Raynham in Norfolk. However, due to some policy change, the next DFLS course, due to start in late August, was to be the last one for some time. So although I was still getting to grips with simply flying the Hunter I joined the course. I performed just about adequately but it would clearly have been much better if I had gone there with at least a few more hours experience on type—or had done a proper Hunter conversion.

The last phase of the course was "streaks and swipes," actually sweeps and strikes. For this exercise each student in turn led a formation of eight aeroplanes; two finger fours, on either a strike, if one was destined for a ground attack unit; or a sweep, if one was going to be an interceptor. I was tasked to lead a strike. This entailed climbing to altitude, before "letting down"; coming down over the sea and approaching the "enemy" coast (still East Anglia) at low level. Having pinpointed your position you then led the formation at low level to

119

your designated target and zoomed up at the last moment to dive down on to it in a simulated cannon and rocket attack. The staff would have arranged for the target to be defended, by notifying some neighbouring squadrons of your intended target and the time that you were planning to strike it. You could therefore expect that the defending fighters would be circling overhead and that you would have to fight your way out.

The exercise required detailed planning, you then briefed the rest of the pilots, led the sortie and ran the debrief, after which the member of the DFLS staff who had flown as one of the formation debriefed you. It was an exciting, realistic and quite stressful exercise. I just about coped but found I certainly had my hands full and my thought processes fully stretched. We climbed away from the target, my sub-formation leader, Charlie Slade, helpfully suggesting that I detach his four to recover to base independently. We four arrived back in the West Raynham circuit and landed. After all the excitement I landed a bit hot and fast, and then discovered that Air Traffic had unhelpfully not told us that there had been a wind change since we had taken off nor that we were landing with a ten knot tail-wind. I failed to stop in the distance available and went off the end of the runway on to the grass. The Hunter's high-pressure tyres sank straight in and I had to stop the engine and wait ignominiously for a tractor. It hardly put me in the right frame of mind to conduct an incisive debrief of the whole sortie. But overall it had been a good course and a very steep learning experience.

By December I was just about fully at home on the Hunter and as air gunnery had always been a particular interest I jumped at the opportunity to go to Driffield to the Fighter Weapons School to get qualified as a PAI—a Pilot Attack Instructor. For some reason the course proved especially enjoyable. My fellow students and many of the staff became very good friends. The whole station had a positive, lively atmosphere, largely due to the personality of the Station Commander, Group Captain Deacon-Elliott, otherwise "The Wedge." He was not the only short, stocky man I have known who was a very considerable squash player. I managed to squeeze into the station squash team and while I was at Driffield enjoyed some splendid evenings of fixtures against civilian teams in Hull, Beverley and the neighbourhood.

I had decided to replace my MG. I went into a car dealer in Driffield originally to enquire about a Morris Minor. Due to some expert salesmanship by the dealer I emerged a week later with British Racing Green Triumph TR2. Shortly after I had bought it Bill Shepperd happened to come up to Driffield on some errand and stayed the night. Of course I had to show off my new car and we had a run into Hull and around a few of the pubs. Driving back to Driffield through a village just north of Beverley I took a sharpish curve much too fast, lost it and spun. Bill said afterward that it was better than Cinerama. The view in front went road–hedge–wall–shop–hedge (again) ... and so on! By rights we should have expensively clouted the very solid brick wall, instead of which we spun on parallel to the wall and eventually slithered across a grass verge into the hedge—and broke a headlight. The total cost of the damage was about £20. The incident had happened at about eleven o'clock at night, so I was very impressed when at met. briefing the following morning the Station Commander greeted me with, "Good morning, Boult, not too much damage to your car last night I hope!" The Wedge was clearly a man who had his finger very firmly on the pulse of what went on round his station.

The gunnery exercises were fascinating and the course, aiming to prepare students to run gunnery training back on their squadrons, also included instructional technique. During one session I learned an unforgettable lesson on not getting over engrossed in what one was saying, but to spare a thought for the listeners too. I had worked hard to write and deliver a certain lecture, and had laboriously drawn some relevant diagrams on the blackboard. When I had finished my talk our instructor, without a word, walked over to the door and switched on the room lights. In my concentration on what I was saying I had simply not noticed the deepening gloom of the January afternoon. "Yes," he said," I think your diagrams are splendid—now that we can see them!"

The gun-sight in the Hunter was basically similar to that in the Meteor in that its gyroscopically-controlled aiming system automatically indicated the appropriate deflection with one proviso. The pilot still had to assess the range of the target. You needed to know the wing-span of the target aircraft. With this figure set on it, the gunsight then projected with the aiming pipper, an ingenious sort of optical callipers. You moved the twist-grip on the throttle control to adjust the sighting picture until the callipers appeared just to bracket the target and you were then feeding the correct range into the sight. A fair degree of accuracy could eventually be achieved with practice but a great improvement was offered with the introduction of Radar Ranging. Once the radar had locked on to the target, indicated by a small green light within your field of vision as you peered through the sight, its range was fed into the sight with complete accuracy.

The detailed design of the Radar Ranging threw up an example of the poor communications which too often existed between boffins and aircrew. The radar set was about the size of a shoe box and was quite a tight fit, located right in the nose of the Hunter with the 8 inch radar dish directly behind the plastic nose fairing. The radar was installed with the dish aiming or "looking" directly ahead along the axis of the aircraft. Knowing that the guns were aimed by aiming the aeroplane this presumably seemed to the designers entirely logical. However, had they talked to the fighter pilots who were going to use the sight, the flaw in this reasoning would at once have been revealed. The only time that the target was going to be directly ahead of the fighter was when you were line astern of it, and in this case no deflection was needed. In all other cases the fighter would be turning and aiming ahead of the target aircraft to allow the necessary deflection and the target was going to be below the nose. The longer the range and the tighter the turn the more would this be the case. A radar dish operates best along its axis and so the optimum performance of the radar ranging was going to be confined to the very case when it was not needed.

When I got to the Air Gunnery School at Driffield and became immersed in all the interesting details of air gunnery I found that they were working to overcome this problem. The obvious solution would have been to mount the radar set so that its dish pointed down at a small angle below the aircraft's axis. However such was the tightness of the fit that this was not possible. Instead of this the studs on which the actual dish was mounted were being fitted with small shims or washers to tilt just the dish down. The wave-guide which powered the dish could not, however, be moved and so the two elements were going to be out of alignment. This was inevitably going to degrade the performance of the equipment by a certain amount and Driffield were doing trials to find the best compromise. Of course the whole problem could have been avoided had the designers of the radar ranging come to consult the users before they completed the detailed design. Later in my career and particularly at Boscombe Down I saw other situations where ostensibly technical problems were actually people problems.

I greatly enjoyed Driffield and just missed winning the Leconfield Trophy for the most marks on the course. We all received beautifully written certificates, written in elegant copper-plate by Dickie Doe, one of the navigators who had accompanied the night/all weather-fighter pilots on the course. Our certificates stated that we had qualified as PAIs. Dickie also produced certificates for himself and his fellow navigators stating that they too had qualified as "PAI's Mates."

No sooner had I got back to the 'beach than we heard that the squadron had won the Dacre Trophy for our year's air gunnery scores and we had a party to celebrate. Not long previously we had done a short attachment to the Belgian Air Force base at Beauvechain near Brussels and we had brought back various goodies. At the party the tastefully displayed Dacre Trophy was somewhat over-shadowed by our fully working model of Brussel's best-known statue—Mannikin Pis.

Shortly after the PAI course I was up in London one weekend and staying in the RAF Club. I came down from my room intending to have a quiet drink in the bar before dinner and there in the corridor was Jack Sherburn. I had heard on the grapevine that he had been commissioned and there he was. He had recently come back from Africa where he had been flying Harvards in operations against the Mau Mau terrorists. This called for a not-so-quiet drink but we paused on the way to the bar for Jack to check his letter rack. He picked up a letter and turned it over thoughtfully. It was addressed to "Flight Lieutenant Sherburn, DFC." It was an official notification from the Ministry of Defence informing Jack, "that the Queen has been graciously pleased to approve the award of the Distinguished Flying Cross for services..." This called for a series of not-at-all-quiet drinks and we had a delightful evening celebration. I was so pleased that I had happened to run into Jack at just the right moment.

The two day-fighter squadrons, 56 and 63, now shared Waterbeach with No 253 (Hyderabad) Squadron, a night/all-weather outfit who flew two-seat Venoms. They had acquired their title while serving between the wars in India and had carried out some service for the Nizam of Hyderabad. He had presented the Squadron with an ornate and quite valuable ornamental axe that was kept in a glass case opposite that containing Albert Ball's uniform. Unfortunately at Dining In Nights both trophies were likely to become the object of various escapades by the more boisterous members of the other squadrons. A great comedian on 56 Squadron was Alan Harvey or "Harv." On one memorable night Harv appeared late on at a very good party actually wearing Albert Ball's uniform, at which various senior officers went apoplectic at this desecration of such a valuable and almost sacred relic. But as Harv himself said, "I don't know what all the fuss was about. Do you know it fitted me perfectly, just shows what an ace I must be too!"

No 253 Squadron's axe was not held in quite such reverence, but their boss always had visions of hefty insurance claims whenever the cry went up from the day-boys of "Let's get the axe!" We more sober types often took the cry as a signal that it was time for bed before any real trouble started. However we were on generally good terms with 253 and many of the more experienced of us managed to chat up their boss and organise a trip in a Venom before the end of our tours. There was, as with the Hunter, no dual-control version and one had to talk some long-suffering navigator into coming along for the ride. The Venom was an improved and much more powerful version of the Vampire, and often described as a Vampire with hair on its chest.

Each of the day squadrons had a Vampire T11 two-seater for instrument flying and other odd jobs. At the start of '58 our new boss on 63 decided we ought to start an aerobatic team. I would dearly have liked to have been a member, but others had been on the squadron ever since the arrival of the Hunter, had many more hours on it and so a better claim. We had at the time a naval officer attached to us, a Lieutenant Paul Perks, and he and I appointed ourselves as chase pilots for the team. We flew the T11 which being considerably slower than the Hunters was ideal. As the team for example flew a loop, we could fly a much smaller loop keeping inside them rather like a terrier chasing a greyhound. We could thus keep them in view with our gun-sight cine camera. We filmed all their manoeuvres and the film was a considerable aid at the de-briefs for analysing their station keeping and revealing faults.

During my previous tour at the 'beach there had been the eventful escape and evasion exercise, but that had only introduced us to the general feeling of trying to evade and of coping with fatigue and stress. It had now been realised that much of the chance of success in evading depended not just on grimly carrying on but on understanding some well-proven techniques, for example of finding and preparing food, making shelters and so on. A course on these elements was being run in Scotland and three of us from the squadron decided to do it. This was how I made my first visit to the Rothiemurchus Hut. The hut was a simple wood cabin three miles from the nearest road in the valley of the river Spey on the northern edge of the Cairngorm Mountains. Sleeping accommodation was in tiers of bunks and there was a comfortable if cluttered and smoky central room. The main thing after a day on the hills was that it was warm, and there was a drying room for wet clothes. A Major Ward ran the course and in spite of it being in November and not in mid-summer it was great fun. We got soaked and frozen paddling across Loch Morlich in aircrew one-man inflatable dinghies, and suitably exhausted climbing over the Cairngorms.

One exercise on what looked at first sight to be an area of completely bare hillside consisted of our having to conceal ourselves well enough to be missed by a line search. We found that it is surprising how well one can hide under the smallest clumps of heather so long as you stayed absolutely still; it is the slightest movement that attracts the searchers' eyes. One course member did better. When the search party had passed and Major Ward declared the exercise to be over, a soaking, mud-coated figure emerged from the bed of a burn. He had lain completely submerged, with a bunch of weeds over his face to breathe through. That was acknowledged as real dedication. On the Sunday evening we walked the three miles down the hill to the Outdoor Activities Centre beside Loch Morlich for the short church service and the minister's sermon. After the service Ken Petrie and I took turns between us to carry on our backs a new, full Calor gas container back up the hill to the hut. That was acknowledged as real dedication too.

I hardly had enough time back at the 'beach to pass on all the good "gen" from the Fighter Weapons School when I heard that I was posted. When I had re-joined 63 I had been so pleased to be on Hunters that I was not unduly concerned that I was just a squadron pilot again rather than even a Deputy Flight Commander. The previous year the government had introduced a series of economy measures, known as the Sandys Axe, after the then Secretary of State for Defence, Duncan Sandys. One of the cuts had been to reduce the RAF's commitment in Germany and to disband one of the Hunter squadrons. Now, a year later, with a re-assessment of priorities, or the re-shuffling of politicians, it was decided to re-form the squadron. No 26 Squadron

125

was to re-form in May '58 at RAF Ahlhorn and I was posted there as OC A Flight. This meant my own Flight, cheap continental holidays and a new (purchase tax free) car, so it all sounded a very good idea.

# No 26 Squadron

## R A F Ahlhorn & R A F Gütersloh

I DISPOSED OF the TR2, made my farewells to 63 Squadron and caught the boat to the Hook of Holland. The train wound its way through the Netherlands and eventually across the north German plain. Ahlhorn was an ex-Luftwaffe airfield halfway between Bremen and the Dutch border. It was surrounded by open, flat, sparsely populated countryside and large areas of pinewoods. The few villages were often of attractive half-timbered houses and farm buildings but were invariably run down and shabby. Ahlhorn camp itself was unremarkable but the Officers' Mess was airy and spacious, typically German. The accommodation bungalows were surrounded by glades of pine trees and the whole station had a pleasant, rural ambience. As a lover of wide-open spaces I immediately liked it.

I reported to the Station Commander, Group Captain Peter Cribb, and he pointed out the hangar that was to accommodate No 26 Squadron. We were to share the station with Nos 14 and 20 Squadrons and so again make up a Wing which had managed to retain its identity since the end of the Second World War—No 124 Wing.

I was the first of the squadron pilots to arrive. The hangar appeared to be completely empty until I heard voices coming from one of the offices. In the office I found two Flight Sergeants, three aircraftmen, a packing case being used as a table and not much else. "Good morning, sir, what about cup of tea?" And so I first met Chiefies Mackintosh and Anstey and some of the troops who were to become very good friends and colleagues on the brand new 26 Squadron which we put together over the next few months.

The following day the boss, Squadron Leader Eddie Edmunds, arrived and over the next couple of weeks the rest of the pilots and ground crew followed. We were too busy to reflect much about it at the time but setting up the squadron from scratch, seeing it come together as a blend of all the individuals as they arrived and develop its own distinctive personality, was a unique and fascinating experience. The first job was to walk round the empty hangar deciding which rooms were to be the boss's, Flight Commanders' and Flight Sergeants' offices, and then the electricians and engine mechs' lairs, the pneumatic and hydraulics bays and all the rest. Mike Read, OC B Flight, the boss and I were all new to the Squadron and to RAF Germany, but about half the rest of the pilots had been on the old 26 before it was disbanded. Willie Wilmot and Phil Alston re-joined us from 20, Fred Daley, John Merry, Chris Cowper and the irrepressible Bill Bailey from 14 and Al Pollock from No 4 at "Jeever's Field" (RAF Jever). Experienced Hunter pilots from UK included Tony Chambers, Dave Whitaker and Chris Strong. Less experienced new comers were Bill Stoker and Gil McCluney. Remembering his expertise in gunnery I told the boss about Mick Davis. He pulled some strings and Mick duly arrived. We took over aeroplanes from the other squadrons and for a time flew a motley looking collection carrying many different squadron markings.

No 26 Squadron had originally been formed in South Africa as an observation unit working with the army, and our full title was still No 26 (Army Co-operation) Squadron. Our crest was a springbok's head and our motto, in Afrikaans " 'n wagter in die lug"; the watcher or the sentinel in the sky. We were keen to re-establish the Squadron's distinct personality as soon as possible and we delved around in the archives to see what goodies we had inherited. One of these turned out to be a beautifully mounted springbok's head which was proudly displayed on the wall of the aircrew coffee bar. Regimental and unit ties were then fashionable and we discovered that 26 Squadron had two. Somewhere lost in the mists of our earliest history in "Army Co-operation" we had acquired a striped tie of alternate broad and narrow stripes of dark green and black. There was also a conventional dark blue tie decorated with small silver springbok heads. I think it was the boss who came up with a novel way to use both. The dark blue tie with its springbok crests could be worn by everyone on the squadron, including all our ground-crew and the most junior pilots. After having been on the Squadron for about four months a pilot would be declared "operational." He would than be awarded the black and green tie to mark the occasion.

We discovered that our traditional aircraft insignia was a green lightning flash on a black ground. I produced a sketch of the springbok head between two such flashes which Corporal Harnden laboriously and expertly reproduced on all our aircraft. The large white disk bearing the Springbok head stood out well and turned out to be most useful in letting us instantly identify our aeroplanes as they re-entered the circuit.

No 26 had only been in existence for a couple of months when the Station Athletic Sports Day arrived. Feeling concerned for us new-boys the organisers suggested that the very small Air Traffic Controllers team should join us to even things up a bit. We won the Inter-Unit Competition. Even I contributed one point by puffing slowly round the three-mile steeplechase. The average age of the squadron pilots must have been about twenty-two. In the station cinema one night the 26 Squadron contingent was reduced to helpless laughter when the advertisements were interrupted by a slide which said simply, "Guess who's getting old?" At twenty-six I was regarded as positively geriatric.

Back at Waterbeach 63 Squadron had been big enough to operate as two virtually independent flights. 26 was not big enough for that and although for organisational purposes Mike Read and I each managed our own pilots, our flying programme had to be a single operation. Mike and I took it in turn to plan and run the programme and any formation would be made up of pilots from both flights. Mike's background was as a flying instructor, he had plenty of experience of this and I learned a great deal from him.

As part of RAF Germany we were also part of the broader defence system of Western Europe which was NATO. Such has been the success of the North Atlantic Treaty Organisation that we have tended to take it for granted. It is nowadays easy to forget that it was set up in response to increasingly threatening behaviour by the Soviet Union, actions such as the Berlin blockade. As squadron pilots we were not involved in issues of higher strategy but a pleasant aspect of the job was the feeling of camaraderie we enjoyed with the Dutch, Belgian, Danish, Norwegian, Canadian and of course United States Air Forces. When we encountered people around the station or in the Mess wearing different uniforms our first question was always what type of aeroplane they flew. Quite as an afterthought, if we remembered to ask at all, we might wonder what nationality they were.

Our tactical flying exercises were much the same as we had practiced on 63 Squadron's Hunters and for that matter on the Meteors. Battle Formation does not convey much but it was the basis of how to manoeuvre two, four or more aeroplanes around the sky in an efficient way maintaining the best combination of flexibility and mutual cross cover, to avoid the possibility of being "bounced" unexpectedly. One tactic was to leave a pair at the height where they were making contrails to act as bait. Often this was quite a narrow height band, and the rest of the formation climbed a few thousand feet higher where, if there were no trails, and especially up sun, one became almost invisible. We tried to remember and to put into practice all the old adages such as, "The Man with the Height Controls the Fight" and, "Beware of the Hun in the Sun," except that in our case it would have been the Mig in the sun.

It is hard for those without the experience of it to appreciate how difficult it is to see properly at height. Far above cloud and also above most of the atmosphere the sunlight is intense but the rest of the sky is almost black. On the instrument panel half of an instrument will be intensely illuminated while the other half, where the shadow of the cockpit arch falls, will be quite invisible. For years many of us agitated for the interiors of cockpits to be painted pale grey to allow some diffusion of light but at the time black was traditional so black they remained.

The high performance of the Hunter and the delightful lightness of the powered controls made it a joy to fly and if at, say 40,000 ft, one put the nose down a bit in no time at all one had, without noticing it, gone supersonic and planted a sonic bang on the ground below. One day Fred Daley and I were flying as a pair when we came across a four of No 20 Squadron flying around, as one of our squadron songs averred, "with their eyes up their arses." We stalked them, successfully bounced them and then reckoning that two against four was not really a good idea headed for home flat out with an indignant 20 Squadron in hot pursuit. It was a gin clear day and we could see base from thirty miles away so we popped our airbrakes and came straight down into the circuit. As we taxied in and on to the chocks Flight Sergeant George Anstey came out to meet us grinning broadly and pretending to massage his ears. Apparently all six of us must have planted a bang simultaneously which had lifted Ahlhorn about a foot in the air. In later years back in UK it became "streng verboten" to go supersonic over land as farmers and other owners of greenhouses got upset, but in those days if the locals didn't like it that was just too bad. Of course we were young, insensitive and irresponsible but in the late fifties our relationships with the Germans were only slowly changing to our being friendly allies from our earlier role as conquering invaders. In common with the rest of the RAF all the stations in RAF Germany celebrated Battle of Britain Day each year on September 15th. That year, 1958, Group Captain Sid Hughes at Jever decided that, to mark the new relationship, the air fair, aerobatic displays, swings and roundabouts for the kids etc would not be Battle of Britain Day any more but would be an Anglo-German Air Day. But it was still held on September 15th.

Flight Sergeants Mackintosh and Anstey were to become particularly valued colleagues. George Anstey was the extrovert, a large, genial, ginger-haired Glaswegian he was, just like Bob Jude, no sufferer of fools but endlessly patient of human foibles in others. As far as I remember, in all the time I served on 26 Squadron we never had an airman on a disciplinary charge. But there were occasions when one of the lads would emerge from the Flight Sergeants' office looking distinctly sheepish and with rather watery eyes.

One morning Mike Read was airborne and I was in the Ops Room as duty Flight Commander. We got a message asking us to despatch one of our aeroplanes up to Sylt where it was needed for some air gunnery event. We had been warned in advance that this request was pending so all that was needed was to select which of the aeroplanes on the line to send and to brief a pilot. I had been a Flight Commander for all of two months so I duly made the appropriate decisions, the aeroplane departed and I made myself a cup of coffee. Flight Sergeant Anstey arrived in the Ops Room and accepted the offer of another coffee. He then said, "Sir, that aeroplane that has just gone to Sylt. How many hours does it have left before its next inspection is due?" Before I had time to answer he continued, "Did it have the appropriate radio crystals

131

fitted that it will need when it gets there? And incidentally how recently was the gun harmonisation checked?" By this time I needed scraping off the floor and had learned the very basic management lesson of the importance of consulting before deciding. George Anstey concluded, "You see, sir, that's what Flight Sergeants are for!" I can't remember if he actually laid a fatherly hand on my shoulder but he would have been fully justified in doing so. Later in my tour I got into the habit when returning from leave of dropping in to Flight Sergeant and Mrs Anstey's married quarter to get brought up to date on the Squadron's state of play and the current gossip.

One item in the Flight Office of on-going interest was the stagger chart. The servicing schedule of our Hunters was based on the number of hours they flew. The most frequent, very simple inspection was the Primary, then the Primary Star, then the Minor and so on. We tended to fly rather in fits and starts depending mainly on the weather, but the engineers' aim was to maintain a steady flow of work through the hangar. Unless they achieved this they either had technicians sitting around or aeroplanes awaiting servicing with no one available to work on them. The main planning aid was a chart, painted on a large blackboard, listing all the aeroplanes and showing how many flying hours each one had left before it was due for its next inspection. The Flight Sergeants' aim was to have the aluminium disks representing each aeroplane distributed across the pins on the board in a perfectly regular diagonal line. This showed that one aeroplane would be out of hours and due for inspection by the end of today, the next early next week and so on. Often the Chiefies would say to Mike Read and me, "Can you fly F-Foxtrot as much as possible for the next couple of days but use C-Charlie as a spare and only fly it if you really need to." It all reinforced the need for the Flight Commanders to keep closely in touch with the Flight Office while planning the flying programme. The pay-off was that the Flight Sergeants took pride in their ability to have the whole twelve aeroplanes serviceable and all available to fly up to Sylt for the air gunnery attachment in one formation.

In spite of the excellent relationships we enjoyed with our Squadron engineers we encountered one interesting difference of perspective with them which I have come across on other flying units too. An aeroplane would come down with some minor snag, but one that needed rectifying before it could fly again. The Fight Commander running the flying programme wanted to know an estimate of how long it would take to fix. Perhaps it was needed to make up the next four we were planning to fly. Should we wait for it or change our plans? If we could plan on the probability of it being available at a certain time we could select the pilots, they could get changed into flying kit, hold their pre-flight briefing and be ready to walk out as soon as the Flight Office called up that the aeroplane was being signed up.

The Flight Sergeants were most reluctant to give us that sort of forecast. They would promise to let us know the very minute it was serviceable and would in due course often appear in person to present the Form 700 all signed up like a rabbit out of a hat. But it went against their professional pride to make a forecast which in the event they might not be able to fulfil, although we knew as well as they did that it was only a forecast and we understood completely that unforeseen problems could prevent it being met. It was difficult to get them to see that by getting ourselves ready to fly on spec might let us get in an extra sortie whereas if we waited until the aeroplane was actually available we might have missed the latest available afternoon slot. It illustrated the difficulties which arise in running an inter-dependent team of people from different backgrounds and with different perspectives.

Our monthly flying programmes consisted of a standard set of exercises. Most of our flying was in sections of four practising battle formation, PIs (practice interceptions) for the benefit of the controllers and then cine gunnery, low flying, tail-chases, QGH/GCAs and some close formation. Until they gained experience the newcomers flew as wingmen. Then they would fly as a number 3, that is as element leader of the second pair, and in due course as the formation leader with an old hand as wingman and who would run the debrief. As I had discovered back at Waterbeach there was much to learn. In addition we all flew a couple of individual trips each month, for some aerobatics and to practise the procedures for various emergencies. For a flameout recovery and landing, pretending to take yourself by surprise, you closed the throttle to simulate having suddenly lost the engine and called the tower asking for a simulated flameout recovery. Your engine, even though it was just idling, was still producing quite bit of thrust so to give yourself a more realistic angle of glide you dumped 10° of flap. Unless you could see the ground, the Air Traffic radar brought you overhead and you then descended in a high-speed spiral in the hope that once you broke cloud you would have enough height and speed to position yourself on the approach to a runway.

Another exercise which I found to my surprise was regarded by some of the younger pilots with some apprehension was to de-select the hydraulic power to the controls, fly around for a bit in manual to get used to what it felt like and then to re-join the circuit for a manual landing. It struck me after a time that the apprehension was because none of their generation had ever flown an old gear-tabbed Meteor and so were not so used to aching arm muscles as we old-timers were. Almost every month too there would be a NATO exercise, sometimes good fun but sometimes involving much time sitting around on the ground waiting to be scrambled.

The element which kept us all on our toes, especially in the winter, was the weather. We had a map on the wall of the Ops Room of our area of North Germany showing all the airfields and the duty pilot kept this up-to-date with their current weather states which were displayed by coloured counters—green if their weather was clear, amber 1, ...2, or ...3 denoting progressively lower cloud and reduced visibility and red if it was clagged in and even the birds there were walking. If the weather forecast at base was at all doubtful we never got airborne without a cast-iron diversion where we could have got down if we had needed to. We also made sure that we recovered with plenty of fuel in case of unforeseen delays.

If first thing in the morning the weather looked marginal for any flying at all the Flight Commanders had an interesting and tantalising decision to make. You rang the met office and tried to wheedle out of them a firm opinion on what it was going to do during the morning and the rest of the day. Was it going to clear and if so when? All you were likely to get was a definite maybe. On some winter days they explained that their problem in making a forecast was that if the sun got even a small break in the clouds and could warm the ground the cloud might all burn off within half an hour. But on the other hand if no break occurred all the heat would continue to be reflected up off the white cloud-tops and it might stay "clagged in" all day. By now the Flight Sergeant was on the phone asking if you wanted the aeroplanes out on the line or whether he could get on with routine servicing. At the same time the pilots detailed for the first sorties were agitating to know if we were going to fly or if they could go off and get on with some of their secondary duties, checking inventories and the like. I quickly learned that the least helpful response was to say that you would check with the met in an hour and then make a decision. If you did that, at the end of the hour you would be tempted to wait another hour … and so on!

You had to be brave enough to take a deep breath, perhaps even flip a coin, and make a decision. "OK, we'll fly." If then it did clear, our aeroplanes would already be out on the line, pre-flight inspections done; 26 would be airborne at least forty minutes before the other squadrons and the Wing Commander much pleased. Or you said, "Chiefy, the aeroplanes are yours for the day." Then if it cleared, although the pilots were much disgruntled, at least the ground-crews had got on with a full day's servicing. It was a good lesson on an important principle of management. Wherever possible make a decision. With even a small amount of luck you will get more than 50% right and at least something gets done. Dither about and nothing gets done at all.

As the Squadron developed its own personality the pilots emerged as the usual mix of characters, some reasonably normal, some decidedly eccentric. Chris Cowper was the car enthusiast; John Merry, a good administrator, became Squadron Adjutant and kept the boss' paper work in order. We had a number of rugby players and some of us tried to keep as high as possible on the Station Squash Ladder. It was intended that the only flight lieutenants were the flight commanders and their deputies, all the other pilots were flying officers or pilot officers. Except that for a time there was one extra flight lieutenant, for whom there was for the time being no proper post. Chris Cowper, as ever thinking about cars, had already christened the boss the Steering Wheel, Mike Read and me the Driving Wheels, thus inevitably Flt Lt Mike Hall became the Spare Wheel. Willy Wilmot, a lean-faced fellow, had a special party trick. He would dunk his chin in the foam on the top of a can of beer, leaving himself a neat, white, wedge-shaped beard. "There you are," he would say, "General Smuts!" It was a surprisingly good likeness.

The technique of subliminal advertising was then in the news, and it was being suggested that a brief message flashed on to a cinema or TV screen could influence people without their realising it. The fleeting single word "thirsty" might thus increase sales of soft drinks! At the end of the day Mike Read or I would be planning the following day's flying programme and deciding who should fly. While doing so we often stood at the window gazing across the airfield. One day I idly noticed what I took to be a small smudge of dirt on the window. Something prompted me to look closer and I could then see that it was a tiny, minute message written on the glass with a Chinagraph wax pencil reading, "Bailey should fly." On another window I found "Bailey needs hours." Bill Bailey reckoned he got himself a couple of extra trips a week by such subliminal advertising.

But the most amusing humorist on the Wing was Chris Golds on 14 Squadron. His party trick was much more elaborate. He would seat himself on a bar stool and then silently mime a pilot strapping in and preparing for his first trip in a Hunter. Unless you were yourself familiar with the Hunter cockpit and its equipment the whole thing would have been meaningless. But if you flew Hunters you too had experienced the irritation of settling yourself in the ejector seat and then having to wriggle about to release the parachute straps which you couldn't now reach because you were sitting on them. You too had overshot once or twice while trying to raise or lower the seat to a comfortable height, or if you were tall, of finding that the adjustable rudder pedals had been left so close to you that your knees were almost up to your ears or, best of all, of the sudden panic of thinking you were suffocating because you had put on your oxygen mask before you had connected it to the aircraft's oxygen supply pipe. It was a masterly performance, and you got so weak from laughing that you had to look away to get your breathe back. We used to say to Chris, "Why don't you go on the stage, man, you'd be a sensation." To which he always replied, "No way, I'm afraid—I can only do it when I'm pissed!" Chris was also a talented artist. After he had left the RAF he for a time supported himself by selling paintings of aeroplanes. You sent him the details of the particular aeroplane you wanted in the picture, its serial number, special markings, and the appropriate background and he reproduced them all in the picture. I have one of his pictures of the Beaver in which I flew round the Arabian Desert.

The date approached for the Officers' Mess summer ball. We got hold of large rolls of brown paper to cover the walls of some of the rooms so that the artistic could then paint on them scenes of Parisian cafes and nightclubs or Wild West saloons. But before the real artists could get to work some late night revellers produced a bit of graffiti of their own. One of the most popular officers at Ahlhorn was the Roman Catholic padre, Gerry Aspinall. We were not therefore too surprised to come in to breakfast the next morning to find on one wall the large white-painted message "Aspinall for Pope." Amusement turned to horrified embarrassment when we opened the morning papers to read that the real pope had in fact died the previous day. The least embarrassed person was Gerry Aspinall who however had some choice remarks to make about, "You terrible heathen blighters, I suppose the Good Lord will forgive you although I can't for the life of me think why He should!"

The majority of pilots on the Wing were bachelors, but those who were married all seemed to have found wives who were perfectly happy to join in the sometimes boisterous parties that were a regular part of the social scene. One of the quieter young members of No 26 Squadron went home on leave and reappeared some weeks later with a brand new bride. She was a vicar's daughter and on first acquaintanceship it seemed that butter wouldn't melt in her mouth. She sat demurely on the sidelines with not a word to say and looking quite out of her depth. We wondered if Pete had not made, socially, a serious mistake. We need not have worried. Within a few weeks when the newly-weds arrived in the Mess on a Saturday evening, she would sling her handbag into an armchair and announce loudly, "Where's Gil? I want to dance with Gil McCluney!"

As the wives of course all put on smart dresses and dolled them-selves up a bit for Saturday night, someone suggested that we chaps should make an effort to smarten up too. We decided as an experiment to make it a Squadron custom to wear dinner jackets. It was quite remarkable what a lift this gave. Even if the programme remained the same as usual—a few Carlsbergs and perhaps a steak sandwich, before a bit of dancing—the whole evening took on a more festive and enjoyable atmosphere and we decided to make the custom permanent. Even so it did not inhibit some of the sillier games that the Wing played. Most memorable was "Dead Ants." For those who have never studied the matter, a dead ant usually lies on its back with its arms and legs in the air. The game was that at any social gathering at all anyone could call out "Dead Ants" and the last person down on the floor in the dead ant position bought the next round. This could be an expensive penalty and so it became a completely instinctive reaction that you flung yourself down quite regardless of your surroundings or who you were talking to. Most embarrassing!

Arriving in Germany I had needed a car. The drill was to get a new one just over a year before one came home, a year of ownership abroad being the minimum required to avoid purchase tax on return to UK. In the meantime one got an economical banger, although that hardly describes the sedate, dignified elderly "Petronella," the black Mercedes saloon I bought from Ian Stanway for £70. It had the spare wheel in a shaped container on the boot and was the sort of car which, for those who can remember him, Inspector Maigret used to drive around Paris. Later, with just over a year of my tour to go I came back to UK one weekend to collect a brand new TR3. It was the only new car I have ever owned and it eventually covered 150,000 miles before I reluctantly parted with it. I managed to sell Petronella—for £70.

The Cold War was by now an unpleasant reality and the political calculation was that it was going to be better to have the Germans as allies rather than to drive them into the arms of the Russians. No 26 Squadron had no sooner settled in to Ahlhorn and into 124 Wing when we heard that the station was to be given back to the re-born German Air Force and that the Wing was to move fifty miles south east to Gütersloh. We moved in September and although I had nothing against Gütersloh, for me it never equalled the peaceful country atmosphere of Ahlhorn. At Gütersloh the wing joined No 79 Fighter Reconnaissance Squadron already in residence with their Swift Mk 5s.

The move had minimal effect on our flying operations, we continued to range over the north German plain, but having moved a bit further east were now even more conscious of the Iron Curtain, in terms of flying time, not all that far away. On more than one occasion we would be up at around 40,000 ft trailing, and would see perhaps a further fifty miles further east four distant but distinct trails. We speculated on how interesting it would have been if we could have landed somewhere to meet and share a beer with the Mig pilots and to talk shop with them.

Some people worked hard to promote Anglo-German relations. In the Station Flight hangar an elderly German civilian was employed as general odd-job man and floor sweeper. Smart and, as far as his arthritis would allow, efficient he was clearly of the old school of German military manners, and unfailingly correct and respectful of all officers. One day I had occasion to go back after morning briefing to his hangar with the Station Flight boss, Flight Lieutenant Law Liversidge. Half way up the stairs we met the sweeper who sprang to attention, almost performed a present arms with his broom and rapped out something like, "Guten Morgan, Herr Officieren." Law stopped, raised his cap as if it had been a bowler and replied, "Good morning to you, Herr Sweeper." The old man's eyes almost popped out of his head although Law told me that they had similar encounters almost every morning.

An incident occurred not long after we arrived at Gütersloh that highlighted the importance of keeping one's wits about one even in very routine flying. We had been warned at the morning briefing that Air Traffic Control would be manned for some of the day by new, inexperienced controllers under training. I went off leading a section of four for a standard sortie of battle formation and cine gunnery planning to recover visually as, although it was a day of unbroken medium level cloud, the cloud-base was up at around 20,000 ft. Once we were below that we would need no further help. As we flew the sortie I was, of course, keeping a mental dead reckoning plot of where we were. By the time we were due to come home I judged that we were about thirty miles north east of base and had already turned us on to a south westerly heading and was preparing to start letting down.

I judged that we would arrive back in the circuit as usual with comfortably enough fuel for the circuit and landing. Just to make sure I called Gütersloh for a course to steer. Normally one could reckon to have got it right to within about twenty degrees, so I was somewhat shaken to be given a course to steer of north-east. In spite of this I was confident enough of my own mental navigation to call the descent the way we were going. Sure enough we broke out below cloud just about where I had calculated we should be. The set up in the Air Traffic Control tower for the CRDF—the Cathode Ray Direction Finding gear—was such that by simply throwing a switch the controller could select either the bearing of the aeroplane from base or its reciprocal, the course to steer towards base. The inexperienced controller had left the switch in the wrong position and had we turned on to the course he gave us we might, by the time we had realised our plight, have been across the Iron Curtain and without enough fuel to get home.

In our new Squadron hangar at Gütersloh the Ops Room and pilots' coffee bar were on the first floor down one side of the hangar facing the similar set of rooms of No 14 Squadron in their hangar, thirty yards away. Dialling telephones were something of a novelty at the time and with them we discovered a new game. Through the windows of No 14 squadron we could see the squadron adjutant sitting at his desk with his back to the window. The boss's office was empty so we dialled his number. The adj. got up from his desk and went down the corridor to answer the boss's telephone. Just as he reached across the desk to pick it up we rang off and dialled the Squadron Orderly Room at the other end of the corridor. The adj. dropped the boss's phone and went down the corridor to the orderly room where the phone, amazingly, stopped ringing just as he got there ... and so on. He did quite a few circuits before he happened to look out of the window to see half of 26 Squadron hanging out of our windows laughing ourselves silly. In due course the adj. retired as an Air Vice-Marshal. Strange old world... .

Just as with 63 Squadron, the whole purpose of our existence was air defence and hence air gunnery. The Hunters' gyro gun-sights were similar to those in the Meteor but we now had four 30mm Aden cannons in the nose. The change up from the Meteor's 20mm cannons gave a far heavier and more lethal shell, the rate of fire was much higher and the Hunters had a novel time-saving system of re-arming. With the Meteor the armourers had to lift new boxes of the belts of shells on to the top of the fuselage, fit the boxes down into the ammunition bays and thread up the belts into the gun breeches. With the Hunter the whole gun pack, with the storage tanks and the guns themselves, less their barrels, dropped out of the bottom of the fuselage on to a special trolley. Thus the ammunition belts could be assembled and the first shells threaded into the breeches back in the armament bay before the pack was wheeled out to the aeroplane and substituted for the old pack and the barrels refitted in just a few minutes.

At Waterbeach we had been near enough to the coast to fly down to Knock Deep gunnery range for live air firing. However at Gütersloh this was not possible and this entailed a twice-yearly attachment to the Armament Practice Station at Sylt, an airfield on the German island just south of the Danish border. Sylt was set up to provide all the facilities, the tug aircraft, the flags, the marking system and so on. All we had to do was to get airborne and shoot. In summer the island, which was joined to the mainland by a railway causeway, was a favourite holiday resort and the town of Westerland was crammed with bars, nightclubs and discos. The rest of the island consisted mainly of sand dunes and many miles of sandy beaches, many of them designated as nude only. A fat lot of good that did us however as our first attachment to Sylt had been arranged by some humorist at RAF Germany Headquarters for January 1st. Westerland was like a ghost town and to add to the excitement there was a snowfall soon after we arrived and then a freeze which made the runway unusable. Many of us were beginning to think about our Promotion Exams so the enforced idleness was put to good use and we got down to trying to learn up Air Force Law and all the other subjects we would be examined on. As Willie Wilmot complained one evening, "I'm even having to learn mnemonics to remember the mnemonics!" We returned to Gütersloh at the beginning of February.

It was while we were at Sylt that we heard the news that Mike Hawthorn, having a couple of months earlier won the Formula One World Championship, had been killed on the Guildford Bypass. Many of us took more than a passing interest in Formula One motor racing and it was like hearing that a personal friend had been killed.

The boss of No 79 Squadron was Squadron Leader Buck Buchanan. He was an outdoor type, a keen sportsman with rod and gun and invariably accompanied by his faithful black Labrador, Pluto. A few weeks after we had returned 79 with their Swifts went up to Sylt for their gunnery attachment. While they were there Buck came back to Gütersloh for a weekend and seeing him in the mess someone asked him how the shooting was going. "Oh its very good," he said, "There are plenty of ducks down on the marshes and some snipe and of course plenty of rabbits on the airfield if you can't find anything else … ."

Being on the continent made it very easy to get down to Switzerland for the skiing, so Tony Chambers and I decided to drive down in my TR3. Anticipating a fair amount of snow on the roads especially after we would be leaving the autobahn I was concerned that my tyres were by now showing signs of wear. Alan Ginn of 14 Squadron owned another TR, and hearing about this lent me his wheels for the trip. This was much appreciated and was typical of the good fellowship we enjoyed around Gütersloh. We strapped our skis on to the hard-top, crammed ourselves in, Tony being a good inch taller than me, and set off. On the second day we had a most exciting drive on packed snow up the valley to Kandersteg. We loaded the car onto the train for the fifteen-minute trip through the Lotschberg Tunnel and drove down to

Brig, where we would leave the car, as Brig is the boarding point for the mountain railway up to Zermatt. Shortly after leaving Brig the railway turns south and heads up a narrow valley down which tumbles a mountain torrent. The gradient suddenly steepens and the train pauses to engage the rack and pinion system. Between the running rails is a third rail equipped with cogs, a cogwheel under the electric engine engages those on the rail and up you go.

Zermatt is the original picture postcard Swiss mountain village. It is crammed into a narrow valley surrounded by towering mountains and dominated by the theatrically spectacular Matterhorn, the subject of countless chocolate box photographs. No wheeled vehicles are allowed in the streets which in winter are covered in packed snow and horse-drawn sleighs provide the taxi services from the station to all the hotels. Our fortnight on skis passed in a flash and it seemed that in no time we were heading north up the autobahn again to Gütersloh.

We were fortunate that the autobahn passed so close to the airfield. Many of our leave destinations were either in Scandinavia or in the Alps, you simply went ten minutes down the road, through Gütersloh town, and then turned north or south. Quite near to us too was one of the autobahn restaurants. The contrast with the modern, trashy motorway cafes in England could hardly have been greater. The buildings were well designed, restrained, spotlessly clean, the dining rooms quiet, tastefully decorated, with snowy white tablecloths and the waiters, in their dinner jackets, alert, courteous and efficient. Often in looking for somewhere near the airfield for a pleasant dinner out we would choose the autobahn restaurant as the best in the area. Eating out was straightforward although many of us were too lazy to learn properly to speak German. Our excuse was that every German we met wanted to practise their English, and anyway one could go a long way with Ochsen Schwanz Suppe (oxtail soup), Spiegel Eie mit Shinken (bacon and eggs) und Noch Zwei Biere (two more beers), bitte.

One summer afternoon a crowd of us, motoring around the picturesque countryside south of Gütersloh, stopped at a pleasant woodside cafe for tea and cakes. Someone, keen to show off their German-speaking prowess, emphatically ordered Erdbeeren mit Sahne, and impatiently waved aside the fraulein's attempts to remonstrate. What he should have asked for was Erdbern mit Sahne— strawberries and cream. He was duly served with exactly what he had asked for—boiled peas and cream. We said "Well you were so damn rude to the fraulein about it, now you jolly well eat it!"

With its crisp controls and graceful appearance the Hunter had always been a favourite at aerobatic displays. From its first appearance at Farnborough in the hands of Neville Duke, Bill Bedford and Duncan Simpson, the Hawker Company Test Pilots, it had been a show stopper. In March '59 RAF Germany wanted someone to get trained ready to provide Hunter aerobatic displays around the summer programme of air shows. Mick Davis and I both expressed an interest and so, if at the end of the day there was a spare aircraft available after the last normal training four were airborne, one of us would take it for an aerobatic practice trip.

Solo aerobatics in an aeroplane with the performance of a Hunter are mainly a matter of working out how to keep the show tight, over the airfield and in front of the crowd. It is extremely hard work, both because snappy, precise manoeuvres require abrupt even brutal control movements and because of the need to keep pulling high "g." The moment you relax you are liable to find yourself in the next county, much pleasanter for you but boring for the spectators. It is rather like trying to demonstrate the performance of a Ferrari within a school playground. Having worked out a sequence one practises it first above about 8,000 ft. Ideally one looks for an area of perfectly level cloud tops to represent your planned minimum height. Manoeuvres can then be tried out and if you make a mistake and come too low you simply pop into cloud for a few moments, climb up and try again. As you gain experience you lower your minimum height to, say 6,000 ft and so on. The lower you come the easier it becomes. At lower heights the actual ground gives a better perspective and in the thicker air the aeroplane performs better allowing tighter and more precise manoeuvres

On 24th March at the end of the afternoon there were two spare Hunters available. Mick Davis and I signed them out for solo aeros trips, strapped in and prepared to start up. I found that there was some minor unserviceability in my aeroplane and so I unstrapped and sprinted across to his. It happened that Mick had already had a solo trip that day so I persuaded him to let me take his aeroplane. I climbed out of the circuit and headed west to an open country area, about fifteen miles away where I would not be disturbing too many people on the ground. I tightened my straps, had a careful look round and started my planned sequence, staying above 6,000 ft. I came out of a loop and pulled up into what I intended to be a "hesitation barrel roll." This entailed whacking on 45° of bank, pausing, whacking on a further 45° and so on. I never got beyond the first pause. As I described it subsequently it was like driving a car along a smooth road and suddenly finding oneself bucketing noisily over old, badly maintained cobbles. Instead of the normal silky smoothness of a Hunter there was an ominous rumbling and vibration, felt as much as heard. I was still in a slight climb and so I levelled the wings and looked round the dials. I mainly remember that the fuel gauges indicated zero. This was plainly silly as I had taken off with full tanks and had hardly yet been airborne for a quarter of an hour. Even more ominously the Fire Warning Light was on.

The drill was that if the light came on it might just indicate a split in one of the flame tubes in the engine. In that case one closed the throttle and if the light went out within eight seconds it was OK to open up again and to use the engine to get home, throttling back every few minutes again to check that nothing more serious had happened. If the light did not go out after eight seconds it indicated a real engine fire. Then there was nothing for it but to turn off the fuel to the engine and glide. In spite of what the producers of television dramas would have us believe an aeroplane losing engine power does not dive helplessly into the ground. It glides perfectly well, steadily losing height, and depending on how high it is can cover many miles.

The Hunter glides perfectly well, although without hydraulic pressure the flying controls revert to manual, heavy to move but quite safe. In fact every month we practised the technique for a "flame-out" landing for just this situation. We would aim to touch down one third of the distance along the runway on the theory that it would be better to go through the far hedge at 40 knots rather than the near hedge at 140 knots. This, however, depended on whether one could reach an airfield. We reckoned that we could cover a mile per thousand feet. Putting a Hunter down without power on a runway was one thing, but it was strongly recommended that one did not attempt to put one down otherwise. If one lowered the wheels they would almost certainly have been torn off by digging into the ground and if one left them retracted, the aeroplane would in any case have touched down tail first and then slammed the rest of the fuselage down on to the ground, probably tearing off the nose, where the cockpit, and you, were situated. So the message was clear—if you lose your engine, get to a runway or bail out.

I closed the throttle and waited eight and then just a few more seconds, actually lots more seconds willing the light to go out. It stayed relentlessly on and so with a deep breath I closed the fuel cock, at the same time levelling out, trimming into a shallow dive to maintain speed in the glide and turned east towards the airfield. I called the tower, told them what had happened and got a steer to confirm that I was heading exactly the right way. There was the usual "clunk" as the controls lost hydraulic power and reverted to manual and I concentrated on maintaining 210 knots, the speed which would give the greatest distance covered for every thousand feet of height. I racked my apparently paralysed brain without success for anything stupid I was overlooking which could have recovered the situation. Other aircraft had heard my emergency call and in particular Nick Carter of 79 Squadron who was airborne in a Swift called to ask me where I was. Others who have been in similar situations have confirmed that the main mental anguish comes not from any thought of physical injury but from the fear that someone will say later "Why on earth didn't you try ... ." And you will think, "Oh God, I never thought of that!"

The altimeter wound down steadily. At 3,000 feet I could actually see Gütersloh airfield straight ahead and I was nicely lined up with the runway. However it was also becoming ever more obvious that I was too low and I was simply not going to get there. The strong temptation is to raise the nose and try to eke out a bit more distance, but this is counter-productive because although the aeroplane is in a more nose-up attitude the speed falls off and it is actually sinking faster. At about 1,200 feet I was trying to make the decision to use the ejector seat when Gütersloh Tower called and asked, "Do you still have your emergency?" Before I could say more than "Affirmative, I ..." the aeroplane suddenly dropped its port wing. Whether I had in fact tried to stretch the glide and this was the start of a stall I never knew. I reached up and pulled the ejector seat blind. The canopy blew off immediately but to ensure that it is well clear there is a one second delay designed into the system before the seat fires. We had endlessly been told that in the heat of the moment, with one's adrenalin up, it seems very much longer than one second. In spite of this and having waited for what seemed an absolute age, I decided that the seat was not going to work. I started to move the blind away from my face to see what was going on, and at that moment the seat fired.

I had a momentary glimpse of the aeroplane below me and had the stupid thought, "Oh, look, there's no cockpit canopy!" before I was tipped out of the seat and was swinging thankfully below the parachute. I landed in a grass field and had a second stupid thought, "Well, now I can wear the caterpillar club tie!" The Caterpillar Club was originally started as a publicity idea by one of the parachute manufacturers. The original parachutes having been made from silk, the caterpillar is actually a silkworm.

The aeroplane had crunched into a field about half a mile further on and started to burn fiercely as it still had, of course, almost full tanks. As invariably happens half a dozen children had materialised from nowhere and were now prancing round it clearly thinking that 5th November, or whatever is its German equivalent, had come early. A German farmer got to me, took me the few hundred yards to his farmhouse and gave me a welcome glass of something fairly strong. Before I had time to gather my wits a car pulled up, Group Captain Cribb walked into the room and said casually, "Hullo, Bill. I'd better give you a lift back to the station."

The doc. said I had compression fractures in a couple of vertebrae, so I had two weeks' lying on fracture boards in the RAF Hospital at Wegburg, two more weeks' sick leave and rejoined the Squadron. Perhaps I have been lucky because I have never had the slightest trouble from my back from that day to this. Nick Carter in his Swift took a couple of excellent aerial photos of Hunter XG 208 lying on the ground burning merrily with Gütersloh runway visible in the distance.

Before being carted off to hospital I had told my story to the Inquiry. It was there that I thought of the description of suddenly finding myself driving over old cobbles, it was the best I could think of to describe what it had felt like. My main memory was of all the instruments having gone haywire, in particular zero fuel indicated and the fire warning light. But having stopped the engine I lost interest inside the cockpit and was concentrating on trying to glide back to the runway.

An axial-flow jet engine has in principle just one moving part, the central shaft with the compressor at the front and, at the back, extracting power from the hot gasses to drive it, the turbine. But in addition to this there has to be a means of obtaining power to run all the aircraft systems, electric power for the radio and all the other electric services, a hydraulic pump for the powered flying controls, and pneumatic power for the brakes. A small drive shaft, known as the turret drive takes power out to a gearbox to drive all these services. There had been a number of instances in the Hunter of this gearbox fracturing, leaving the unattached end of the turret drive thrashing around cutting and disrupting electric wires, hydraulic pipes or anything else it happens to hit. The Inquiry concluded that I had suffered a turret drive failure, and that this would account for all the symptoms I had encountered.

There was one other member of the squadron who took almost as close a personal interest in my bail-out as I did. This was the armament technician who had serviced the seat before my trip and who had fitted the explosive cartridge which fired the seat up the rails and out of the aeroplane. Corporal Fosh naturally took an acute interest in how the seat had performed and when it was recovered from the field in which it had landed, made sure that he carefully removed the spent brass cartridge case. When I returned to the squadron he kindly gave it to me, with the details of the ejection and the date recorded in neat writing on it. Bob Fosh and I now live not too far apart and at squadron reunions we always spend a few minutes recalling the events of 24th March 1959, and I am able to thank him again for such a smooth, trouble free hot-seat ride.

Mine had been a very straightforward bail out, the Martin Baker seat had operated exactly as the makers said it would and there had been no complications. Not many months later Tony Rimmington of 79 Squadron had a much more exciting ride. It all started when 79 Squadron, the fighter recce boys, were discussing in the bar one autumn evening what sort of original photograph they could produce for their squadron Christmas card. About thirty miles from Gütersloh the river Weser runs through the Minden Gap, a gorge through some pretty beech-covered hills. On one of the spurs overlooking the river is a large monument, a statue of a helmeted warrior, probably Siegfried, with a shield and waving a sword. It was a well-known landmark and we always referred to him as Herman the Kraut. 79 decided that it would be nice to have a picture for their Christmas card of one of their Swifts flying past Herman the Kraut, with the hills and the river all picturesque in the background. A few beers later someone suggested that the picture would be really spectacular if the aeroplane was flying past inverted. This seemed like good idea at the time and Rimmy duly agreed to fly it while someone else took another aeroplane and took the pictures.

147

Flying inverted for a short time in a high-performance jet is a perfectly satisfactory business just as long as you are properly strapped in and that you take a bit of care. But just as a carburettor on a normal piston engine will not work inverted unless it has been specially modified to do so, a jet too has to have a special gadget to let it go on working inverted. This consists of a fuel recuperator. When you roll upside down fuel no longer feeds from the tanks in the normal way, but comes from the recuperator and is available for about twenty seconds. This is normally quite as much as you need before you roll the right way up again. But there is still one snag. If a piston engine cuts out while inverted it re-starts automatically, with a couple of coughs, once you are the right way up again. But with a jet, once it has flamed out it has to be re-started again and this takes quite a few seconds.

Of course the inevitable happened. The pilot taking the pictures took a bit too long getting ideally positioned, Rimmy stayed inverted too long and his engine flamed out. He rolled out and started to try a re-light. But he was too low, the engine was simply not going to light up in time and Rimmy ejected. But then the fun started. What nobody had realised until then was that in certain circumstances the jolt of the ejection could unfasten the parachute straps even though the release box should have kept them done up. Rimmy was tipped out of his seat in the normal way but then found that his parachute straps had released, that he was still attached to his parachute at all only because one of the side straps had snagged the leg strap and his flying overalls and that he was hanging from his parachute head downwards. Although he realised that this was a far from ideal way to hit the ground he was naturally scared even to move a muscle in case the straps were jerked free. He didn't hit the ground and break his neck; he went straight into the middle of the Weser River. What on earth must be the mathematical odds against surviving all that!

But the most amazing escape of the time must have been that of Pete Underdown of 14 Squadron during a previous tour. Pete got airborne one day in an F86 Sabre. Just as he reached climbing speed and raised the nose into the climb there was some very catastrophic failure in the engine causing the whole aeroplane to break up. Pete, very concussed, was thrown out still strapped in his seat. Against another astronomical set of odds his trajectory through the air coincided exactly with a steep hillside on which was planted an orchard of young trees. A farmer found him, still concussed and still in his seat, safely entangled in one of the trees at the bottom of the slope. He was not accepted into the Caterpillar Club because as it was quite truthfully claimed he had not actually used his parachute.

Many members of 124 Wing were avid motor racing fans. They would arrange a fortnight's leave to include the weekends of, say, the Dutch Grand Prix at Zandfoort, the French at Reims and the Italian at Monza. At the time there was a well-known Scottish sports car team racing their immaculate dark blue D Type Jaguars called Ecurie Ecosse. Chris Cowper was one of the most avid racing fans and it was he who founded "Ecurie Bloggs." To join you had "to have applied full opposite lock, and left the road going sideways." Due to my Driffield experience I was judged to have qualified.

One weekend Tony Chambers and I made the trip down to the Nurburgring for the Thousand Kilometre Sports Car Race. The afternoon before the race you could, for a small fee, drive on to the famous 14 kilometre circuit and go dicing with death round it, seeing what sort of time you could achieve and how it compared with the likes of Stirling Moss. On another weekend Tony Netherton had managed to roll his TR into a ditch but without serious injury. We stayed with some others for the night before the race at a hotel in a pretty spa town on the Mosel. The very correct, rather dim German waiter could not work out how, as dinner proceeded, six of us got progressively more and more smashed on one bottle of wine. He never switched on to the fact that we had quite a few more bottles on the floor under the table. The great length of the Nurburgring circuit meant that by simply walking a bit through the woods you could get right to the edge of the track and an excellent view. Stirling Moss in an Aston Martin was the runaway winner.

The following month Fred Daley and I drove down to Reims for the French Grand Prix. It was a swelteringly hot day and the race was won, as far as I remember, by Jack Brabham. On the way back driving through the French countryside we came across a small, sleepy village called Boult aux Bois–Boult in the Woods! My dad had always maintained that our family were Hugenots chucked out of France so maybe that is where we came from. In those days the French had apparently been a rather prickly lot.

As part of NATO it was important that we in RAF Germany developed links with the other air forces in the alliance. But the close co-operation that was intended did not always work out exactly in practice and one example of this was with the radar fixer services. Just as in UK the intention was that you had with you in the cockpit a list of their radio frequencies and as English was the universal language laid down for all Air Traffic Control uses, you could call them up at any time to get a fix. In some cases this worked well. Getting airborne from Gütersloh you could call up the German fixers and they would respond promptly, although of course with German accents. Heading north over Denmark or west over Holland the response was the same with Danish or Dutch accents as appropriate. You might than head south-west over France, call a French fixer and they would answer—in French. To most of us being told that we were "cinquante-quatre kilometres de la sud de la somewhere" was not all that helpful. The French are still a prickly lot.

Our best friends on the continent were the Dutch. We found them so much on our wavelengths that we used to refer to them, although I doubt if they were much flattered by it, as being just like Englishmen with funny accents. In the spring of '59 Second TAF Headquarters arranged an exchange attachment for No 26 Squadron with a Dutch squadron flying Hunters and based at Woenstrecht. During the Second World War, after Holland had been over-run by the Nazis, many Dutch pilots came over to UK to continue to fly with the RAF. They were allotted as squadron numbers the block of 300s. We were therefore delighted to discover that the outfit we were to exchange with was No 326 Squadron of the Royal Netherlands Air Force—the Dutch 26 Squadron.

The boss was going to be on leave during the attachment so I took four Hunters and six pilots over to Woenstrecht for the ten days, while they sent theirs to operate from Gütersloh. We were taking part in a NATO exercise involving being scrambled off to intercept a variety of raiders and the Dutch generously kept putting us at the front of the Readiness State so that we got many more than our fair share of trips. The Dutch squadron ops room was equipped, just like ours back at base, with extensive areas of perspex on the walls and the times of sorties, lists of airfields, pilot states, aircraft availability, weather states and the rest were all kept up to date by the lavish use of chinagraph wax pencils. One of the Dutch pilots who had stayed behind at Woenstrecht to look after us was a Lieutenant Mina Hannagraff. As he spent much time running the ops room for us he was promptly christened 'Lootenant Chinagraph'. We made some good friends on the "Dutch 26" and kept in touch long afterwards.

# Second Tactical Air Force
## Air Gunnery Team

During our winter gunnery attachment to Sylt I had really struck form. My average hits on the flag for all my live firing sorties was 35% and the highest individual score was a 64%. The boss had recorded in my log book that on the attachment my scores had rated the assessment of Exceptional. We were due for our next trip to Sylt in July but when we got there I was detached from 26 Squadron to lead the 2nd TAF Gunnery Team. The term "Second Tactical Air Force" was a pleasant hangover from the war when that had been the name of the air element supporting the Second Front and the allied advance into Germany. The team was being formed to practise concentrated air firing and cine simulated firing in preparation for the annual Aircent Air Firing Competition against the Dutch and Belgian Air Forces. The competition would be held in late August at Cazaux, a French airfield near the Atlantic coast and just north of the Spanish border. I was team captain and I was joined by Al Pollock, Phil Alston, Gil McCluney and Mick Davis from 26 Squadron and by Jock McVie, Ron Stuart-Paul, John Preece and Ian Rothwell all from our next door (next hangar) neighbours, No 14 Squadron. We became a close-knit team, all committed to helping each other to do as well as possible. The guys from 26 squadron I already knew well, although least the comparative new-boy Gil McCluney. He was the typical enthusiastic, energetic rugby-playing Scot. He threw himself enthusiastically into everything he did. He could be found in the bar on a Sunday evening pounding his fist into his other hand, muttering to himself "Tomorrow we get airborne. Tomorrow we are going to hit that flag like never before … ."

The competition consisted of two elements. For the "cine weave" element a stooge aeroplane had to fly a prescribed manoeuvre—diving, climbing and turning while the chaser tracked him, filming as he did so in order that the percentage of the time his sights were "on" could be assessed. This required close concentration and ultra smooth handling of the controls and was a skill at which Mick Davis was quite exceptional. During the actual competition a Turkish officer, one of the assessing judges, sought me out to tell me that he had never before seen films like Mick's for their smoothness and accuracy. He said that had they been created on the ground by some special demonstration mechanism they could not have been better.

The second element was much more fun. For normal air-to-air gunnery practice the tug aircraft stooged up and down the range and the attackers had about ten minutes in which to settle themselves on "the perch," adjust their position relative to the tug and then turn in to fire on the flag, discarding any attack which did not turn out exactly to their liking, rather like a batsman selecting which balls to block or leave and which to clout to the boundary. For the competition we had just two passes. Having called that you were turning in for your first attack you had just four minutes or two passes to fire off all 120 rounds of ammunition. This meant that you had to fire on both attacks or be left with unused rounds that would be counted as having missed. It was a much more challenging exercise.

One evening while we were at Sylt I actually saw, the only time I ever did, a mid-air collision. The Sylt tug pilots with their Meteors, released from their boring job of towing targets for us, had put together a four-ship aerobatic team. As we watched them practising their routine over the airfield they pulled up in box formation into a barrel roll. Perhaps the leader did not keep enough "g" on but for whatever reason as they went over the top one of the wingmen slipped in and knocked the leader's tail off with his wing tip. The wingman himself was only slightly damaged and landed safely but the leader's aeroplane deprived of its tail did a classic falling leaf, wallowing down flicking lazily from side to side. People were calling out, "Get out, man, get out," and he did, ejecting safely and landing on the airfield.

As the Gunnery Team we came under the direct supervision of Wing Commander Pete Thorne, the OC Ops at Sylt, an ebullient, enthusiastic extravert and constant user of apt and memorable phrases. "That man," a fairly useless air gunnery pilot, "couldn't hit an elephant's arse with a handful of rice." A Friday night party to wind down was a "small manifestation of joy." He invited the team to dinner at his house and throughout dinner Jock McVie insisted on keeping a notebook by his elbow and could hardly keep up trying to jot down the stream of memorable remarks and comments. Some years later I met Wing Commander Thorne then languishing in a ground tour at the MOD. He had by then collected the Air Force Cross and two bars for his flying contributions and was recounting indignantly how some very young flying instructor, when he had appeared at White Waltham to fly a Chipmunk, had insisted on giving him a dual check. "A dual check!" he said, "For me! Good grief, I've got enough red and white ribbon here," indicating his chest, "to hang that young man."

Our training and preparations complete, we flew down from Sylt, re-fuelling at Wildenrath and on to Cazaux. Letting down we called Cazaux Air Traffic Control and asked for landing instruction. "Alors!" they said, "Please to make a right-hand circuit because we have an air-to-ground gunnery range on ze left-hand side of the airfield … . And please to make a very wide right-hand circuit because we have a bombing range on ze right-hand side of the airfield." We duly landed, hoping that both the air-to-ground gunners and the bombers were reasonably accurate.

We had an interesting week in France, but were a bit shaken to find that even if we were flying again in the afternoons there were, instead of water on the tables at lunch, bottles of red wine. Our performance in the competition was disappointing, however we greatly enjoyed ourselves and flew home reckoning that we had not disgraced 2 TAF. When signing up my flying logbook Wing Commander Thorne wrote in it, "You've done a splendid job as Team Leader, Bill. Thanks for all your help. PDT"

\*　　\*　　\*

A couple of weeks later I came in from a sortie back on 26 Squadron, slumped into an armchair and said to no-one in particular, "I'm due for some leave. I think I'll go to Switzerland and climb the Matterhorn." In the same way that I might have said row across the Atlantic or fly to the moon. One should not however make such facetious remarks within the hearing of Alan Pollock, and the following week we were driving down the autobahn with me still saying, "Look, Al, I didn't mean it. Al, you are a headstrong, stubborn and impetuous lunatic. Pollock, will you LISTEN a minute." To no avail. We had a splendid week climbing around Zermatt, now in midsummer looking quite different from its winter set up. There was not a ski to be seen, the shops being instead full of climbing ropes, ice axes and crampons.

With just a few days still left of our leave, and now feeling reasonably fit, we persuaded Gotfried Perren, the sixty-year-old father of Gotlieb, Director of the Ski School, that we were both experienced mountaineers (Oh Yeah, big deal!) and would only need the one guide on the Matterhorn between the two of us. It was all that we could afford. We set off one afternoon and walked up to the Hornli Hut, the hotel where one spends the night before setting off, before the dawn, on the Hornli Ridge, the tourist route up the mountain. The next morning dawned grey, foggy and with drizzle. Climbing was out of the question so we retired disappointed to the village. The next day was going to be our last chance, so with fingers crossed we went up to the Hornli Hut again and this time everything came right. We set off in the dark and as we mounted higher and higher the dawn came up crimson and gold and then turned into a brilliant, calm, sunny day. Zermatt and all our familiar skiing runs around the Gornergrat, the Riffelberg, Tuftern and Sunnega looked like a tiny model far below while all around us the giants of the Valais shimmered in the sun, from the Obergabelhorn and Weisshorn in the north to the Breithorn and Monte Rosa in the east.

The view of the Matterhorn from the north-east, that is from Zermatt, presents a now well-known optical illusion. The dominant east face sweeping up to just below the summit, which is seen on all the photographs of this so photogenic mountain, looks to be of precipitous steepness. In fact its average angle is just less than 45°. The Hornli Ridge on its northern edge is an energetic scramble but only becomes a real rock climb for a few hundred feet over the shoulder above the Solvay Hut. It is here that, with tourists in mind, the Swiss guides have installed fixed ropes. Gotfried led us steadily and safely upwards until the angle of the rocks eased off and then suddenly there was nothing above us and a precipice yawned at our feet dropping away towards Cervinia in Italy. We had climbed the Matterhorn. On the summit we enjoyed a brief stop and gazed down into Italy fading into the southern haze. In fine weather and for reasonably fit young men it was no outstanding achievement, but a memorable one. It was Gotfried's one-hundred-and-fifth ascent.

Over the years I have frequently seen the marked influence on not just the dry statistical performance of a unit but on the whole atmosphere and ambience of the place which is generated by the personality of the leadership and in particular of the Station Commander. When the boss is good the more junior types tend not to notice him, they just get on with their jobs, do them well and enjoy them. This was certainly the case at Gütersloh. The Wing Commander Flying, Wing Commander Ian Butler, affected an air of genial vagueness, which for a time took me in. He had his favourite corner of the bar where he would puff quietly at his pipe and fondle a litre of Herforder Silver Top, the local brew, while disparaging our preferred Carlsberg as "Danish Mineral Water." If you paused to pass the time of day with him, he would greet you casually and then suddenly ask a most penetrating question perhaps about one of your junior pilots who might have been having problems, revealing that the casualness was a complete pose and that he had his finger exactly on the pulse and knew precisely what was going on around the wing.

He did tell one joke against himself. A year or so previously No 20 Squadron had adopted as a Squadron mascot a very small terrapin or tortoise. This lived in a glass-fronted box in the Squadron Crew Room, was looked after as a proper official duty by one of the junior pilots and regularly fed on lettuce leaves and other goodies. The Squadron number, 20, written in Latin was of course XX or two crosses so the mascot was called Flying Officer Elbert Du Croisses. He also occasionally went flying in a Hunter and so was able to boast that he was the only supersonic tortoise in the world. As he flew in RAF aircraft he had to have, just like the rest of us, an official Flying Log Book to keep a record of his flying hours. The drill was that at the end of every month our Log Books were brought up to date to be signed by the Squadron Commander and at the end of three months looked at and signed by the Wing Commander Flying. By mistake Elbert's Log Book was sent across to Flying Wing Headquarters with the rest from 20 Squadron. Wing Commander Butler loved to recount how he came across a Log Book for an apparently operational squadron pilot who had a grand total of about eight flying hours. He rang up OC 20, Squadron Leader Roy Bowie for enlightenment. Boss Bowie was having a busy day and for the moment could not think what went on. Apparently there was an embarrassing half hour until it was all sorted out. Elbert hibernated during the winter and one year happened to wake up on the day of the AOC's annual inspection. The AOC was so impressed that he awarded Elbert a Green Endorsement.

The Station Commander was Group Captain Peter Cribb. On one occasion when Wing Commander Butler happened to be away, one of our Hunters encountered a minor emergency and as his Flight Commander I was summoned to the Control Tower to be able to talk to the pilot by radio if need be. I had only been in the tower a few minutes when the Hadley Box connected to the Station Commander's office sounded. "Oh, Bill, I hear Fred Daley is having a spot of bother. I expect you have it in hand, I was just calling to let you know I'm here if you need me." Other bosses I have known would either have diverted your attention from dealing with the emergency and distracted you with a string of questions or would have turned up in person and been frankly a damn nuisance.

Group Captain Cribb had served at some time previously as the RAF liaison officer at one of the USAF bomber bases in East Anglia. He had some interesting stories to tell about the Americans, one in particular illustrating their ruthless hire and fire attitude towards their people. The biggest of the USAF long-range strategic bombers was the Stratofortress, powered by four jets and six propeller engines; "Four burning, six turning" as they put it. A formation of Stratofortresses was due to come in, having flown direct from their base in Texas, a trip of some 8,000 miles. General Curtis le May, the legendary and fire-eating boss of the USAF Strategic Bomber Force had also flown in to watch their arrival. All the Stratofortresses touched down precisely on their planned ETAs (estimate times of arrival) except for one which arrived some ten minutes later. General le May ordered that the pilot should report to him in the tower. A few minutes later a major arrived still of course somewhat sweaty and with the marks of his oxygen mask firmly imprinted on his face. The general turned to him, removed the cigar from his mouth and said, "You're late ... Captain." He turned away and replaced the cigar. Before entering into detailed discussions on motivation and passing judgment on how to get the best out of people it is important to remember the different national characteristics and traditions involved. I was once warned never to regard Americans as Englishmen with funny accents. It is much more helpful to regard them as a completely foreign people who just happen to speak a sort of English.

We did not have many opportunities to meet the Americans stationed in Germany, as their zone was in the south of the country, but occasionally a USAF aeroplane dropped in to Gütersloh and we entertained the crews while they were with us. One of the most sociable members of 26 was Nigel Bacon and people like him could always be relied on to make the visitors feel welcome. Nigel had a fund of good anecdotes but at the time had developed an irritating habit of always needing to act out his stories especially if they involved some fisticuffs. "This chap gets angry, see, and hits him. POW!" jerking his head back to illustrate the action. "So the first chap of course retaliates, POW, POW!" with more histrionics. All most tiresome.

A couple of Americans had dropped in to Gütersloh and were staying the night. Late in the evening Nigel was entertaining them down in the popular Officers' Mess cellar bar. One of the Americans, perched on a tall bar stool had apparently dozed off. The cellar bar had a stone floor and Nigel thought to himself that if the chap actually fell off the stool he could injure himself quite badly. Generously solicitous Nigel went across the bar and shook him gently by the shoulder. The American woke up suddenly, thought he was being attacked and delivered a swift straight left straight into Nigel's face. Nigel appeared in the Squadron the next morning with a most prominent black eye. "Hey, Nigel, tell us again, man, what actually happened, what did he do?" I'm afraid we just couldn't stop laughing.

In Germany as elsewhere low flying was strictly controlled and unauthorised low flying much frowned on. Right up in the north of the country, just short of the Danish border there was a long, spectacular high-level railway bridge spanning some river valley. It was whispered that occasionally some people, greatly daring, had been known to swoop down and fly under the bridge. Presumably this foolhardy behaviour must have considerably angered the local inhabitants. A couple of the chaps on leave were motoring that way, returning from a visit to Copenhagen. Passing a pleasant roadside restaurant they decided to stop for beer. They parked the car and walked back to the restaurant, only then noticing the prominent sign which said, in German, "Come in and sample our food, enjoy the marvellous views and watch the aeroplanes fly under the bridge."

For quite a few years I had nursed the ambition to become a Test Pilot. Having always been interested in science, especially physics, the way aeroplanes behaved in the air was just physics come to life. On many occasions one saw a fleeting phenomenon, the way a wing-tip streamer formed, or an unusual reaction to control movements and would have liked to stop the clock and examine it properly. Approaching the end of my second flying tour, this was clearly the moment to apply to join the next course at the Empire Test Pilots' School at Farnborough which would start in February. Having discussed it with the boss, I found the relevant regulations, sent off the application forms and was invited over to Farnborough to sit an exam and to be interviewed. At the beginning of December I heard that I had been accepted and in the New Year made my farewells to 26. Before I left the boss asked me my views on who should succeed me as OC A Flight. We discussed it and he selected Bill Dodds, an experienced, forthright, not to say blunt north countryman. He was a good choice. Just before I left I heard him in the crew-room one morning with Mike Read, the other Flight Commander, discussing with the boss some aspect of forthcoming plans for the squadron. Gil McCluney, still a relatively junior pilot, but as bursting with enthusiasm as ever, bounced up to them and joined in the conversation. Hardly looking up Bill said, "McCluney, when we want your views we'll rattle your ****** cage." Gil, good-natured as ever, retired grinning while the rest of us fell about laughing. Clearly I was leaving my Flight in good hands.

We, 124 Wing, shared the airfield at Gütersloh with No 79 Squadron who flew the Supermarine Swift Mk 5. After having been found wanting as a high-level interceptor the Swift had been fitted with cameras and given the role of low-level reconnaissance. It was a heavily built, solid aeroplane, one of its handicaps at high level, but it made a good steady camera platform, not disturbed by air turbulence—or in fact by anything much else. When the Swift finally retired an amusing article "In Memoriam" appeared in a 2 TAF magazine which started, "Stories about how the Swift killed its pilots are untrue. Actually it just frightened them to death and left them with the blame."

I went down to 79 Squadron to cadge a ride in a Swift before I left for UK and happened to meet Alan Harvey, my old friend from 56, now on 79, in their hangar. Just then I caught sight of one of their aeroplanes propped up on jacks, a bit scratched, dripping hydraulic fluid and looking rather sorry for itself. I asked Harv what had happened to it. "Oh that one—it hit a bird." I started to express my disbelief and he added, "Mind you, the bird was in its nest at the time!" In fact it was being flown by Pat King of 79 Squadron at low level and he said afterwards that he looked down to write some note on his kneepad, "And before I could look up again everything went green!" With only the slightest jolt his Swift had flown straight through a hilltop clump of trees leaving a Swift-shaped dent in them and returning to base not really all that badly damaged.

Another of the characters on 79 was a native New Zealander, a Flight Lieutenant "Kiwi" Graves. Later on he came back to UK on posting to a new job and found himself a house to rent in a local town which just happened to be in a Cemetery Road. Entering into the spirit of the thing he and his wife re-named the house Tombstone View. The neighbours all promptly wrote to object. They said it lowered the tone. I got my trip in a Swift without either breaking anything or frightening myself to death.

Before I left Germany I just had time for one more spot of leave and having been dragged up the Matterhorn by Pollock in the summer I persuaded him that he ought to have a go at skiing, which up to then he had not tried. We duly trekked down the autobahn, across Switzerland, past Lake Geneva and up the rack and pinion railway to Zermatt again, this time with me, as a reasonably experienced skier, calling the shots. We had the usual most enjoyable fortnight, which Al, of course, spent in the beginners' class. When we got back to Gütersloh I left almost immediately for England. I heard subsequently that the following year Al arranged his winter holiday, just his second fortnight ever on skis, to coincide with the dates of the RAF Alpine Skiing Championships. He won the Downhill.

I kept in touch with Al and was vastly pleased the following year to be his best man for his wedding. Various stories filtered back about him. He became a QFI, a Qualified Flying Instructor, just at the time that the air force was making rather a meal of introducing the Gnat Trainer, an episode of which I saw something at Boscombe Down. One story that we heard was that Alan took a section of three and had the flaps loaded up with rolls of lavatory paper. He then flew the section over HQ Flying Training Command, opened the flaps at the right moment and festooned most of the county with confetti. Air Marshal Paddy Dunn, the Commander–in–Chief was said to have had a sense of humour failure and demanded to interview the culprit. While Al, in his best uniform, was standing to attention on Air Marshal Dunn's mat, the ADC came in, handed the Air Marshal a piece of paper and said, "Excuse me, sir, I expect you would like to deal with this at the same time." The Sopwith Camel had been a well-known training type in the 1930s. Alan had sent Air Marshal Dunn a signal quoting the Biblical reference which read:—"You swallow a camel and strain at a gnat."

# The Empire Test Pilots' School

## R A E Farnborough

On 1st February 1960 I joined No 19 Course at the Empire Test Pilots' School. Farnborough, the Royal Aircraft Establishment, could be called the cradle of aviation in Britain. The old dead tree to which, well before the First World War, Colonel Cody used to tether his aeroplanes is still carefully preserved. For many years the crowds have flocked to the Air Show and listened to the commentator introducing some of the newest and most exciting aeroplanes in the world as they approached either "over the black sheds" or "over Laffan's Plain." When sonic bangs were a novelty I had stood in the crowds as the commentator said, "Neville Duke ... or Mike Lithgow ... or whoever is starting his dive now," and we all waited with bated breath for the bang to arrive.

The firms' test pilots are pilots of outstanding ability and many year' experience. They have grown up with the aeroplane they are testing and then demonstrating to potential customers at Farnborough and similar air shows. They know intimately every aspect of its behaviour and have had time to investigate all the corners of its performance envelope. They know in detail how all its systems work and have probably played a part in their design. For all these reasons they are not the best judges of how the ordinary squadron pilot will cope with the new aeroplane when it enters service.

I and my fellow students at ETPS were not mainly destined to join one of the manufacturing companies building the new aircraft. Our role was to be a more humble one. We were to represent the ordinary squadron pilot who would meet the aeroplane as I, for example, had met first the Meteor and then the Hunter at the completion of training or operational flying on simpler types, bringing with us no special skill and not all that much experience. I have heard it said that our jobs, once we had completed the Farnborough course, would be analogous to the "Which" magazine, investigating and then reporting on new products from the point of view of the customer and occasionally having to water down some of the hype in the glossy brochures from the manufacturers.

One of the most interesting aspects of the course was the opportunity to fly a selection of new types. Pilots, even the most sophisticated, are eager to collect new types in the way that schoolboys collect stamps. My log book records that my first two trips at ETPS were a dual demo and then a left-hand seat ride in a Canberra, in fact the biggest aeroplane I ever flew as first pilot. By the end of March I had also flown the Meteor Mks 7, 12 and 14, Hunter Mk 4, Vampire T11, Varsity, Provost and Chipmunk. In the next few months I added the Devon, Tiger Moth and an amazing little aeroplane called the Tipsy Bee, and (as second pilot) the Hastings, Shackleton and the Vulcan V-bomber.

I flew my first left-hand seat trip in the Canberra with an experienced pilot on the type, Murphy Morrison. However this Canberra was a Mk B2, the bomber version, so there were no dual controls as there are on the trainer, the Mk T4. Beside the pilot's seat in the B2 Canberra there is what is known as the rumble seat. This is a simple metal frame that normally folds and is clipped out of the way when the navigator is at his proper position down behind with his charts and books and radar displays. It is just used when the navigator needs to come up and perch on it to work his sextant or to see out for a bit. Murphy was sitting there while I flew the aeroplane. We were returning to base when he said, "We've got a few minutes in hand, do a loop." I replied, "I can't with you sitting there. You're not strapped in, you'll fall out." "I won't if you do it properly!" We have all had demonstrated to us at school how you can swing a bucket of water round in a loop without spilling the water. So we demonstrated to each other how, if you do it properly, you can fly a Canberra light bomber round in a loop without losing the chap sitting on the rumble seat.

Later in the year we each got a ride in the Swift Mk 7 to let us experience a certain defect in its design. You were carefully briefed that the Mk 7, a development of the familiar Mk 5 of No 79 and other squadrons, had had a longer nose fitted to accommodate extra cameras, but that the size of the tail fin had not been increased to compensate. It therefore had only a minimum amount of directional stability. Having climbed up and trimmed for straight and level flight you gave the rudder a gentle kick. Instead of simply yawing briefly and returning to normal flight the nose weaved from side to side and the yawing oscillations took quite some seconds to die away. Directional stability is often something of a headache for high-performance aeroplanes, particularly when modifications are introduced on later marks and more demanding weapon loads are fitted. I was to encounter the topic again at Boscombe Down with the later marks of the Lightning. In common with some other types the later marks of Lightnings had progressively bigger fins.

At the Test Pilots' School our flying, once we had been checked out on a type, was only part of an exercise. The phase would start with a series of lectures on the subject which might be Take-Offs and Landings, Stalling, Stick Force per G, Spinning or some other specific aspect of its performance. We would then, with guidance from our tutor, plan one or more sorties designed to investigate this. We would prepare a series of test cards, to be clipped to our kneepad, to act in the air as an aide memoir and as somewhere to record our findings. Many of the aeroplanes were equipped with wire recorders, a primitive kind of tape recorder, but we were warned of their unreliability and of the danger of relying on them too much and having nothing to show for a test sortie but a mass of tangled wire. After completing our planned sorties we wrote up our results as a report with conclusions and recommendations. Some of the exercises were technical and mathematical and this being before the days of pocket calculators they involved many hours of midnight oil and work with a slide rule.

My tutor for the first part of the course was Squadron Leader John Crowley. He was in fact my direct predecessor on 26 Squadron in that he had been OC A Flight on the old 26 until it had been disbanded in 1957. During his time at Boscombe Down he had fought a vigorous battle to have the Hunter fitted with a modification to its fuel system. The Hunter's electrical fuel contents measuring system was prone to various errors and John had insisted that this should be augmented by a simple mechanical float system that lit two very visible lights in the cockpit when the fuel was down to a certain level. They were known as the Bingo Lights.

The main interest in the test pilots' course was provided by the fact that we now set off to fly an aeroplane with the specific purpose of investigating some aspect of its performance. Perhaps it was something quite mundane and straightforward, such as the layout of instruments in the cockpit, so that back on the ground you could then report on it accurately and, if appropriate, make recommendations on anything that needed to be done about it. Our brief as service pilots was that we never selected any configuration or carried out any manoeuvre that had not previously been demonstrated by the company. An exercise on an aeroplane in which we had already flown many hours and so already knew well presented a special problem. For me that was mainly the Hunter and the Vampire. You were then liable to take for granted some characteristic that deserved critical comment or to plunge into something that on a type you didn't know well you would have approached more cautiously. As we developed our awareness we started even in types we knew well to say to ourselves, "Well, I've never noticed that before." This analytical approach to flying was a new and absorbing dimension but could get out of proportion unless, as our tutors reminded us, it was constantly balanced by saying to ourselves, "How will this strike the ordinary squadron pilot or will this be important when the aeroplane is in squadron service?" We were not being trained to become academics or experimental test pilots, simply to apply commonsense opinions on behalf of our colleagues back on the squadrons. It was a responsibility to be taken seriously and we realised how lucky we were to be here.

As the course got under way I had become friendly with Jimmy Aitken, a Scot, a mountaineer and a keen skier. For our Easter break we went up to his native Scotland to sample the Scottish skiing. We took the sleeper to Edinburgh, were met on Waverley Station by his father, and taken home for a sumptuous breakfast before picking up the car we had arranged to hire. Driving around the Highlands with someone so knowledgeable was highly educational. "That's Rob Roy's cave where he hid from ..." potted story of Rob Roy. "That's the island where Prince Charlie, after Culloden ..." condensed history of the Forty Five. We stayed a few days at the luxurious Bridge of Orchy Hotel and skied the "White Corries" in Glencoe before moving on to Aviemore and the Cairngorms. Here the skiing installations were in their absolute infancy. The road had only just been built beyond Loch Morlich up to the site of the present car park. It was only open to constructors' vehicles on which you hitched a lift if you were lucky. On the site of the present Shieling at the bottom of Coire Cas and the White Lady runs some enterprising students had installed an old car engine with a rope wound round a back wheel. You picked the rope up out of the slush and were dragged precariously up the hill for a few hundred yards. That was the sum total of the uplift on Cairngorm. As we drove back to Edinburgh we crossed the Forth by the Queensferry and had a close-up view of the early stages of the building of the towers for the new road suspension bridge.

The Farnborough course included as students, in addition to those from the RAF, representatives of the Indian and Royal Australian Air Forces, the Royal Navy and also from the United States Air Force and Navy. With this mix it was socially a most enjoyable year. I flew many exercises with Lieutenant Commander Lloyd Hoover of the U.S. Navy as co-student. This was in the era of much silly graffiti around England saying, "Go Home, Yanks." For our summer leave Lloyd and his wife and family toured Scotland and somewhere in the highlands found to their delight a scrawled whitewash sign "Go Home, English." They were vastly amused and brought back photos to show us. Lieutenant Neddy Hogan also of the U.S. Navy became the course character.

As the summer approached we took advantage at weekends of the ETPS fleet of gliders—Sedburghs, Skys and Olympias. We learned the rudiments of the sport of gliding, of holding position behind the tug aeroplane as it whisked you up to the cloud base, of watching intently the sensitive climb and descent indicator with its two little balls, red for "sink" and green for "lift." The various qualifications which glider pilots strive to gain consist mainly of specific achievements in three elements: height above launch, point-to-point distance and endurance. I was lucky enough to be airborne in a glider on a day of an unstable air mass, towering cumulus clouds and lots of lift. I got into some nice strong lift, started circling to stay in it and, with the altimeter winding up nicely, was soon in cloud and a few minutes later in hail, hissing against the windshield, and still climbing fast. The cloud spat me out, freezing cold but exhilarated, at about 9,000 ft. Back on the ground we consulted the barograph which we always carried and I found I had achieved enough height for that element of my Silver C badge.

Another element was the five-hour endurance flight and to try to achieve these, a party of us took the gliders up to the Long Mynd, an attractive, wild upland area in South Shropshire. This well-known gliding venue has a long, west facing escarpment running for some seven miles north and south. All that was needed was a steady westerly wind and the endurance flight was more or less guaranteed. We found on the Long Mynd another facility that, coming from the flatter Hampshire countryside, we had not seen before. The gliding club owned a west facing field, sloping down from the hill top, at an ever increasing angle until the ground dropped steeply away to some woods far below. With a west wind blowing up the slope they could launch their gliders without mechanical aids, by simply pointing them down the slope, pushing them gently over the edge and letting them trundle off down the hill until they soared into the air and were carried up with the wind soon to be well above their launch point. Unfortunately on our weekend the wind stayed stubbornly in the south-east. We had taken a Chipmunk with us as a tug and so we had a pleasant weekend of some aero-towed trips but there was no chance of the endurance flights.

We made a number of visits to aircraft manufacturers. One memorable dinner party in Stratford-on-Avon ended with most of us swimming cross the Avon or jumping off the bridge into the river. I have to confess I cannot remember which aircraft company were our hosts on this occasion. We met most of the well-known company test pilots and had to be careful not to indulge in name-dropping. But I must mention Bill Bedford of Hawkers who did most of the early flying of the Harrier, including its first flight with his foot in plaster due to a car accident. In fact the historic film of the first flight then shows Bill emerging from the cockpit, hopping on one leg and his toe adorned with a bright red sock. He had a laconic turn of phrase and when asked how he had enjoyed a recent holiday somewhere in the tropics replied, "Generally very pleasant, but as for the swimming, the shark/water ratio was a bit high."

Lieutenant John Carrodus RN, another ETPS student drove a red AC Ace. He quietly went off and passed the Institute of Advanced Motorists driving test and then loudly twitted the rest of the sports car owners about it. He mounted his IAM badge above his car's logo so that it could be read as "I am ace."

The social highlight of the year was the, at that time annual, SBAC Farnborough air show in September. The British aircraft industry was at the time going through a difficult period. SBAC actually stands for the Society of British Aircraft Constructors, but there had been so many recent mergers and take-overs that it was popularly said now to be the Society of Both Aircraft Constructors. The Dutch Fokker Friendship was a small, popular twin-engine, medium range airliner. The Avro Company was just unveiling a very similar but arguably not quite so good equivalent and were said to be canvassing suggestions for a name for it. Someone met an Avro representative in the bar and unkindly said, "Why not call it the Avro Acquaintance. After all it's only a poor man's Friendship." The ETPS Mess became the gathering place for all the ex-students which included almost all the company test pilots in this country and quite a few from America. The bar stayed open far into the night and breakfast was an affair of funereal silence and black coffee.

The end of the course approached and we enjoyed an evening entertaining a number of VIPs from the aircraft industry at the McKenna Dinner. The prizes were presented and Lloyd Hoover won the McKenna Trophy for the best overall student. Lieutenant Neddy Hogan USN insisted he have his say. He announced that he was himself presenting an additional trophy to the test pilots' school, "For the most handsome student on the course; and for this year I've awarded it to—me!"

We got our postings to the various jobs where we would be for the next three years. Jimmy Aitken was to stay at Farnborough and join RAE, the Royal Aircraft Establishment while I, with half a dozen others, was to move to Boscombe Down, to A&AEE or, according to the mathematical comedians A $(1 + E^2)$, the Aeroplane and Armament Experimental Establishment. As you drive down the A30 and approach Salisbury from the east, Boscombe Down's large hangars stand out conspicuously to the north on the heights of Salisbury Plain. Often while I had been at Upavon at HQ Transport Command I had gazed enviously across the Plain, imagining the newest generation of aero-planes in its circuit and wondering if I would ever get there too. Now I would be doing just that.

Before I took up my new post I was due for some leave. Ever since I had first been skiing from Cranwell I had tried every winter to get a holiday in the Alps. Being young and reasonably fit I could now ski moderately well and during the autumn at Farnborough I had spent almost every evening seriously training. In the RAF Ski Championships at the start of 1961 I intended really to give it a go.

The army, for various reasons, is able to attract many hundreds of soldiers first to their regimental races and then to the Army Championships at which they can select the army team for the Inter-Service Championships. By contrast only a small group of us, about two dozen, made up the RAF ski racing community. The Navy came somewhere between these two. The Inter-Service event was always going to be for us a David and Goliath affair, but each year we set out with high hopes to produce the best possible team.

We trained hard and given our level of ability this meant that we often skied above our ability and suffered injuries accordingly. In spite of, or perhaps because of this, it was all the greatest fun and the skiing crowd became among my closest friends. In the normal style of macabre air crew humour every ski run around Zermatt got many of its features christened in memory of various crashes—Galpin's Gulch, Hare's Hollow, Tite's Folly or Ferrier's Furrow. Nick Galpin summed up our approach. Having set off one morning to ski down far too fast for the first run of the day before being properly warmed up he had crashed and not surprisingly done something serious to one leg, probably broken it. He was being strapped on to the blood wagon, the sledge-borne stretcher, used to bring casualties down to the village. As we gathered round to commiserate he commented, "Ah well, boy, got to live you know, can't just exist."

Nick was a talented pianist/organist as well as an ace skier. In Zermatt village there was a small English church which over Christmas held the usual programme of services for the many English visitors. Nick was invited to play the organ for the services, there was no choir and Nick sat up at the front of the aisle in view of us all. The parson this year was a large imposing man with a rich baritone voice. He stood up to announce the next hymn, which happened to be one of those that has two alternative, equally well-known tunes. While Nick played the introductory verse of one of the tunes, we all found the place in our hymn books and got to our feet. The parson then led off sonorously on the first line, singing the other tune … . He and Nick got to the end of the line roughly together and Nick, turning to the congregation and miming with violently raised shoulders and eyebrows, "Oh well, if you can't beat 'em, join em!" launched straight into the other tune. The congregation, shaking with laughter, eventually managed to catch up and to join in too.

The Director of the Zermatt Ski School was Gotleib Perren, a friendly, relaxed, unassuming individual. One bright, sunny day up on the ski slopes above Zermatt I arrived at the foot of a T-bar lift and joined the queue to go back up. There, manning the lift, helping skiers to take hold of the tow bars, was the Director of the Ski School. "Gotlieb! Good Morning, what on earth are you doing here?" He made a dismissive gesture with his hand. "Oh, down in the willage they argue, always argue." Many times since in busy managerial jobs I have remembered Gotlieb Perren's excellent example and wished I too could spend the day out in the sunshine away from the telephones and visitors and paper work and arguments.

We became good friends with many of the Zermatt Ski School instructors. One year I was in a class with Herbert, renowned for a rather short temper first thing in the mornings and no sufferer of fools, or of over-talkative female pupils. One morning we sat dozing as the train wound its way up the mountain past Riffelberg to the top of the Gornergrat. Or rather we would have been comfortably dozing, had it not been for the endless prattle of one particular pupil. "Oh, Herbert, doesn't the Matterhorn look so exciting. Do tell me, Herbert, could you ski down the Matterhorn?" Long pause. "Yes, but only once."

Our other great friend in Zermatt was Mr Roman Perren-Fux owner of Glacier Sports. Like many able businessmen he affected an air of genial vagueness, with his dusty grey coat, battered felt hat, steel-rimmed spectacles and shy smile. He took a fatherly and benevolent view of the RAF racing crowd and would always let us choose brand new skis from the racks in his shop and then hire them out to us rather than our having to buy them, declaring stoutly that they were now part of his "for hire" stock. Mrs P-F was not so generously oriented towards the RAF and if she was hovering around Mr P-F would often invite us into the lift and close the door while we discussed a deal and he told us in his broken English his latest joke about American tourists. Like the American who returned a pair of skis he had just hired with, "Mr Perren. I want to replace these skis, they don't turn properly!" For Americans he sometimes pretended to have almost no English at all. "Ach so, are you vanting new skis or blue skis?"

Our favourite evening haunt was the Walliserkanne, otherwise the Jug. We sometimes felt that, unlike Mr Perren-Fux, some of the Swiss were too keen on a fast buck and, ensuring that everyone else in the bar could hear too, we would loudly tell each other the story about when God was creating the world. He gave each country three wishes and when it came to the Swiss their first two wishes were, "Some mountains, please, and then some cows to live on the mountains." They then said, "Can we have a bit of time to think about our last wish." "Certainly," said God, "and while you are thinking can I have a glass of milk from one of those cows." A few minutes the Swiss came back and God said, "Right, have you decided on your third wish then?" "Well no," said the Swiss, "But can we have 5 Francs for the milk."

In the Championships I skied about as well as I could expect to do and at the end of them while the selection committee retired to choose the team to represent the RAF at St Moritz I sat with my fingers crossed thinking that I might, just might, get selected. It was not to be, but by way of consolation I picked up the Novices' Slalom Cup and the Collins Jug "For the most promising newcomer to RAF Ski Racing." There was always next year and in the meantime I had an exciting new flying post to take up.

# The Aeroplane & Armament
# Experimental Establishment

## R A F Boscombe Down

THE VILLAGE OF Amesbury, ten miles north of Salisbury, nestles in the valley of the Hampshire Avon where the river winds its way south, from the Vale of Pewsey, below the open, wind-swept spaces of Salisbury Plain. Above Amesbury lie the airfield, hangars, laboratories, workshops and offices of the Aeroplane and Armament Experimental Establishment, Boscombe Down. The station enjoys sweeping views in all directions across the wide gallops and pastures. Just as at Upavon, a few miles to the north, I found the situation ideal, it was just my sort of open, peaceful countryside and it was enhanced by its collection of attractive villages scattered along the various river valleys. The Plain was an archaeological treasure house, long and round barrows and other relics of prehistory were everywhere and three miles away across the Avon valley stood the grey, brooding stones of Stonehenge. I was pleased to be back on Salisbury Plain and I could not have asked for a more interesting job.

On my previous squadron tours we had flown just two or three types of aeroplane. On 63 Squadron these had been single- and two-seat Meteors with the occasional jolly in the T11 Vampire, Oxford or Tiger Moth. On 26 it had been almost exclusively single- and two-seat

Hunters. Our job on the squadrons was simply to keep ourselves and the junior pilots who joined us, up to scratch and efficient in our operational role as Interceptor Day Fighters.

At Boscombe Down our role, as had been explained to us at ETPS, was much more interesting. We were there to represent the views of the average front line squadron pilot on any new type entering service and on the many modifications or new pieces of equipment which were being fitted to existing types, to comment on any undesirable features, to suggest how they could be rectified and to check the findings and conclusions of the manufacturers' own test pilots. Previously on meeting a new type we would have expected to attend a conversion unit, with a comprehensive ground school and some hours dual before being launched off solo. At Boscombe it was taken for granted that we would familiarise ourselves with the cockpit, locate the manuals and other literature and talk to other pilots who had flown the aircraft to get ourselves acquainted with all the systems and drills. As likely as not there was no two-seat version available. It was very satisfying to be treated in an entirely adult way.

There was a marvellous variety of types to fly, some that we were familiar with, some that we might never have happened to come across before and, best of all, the new ones just entering or about to enter service. During my time on A Squadron we had there at various times the Hunter, Javelin, Gnat, Jet- and Piston-Provost, Meteor, Beaver, Auster and all the marks of Lightnings from the Mk 1 to the Mk 5, as well as one pre-production version. The latter was distinctive compared with all the later versions by having a tiny tail-fin. Directional stability problems appeared as the later marks were produced resulting in an ever bigger tail fin. We made frequent visits to English Electric's factory at Wharton near Preston and to Hawker's at Dunsfold, using as runabouts Harvards, Ansons or the ubiquitous Meteors. By visiting the other squadrons we could get airborne, at least as second pilot, in a variety of choppers, as well as the Beverley, Canberra, Varsity and the occasional V-Bomber. Variety is the spice of life and it was most satisfying being able to jump into a different type almost every week.

The Javelin, most of us would agree, was as ungainly as it looked. It was a contemporary of the Vulcan bomber and had delta-shaped wings, once thought to be very much the shape of things to come. At the top of the enormous fin it had a small delta-shaped tail-plane. This had originally been fitted as a precautionary addition for the initial handling trials, but the slow speed handling had been found dubious and the tail-plane had become a permanent feature. The Javelin was designated as a night/all-weather fighter, it had a curious, cavernously roomy cockpit and was fitted with a massive radar set in the nose and of course carried a radar operator/navigator. For some reason it had a very long nose-wheel undercarriage leg and an awkward nose-up posture on the ground. We used it when we needed an airborne observer for some trial and took along a photographer or cameraman in the roomy rear cockpit.

At the other extreme was the Folland Gnat. It had originally been intended as an Interceptor Day Fighter. The theory was that its being so much smaller than its contemporaries, the Hunter and Swift, its adoption would lead to great economies and so allow for much greater numbers of Gnats to be ordered. However the Gnat only carried two guns as against the conventional interceptors' four and evaluation trials had led to the conclusion that a good big'un will always beat a good little'un. It was decided that the Gnat as a fighter was a non-starter, but it was then given a slightly longer fuselage to fit in two seats and was now destined to become the RAF's standard advanced jet trainer. Compared to the Hunter it was tiny; it felt as if you didn't really get into it, more that you put it on. But the cockpit was surprisingly roomy-roomier than the Lightning's! The Gnat seemed to have a similar appeal to the Austin Mini, not perhaps to be taken too seriously but nippy, cheeky and fun. Eventually for many years it equipped the Red Arrows, but it is really necessary to see a photograph of the aeroplane showing the pilot's head to appreciate the Gnat's very small size.

I am not sure why we had an Auster sent to us on A Squadron, presumably for us to look at some new radio fit or the like. It was a slow, short landing and take-off little aeroplane. Its high wings gave an excellent downward view but because the wings were so long its rate of roll was sluggish and its ailerons seemed underpowered, otherwise it was undistinguished. All I remember about it was that the throttle control was a strange mushroom-shaped knob protruding from the instrument panel like a displaced organ stop. The Beaver, on which I did a most interesting trial in the Middle East, was a worldwide success. It could only be described as an aerial Landrover and was successful for all the same reasons. It had a fixed undercarriage; it was simple, rugged, reliable, undemanding and could operate almost anywhere. There was a variant used around the lakes of the Canadian wilderness fitted with floats and known as the Otter.

A&AEE, the Aeroplane and Armament Experimental Establishment, was part of the Ministry of Aviation, a civil service responsibility and we service people were attached there. It was my first and only experience of working in a civil service outfit and in particular in one which practised what I later came to understand as matrix management, but of that more later. In those days the Establishment was divided into four squadrons: A—fighters and light aircraft, B—Bombers and large aircraft, C—Naval Aircraft and D—Helicopters. In addition there was the Handling Squadron, responsible for writing Pilots' Notes for aeroplanes entering service. Naturally I joined A Squadron, where our boss was Wing Commander "Red" Evans and the Senior Pilot Jack Fryer. I shared an office with Ronnie Lees, an old skiing friend, and for the third time met up with Don Hall, whom I had known at both Cranwell and Waterbeach. But thereafter our careers moved a bit apart. Don retired as Air Marshal Sir Donald Hall, but whenever I subsequently met him he remained the same cheerful, courteous, utterly unaffected friend he had always been. A truly great man. John Hewitt had been just ahead of me on 55 Entry C Squadron at Cranwell, Geoff Talbot was from the Royal Australian Air Force. Although actually a perfectly relaxed, friendly Aussie, Geoff had a solemn, rather unsmiling manner, so I nicknamed him "Sunbeam" Talbot. John Barwell, Dave Samuels and George Cannon arrived with me from ETPS. We had a couple of navigators on A Squadron, Jock McCabe and Jess Pudwell.

Wing Commander "Red" Evans was a charming boss. It was the squadron custom on wet Fridays when there was clearly no more flying in prospect to depart to the Red Lion in Amesbury for some beers and a spaghetti bolognese lunch. The two navigators took it in turns to stay behind and man the telephones, and we would occasionally get a frantic call from them saying that the Group Captain, the Superintendent of Flying, wanted to talk to the boss. Red kept a tube of toothpaste in his car which we would munch driving up the hill in an attempt to hide the wafts of "spag bol" before he got to the Group Captain's office.

Highly efficient in the air, Red was not really at his best on the parade square. We were preparing for an annual station inspection and he was commanding the parade. He faced us, all drawn up in line, intending to order us to turn ready to march past, but momentarily forgot that what was to him the right-hand side of the parade ground was to us the left-hand end. He gave the order "Right Turn" and we all promptly turned the opposite way to that which he had intended. Acutely sympathetic to his predicament we waited with bated breath to see what he would do to rectify matters. The appropriate order would have been "As you were" but the boss, being much more familiar with R/T nomenclature than that of the parade ground rapped out in his best Brigade of Guards voice, "I say again." Thank goodness it was only a practice parade.

Within weeks of joining A Squadron I had added the Jet Provost, Javelin, Freighter and Gnat to my list of types. None of them compared with the excitement of flying the Lightning but that was to come a bit later. Much test flying work is far removed from the dramatic "frontiers of space" dramas of the cinema and TV screens. In many trials the main satisfaction derives simply from flying the aeroplane as smoothly and accurately as possible in order that the boffins could get consistent results and nice smooth curves on their graphs. One such trial was a radio transmission trial needed whenever a new piece of radio equipment was to be fitted in a current type. About twenty miles west of Boscombe Down north of Wincanton, there is a curious triangular brick tower, probably somebody's folly. The point for us was that, rising above its surrounding trees, it was a clearly recognisable landmark, visible for miles around, on a hilltop and not near any town or centre of population. The radio engineers could therefore use it as a fixed, standard location a known distance from their receivers, for measuring radio performance. They needed to measure the strength of the transmission all around the aircraft, and this entailed our flying over the tower and making a transmission as we did so, on all points of the compass at ten degree intervals right round the 360°. We amused ourselves working out the best pattern to achieve this in the minimum time.

A recent variant of the Hunter had a new radio fit installed and trials were needed to check that its temperature control could cope with long low-level flights. In addition to the familiar 100 gallon drop tanks on the outboard pylons the test aircraft was fitted with two additional 230-gallon drop tanks inboard and I enjoyed some days of boring up and down the south coast at low level periodically switching on the temperature recorders.

The Folland Gnat was one of the new aeroplanes going through Boscombe Down prior to its introduction as the RAF's new advanced jet trainer. It was a particularly delightful aeroplane to fly. Its very small size made it handy and manoeuvrable on the ground and in the air, its comfortable, pale grey (at last!) cockpit was well laid out and its clear bubble canopy gave excellent all-round visibility—although Flying Instructors regarded the tandem seating as less satisfactory than side-by-side. However, its spinning characteristics were causing concern, especially as in service it would be flown by inexperienced students. The point about clearing an aeroplane, especially a trainer, for spinning is that when an aeroplane is mishandled or gets into a really unusual position the worst thing that can happen is that it goes into a spin. Thus if the student pilot, or any other pilot for that matter, can recover from a spin, and assuming that he has enough height to do so, all will be well.

The pilots actually conducting the spinning trials sometimes felt that they could no longer see the wood for the trees, in that they had become so involved with the subject that they found it hard to be objective and that they needed others to take a fresh look. They had concluded that the Gnat, apparently at random, could enter either a normal spin or an oscillatory spin or occasionally a very flat spin from which it was difficult to recover. The main point was that for student pilots the fact that the spinning characteristics were unpredictable was itself a serious drawback. Student pilots (and not only students!) meeting an unusual situation like to have a drill available which can be learned and memorised. If the situation cannot be predicted with any certainty a drill is not going to be of much use. Experienced pilots with many flying hours behind them have a better chance of remaining cool and analytical when faced with the unexpected, but even for them I felt that I knew from personal experience something of the feeling of mental paralysis that an emergency can induce.

The Gnat spinning trial pilots thus occasionally asked the rest of us on A Squadron to go and spin a Gnat in some particular configuration and tell them how we found it. A couple of months or so after I had first flown the Gnat, I had about ten hours on the type and so I represented quite well the sort of experience on it that a flying instructor or his student might have. I took a Gnat up to 30,000 ft closed the throttle, raised the nose and at the stall applied stick right back and full left rudder to enter what I expected would be a normal left-hand spin. The aeroplane made one turn to the left, paused, and then without my moving the controls in any way made one complete turn of a right hand spin, against the applied rudder. As it paused again I concluded that I had seen enough to agree that it indeed had very peculiar spin characteristics. I recovered and went home to tell the story. Because of many instances such as that, as far as I recall, the Gnat was never cleared for spinning in normal service.

The skiing season had come round again. I took a month's leave and headed once more for Zermatt, determined to have another serious go at getting into the RAF Team. On just the fourth day of the holiday I caught a ski in frozen ruts in Galpin's Gulch on the Sunnega—Blauherd run and tore a cartilage in my left knee. I tried to kid myself that with a few days' rest it would recover but of course it didn't. I came home and went in to the RAF Hospital at Wroughton to have the cartilage removed.

Straight out of Wroughton I was taken, with my leg still in a splint, to the RAF Rehabilitation Unit at Headley Court near Leatherhead in Surrey. Headley Court is an imposing mock-Tudor house surrounded by lawns, formal gardens, lily ponds and elegantly trimmed yew trees. It has a large, well-equipped gymnasium, a physiotherapist's wing and hydrotherapy heated swimming pool. Its purpose is to speed up recovery from operations or accident injuries. Compared with some of the patients there my injury was trivial and it was both humbling and inspiring to meet them and to hear some of their stories. In time I concluded a number of skiing seasons there and so got to know the place quite well and I always enjoyed my time there. Although we were patients, Headley Court was run on military lines in that the programme ran to a strict time-table, sessions in the gym, the pool or on "remedial strolls" up to the pub in the village which were managed by Physical Education NCOs. All patients were required to wear at least some article of uniform, usually a service blouse or hat.

Every morning there was a proper colour hoisting parade. The Orderly Officer might stump out on crutches or even trundle himself out in a wheel-chair, before standing, or sitting, to attention and at the salute as the flag was raised. With my injured knee I was in the class known as "Static Quads." Having limped into the gym you sat down on

177

the floor mats, carefully unbandaged your leg and joined in a series of exercises designed to start building up the muscles again but without allowing your knee to bend. Eventually you progressed to "Early Legs" to start bending the knee. Here the hydro pool sessions were the key as the water took most of the weight of the leg and you could control exactly how much stress you put on it. Everything at Headley Court was done professionally, pushing the patient as far as was sensible but taking great care not to overdo it. One of the gravest crimes one could commit was to walk into the gym wearing probably muddy outdoor shoes. At once the chant went up, "Shoes in the gym, shoes in the gym … ." The culprit, be he pilot officer or group captain was required to pay a penalty of ten press-ups. Just about any misdemeanour incurred a penalty of ten press-ups!

By the end of my stay I was walking normally except that, having worn a splint for so long I had got into the habit, now quite unnecessary, of limping. At any moment one of the PTIs was liable to call out, "Mr Boult, sir, did I see you limping, sir? That will be ten press-ups, please, sir!" "Hey, come on, Flight, I was only walking up these steps." "Oh, arguing with the staff are we, sir, that will be another ten, please, sir!" It was all done in the best of spirits, everyone joined in the fun and some of the recoveries one saw in really badly injured people were quite remarkable. I saw an elderly sergeant, recovering from a bad stroke, manage to walk slowly, almost for the first time during his recovery, the whole length of the gym on his way to the tea break and then slump down exhausted in a chair. One of his friends turned to him and said, "What's the matter with you today, Robbie? You're walking like a spastic crab!" He got an equally robust rejoinder. By the end of the month the Headley Court doc concluded I was sufficiently recovered and I was discharged back to work.

A group of senior scientists and other officials was to visit A & AEE to be given a series of presentations about our work. It was realised that while the other divisions could adequately explain this in their workshops and laboratories, Flying Division needed something more. We were therefore asked to make a short film about one of our trials and I grabbed the job of doing so. As it was about our hottest current topic the Gnat spinning programme was selected as the subject.

We decided that an interesting aspect of the trial, although primitive by today's standards, was the telemetry which was fitted to the trials aeroplane. This recorded many of the relevant conditions in flight such as height and speed, rates of roll, pitch and yaw and the positions of the flying controls and then transmitted these items to the ground where they were displayed and recorded. Our film set out to explain why this was valuable and then how all this information could be transmitted from the aeroplane on just one radio channel. We had no sophisticated film laboratory and so we drew a complete block diagram on a large sheet of paper and then worked out how the diagram could be built up one item at a time on the film. We set up the projector facing the completed diagram but with all except the first item hidden by another sheet. We ran a few seconds of film, cut away the covering sheet to show the next item, ran a few more seconds and so on. It was all very home-made and would have been laughed at by proper film-makers but on the finished film the sequence came out exactly as we had planned and we were very pleased with ourselves.

Having explained all this in our film we then needed to show an actual spinning sortie. Our civil servant cameraman found to his dismay, as he had become as enthusiastic on the project as any of us, that his contract of employment did not allow him to fly on "High Risk" sorties. Spinning in any aircraft was regarded as high risk. He gave me a quick coaching on how to work the 16 m/m camera and I loaded it up with film and flew a couple of trips in the back seat of a Gnat while boss Evans flew and spun it. We then filmed some more shots in the ground cabin where the telemetry outputs were displayed on dials and recorded by moving pens on a paper roll. We worked out the logical sequence for our material and spliced all the film together. The end result was most satisfactory. For the presentation to the visiting boffins I had more or less learned the commentary by heart and was able, with just the occasional glance at my notes, to narrate it in sync with the film. It was decided to record the commentary properly and I went down to a government film laboratory to make a recording which was properly dubbed on to the film. Later I was flattered to hear that the film was to be kept in the archives but also somewhat miffed to hear that the commentary was to be re-recorded by a professional. I believe it was Richard Baker.

Partly because of the Gnat's unpredictable spinning characteristics a controversy was in progress at the time on whether it was really the best choice for the new advanced jet trainer. The other candidate was the

179

two-seat version of the Hunter, the Mark 7. This had completely predictable handling characteristics and the additional advantage of side-by-side seating. In addition the RAF had operated Hunters for many years, spares were held in abundance and there were dozens of trained tradesmen experienced in its servicing. The problems with the Gnat's spinning were by now well known and at that year's Farnborough Air Show Bill Bedford, Hawker's Chief Test Pilot, gave a perfect demonstration of the complete predictability of the Hunter. It was a clear, cloudless day and he ran in at high speed, sweeping up the line of the runway and turning on his smoke generator as he pulled up into a long, straight almost vertical climb. At about 20,000 ft, still clearly visible against the blue sky, he entered a spin. The Hunter came spinning down, forming a clear corkscrew trail of white smoke. After some eight turns of the spin Bill neatly recovered and dived out of the manoeuvre once more exactly down the centre-line of the runway. We felt it rather clinched the case. However we were eventually told that while Hawkers didn't need the additional employment in their area, Follands did. The economic and political factors were to over-ride the operational considerations of which was the appropriate choice of aeroplane.

One day Jimmy Aitken rang me up from Farnborough and asked me to go over and fly a trip for him in a Canberra. The trial he was conducting provided another example of the need to get the views of someone coming new to a piece of equipment and who was not familiar with all the ongoing arguments about it. The purpose of the trip was to form an initial impression of a map projection system. This was many years before modern IT was available and at the time it was state-of-the-art stuff. The equipment used a series of ordinary 1:500,000 scale maps which had been converted into 35mm slides. The selected slide was projected on to an eight-inch diameter screen in the cockpit and the cunning bit was that it was adjusted so that the present position of the aircraft was always at the centre of the screen. Some of the questions we were asked to comment on were, given the limited size of the screen, what scale should the projection be, was the illumination the right brightness and should the display be north-oriented or track-oriented? That is to say should the display always show the aeroplane flying up the map or should it always have north at the top? Different pilots held strong views on each side of the question and arguments were fierce. In fact we used to say on A Squadron that if you put any

180

question of this sort to four TPs you would get four different opinions—unless Ronnie Lees was one of them in which case you got five, because Ronnie talked everyone else round to his point of view—and then changed his mind.

I grabbed a Meteor, flew over to Farnborough and Jimmy briefed me on what he wanted from the trip. I had at the time about a dozen hours on Canberras so although comfortably familiar with the aeroplane and its cockpit I was not well up in all its possible configurations, fuel loads and so on. This particular aeroplane was fitted with wing-tip fuel tanks giving it an extended range. Jimmy explained that my navigator had already worked out a route for us around the Scottish lowlands and over appropriate types of terrain. He was apparently an experienced Canberra man and knew all about the aeroplane. Jimmy added that he wanted us to get off without delay so that the aeroplane could do another sortie in the afternoon. We started up, taxied, got airborne, climbed to height and headed for Scotland. We let down over the lowlands and I tried out the map projection system as an aid to low level navigation. Having formed some opinions I jotted down some notes and we climbed up and headed south for Farnborough.

The drill was to use about half the internal fuel before switching over to the wing tanks. As we flew down over the north of England I therefore decided to start using fuel from the wing tanks, so I moved the left hand switch to select wing-tip fuel for the port engine. The fuel low pressure warning light for that engine promptly came on, so I switched straight back to internal fuel. The same thing happened for the starboard engine. It was clear that for some reason we were not getting tip-tank fuel for either engine. What was equally obvious was that without it we could not reach Farnborough. My poor navigator searched franticly through the Pilots' Notes to see what aspect of fuel system handling we had overlooked. No joy, so we were going to have to divert. With fingers crossed and trying to sound nicely casual I called Waddington in Lincolnshire, a Master Airfield, for a "practise diversion." Had they answered that they were too busy to accept a practise I should have had to swallow my pride and admit that it was a real one. But all was well, they accepted our practise, gave us a course to steer and we descended through cloud while I reflected on how pleased Jimmy was going to be to lose his aeroplane for most of the day, while we sat at Waddington getting re-fuelled.

We were just joining Waddington's circuit when my navigator finally found a reference to an obscure fuel transfer pressure switch, well hidden—as vital switches so often are. We tried it, we could now use our wing-tip fuel and so we could go home. We thanked Waddington and climbed away. Before Jimmy could say anything about our wasting time while he was waiting for his aeroplane, I explained rather vigorously to him my views about skimping briefings and assuming that navigators knew anything at all about the management of such things as fuel systems.

By far the most interesting and exciting aeroplane we had on A Squadron while I was at Boscombe Down was the English Electric Lightning. It could never have been called beautiful but with its angular lines, slab sides and very sharply swept wings it exuded power. A sharply pointed, conical nose fairing, within the circular air intake, housed the radar and behind this the air was fed under the cockpit floor into the two Avon engines. The engines were mounted one above the other so that there were no asymmetric handling problems. To allow the frontal area of the aeroplane to be reduced to an absolute minimum the two engines were mounted not exactly one above the other but staggered so the wide part of one engine fitted snugly into the narrower part of the other. The aeroplane was, however, something of a challenge to the engineers and Houdini-like feats of dexterity were needed to carry out servicing and component changes. The outer skin wrapped so closely round the engines that the control runs to the rear fuselage had to be incorporated in the narrow spine running back from the cockpit. The wings were of a very narrow thickness/chord ratio and swept back at 60°. The Lightning was the ultimate in the specialist role of interceptor. Its primary armament was a pair of heat-seeking missiles, its rate of climb was phenomenal and as it was a single-seater the pilot operated the search radar as well as flying the aeroplane

At Boscombe all the aircraft on the squadron were engaged in busy test-flying programmes, although as this sometimes involved engineering modifications, such as fitting special recorders it could mean lengthy periods in the hangar with the panels off. They could not easily be spared for providing first solos on type and familiarisation rides for newcomers. Often the opportunity for a first trip came up at the end of the day once the planned test-flying programme for the day had been completed. It became a squadron joke, with an element of truth in it, that on your first trip on a new type you would probably have to land in the dark. There was no Lightning simulator available so you strapped in hoping fervently that you were going to be able to recall enough of your many days' study of Pilots' Notes.

The Lightning was basically a simple and delightful aeroplane to fly. As someone said, "Hell, it's got a stick and throttles, what more do you want?" True enough, but the cockpit was cramped and the aircraft systems were undeniably complicated. You hoped that none of them was going to play silly buggers on your first trip. To help you cope there were two centralised warning panels. The secondary warning panel of amber lights alerted you about a number of non-critical malfunctions and a thankfully smaller panel of red lights for the serious stuff—engine fires and the like. What was more, to draw your attention to primary warnings a couple of red attention-getters flashed straight in your eyes and, even more alarming, a loud fire-bell-like clanging went off in your headset. Even when you were just testing its operation, this latter was enough to produce heart palpitations.

One day a Lightning became available for my first ride. It was with a certain feeling of mainly pleasant anticipation that I climbed into my "g" suit and overalls, collected my flying helmet and Mae West, signed the authorisation book and walked out to the aeroplane. I made a brief walk-round check, climbed up the ladder and started to strap in. My ground-crewman handed me my helmet, connected the radio pigtail, removed and stowed the hot-seat (ejection seat) safety pin, unhooked the ladder—and I was on my own. Having started the engines and, trying to sound suitably casual, I called the tower for taxi clearance. I taxied down to the threshold, completing the pre-take off checks as I went, called for take off clearance, turned onto the runway and lined up on the centreline. I took a final look round the cockpit, took a deep breath and released the brakes.

The acceleration on take-off and in the initial climb, even without re-heat, was absolutely breathtaking. In fact you had to be quite sharp, immediately you were airborne, in order to select wheels up for them to be retracted before you reached the maximum permitted speed for the unlocked undercarriage. In time the Lightning became just one of the types we flew regularly, but it was always special, something like a Ferrari among Ford Mondeos!

Having done a few familiarisation trips in the Lightning I became engaged in a programme of engine-handling trials at high altitudes and high Mach Numbers. As you climb from ground level the air pressure, which only depends on the amount of air still above you, drops steadily. The air temperature also at first drops off with height but only up to about 36,000 ft. From here on up it remains constant. The height at which the temperature suddenly ceases to fall is called the tropopause, and this is the altitude at which a jet engine performs best. The Machmeter displays your speed as a decimal part of the speed of sound and at high altitude and high speeds this was the measure of speed we mostly used.

For a typical high-altitude test sortie we took off from Boscombe, usually to the south-west, and at 400 kts raised the nose into the climb to maintain that speed. To do so you were climbing at quite a steep angle and such was the power of the Lightning that if you let your attention wander and eased off the angle of climb you suddenly found that you had gone supersonic and despatched a sonic bang somewhere towards Dorset and Somerset. As you climbed the Machmeter started to register and, for the best climbing performance in the Lightning, once 400 kts IAS equated to .9 Mach you maintained that, until you levelled out at the tropopause. You throttled back to maintain Mach .9 and turned out to sea over Torbay but once you were pointing away from the land you could open the throttles again and engage re-heat. Re-heat or after-burning as the Americans call it is a system of feeding extra fuel straight into the jet pipe behind the engine and igniting it there. It is naturally expensive in fuel but by raising the temperature and so the velocity of the jet it gives a marked increase in power. Having gone supersonic you continued the turn round on to east and aimed between the southern tip of the Isle of Wight and the Channel Islands. You could often see the sun glinting on the many acres of greenhouses on the latter and to drop a bang there would have been highly unpopular. Because the tropopause is the height at which a jet performs best the technique was to take a sort of running jump from that height, getting up to maximum speed there and then easing up to a much higher altitude while letting the speed fall slowly off in the process.

On a couple of occasions on nice cold days, which allowed the engines to generate their maximum power, I got the Machmeter up to the magic figure of M2, twice the speed of sound and about 1,400 mph, before climbing. At that height and with the air absolutely smooth you were really not conscious of the speed, except that the south coast of

England, if you could see it, was slipping past quite fast, and even more noticeably the fuel gauges were visibly going down. You pulled up to something well above 45,000 ft, switched on your recorders and carried out the engine-handling checks that you had been briefed for and made appropriate notes on your test cards.

Having finished the trials you throttled back and turned gently left again, coming subsonic over the Isle of Wight and using the speed to get a bit more height and so into a nice economical semi-gliding descent back to the airfield. Boscombe Down's radio call-signs were all prefaced with "Evergreen" and finding it was at the time unallocated I naturally grabbed "26" as my individual call-sign. We enjoyed the luxury of our own radar cabin so that you only had to say, "Evergreen 26, pigeons to base, please," to be instantly given your heading and distance back to the circuit. You popped the airbrakes, skirted Salisbury, called "Boscombe, Evergreen 26, rejoining from the south," dived into the circuit, round on to the downwind leg and dropped your wheels and flaps. You called, "Finals," came round the turn, over the hedge, and on to the runway, streaming the tail parachute. Even with the length of Boscombe's runway the braking parachute greatly lessened the wear on the brakes. Taxi-ing in you noted your flying time for the trip and would be slightly amazed to see that it was just thirty or maybe thirty-five minutes.

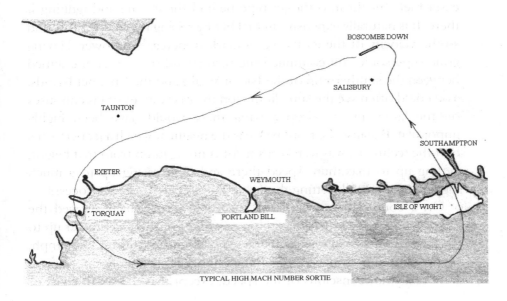

TYPICAL HIGH MACH NUMBER SORTIE

I flew many hours in different marks of Lightning in connection with the various radar fits. The progress of some of these trials was slow because of the need for special instrumentation to be designed and installed to measure different aspects of the performance of the radar. This entailed many days of the aeroplane sitting in the hangar with its panels off and sprouting wires and electrical rigs and looking like a patient in intensive care, which in a sense it was! We worked in close co-operation with the scientists and engineers and often had to curb our impatience to get on with the trial to accommodate their more leisurely but also more meticulous and careful approach. It was an interesting experience of the difficulties of working in a team with those from very different backgrounds and training. By the time that I left Boscombe Down I had flown all the Marks of Lightning from the Mk 1 to the Mk 5 as well as the Development Batch prototype.

For some very high altitude trips in the Lightning, had you suffered a loss of cabin pressure at height even breathing 100% oxygen would not have saved you from unconsciousness while you let down to a more benign height. We therefore wore special goldfish-bowl helmets a bit like astronauts. The helmets were designed to be pressurised for that situation, but they provided much less sound-proofing than our normal ones. The first time I flew with one was nerve-wracking. Every time I operated some cockpit selector switch or moved a trimmer or such like I heard an unusual and hence alarming buzz or click or whirring noise. After a time I realised that the aeroplane was in fact behaving entirely normally, but previously with a normal helmet, I hadn't been able to hear all the plumbing at work.

Operating at very high altitude, as it was intended to do, the Lightning could encounter a rather special handling problem. At those heights the air is very rarefied and stability has to be carefully considered. Many aeroplanes have a considerable amount of their weight, or more accurately their mass, out in the wings, that is a fair distance from the central axis of the fuselage. The wingspan is also usually greater than the length of the fuselage. When such an aeroplane rolls rapidly this widely- spread mass acts like a flywheel and tends to keep the aeroplane pointing along the direction of flight. But the Lighting, with its thin, very sharply swept wings, and short wingspan, has very little of its mass distributed in this way. Moreover, at height in the thin air and especially if it is pulling some "g" it may be flying at a

186

considerable angle of attack, that is with the fuselage inclined above its flight path. If it now rolls fast the masses concentrated in the ends of the fuselage tend to act as a destabilising flywheel and to cause the aeroplane to yaw away from the line of the flight path. This is called roll-yaw-coupling. There was at least one known instance of a Lightning, flying at a high supersonic speed, being so far destabilised that it in effect went sideways, the fin broke off and the pilot got out on his hot-seat just an instant before the aeroplane disintegrated. As a result of this characteristic there were a number of laid-down limitations about avoiding high rates of roll at altitude which we were all most careful to observe.

Alternately flying the Lightning and the Gnat was an odd experience. The nice judgement required for a smooth landing is at the round out. This is the point at which you checked the rate of descent and felt for the ground, aiming to grease the wheels on to the concrete without a jolt. With the Lightning, in the landing attitude, your eye level was a good twelve feet above the ground while in the Gnat not more than about six feet. Depending on which of the two so dissimilar types you had recently flown most, you either rounded out in the Gnat high above the ground and floated half way down the runway while it felt as if the concrete was coming up round your ears, or in the Lightning just as you were thinking of starting to round out you arrived unexpectedly on the ground with an undignified crunch.

In addition to the primary armament of its heat-seeking missiles the secondary armament of the Lightning was a pair of Aden 30 mm cannons. An aircraft can be set up in butts on the ground and the bullet pattern established, but this is no substitute for a check in the air where factors such as some minute flexing of the airframe or the airflow over the gun muzzles may introduce significant differences and so another trial that I was involved in was to provide an airborne check of the gun harmonisation. The trial, while technically simple, was a complicated affair to arrange and conduct.

The guns were loaded with tracer ammunition, so that the bullets could be filmed from a nose-mounted camera loaded with colour film and fitted with a very long-range telephoto lens. Colour film has no grain and this was required in order to achieve the very high definition needed to be able to see the bullets. The firing had to be done over the authorised gunnery area in Lyme Bay off the Dorset coast. A target which looked like a dart was towed, on a very long cable, by a Canberra. For safety the Canberra was never permitted to tow the target through cloud and it also had to be accompanied at all times by a chase aeroplane to keep an eye on the dart. The intention, once the cliff-top shipping search radar had confirmed that the range area was clear, was to close in line astern on the target, to sight very accurately and to fire short bursts at the dart which the nose-mounted camera would automatically film, so that we could actually see where the bullets went. A complicated radio arrangement also allowed the range to be worked out.

For every trial a Test Instruction was issued to all concerned, but due to the matrix organisation, it was never actually clear who was in charge or accountable for getting the trial progressed. For this gun harmonisation trial on the Lightning four of the A&AEEs divisions were involved. In addition to us, the pilots from Flying Division, there were the contributions from the Armament, Radio and Photographic Divisions. Although the pilot flying the trial was the person attempting to get it done, due to the matrix setup, he had no formal authority over people in the other divisions. You just hoped that the others would carry out the requirements of the Test Instruction.

Given the intermittent availability of the Lightning, the Canberra, the firing range area radar and the chase aeroplane (and skies sufficiently clear of cloud on a typical English summer day) it was quite an occasion when finally everything came together and, having found someone to fly the Canberra and the chase and having briefed them on the plan for the sortie, you actually got airborne and headed for Lyme Bay. I finally did so, fired off the necessary rounds and came thankfully back to await with great interest the results when the films came back from being developed.

The films came back and it was then discovered that a junior technician in Photographic Division, feeling that his stocks of colour film were rather low had on his own initiative, and without checking with the office which had issued the Test Instruction, loaded the camera with ordinary monochrome stock. The normal grain on the films rendered the results quite useless. Taking a deep breath we went through the process again, eventually found a day when all the components came together and got airborne once more. When the films came back this time it was discovered that instead of the long telephoto a wide-angle lens had been fitted. The Canberra itself was hardly visible let alone the dart which was the target and as for the bullets … . So much for matrix management.

Managerial issues intruded on the ground just as in the air. On one occasion I was sent up to the Ministry of Defence to attend a meeting called to review the introduction of some piece of electronic equipment. My job was simply to listen and to report back so I was not going to have to take part in the discussion but clearly I needed to take an interest in who attended and note who said what. The meeting was chaired by a Group Captain and in the light of my later experiences and the beginnings of some understanding of the business of management I can only describe his chairing of the meeting as—incredible.

There were no name cards and no introductions. I found it difficult to keep up, as there was no written agenda and no summaries to punctuate or finalise topics being discussed. Of the eight or so round the table most seemed to know each other already. Two very smartly dressed and cultured young men seemed to have the most to say and in fact dominated the talk, simply raising their voices whenever someone else tried to comment. But as the meeting proceeded it emerged that they only talked about the financial aspects of the programme. The Group Captain said little but, hardly looking up, scribbled busily away, himself taking the minutes. At the bottom of the table, apparently in shy silence, sat an elderly, rather scruffy man wearing a poorly-fitting suit and woolly pullover. He had a little kit for rolling his own cigarettes and this he did most skilfully. The nicotine on his fingers told their own tale and I was fascinated in his skill with the machine. As far as I can recall he hardly actually said anything at all. I idly wondered why he was there, perhaps to straighten the chairs and empty the ashtrays when the meeting finished? He seemed as out of place as I was. When the meeting ended the man sitting next to me suggested I join him for a pub lunch. As he was clearly a friendly type I eagerly quizzed him about what he had got out of the meeting and about our fellow attendees. The two cultured young men he dismissed as of no importance, they were only people from the Treasury. And the old guy with the woolly? He was the eminent scientist who had actually designed the bit of electronic kit we had been discussing, far and away the most important person there. I really have not exaggerated the story of that meeting and it still stands out in my memory for that Group Captain's unbelievably incompetent chairmanship.

It was through experiences such as these, that MOD meeting and the muddle over the gun harmonisation trial, that it began to dawn on me that this whole business of management was of the most fundamental importance. With hindsight I suppose that is terribly obvious but in the years which followed I have discovered that I was by no means alone in my previous ignorance. It eventually came home to me that the whole business of running meetings, of communication, of resolving mis-understandings, of co-ordinating the work of a number of people, of avoiding muddle and confusion, deserved much more attention than it seemed to get. With increasing frequency I have come across organisa-tions which regarded muddle as something inevitable. It became apparent that it was often seen as regrettable but unavoidable, rather like the English summer weather, something you joked about but had to put up with.

We were not alone with our organisational problems. All of us on the Lightning trials made periodic trips up to Wharton near Preston to talk to the English Electric Test Pilots, often their Chief TP, Jimmy Dell. One day I was up at Wharton to discuss with him some detail of a simple piece of cockpit equipment. We needed to look at an actual example so when Jimmy was called to the telephone I grabbed a screwdriver and, to save time, nipped out into the hangar, hopped into an aeroplane and brought back the item for us to examine. Our resumed discussion was abruptly interrupted. The thirty second job of unscrewing a couple of screws and bringing into the office the piece of kit was by rights the job of a civilian fitter and I had transgressed union demarcation rules. No matter that it could have taken half-an-hour to find an available fitter, to explain to him what we wanted and to wait for him to get it. Perhaps peoples' attitudes and their ability to ignore the perfectly obvious was something to do with management too. It also began to dawn on me that this might have something to do with why Britain was no longer at the forefront of aircraft development.

Jimmy Dell told us about another example of a simple failure of communication which some months previously had wasted many days. They were checking out a new arrangement for some cockpit night lighting and discovered that it was getting reflected in the windscreen and producing confusing spots of light apparently ahead of the aircraft and in the pilot's field of vision. The solution was a simple metal mask fitted under the windscreen to prevent this, a bit of tin would have done, something that could be cut out in a few minutes with a pair of tin snips. The difficulty was to indicate to the workshops the actual shape needed. They got hold of a bit of plasticine, wedged it in place and phoned the workshops to tell them what was needed, to say that we had left it in the aeroplane to show them what we need, could they please knock us up a metal one. Another job diverted their attention and a week later it occurred to them that they had still not heard from the workshops. They went over to check what was causing the delay. The aeroplane had been standing out in the sun, the plasticine had melted into an interesting and intricate three-dimensional shape, which the workshops were carefully reproducing, machining it accurately out of a solid block. They reckoned it would be finished by the end of the week.

However on another occasion Jimmy encountered exactly the sort of problem that test flying is intended to discover. A new item of navigational equipment allowed one to lock on to one of a series of ground beacons and then to read off one's range from it. The cockpit indicator displayed the code number of the selected beacon and in the two-seat Lightning the only place that could be found for it was right over on the second pilot's side of the instrument panel. This meant that when flying solo the pilot in the left-hand seat had to look across the cockpit at it diagonally. The depth of the instrument meant that the first digit, for example the 1 in 18, was obscured and Jimmy read it as 8, the first digit being hidden by the rim of the instrument. Knowing the range from the beacon was of no use if one had misread which beacon it was, but in this instance the danger was discovered and rectified. Such instances sound, with the benefit of hindsight, so trivial and obvious that it is hard to get people to understand why development test flying by critical and experienced pilots is so important. Unfortunately on some occasions a defect such as this in an instrument or other piece of equipment has been brushed aside and a subsequent incident then blamed on pilot error.

Another more frightening instance Jimmy encountered was on a trip wearing a new, bulky, high-altitude flying suit. He landed and moved his left hand forward to press the braking parachute selector button. As he did so his bulky cuff caught the starboard throttle lever and pushed it right forward to select full power and re-heat. Of course this ripped off the braking parachute and Jimmy just, only just, came to a very breathless stop inches from the end of the runway.

Exciting as the Lightning was, we still enjoyed variety and we all queued up for a ride in a small, simple primary trainer when it made its appearance on A Squadron. The original Percival Provost had been a standard if rather boring and undistinguished propeller-driven side-by-side seating trainer with a fixed under-carriage. It was then re-designed, and the piston engine was replaced by a small jet. This allowed a low tricycle undercarriage, which now retracted and it became, as the Jet Provost, a much more attractive machine. We had one on A Squadron for some weeks and it proved a most popular and relaxing diversion. The Jet Provost had a large, unusually comfortable, roomy cockpit but this very characteristic was to be the cause of an embarrassing incident which I heard about some years later.

New items of equipment, navigation and landing aids and the like do not have to be expensive and complicated to be effective. A new landing aid which appeared at about this time was the VASI, the Visual Approach Slope Indicator. In bad weather, poor visibility and heavy rain it may be difficult to judge the angle of your final approach to the runway threshold. The VASI consisted in effect of two large tin boxes placed beside the runway, one near the touchdown point and the other some distance along the runway. In each box was a light and facing the approaching aircraft was a horizontal slit, like a long thin letterbox. The key element was that behind the slits and parallel to them was a light filter, the top half coloured red and the lower half clear. Viewed from a shallow angle the light strip from a box was seen as red and from a steeper angle as white.

The boxes were adjusted so that if you were approaching at too steep an angle both light strips appeared white, if at too shallow an angle, because you were too low, both as red, but that if you were at the correct angle of approach the near light appeared white and the far one red. The system was simple, effective and very helpful. On this occasion well done the boffins!

I still regarded skiing as my main sporting interest and the skiing crowd were among my closest friends. One of the prominent members of the RAF Ski Team was Corporal Rudi Prochazka. He was of mid-European origin but had been brought up in the north east of England. He had a strong personality, a delightful sense of humour and a marked Geordie accent. He had a number of times been put up for a commission, but had regularly declined saying he was quite happy

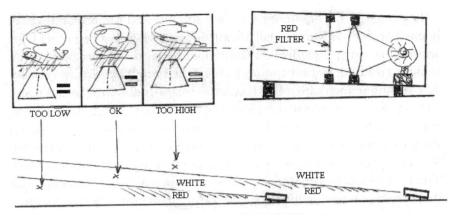

VISUAL APPROACH SLOPE INDICATOR.

doing jobs he liked and letting others take all the hassle. I was pleased and flattered when in April '61 Rudi rang me up, told me he was to get married in the coming June and asked me to be his best man. In suggesting to him that we meet at the RAF (Officers') Club in Piccadilly I had completely forgotten that as a corporal this was hardly his normal scene, until as we strolled into the bar he muttered, "If we meet some officer I know, I'll just die!" Anyway we didn't. The wedding was to be in Kerriemuir in eastern Scotland and the original plan had been for us to meet various other members of the party, bridesmaids and others that evening, catch the sleeper to Edinburgh and then go on by train to Forfar on the following, Friday morning. It was absolutely sweltering and the more we considered it, the more unattractive sounded a stiflingly hot night in the sleeper. Almost without realising it we found we had decided to drive up instead. We made contact with the bridesmaids to say, "Tell Barbara (the bride) that it's OK. Just because the groom is not on the train it doesn't mean he's welshed on you! He's coming up by car."

This was before the days of motorways, but also an era of far less traffic and the first part of the drive in my TR3 up the almost empty Great North Road in the early part of the night was fine. Through Otterburn, over Carter Bar and through the lowlands into Edinburgh was wearying and by the time we were in Angus the idea didn't seem quite such a jolly jape. We arrived at Barbara's house in time for breakfast, she took one look at us and said, "You need sleep." We re-appeared refreshed in time for the rehearsal and the wedding went off fine. Rudi and Barbara duly departed for their honeymoon and on Sunday morning her two brothers decided that water-skiing at Lochearn would be appropriate. I left Lochearnhead at four that afternoon and was back at Boscombe by two am Monday morning and that, as I have said, in the days before motorways.

I got back to Boscombe Down to find some pleasant news of my own. It being the start of July the half-yearly promotion list had appeared over the weekend and together with a large contingent of No 57 Entry I was promoted to Squadron Leader. I had my scraper—and some months later it dawned on me where the expression came from!

In June 1962 a trial of a very different nature came my way. The Sultan of Oman's Air Force operated Beavers, the well-known "aerial Landrovers." They were concerned that operating around the mountains of Oman, carrying heavy loads of troops and supplies, they were often exceeding the laid down engine temperature limits. Quite apart from the probable presence of unfriendly tribesman with long sharp knives, a more inhospitable location for any forced landing could hardly be imagined. Very sensibly they wanted to know how serious the overheating was and what they should do about it. There was a British Army unit in Aden also operating Beavers and it was arranged that John Smith, one of the Performance Division boffins, and I should go out to borrow one of their aeroplanes and study the problem. Because clearly we needed to study the "worst case" the trial was planned for July, the hottest time of the year. Before we arrived all the critical spots on the engine of one of the army's Beavers had been covered with an additional array of temperature sensors. In the cockpit were a sensitive temperature gauge and a ten-position selector switch. John Smith selected a series of representative conditions of aircraft weight, altitude, speed and engine settings and then all I had to do was get airborne, climb to the necessary height and trim the aeroplane into the appropriate setting, let everything stabilise and then select in turn each of the ten positions of the switch and read off the indicated temperatures.

John and I arrived in Aden and were greeted by the army who were actually based at Falaise Camp, in Little Aden. It was my first experience of the Arab world and the desert, and I found it quite fascinating. The heat of the day was best avoided whenever possible but the cool, silent evenings as the sun sank over the desert and all the colours slowly changed and faded were magical. Aden town itself was a crowded, bustling, typical Arab city strung along the shore of the bay under the craggy slopes of the peak. A narrow road wound over a spur into the original Arab town of Crater, so named because it was crammed into the actual crater of the long dead volcano. It was a seven-mile drive across the causeway, past the big RAF base of Khormaksar and through the "silent valley" where among the steep volcanic peaks vehicle radios gave up, to the Army Air Corps base. As I was to find later in Singapore the army had a laid-back, unflustered way of keeping everything organised in meticulous and exact detail with the minimum of fuss. I found their approach greatly to my liking. The army greeted John Smith and me warmly; I flew a sector recce with Sergeant Harris to be shown the local area and we were in business.

To conduct the trials we wanted to see just how hot the aeroplane got so we left it standing in the sun until mid-day and then, arming ourselves with the seat cushions which we had stored in the fridge, we started up, took off and flew the planned set of conditions, keeping a close watch on all the engine temperatures as we did so. Had one of the Sultan of Oman's Beavers developed serious overheating out over some craggy mountains or desert wadi it could have been a very nasty emergency. By contrast we took care always to remain within gliding distance of Khormaksar, so that even if we had had to stop the engine immediately, putting a slow landing Beaver down on that 2,000-yard runway would have been no cause for concern.

We completed all the sorties that John Smith had planned but once he had studied the results of his sums he came to the conclusion that Aden happened to be enjoying an unusually cool summer and that we had not really tested the hottest conditions that could be met in the Oman. The answer was to make a few more sorties at somewhere really hot, and that was likely to be Sharjah, 1,000 miles away on the other side of the Arabian peninsula at the entrance of the Persian Gulf. However, it was obvious that flying around the Arabian Desert was a very different proposition from flying in Europe under the watchful eye of the radar fixer services. I therefore went to see the Army Air Corps, pointed out that I was a novice to their area and they kindly lent us an experienced desert pilot and an airframe mechanic. Lieutenant Michael Ashley, Corporal Drake and I set off to fly round the coast of the Rub al Khali, the Empty Quarter of Arabia. I really felt that we were on the edges of civilisation. On the map even the coast was in places only depicted as a rather provisional dotted line. At the height we would be flying we would be out of radio contact for about one third of each leg both with the airfield we had just left and the one which we were flying towards. Had we experienced engine trouble during that time and had to make a forced landing no-one would have known where to start looking for us. We therefore took the precaution of getting in touch with Aden Airways and making arrangements with them that we would set off on each leg just an hour before their regular daily Dakota flight up the coast. The plan worked well and just as our radio contact with Aden started to fade we could hear on the R/T the Dakota getting airborne behind us. We remained in contact with it as it overhauled us and before it faded ahead we were in contact with our destination. We were very grateful for the link. We refuelled and took a quick lunch at Riyan and then in the afternoon flew on to Salalah.

Salalah is in the unusual situation that although it is on a generally dry, sandy desert plain, for two months of the year it experiences a brief south westerly monsoon, bringing low cloud, poor visibility and almost continuous drizzle. It is certainly unusual to see airmen in khaki, desert uniforms walking about the sand carrying dripping umbrellas. Salalah gave us some sort of ground-controlled approach and we planned to stop for the night. We checked in to the pre-fab hut which was their Air Traffic Control Tower and were amused at the primitive looking direction-finding system they used for controlled approaches. It looked rather like a submarine periscope that the controller squinted through.

The following morning I so nearly made a very unwise decision, and even today it disturbs me to remember how nearly I did. While Corporal Drake carried out the pre-flight inspection on the aeroplane Mike Ashley and I passed our air movement information to Air Traffic Control for the next leg to Masirah Island. We climbed aboard the Beaver and started up. Having allowed the engine to warm up to its normal operating temperatures we started the run-up. We ran up to 2,000 RPM and checked for the "mag. drop." Aero engines have two electrical systems—magnetos and sets of plugs—because the electrics were reckoned to be the least robust and reliable part of an aero engine. It was considered important always to have the two fully functioning sets in case one gave out in the air. It is important to check that each system on its own gives a satisfactory performance. The revs obtained will be less with only one set of plugs firing than with both systems operating and so a small drop in revs when one magneto is switched off is acceptable. On this occasion with the engine running on the port magneto alone the drop in revs was right on, or was it just above, the acceptable limit? It depended on the angle from which you looked at the gauge. It was difficult to tell, but as Corporal Drake pointed out, the aeroplane had stood out in the drizzle all night and so it was almost certain that moisture had got into the system. By the time we had taxied out to the take-off point it would have dried off and cured itself.

We taxied out to the downwind end of the airfield, completed our pre-take-off checks and took one more quick look at mag drop. It really had not improved. It was still just about on the acceptable limit. What to do? It was still most probable that it was a bit of moisture, by the time we had climbed a few thousand feet it would surely be OK—or would it? The visibility was indifferent, the cloud base was still around or below 1,000 ft, Salalah is ringed inland by hills much higher than that— and what about their rather rudimentary Air Traffic Control facilities and that periscope?

To go or not to go? I decided not to go. It still disturbs me to remember how very nearly I decided the opposite. We taxied in again in a rather prim silence from Mike and the Corporal and with me feeling all sorts of wimp. That was until we had taken off the engine cover and removed the offending magneto. The oil seal had gone and it was dripping oil. In the air it would have got steadily worse and would soon have packed up completely—leaving us heading out over the desert with only one set of functioning electrics. We signalled Aden for new magneto, relaxed at Salalah until it arrived and once it had been fitted and tested flew on to Sharjah without further incident.

While we were completing our trials at Sharjah a colonel from the Trucial Oman Scouts asked if we could give him a lift out to Buraimi Oasis. For a bit of sightseeing it was too good an opportunity to miss. The fort at Buraimi was like something out of Beau Geste, the airfield was just an area of desert which had been cleared of the bigger stones. The total Air Traffic facilities consisted of a wind-sock. This had been made by lashing an old palm tree upright against a derelict bulldozer and attaching the actual wind-sock to the top of it. The curry lunch we enjoyed in the Omani Scouts' mess was excellent.

For the last couple of trips we had been worried that there was still something wrong with one of the ignition systems of the Beaver and this was producing an increasingly loud background crackle on the radio. Clearly it would need careful checking before we set off again on the trip round that long, deserted coast back to Aden. On doing the check Corporal Drake made a truly interesting discovery.

Some months previously this particular aeroplane had been on the ground somewhere up country and a local tribesman had taken a few casual pot shots at it with his rifle. To the army this was nothing unusual, they were quite used to occasional rifle fire from nearby hills which they knew that the tribesmen regarded as just a bit of sport and was certainly nothing personal. One round had glanced off the engine block and only left a small, quite insignificant scar about an inch long. However, on checking more carefully Corporal Drake had found that the round had in fact also gouged a deep groove out of the rear, hidden side of the high tension cable of one of the ignition harnesses. The metal mesh cover and the rubber sleeve behind it had been stripped away over about four inches and the insulation had gradually completely broken down. As bad luck would have it, it was the rear cable which, because it encircled the engine, could only be replaced by first removing the engine itself. The next difficulty was that Sharjah, not accustomed to servicing the Beaver, had no suitable means of lifting the engine and something would have to be cobbled together using some palm tree trunks and baulks of timber. I would happily have stayed around to see the fun but Boscombe Down was agitating for me to come home as soon as possible and so I had to dessert the Beaver and cadge a lift back to Aden in a passing Beverley.

Back in Aden I asked the army if I could do one last sightseeing trip in a Beaver up into the Protectorate to see the famous Dhala Road. Some twenty miles inland from Aden is an escarpment about 5,000 ft high and up this the Royal Engineers had built a road for the use of the units up on the border. We flew up and over it and it was a truly remarkable piece of engineering. From the air it looked initially like a tiny footpath winding backwards and forwards as it climbed steadily up the cliffs in a succession of hairpin bends, until one realised that the little beetles climbing it were actually army 3-ton trucks. Only then did the scale of the mountains and of the road become apparent.

When we got back to Boscombe John Smith entered into a discussion with the makers. The conclusion was that we were able to reassure the Omanis that although their Beavers were exceeding the nominal engine temperature limits, these had been set very conservatively and in fact there was no problem.

I got back to Boscombe Down to find waiting for me a letter from the Air Secretary. The Air Sec is the Air Marshal who deals with officers' careers and the letter stated that a squadron leader with about my seniority was needed for a certain post which would probably be of three years' duration and the details of which would be explained at the Ministry of Defence at interview. Would I please present myself at Adastral House on a certain date. It all sounded most mysterious. I tried to find out if anyone else I knew had received a similar letter. It turned out that Jimmy Aitken at Farnborough had. Ever since we had left ETPS Jimmy and I had been in the habit of meeting periodically at the Wheatsheaf pub on the A30 west of Basingstoke, which

happened to be about half way between Farnborough and Boscombe, for a meal and a pint. We quickly arranged another meeting and put our heads together to try to work what, in career terms, we had in common.

The most obvious items were that we were both RAF test pilots and both single. Obviously the job in question was concerned with test flying—and possibly assessed as high risk? Could it be something to do with the American space programme? Until the date of the interviews our imaginations ran riot as more and more exotic possibilities occurred to us. In fact our speculations showed clearly the danger that Sherlock Holmes always talked about, that of constructing hypotheses from insufficient data. The fact that we were both TPs was purely coincidental and arose merely from the fact that the people we each knew well were of course likely to be just that. Quite a number of other squadron leaders had been invited to MOD too and the job on offer, while nothing to do with test flying, was in its way just as exciting. The job on offer was to do three years as an equerry to the Queen.

The job of equerry is shared around the three services and it was the turn of the RAF to provide the next one, which would entail taking up the appointment in the spring of 1963. Having interviewed us the Air Sec announced that those who made it to the short list would be told in due course. A fortnight later I had a letter from Adastral House which started, "I am sure that you have been anxiously awaiting the outcome of your recent interview with the Air Secretary in connection with the appointment of Equerry to H.M. The Queen, and I can now tell you that you are one of the three officers whose names have been accepted for consideration by the Lord Chamberlain."

In his office in St James's Palace Lord Cobbold, the Lord Chamberlain, was quietly charming and explained that the job of an equerry was much like that of an ADC—but rather more so! I waited on tenterhooks for another couple of weeks and then heard that the job had gone to Mike Walmsley, my old friend from Cranwell—whose dad had given us our wings. I had, as Lord Cobbold put it, been pipped at the post. In his letter telling me this, to sugar the pill, he added, "if it is any satisfaction to you it must be that you are considered as one of the three best Officers of your rank in the Royal Air Force ..." For the next couple of years we got some fun during weekends in London by suggesting to friends whenever we were arranging a party that they ring Mike up, without telling them where he was. We would casually pass them the phone number and then watch their consternation when a very posh voice answered with "Buckingham Palace."

During the summer of '62 I came across a pastime that has remained a source of much enjoyment ever since. Someone said to me, "Haven't you done a bit of sailing? A friend of mine is looking for an extra member of crew this weekend." I rang up the number he gave me and so duly met David Kyle, owner of the 9-ton yacht "Swan Lake" and a most experienced and knowledgeable sailor. I discovered that owners of such yachts are often looking for crew members. Even those with teenage sons often find that having taught them all the skills of the game, they then don't want to sail with Dad and would rather take their friends out themselves. This occasion was the Cowes—Dinard Race. I drove down to Poole and located David and Swan Lake. The two other members of the crew arrived and we enjoyed a leisurely sail from Poole while I learned my way around the boat, and what jobs the crew were expected to do. We crossed Bournemouth Bay, passed the Needles, sailed through Hurst Narrows into the Solent and so to Cowes where the skipper stood us a splendid dinner and we spent the night.

It was a clear, bright day next morning and already a brisk south-west wind was blowing. We set off down Spithead to the east from Cowes, reached out to the Nab Tower and then turned south-west, heading straight into the wind and waves and settled down to a long tiring "beat," against a wind now not far short of gale force. The sun set, the wind hardly dropped all night and bracing oneself against the constant pitching motion of the boat, even while trying to get some sleep, was incredibly tiring. In the grey dawn the day ahead hardly seemed as if it were going to be much fun. I am ashamed to say that we, the crew, on the excuse that we were cold, tired, battered and not really enjoying it, voted that instead of slogging on dead to windward for many more hours we ought to pack it in and retire from the race. The skipper, with a certain amount of muttering, accepted the majority vote, we eased sheets, turned away from the wind and set course toward Poole, our home port. A couple of hours later the wind eased, the sun came out and the warmth returned. David vowed never to let us forget it! Although I met other skippers and enjoyed many more weekends on Swan Lake and other boats, for many years people around Dorset would say, "Oh, we've heard of you. Weren't you one of David Kyle's mutineers!"

Among the many sailing friends I made around South Dorset the most memorable were Sir Freddie and Lady Coates. They always raced in a state of hilarious enjoyment and the whole crew always argued vigorously over every course change or other tactical decision. Sir Freddie would forgive me if I say that he sometimes reminded me of the story of the man who was asked by his club if we would mind helping to manage a race by sailing on the Committee Boat. He muttered, "I always sail on a committee boat!" The Coates' boat was called Varthan. They explained that this was a Swedish word which means hence or hither "because we never know whether we are coming or going." I crewed for them or for David Kyle for many years and met a wide circle of interesting south Dorset folk as a result. We used to say that whatever the time of year if you went down to Dorset for a weekend you were well advised always to take sailing oilskins, gardening kit and dinner jackets as you never knew which aspects of the social scene would be on the programme.

A controversy appeared on the letters-to-the-editor page of one of the sailing magazines. It was about how a sail produces the force which drives the boat along when it is sailing against the wind. All the standard but incorrect explanations appeared, including the one about how the soldiers on the outside of the turn have to march faster to keep up— true but irrelevant! The sail of a boat is in many ways scientifically similar to the wing of an aeroplane, which we had learned all about at

201

Cranwell and then again in much more detail as putative test pilots at ETPS. So when a letter appeared with a comprehensive diagram to illustrate it, and with a detailed but still wrong explanation, I felt I had to join in. I wrote to the editor explaining as simply as I could the actual aerodynamics of the situation and for simplicity I reproduced the previous letter's diagram. I explained the science of the situation, referring to the diagram and how the various forces acted "to the left," "upwards" and so on. The following month my letter and the diagram were duly printed. Unfortunately this time the printers had for some unknown reason rotated the diagram through 90° which if course meant that my carefully worded explanation was now complete gibberish. Various Dorset friends said subsequently that they had not surprisingly found my letter "rather difficult to follow."

My Triumph TR3 was of course always a joy to drive and one hot summer weekend I was on my way to some sailing event in Dorset and threading my way through heavy, crawling traffic on the edge of Southampton. When finally we came to a stretch of dual carriageway I thankfully got going and, rather ignoring the speed limit, was at last able to overtake a long queue of dawdling holiday motorists. Just as I happily overtook the leading car I was myself overtaken by a very smart black motorcycle whose rider waved me to stop. The traffic cop parked his bike, propped it up, slowly and deliberately removed his gloves and goggles and walked back to me, getting out his notebook. I patiently sat and waited for him, trying to look suitably chastened. His opening remark was, "Well, sir, for an Advanced Motorist you make remarkably poor use of your rear view mirror!" What a nice man. We both started to laugh. He delivered a long and perfectly justified lecture on how we all knew how irritating holiday motorists were, but how important it was to be patient and to obey the speed limits even if they did seem very conservative for such a nice stretch of road etc etc. All the holiday motorists whom I had just overtaken drove smugly past and only when I was once more right at the back of the queue did he conclude and suggest that in future I should check more carefully to see if I was being followed. He put his notebook away, we wished each other good morning and he departed grinning. I have often reflected how far more effective his "bollocking" was than a long, tedious court case would have been.

Christmas '62 saw the start of the great freeze in southern England. In the week after Christmas heavy snowfalls blanketed southern

England and for a couple of days Boscombe Down airfield and the town of Amesbury were completely isolated. All the roads into the area were blocked with drifts up to the tops of hedges. Every airfield has a "snow plan" which revolves round the top priority of keeping the runway clear. The theory is that by mobilising everyone available as a labour force it will usually be possible to remove the snow off the runway as fast as it falls without ever letting it build up and this will be a much easier job than leaving it to settle and harden. However, not long previously there had been the Munich air disaster which killed so many of the Manchester United players. This was thought to have been caused by slush on the Munich runway and some of the scientists at Boscombe were anxious to do trials under controlled conditions. They persuaded the station to leave the snow on the runway until it melted into slush. There was only one snag—the snow didn't melt. A massive anti-cyclone established itself, the weather got steadily colder and the snow on the runway froze into solid ice. We didn't fly for six weeks. However we did get some excellent skiing. Every morning we would check in at the squadron and say to the boss, "You know where to find us, if you want us you can send a chopper!" Laverstock Down outside Salisbury became so well frequented that the snow got properly beaten down into a very respectable piste. Eventually the snow melted and we started flying again.

Boscombe Down's D Squadron operated the choppers and I arranged a number of dual rides over there in their Whirlwinds and Skeeters. We would go over to Old Sarum airfield which was quiet and I would have a go at hovering and spot turns. If there is any wind these are not as easy as they look. To stay in one spot over the ground the helicopter, as it faces into the wind, has first to fly gently forward. As it turns it has to be flown to one side then, as it faces downwind, backwards and then to the other side at the same time maintaining a constant height. For beginners a few minutes' practise had your brain reeling and greatly increased your admiration for the search and rescue boys who in a gale can hover over sinking ships or within a few feet of cliff faces.

While Boscombe Down and the A&AEE were ostensibly concerned solely with the technicalities of aeroplanes and their weapons and navigation systems, we were never able to ignore human factors—nor human failings. The two are closely related and all we could do was to try to ensure that aeroplanes and their controls were designed to reduce as far as possible the probability of aircrews and others making silly mistakes. We didn't always succeed.

One day Johnnie Mayes got airborne in a Gnat. On returning to the circuit he encountered some problem in trying to lower his wheels. He therefore called the tower and said that he wanted to do a slow fly past so that they could visually check if the wheels appeared to be locked down. He flew past the tower and they said, "Your left wheel appears to be jammed half retracted and is certainly not properly down." John knew that a one-wheel landing should not present too much of a problem but that as his speed dropped off he was liable to swing towards the side with the collapsed wheel. If he swung off the runway to the left he would be going towards a line of parked aircraft, while to the right there was just the open grass of the airfield. The wind was very light so to be on the safe side he elected to land downwind. He landed carefully, held the wings level as long as he could and was greatly surprised when the right wing dropped and he swung off the runway—to the right. In fact he stopped without any problem but when he indignantly tackled Air Traffic Control they said, "Oh gosh, it was the left wheel from where we were looking, so of course from where you were sitting .... Sorry!" Is it any wonder that we often referred to them as Air Traffic Confusers?

The main runway at Boscombe was intersected by a road going over to the control tower, which naturally, was controlled by traffic lights. However on one occasion a Landrover somehow failed to stop and drove straight across the runway only a dozen yards in front of a Naval Buccaneer which was taking off. The Lieutenant Commander flying it saw the Landrover flash under his nose just as he lifted off. He expressed his views to the Tower in suitable naval language and the controller, who happened to be female, responded with, "Aircraft calling Boscombe Down, do you spell that with a capital or two small ffs?"

Having done both my front line tours on single seat fighters, Boscombe Down was my only experience of flying at all regularly with a navigator. I was airborne in a Javelin with Jock McCabe and when we had finished the exercise and wanted to come home I asked Jock for a course to steer. I was very impressed when he responded instantly with, "OK, Steer 113°" when I would really have been satisfied initially with something like "East with a touch of south." A few minutes later he said, "Could you make that 085°"—a heading change of some 30 degrees. When I challenged him about this he explained, "If I had initially said, Oh, about east, I bet you would have started arguing, and wanting something more precise. With all you pilots I find it much better to give you something precise to steer, to keep you occupied, while I sort out the actual heading we need!" Maybe navigators were less stupid that we pretended and we shouldn't really call them the talking ballast.

In spite of this an excellent anti-navigator story was of the famous old single-seater fighter squadron which had recently re-equipped with two-seater aeroplanes and had been joined by navigators. They had just about adjusted to this but were dismayed one day, quite unfairly, to hear that their new boss was to be a navigator. A couple of months after he had assumed command he was sitting in the crew-room one morning with some of the pilots when a very young junior pilot bounced into the room and said, "Hey, chaps, I've just heard a super joke about navigators." The Squadron Commander looked up from his magazine, "Watch it, Pete, don't forget I'm a navigator." "Don't worry, boss, I'll tell it very slowly."

The magazine "Air Clues" used to run a regular column called "I learned about flying from that!" Anyone was invited to write in to the editor recounting some incident that they had experienced and which pointed up a moral about flying for the education, and usually the amusement, of readers. The incidents were invariably the results of our own stupidity, rashness, carelessness, haste, over-confidence, timidity or whatever. One cold spring afternoon I could easily have qualified to get into print in Air Clues … .

The Senior Pilot came into the crew-room and said, "Dave Samuels has had to take an aeroplane up to Coltishall and doesn't want to stay the night. I've booked a Meteor, anyone like to go up and bring him back?" There was usually a selection of aeroplanes in Handling Squadron, from all parts of the RAF including from overseas, for example from Germany, Cyprus, Singapore and elsewhere, with special modifications on them, that the Handlers were working with as they wrote the Pilots' Notes.

I went down to their hanger and signed out the Meteor, which happened to be a very swish Mark 14 Night Fighter. However, I had more hours on Meteors than most folk have had hot dinners so there was no problem on that score. It was, as I have said, a cold, clear afternoon and having started up I pushed forward a couple of levers on the right-hand cockpit wall. On all the Meteors I had flown that was where the pressurisation and cockpit heating controls were located. I could do with some nice heating this afternoon and as I taxied, took off and turned on course for Coltishall there was a satisfying hissing coming from the pressurisation. I climbed to about 30,000ft and was already very unimpressed by the efficiency of the cockpit heating. I got steadily colder and before I started letting down I was perished and banging my hands together to warm them. The cockpit canopy was by this time completely frosted over and the visibility was so bad that I called Coltishall for a Ground Controlled Approach. I finished the approach scraping ice off the windscreen in order to be able to see the runway at all. While taxi-ing in I raised the flaps and started switching things off, including the pressurisation. Once I had moved the lever next to it I could see what it was. It was labelled Refrigeration. This particular Meteor had been modified to operate in the tropics. Dave Samuels came across the tarmac to meet me. "Hullo," he said, greeting a wrinkled, blue, shivering figure, "What on earth's happened to you?"

As the Lightning entered service, improvements were made to the basic layout and modifications continued to appear. At last we got pale grey cockpit interiors instead of black. A steerable nose-wheel was produced and I flew a trip in the aeroplane to which it was fitted. It was very nice, especially for crosswind landings, when the large Lightning fin produced a strong weather-cocking tendency, but it was not considered worth the extra expense. For long range deployments in-flight re-fuelling was going to be needed and a number of us flew some trips to have a go at using the probe and learning the technique of creeping steadily up behind the drogue streaming from a Victor tanker and making contact to allow the fuel to flow down the pipe. At height it was not at all easy but would have no doubt become less difficult with practice.

One day Ronnie Lees and I were getting ready to fly a couple of Lightnings in order to check out some detail of the airborne radar. I was to fly target and he was going to manipulate the set in his aeroplane. We were about to walk out to the aircraft when we had a phone call from some other department saying they needed a photograph of a

Lightning in the air. Would one of us please fly a low pass down the runway after take-off and before we cleared the circuit. They would have a photographer beside the runway all ready. We agreed that Ronnie would start up and take off first and that I would line up ready for take-off and follow him as he came past on his low pass. I started up, taxied out to the threshold, and waited for him.

I turned my head round as far as I could to peer over my shoulder and to see him pass so as to be ready to release my brakes. He came past rather lower than I had anticipated. All I saw was a fleeting glimpse of just the top of his fin. It almost looked as if he was lower than I was! I went to call, "Get up, man!" but then I thought, if I make him jump he will probably hit the ground anyway. In fact he climbed away and I thankfully followed. The photograph is spectacular. Ronnie had perhaps forgotten that although his end of the aeroplane, the front, was almost at a reasonable height, at his low speed and high angle of attack the back was—well the photo says it all. He was actually quite shaken himself when he saw it.

The primary armament of the Lightning was a pair of heat-seeking missiles. The transparent head on the original version was shaped like a tall, narrow pyramid or a sharpened pencil. This was fine aero-dynamically, but not too efficient for the heat-seeking eye. A later version had a visually much improved hemi-spherical head, but this was hardly a good shape aerodynamically, especially for super-sonic flight, and the later Lightning which carried it had a greatly enlarged fin to help restore some directional stability.

The first two-seat Lightning was the Mk 4. The pilots were seated side by side and each had conventional throttle controls for his left hand, needing a centre throttle pedestal and resulting in a very cramped arrangement. For the later two-seater, the Mk 5, the centre pedestal was omitted and the second set of throttles was moved to the right-hand cockpit wall. Thus the second pilot had to fly with his left hand and work the throttles with his right. It was far less troublesome than some of us had anticipated.

Flying the Lightning was in many ways the high spot of my flying but it was not really the most memorable. Compared with the Javelin, the Gnat or even the Hunter its sheer performance was breathtaking, but I got no experience of flying it tactically or, for example, in formation. We never got airborne in a section of four or had an opportunity to engage in tail-chasing. It is when you can see the other aeroplanes in the formation in the sky with you that the visual images are most impressive, and most memorable. Many pilots say that you develop a special regard for the first type on which you fly a large number of hours. For me nothing ever really compared with the Meteor. Even by the standards of the early 60s it was slow and by then completely overshadowed by all the later swept-wing types that I had been lucky enough to fly. However, one day back at Gütersloh Al Pollock had dropped in with a Meteor and I had grabbed a quick ride in it. The weather was pretty thick and I had recovered by calling for a GCA. As I came down the glide-path, in thick cloud, in a bit of turbulence and on instruments, it suddenly struck me that, although I had nothing against the Hunters which I flew every day, I was more comfortable, relaxed and at home in this old Meteor that I hadn't flown for at least three years. However, having been among the first dozen or so pilots in the RAF to fly the Lightning, the English Electric Company presented each of us on A Squadron with a very attractive, chromium-plated model. It is a proud possession and sits beside me now as I write.

My three years at Boscombe Down were coming to an end. During 1963 I had managed to pass the "Q," the qualifying exam for Staff College, so it was no surprise to find that I had been selected to attend the 1964 course at Bracknell. George Cannon had also passed the "Q" and we decided we ought to make some preparations for Staff College. We started to attend weekly typing classes in Salisbury. These were amusing but also an embarrassing failure. All the other students were 16–19 year old girls whose fingers, and brains, were apparently infinitely more nimble than ours. George and I sat at the back of the room and tried to keep up with the metronome and to get our fingers to remember a-s-d-f-j-k-l-. The teacher would call a halt and enquire encouragingly, "And how are Mr Cannon and Mr Boult getting on?"— to the suppressed giggles from the rest of the room.

More usefully I went to Tern Hill for the four week JC&SS, the Junior Command and Staff School course. This was surprisingly enjoyable, largely due, as so often, to the personality of the Station Commander, Group Captain Paxton. His demonstration to the whole course of the correct way to tie a Windsor knot using a length of sacking and a larger red fire extinguisher has become a legend. The staff at Tern Hill knew full well that none of their subjects, for example

Conventions of Service Writing, or Procedures for Orderly Rooms (How to deal with an airman on a disciplinary charge), were remotely exciting intrinsically but somehow managed to make them at least tolerably interesting and often highly entertaining.

One extremely well-taught skill that we learned there and which has been immensely useful to me ever since was public speaking. They were not aiming to turn us into orators, but simply to be able to address an audience on some routine subject without making a great ordeal of it. As the first step we were asked in turn to recount some slight anecdote or story to about five fellow students with all of us sitting around a table. As a second step the speaker would be asked to stand up to do so. This created a quite different atmosphere but one that could be coped with even by the most nervous and self-conscious. By the end of the course we were standing up on the lecture hall stage and addressing the whole course of thirty-odd and even the occasional heckler and, so long as you knew your subject moderately well, not turning a hair. Having seen over the years so many even very senior people who are quite hopelessly bad at speaking in public, it amazes me that they have been perhaps too arrogant ever to have taken the simple steps to learn the drills and to acquire some experience in it.

Another exercise, on stage, was in hearing a disciplinary charge. The student acting as the Section Commander, feeling himself sinking out of his depth and clutching at a straw, announced thankfully, "This is too serious a matter for me to deal with and so I am remanding it to the Station Commander." He slumped gratefully back in his chair. From behind the curtains descended a long pole bearing—a Group Captain's hat—indicating quite clearly, "The ball is still in your court!" The poor student, who couldn't yet see it, could not imagine what the audience was finding so hilarious.

One Friday evening as I drove back to Boscombe Down for the weekend I stopped off at the Seven Stars at Bottlesford. It was there that I heard the news of the assassination of President Kennedy.

I had started my flying career as a student with the rest of 57 Entry on the Prentice at Cranwell in 1951 and for the twelve years since then flying had become simply the job we did. I do not believe we had ever paused to realise how very privileged we were. For a start we were lucky to have been blessed with the necessary general physical fitness and in particular the required standard of eyesight. Over the years I have met many others who had intended to follow a flying career but had been prevented from doing so for a host of apparently minor reasons. Although I happened not to do so, many of my friends had initially suffered from occasional airsickness but most had grown out of it during our first few weeks of training. One cadet, on an Entry just after ours, had never got over it and as a result had eventually been withdrawn from training. For him in particular it was especially disappointing, his father was a senior RAF officer and the son had no doubt been looking forward for many years to following his father. Maybe his very keenness and anxiety to do well had had something to do with his sickness. It was very bad luck.

During these years almost all our professional dealings had been with other aircrew or with those closely related with flying—with our own ground crews, service and civilian, with other aircraft engineers, Air Traffic Controllers, Parachute Packers, Flight Safety people and the like. Their professional concerns and backgrounds were, like ours, therefore entirely practical. Clarity of expression, the facing of facts, total honesty, a complete absence of beating about the bush, were all paramount. The servicing and operating of aeroplanes and their equipment, of radars, guns, parachutes and so on, and also the drills and procedures for their use, could often have lives depending on them. It never entered our heads, any of us, to wrap up uncomfortable facts with diplomatic or reassuring half-truths or tactful white lies.

I once heard a friend of mine, another pilot, being taken to task for his rather brutal description of an incident and of the failings of some of those involved. His response was equally unequivocal. "Look," he said, "Where I come from feelings are less important than funerals." While I believe this was entirely right while we were working with aeroplanes it meant that many of us had to make some radical re-adjustments at least to our phraseology once we had moved on to other parts of the service. Years later after I had joined the staff of the Officer Cadet Training Unit, one of my Flight Commanders, and a very valued colleague, said to me on more than one occasion, "You know, boss, you really can't talk to some people like that. They're not ex-aircrew and they're just not used to it!" He was absolutely right but the re-adjustment was not easy and not always successfully made.

In my flying career luck had played a part many times, quite apart from the occasion when I had just missed those pine trees. I had left school diffident and lacking in self-confidence and had not found it easy to work with all my flying instructors. I owed a lot in particular to Jack Sherburn and to my first 63 Squadron Flight Commander, Joe Blyth. I had, I suspect, come near to being withdrawn from training, at least for jet fighters, due to my initial difficulties with instrument flying. I was lucky to get back on to the Hunter after my brief ground tour and also to get to ETPS when an off day for the exam and interview could so easily have scuppered my chances. I had worked at it a bit but I had been lucky in managing to fly a fair number of types and even though I never flew as first pilot anything bigger than the Canberra it was mainly the smaller types which were the "sharp, pointed" and exciting ones. The Spitfire trip is of course the one that generates the greatest fury and jealousy among my contemporaries.

I missed out on one or two other types. During my first tour at Waterbeach the station maintained one of the last remaining Hurricanes but as a junior pilot I never had a chance of being entrusted with it. During my Instrument Training Course at the Central Fighter Establishment at West Raynham I angled for but missed out on flying their Seahawk, a straight wing fore-runner of the Hunter and Dominie, a delightful hangover from the nineteen thirties, a graceful, twin engine biplane. I only missed out on the latter because someone else made a heavy landing and damaged the tail wheel. When I left Boscombe Down I did not realise that I would not get another flying tour nor that my future flying would consist of the occasional cadged trip in other people's aeroplanes. Some years later when Mike Shaw was flying Harriers with No 1 Squadron at Wittering I paid him a visit and was sitting all kitted up, ready to walk out for a ride in a Harrier. Someone else turned up who had a legitimate reason to take the trip and it was a matter of, "Awfully sorry, old boy. Do come back tomorrow." Tomorrow never came.

Before I left Boscombe I managed to get second pilot rides in the Shackleton, Beverley, Victor and Comet and with Jimmy Aitken at Farnborough in the Avro 707c experimental delta. For the last few months I flew almost exclusively in various marks of Lightning but my very last trip at Boscombe Down, and at what was in effect the end of my flying career was, inevitably, in a Meteor.

# The Staff College

## R A F Bracknell

IN FEBRUARY 1964 I arrived at the RAF Staff College. The college was housed in an attractive estate on the edge of Bracknell new town, the latter currently being transformed from a pleasant if undistinguished old Berkshire town into a collection of by-passes, yellow sodium street lights, shopping malls, high-rise office blocks and hi-tech laboratories. The main college building was 1930s-style cream coloured stucco but the inside was pleasant and quietly elegant. It was surrounded by an area of mature trees and open grass, ideal for those who wanted to practise their golf shots.

The course lasted virtually a year and consisted of a number of elements. Firstly there was the academic study of the techniques that were going to be required of a good staff officer. Secondly, to broaden our understanding of the world in which Air Forces have to operate, there was a brief introduction to the strategic aspects of air operations and of related economic and political questions. Thirdly there was the opportunity to expand one's circle of acquaintances to officers from other parts of the RAF and of the other services, colleagues with whom, as fellow potential high fliers, one was often going to work in the future. The course was considered to have a make or break effect on your future career. There were a few students from the army and the

212

RAF College, Cranwell. (*RB*)

The Junior Entry waiting to fly in an
Anson:-
John Harper, RB, Kiwi Powell,
Benjy Hives, George Coatsworth,
John Dunn. (*RB*)

Flight Cadet. (*RB*)

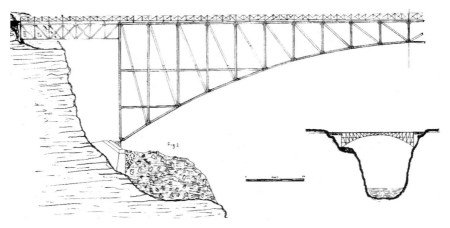

Zambesi Bridge at Victoria Falls
from 1952 Cranwell thesis on long span bridges. (*RB*)

Short Sunderland Flying Boat at RAF Pembroke Dock *c.* 1952.
(© *Crown Copyright/MOD*)

Meteors of No 63 Squadron. (*Russell Adams*)

Meteors of No 63 Squadron on stand-by. n.b. The leading aircraft of the pair joining the circuit has the enlarged air intakes (*Russell Adams*)

de Havilland Vampire T11 trainer. (© *Crown Copyright/MOD*)

The first Supermarine Swift arrives at Waterbeach. (*RB*)

O.C. 'A' Flight No 63 Squadron
Flt. Lt. Joe Blyth (*RB*)

Tiger Moth. (*RB*)

My boss – Air Vice Marshal McKee. (© *Crown Copyright/MOD*)

Air Marshal Sir Andrew McKee. (© *Crown Copyright/MOD*)

Ian Brotherton, honarary uncle to
the Carter children. (*RB*)

Bolton Paul Balliol advanced trainer. (*assumed BAE SYSTEMS*)

Supermarine Spitfire. (© *Crown Copyright/MOD*)

Pat Rooney's view of the Saucy Sally IV
with Graham Tunley, Ian Brotherton, Sid Wilkinson & R.B.

Having reached the sea, we were greeted by the
Mayor of Christchurch. (*unknown tba*)

Some members of No 63 Squadron;-
Alan Cawsey, Derek Hine, Tony Hopkins, Mike Williams. Mick Davis, Pete Jarvis,
Sparrow Smith. (*RB*)

de Havilland Venom night fighter. (© *Crown Copyright/MOD*)

Four Hunters in formation. (*unknown tba*)

No 26 Squadron (Sqn Ldr D L Edmonds RAF Gutersloh 1959) (© *Crown Copyright/MOD*)

OC A Flight, No 26 Squadron. (© *Crown Copyright/MOD*)

Hawker Hunter Mk 6. (*unknown tba*)

Supermarine Swift Mk 5. (© *Crown Copyright/MOD*)

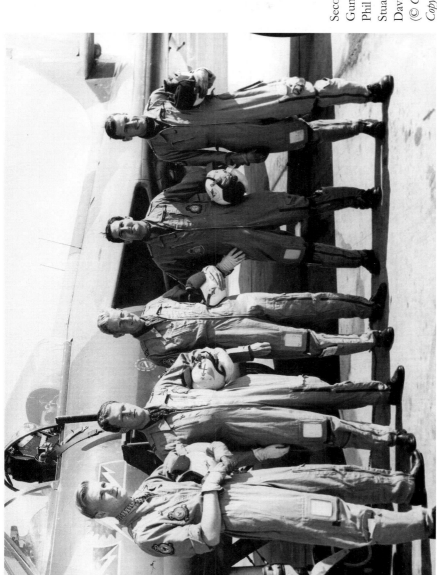

Second TAF Gunnery Team
Phil Alston, Ron Stuart-Paul, RB, Mick Davis, Jock McVie.
(© Crown Copyright/MOD)

Setting off with Al to the Matterhorn. (*RB*)

The Matterhorn from the North East showing the Hornli Ridge. (*RB*)

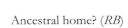

Ancestral home? (*RB*)

Best man at Trish and Alan Pollock's wedding. (*RB*)

Planning meeeting for RAF Ski Championships
Tony Chambers, RB, Bill Duncan (obscured), Make Shaw, Clive Rustin with backs
to camera, Paddy Hughes, Dave Conran Smith. (*RB*)

The first ski-lift on Cairngorm. (*RB*)

Percival Jet Provost (*tba*)

English Electric Lightning Mk 5. (*assumed BAE SYSTEMS*)

de Havilland Beaver. (© *Crown Copyright/MOD*)

Hot weather trials of
the Beaver in the Aden
Protectorate. (*RB*)

Air traffic control facilities – Buraimi
Oasis. (*RB*)

In the Aden
Protectorate.
(*RB*)

Flypast by Ronnie
Lees in a Mk 4
Lightning.
(*unknown tba*)

International Air
Cadet Exchange,
off to Canada.
(*RB*)

Forth Road
Bridge under
construction.
(*RB*)

RAF Gan –
Indian Ocean
staging post.
(*RB*)

North West
beach,
looking
towards
Fedu. (*RB*)

Bugallo –
Maldivian
inter atoll
trading vessel.
(*RB*)

Tree planting on Equator Way while the VC 10 climbs, en route for Singapore, over the resident search and rescue Shackleton. (© *Crown Copyright/MOD*)

RAF Gan Airmen's Christmas dinner, RB leads three cheers for the cooks. (*RB*)

Gan welcomes HRH Prince Charles, Harold Wilson and Ted Heath, enroute to the funeral of the Australian Prime Minister. (© *Crown Copyright/MOD*)

Celebrations for 150th anniversary of the foundation of Singapore (*RB*)

Wessex Helecopter at Green Squadron camp. (*RB*)

Gp Capt Tony Ringer, Reviewing officer, Wing Cdr David Leith, RB. (© *Crown Copyright/MOD*)

Air Vice Marshal Griffiths with Cadet Al Thani of the Qatari Air Force.
(© *Crown Copyright/MOD*)

RAF OCTU Graduation Parade Green Squadron marches past.
(© *Crown Copyright/MOD*)

OCTU No 272 course, Green Squadron, July 1973. (*Studio Five, Thetford, Norfolk*)

Navy and a number of Americans. Quite soon the star students started to emerge and one could see straightaway those who were on their way to the top.

The normal routine was to start the day with a lecture, initially by a member of the Directing Staff and later by some visiting speaker; an air marshal, an admiral, a general, a captain of industry, a politician, a foreign diplomat. Air Vice-Marshal David Lee, the Commandant, would introduce the speaker and at the end of their presentation they would take questions. Often their unrehearsed and spontaneous answers to questions was the most interesting part. At the time there was much discussion going on within the RAF about the large disparity between the salaries of RAF Transport Command pilots flying the VC10 and those of the civilian airline pilots flying the same aircraft. Air Marshal "Bing" Cross, the C-in-C, Transport Command was asked at the end of his lecture if he would comment on the many rumours of very low morale in his Command. He dismissed them airily as not true. The questioner then asked a supplementary. He said, "I have here, sir, the official number of requests for early retirement this year by pilots in your Command. How do you deal with these?" Without batting an eyelid the Air Marshal replied, "We don't accept them." Indicating that as far as he was concerned the problem was solved!

Some speakers were clearly adept at fielding questions and could be amusing and entertaining as well as giving a penetrating analysis of their subject. Dennis Healey was one such. Tony Skingsley asked some very apt and penetrating question and Mr Healey paused before replying, in his well-known tones, "Commandant, before I answer that most interesting question, may I suggest that the student who asked it should be awarded an immediate pass for your course!" Not surprisingly Tony Skingsley retired in due course as an Air Marshal.

Some speakers faced initially a clearly hostile audience. It was a time in Britain of widespread industrial strife and the General Secretary of the TUC could hardly have expected a very sympathetic response from a military Staff College even for an evening lecture when we students had just enjoyed a good dinner. But by the end of the evening Vic Feather had us eating out of his hand. It was an object lesson on how to put across a topic in the best possible light, to face difficult facts, to express possibly unpopular views but to demonstrate sincerity and to create friends at the same time.

One speaker had to be, not exactly rescued, more put into context by the Commandant. He was a diplomat from a certain Middle Eastern country and he delivered what sounded to us an unrealistic, biased, emotional, angry diatribe. After a few perfunctory questions had tailed off into embarrassed silence the Commandant rose to his feet to end the evening and to thank the speaker. We all wondered how he would restore at least a semblance of good relations. He said, "I really do want to thank Mr —— for giving us once again, as he always does, such a vigorous, colourful, thought-provoking, challenging evening. It is all too easy for us sitting comfortably in England to overlook …" It was masterly, the tension and the embarrassment were suddenly gone. We began to understand why people like Air Marshal Lee became Staff College Commandants.

If the questions and answers session ran on, and with many of the best speakers it did, the Commandant could bring it to an end by switching on a red light over the proscenium arch visible to the students but not visible to the speaker at the lectern. Occasionally a speaker who knew the drill, finding that the questions had suddenly dried up, would say with a grin, "Oh, so the red light is on is it! Well, thank you, gentlemen, for such an interesting morning …"

The academic aspect of the course mainly consisted of a series of exercises each of which started with a relevant lecture to set the scene. After the morning lecture we retired to our syndicate rooms for a session with our Syndicate Tutor who would lead a discussion to develop the topic and to hand out the exercise brief. We then dispersed to our own rooms to work on it, possibly getting together periodically to compare our ideas as we progressed. We concluded, perhaps some days later, by handing in our written solution, for the later exercises quite a thick document with attached maps, appendices and graphs and representing many hours of labour. We waited on tenterhooks until the exercise eventually reappeared in our pigeonholes, now covered in the Directing Staff comments—in red ink. DS comments varied considerably, some seemed petty and hair-splitting, some were fair and balanced and provided new perspectives which you had not considered. From these you learned a lot. Often humour provided a welcome sweetening of the pill. A certain exercise concerned a nuclear war in South East Asia and one of the naval students, getting a bit carried away and possibly losing sight of the full enormity of the exercise situation, submitted a solution which involved an over-enthusiastic use of tactical nuclear weapons to stem the advance of the Chinese communist aggressors. His submission was returned with the DS comment, "Thank you. This is not a bad solution, but I think you may have disturbed the rotational axis of the earth."

Finally there was a wash up in our syndicates where the "pink"—the DS suggested solution—was presented and the threads were drawn together. The pink often generated some lively arguments and disagreement, especially from those students who happened to have some specialist knowledge of the particular aspect of air operations being discussed. We were repeatedly warned against "fighting the pink" with our tutor trying to explain that it was only one possible solution and was not intended to discount other approaches. During the year I worked with three different syndicate tutors. They were not all in the same class.

One of the students in my syndicate was Jeremy Hall. Quiet, humorous, most generous to others less able than himself and far and away the sharpest brain in the group, he was clearly destined for the top. Some years later, having distinguished himself in a couple of staff appointments and already having been promoted to Group Captain, Jeremy was doing the Harrier conversion course before taking up the appointment of Station Commander at Wittering, the Harrier base. He was thus in the position of moving back on to flying fast jets after a number of years "flying a desk." He got into some sort of emergency situation, didn't sort it out, crashed and was killed.

This was not the only instance I heard of someone trying to get back into the swing of fast jet flying after a period on the ground and of coming to grief. During my own tour as an ADC, which in any case only lasted fifteen months, I had managed to scrounge enough flying for it hardly to count as a ground tour, so that in effect my flying career was in one continuous period. Remembering my initial difficulties in learning mentally to keep up with the Meteor I have often wondered how I would have coped with re-starting fast jet flying at a later stage of my career had I been given the opportunity to do so. I suspect that in one's thirties one did not pick up speed as easily as one had in one's early twenties and if this was so quite a generous allocation of hours was going to be needed. Of course there was always the pressure for economy and balancing the two requirements was clearly never going

215

to be easy. But I have become convinced that not enough time or flying hours were given in those days to people coming back into demanding flying appointments to allow them to get their reactions fully up to speed again.

An enjoyable part of the Staff College course during the early summer was a whistle-stop tour round a selection of RAF stations on the continent. At each station everyone kindly tried their best to educate and to entertain us. There was so much to absorb and to try to take an interest in, that we were often in need of a respite and some light relief. John Hewitt could always be relied on to provide it. One day some high-powered Headquarters gave us an overwhelming presentation which filled a morning with tables of figures, visuals, graphs, back projection screens and a team of learned and eloquent speakers. We then broke off for a full sit-down lunch with plenty of wine before hurriedly re-assembling for part two. As we tottered back into the lecture theatre John said, "Well, I've got one question I really want to ask these people." Thank goodness that someone was still alert enough to do so. "Yes," he continued, "It's—where are we?" At a front-line fighter and strike station we were shown their new quick reaction hangar where the pilots' ready room was directly above the aircraft readiness platform. On being scrambled the pilots descended through a hole in the floor by sliding down a fireman's pole. We listened gravely to a mass of technical detail and were asked if we had any questions. "Yes," said John, "Can we have another go on the fireman's pole."

A notice went up inviting applications to attend a Buckingham Palace garden party. Strangely, not many people seemed interested. I grabbed one of the available tickets and spent a most enjoyable afternoon in Buckingham Palace and the gardens. I didn't speak to HM but the tea and sticky cakes were excellent.

The final planning exercise of the year, Exercise Triple Crown, was conducted jointly with the army Staff College at Camberley and the Navy's at Greenwich. Camberley was only a few miles down the road from Bracknell but to work with Greenwich entailed a long coach trip right across London. It had been mooted at various times that the Navy should move across to the west of London too to some site near Camberley and Bracknell. However having seen beautiful, historic Greenwich we could quite understand the Navy's stubborn determination to pull rank or to play the "senior service" card. They said, in effect, "You crabs and pongos do what you like—the Navy stays at Greenwich!"

At the end of the joint phase all three colleges held a formal dinner night together in the famous Greenwich painted hall. We all wore mess kit, ours pale blue, the Navy's dark blue and the army's every colour of the rainbow. Admiral of the Fleet Lord Mountbatten was in the chair and it was a truly memorable evening.

As with all such courses, in the final week of the Staff College year, we students produced a course review. One of our army colleagues had a very 'refeened' manner of speech. In one sketch he was acting the part of interrogating an airman on the use of some heavy lift aeroplanes. He asked the question, "Do you take freight?" and was not expecting the answer, "Yes, but only in a heigh wind!" Throughout the year almost every visiting admiral had broken off his presentation to say, "One thing you airmen should remember, you know, is that four-fifths of the earth's surface is covered with salt water!" In the review the curtains opened for another sketch, this time of a naval scene. On the back wall was a poster stating, "Four-fifths of the earth's surface is covered ..." the rest had been amended to read, "... with radio-active Chinese."

Having before I got to Staff College flown almost continuously for the previous dozen years, in fact since I had left Cranwell with a commission, my year at Bracknell was my first opportunity to stand back and try to form a broader view of the service than that which could be seen from the cockpit of a jet aeroplane. I found myself becoming increasingly disillusioned and exasperated with some senior officers as represented by the Staff College Directing Staff. No doubt it was mutual, but a number of incidents, some more significant than others, led to these misgivings.

The Staff College course was deliberately designed to put students for some of the time under stress by the pressure of the workload. When I later joined the Directing Staff of the Officer Cadet Training Unit I came to appreciate more clearly the need for this, but I still believe that it was done crudely and unhelpfully at Bracknell. This was mainly in the case of the written exercises. It was constantly pointed out to us that once we were on the staff of a senior officer, which was what the course was meant to be preparing us for, our written work must be of the highest standard and error free. Layout, typing accuracy and so on was judged harshly and usually attracted much Directing Staff red ink. During my last few months at Boscombe Down I had taken steps to learn to type, but this was before the days of word processors and typing errors still had to be painstakingly corrected with Tipp-ex.

Some of the married students had wives who were expert typists, so that these students could if they wished dictate their work into a tape-recorder and depart for the golf course while their wife produced an immaculately typed exercise with the minimum of effort. Many of us, not so blessed, found that we had to divide the time allotted to an exercise in half. The actual study and writing of the solution, the experience which we were presumably at Staff College for, had to be confined to just half the allotted time and the rest devoted to nothing more constructive than typing it out. We knew perfectly well that in any real staff job we would have the help of professional typists, just as I had already found at both Upavon and Boscombe Down and that our ability as typists would hardly have a make or break influence on our efficiency as staff officers.

During one such written exercise the wife of another student—the student was a particular friend of mine—was about to produce their first-born. There were various difficulties and so it was naturally a very worrying time for John and his wife with late nights, visits to the local hospital and so on. John told me that in the circumstances he had been to see our syndicate tutor to ask for a couple of days extra grace to complete the exercise before handing it in. The request was dismissed out of hand with a short lecture about dedication to one's profession. Was there, we wondered, no difference between the dedication which would rightly be demanded in a real operational situation and the training course we were currently engaged in?

One other incident, in itself trivial, seemed typical. The Staff College was to hold a cocktail party to entertain various dignitaries from around the local area. At the end of the morning lecture a certain Group Captain climbed on to the lecture hall stage and delivered to us students a five-minute lecture on the correct behaviour at cocktail parties. Most of us would have agreed that of all the DS he was about the least qualified of them to do so. He sounded like a petulant schoolteacher lecturing the fifth form. I happened to be sitting next to a naval Lieutenant Commander and, when the Group Captain had finished, he turned to me and said in amazement, "Good God! Do they often treat you like that?"

What was so striking was the stark contrast in the atmosphere here to that at Tern Hill at the Junior Command and Staff School. There, where they were trying to drum into us important but achingly boring bits of admin procedures, one could have expected unimaginative rigidity. We had found exactly the opposite—a genial, amusing staff and excellent relationships between staff and students. All of this reflected exactly the out-going personality of the Station Commander, Group Captain Panton. We had found too, most notably, a great effort by all concerned to make the work as interesting as possible.

At Bracknell there were many examples of lack of imagination, pettiness, negligible understanding of man-management and an unhelpful rigidity of thought which I came to the conclusion were much too prevalent among the Directing Staff. I tried to ignore it, but in the years ahead it was a view that I came to hold increasingly about a number of aspects of the senior management of the RAF. However, I only fully started to crystallise my views on these subjects some years later in Singapore.

I did not do well at Staff College. I suppose I was not sensible enough to conceal my feelings and it was well-known that Staff College was an assessment as well as a training process. I got a thoroughly bad rating and an undemanding posting that reflected this. I was to go just a few miles up the road to White Waltham, to the Headquarters of the Air Cadets.

# Headquarters, The Air Cadets

## R A F White Waltham

W HITE WALTHAM consisted of a grass airfield and an undistinguished collection of brick or pre-fab buildings to the west of Maidenhead and just north of the M4. It housed a variety of units such as Headquarters, No 25 Group, the flying facilities of the London University Air Squadron and the Headquarters of the Air Cadets. The pre-fab accommodation huts in their rural setting, although a comedown from the relative grandeur of Bracknell and Boscombe Down were surprisingly comfortable. The Air Cadets were split into the Air Training Corps and the Air Sections of the Combined Cadet Force, the CCF, and I was concerned with the latter. We organised summer camps and other visits to RAF stations, arrangements for flying scholarships and for the primary gliders which some of the units operated and supervised the arrangements for the appointment of RAF NCOs to work with each of the units. At the time I became quite interested in these aspects of the RAF which I had never encountered before, but the posting was a backwater. I should have been less frank about my views at Bracknell.

One of my jobs was to coordinate the list of senior officers of all three services who would be invited to carry out the annual inspections of school Combined Cadet Forces. This involved many phone calls to their offices to check when they would be available and then the juggling of their availability with the dates the schools wanted for their inspections. The form was for the admiral, air marshal or whoever to be accompanied by officers of the rank of squadron leader or its equivalent to do the detailed inspection of the CCF unit while the star ranking officer reviewed the parade, took the march past and was entertained by the Head. That year one of the schools to be inspected was Shrewsbury School—my old school. Naturally I put myself down to inspect the Air Section.

The senior officer who had been invited to carry out the inspection was General Sir Michael Carver. I was to get to know General Carver quite well later in Singapore but on this, the first time I met him, I quickly discovered the sort of man he was. As the Shrewsbury School CCF consisted of Army, Naval and Air Sections it was arranged that a major and a lieutenant commander came too. The parade proceeded normally and after lunch we three went off to visit our respective sections, before the whole CCF was finally re-assembled in the school hall for the general to say a few words.

As we entered the school hall where the whole CCF and many of the staff were assembled, General Carver excused himself from the Headmaster, drew his three staff officers on one side and asked us to summarise in a few words the views we had formed of our respective sections. He listened carefully to what we had to say, remarked, "Thank you, gentlemen, that's very much the impression I have gained" and stepped on to the rostrum to face the school. He first thanked the Headmaster and the school on behalf of us all for a very enjoyable day. He then said that as he carried out a fair number of such inspections he hoped they would agree that he was well qualified to offer his conclusions on the general standard of the CCF. He said, "I have to say that I have seen better. For a school such as Shrewsbury I would not have expected to find ..." he listed a number of items that could only be regarded at best as mediocre. He had, he said, gained the feeling that Shrewsbury considered itself rather superior to such details and that it seemed to him that the school could not be said to be taking its CCF seriously. You could have heard a pin drop. He concluded by thanking all concerned again for their hospitality, we made our farewells and left. It was all done in the most courteous and charming way but I don't think it left anyone in any doubt about the shortcomings of the

Shrewsbury School CCF. I was not in the least surprised when I discovered much later that General Carver's nickname in the army was Smiling Death.

If a school was not scheduled to have an official inspection that year they sometimes asked one of us at the Air Cadets Headquarters to go along simply as a visiting officer and do an inspection to give them a pretext to get geared up for a smart parade. I duly put on my best uniform, collected my white gloves and sword and went off one summer afternoon to a certain school in north London. Sadly I cannot remember which school it was. I was greeted by the Head, the teacher in charge of the CCF and their visiting RAF NCO. The CCF was drawn up on parade and we set off along the ranks. It is important to show an interest in individuals and to ask a few questions. For sixth formers a standard question was something to the effect of, "Have you decided yet what you are going to do when you leave school?" but it is much harder to think of anything relevant to ask the younger ones.

On this occasion the boys on the main parade were all smartly dressed in khaki battledress uniform. Then at the end of the line was a small squad of clearly the youngest, most junior boys, equally smart in grey shorts, school caps and blazers. I had run out of subjects to ask about when I noticed to my delight a very small boy whose cap bore an unusual crescent shaped badge. I stopped and asked, "What does that badge on your cap mean?" He drew himself up about an inch taller, "It means I have my school colours, sir." I was amazed that one so young had reached this distinction and so I said, "Really! How splendid. What sport is that in?" A pause and he slumped like a pricked balloon. "Actually its not my cap." The Head, the CCF master and the rest of us were totally unable to suppress our giggles. If only I had not asked a second question he would have got away with it, as he fully deserved to. I felt an absolute heel.

The fact that my main job at the Air Cadets was undemanding gave me the opportunity to contribute elsewhere. Quite soon after I got to White Waltham I had a phone call from Tony Back whom I had known as a Flight Commander on No 20 squadron at Gutersloh. He was looking for someone to take over from him the job of Hon Secretary of the RAF Ski and Winter Sports Association. I readily agreed. My being at Waltham was fortuitous as the Chairman of the Association, Air Vice-Marshal Jones was there too, as AOC of No 25 Group. Up to that time the Hon Secretary had been mainly concerned in dealing with travel company Powell Duffryn on the administration of the package holiday scheme we ran at Zermatt for RAF families and their friends. This had been started after the war by a couple of Air Marshals who had gone round a number of alpine resorts to see where they could negotiate the best package deal. Those who know the skiing facilities throughout the alps say that, in order of excellence, there is St Moritz first, Zermatt second and the rest no comparison, so we were fortunate indeed to be so well established at Zermatt.

However, excellent as this scheme was, if I was going to be Hon Sec I was less interested in the family holiday arrangements than in trying to boost the RAF's involvement in the competitive sport of ski racing. All of us connected with RAF skiing had long lamented the very small numbers of serious skiers we were able to assemble at Zermatt each January for the RAF Ski Championships. It was from them that we had to select the RAF team to race against the Army and Navy at St Moritz. As a first move I persuaded Air Marshal Jones to split the Hon Sec's job in two. Someone else became Hon Sec (Holidays) and then I could concentrate on being Hon Sec (Racing). I had discovered that Mike Shaw, one of the Ski Team personalities was stationed nearby and we used to meet at one of the local pubs for a social evening and to discuss what could be done to attract more young RAF people, especially the "other ranks" to the racing scene.

In spite of the good value offered by the Zermatt package holiday scheme, the main obstacle for most serving RAF people, in particular the younger ones who would be the potential racers, was the cost of getting out to the Alps. We realised that for RAF sporting events held within UK, any representative station team could travel on duty and hence at service expense. Why should we not run an Inter-Station Ski Championship within UK—in Scotland? Aviemore was the obvious choice and so over Easter 1965 Mike and I drove up to Scotland to do a reconnaissance and to find out who among the local hotels, ski schools and the like were likely to be helpful. Having got back from Scotland we sat down one evening in one of our local pubs and drafted a letter for our Chairman to send to all UK stations announcing that the First UK Inter-Station Ski Championships would be held in Aviemore the following spring. Almost at once entries started coming in and it was soon clear that we had hit on a popular idea.

In the following months I learned more about management than I had in the previous ten years. Mike was a tower of strength, a born salesman and a universally popular enthusiast who had the knack of getting favours from the most unexpected sources. We started a Royal Air Force Ski and Winter Sports Association magazine, and the following year handed it to Rob Parker to run. Mike tackled the ever difficult task of raising sponsorship. In those days smoking was still socially acceptable and Mike managed to sell the whole back page of our magazine, in colour, to Peter Stuyvesants. Only later did we discover that by a happy coincidence their picture was going to be of a Zermatt Ski School Instructor, in distinctive red jacket, skiing down spectacularly in deep snow. We pressed the Coylumbridge Hotel to lend us race numbers. Without any persuasion ex-corporal Rudi Prochazka, now Director of the Badenoch Ski School in Kingussie, presented us with a handsome silver cup as the main Inter-Station Trophy and lent us a couple of his instructors as course setters. Echoing the Collins Jug presented to "the most promising newcomer to RAF ski racing" in Zermatt, Mike presented "Mike's Mug" as its equivalent in Aviemore.

I pressed RAF Kinloss to provide a helicopter as a stand-by rescue aid in case someone was badly hurt up the hill and the Kinloss Mountain Rescue Team agreed to patrol around the hill during the Championships with their portable radios, in those days quite a novelty, keeping everyone in the picture. As the dates approached Mike and I booked ourselves a week's leave and took off for Scotland, setting up shop in the Craigellachie bed and breakfast hotel. The hotel management were kindness itself as they quickly found that they had taken on almost a full-time job fetching us to take telephone calls. Mike Shaw and I found that we worked well as a team. Adopting the standard French nomenclature for ski race organisations I became Chef de la Race, looking after the general back-up and Mike Chef de la Course and running everything "up the hill." We had invited Stations to enter teams of three and by the time everyone had assembled we found that we had over 90 starters. Numbers like these greatly exceeded our planning expectations and it was wonderfully gratifying how people appeared and took on some vital part of the organisation to help out. A Squadron Leader Bill Norcross turned up, appointed himself Race Starter and endured hours of blizzard condition up the hill at the Start Gate with his stop-watch, meticulously counting down every minute "... three ...

two … one … GO!" Wives, girlfriends and assorted hangers-on came up the hill and braved the conditions to act as gatekeepers. The score-keeping and publishing of the team and individual results was going to be an enormous job and to our great delight another complete stranger, a Group Captain, turned up in Aviemore and said, "My name is Hugh Lynch-Bloss, is there anything I can do to help?" We asked him to become the Chief Score-Keeper, he set up is own crew of helpers in another hotel, the High Range, installed wall charts showing all the teams' results and generally did a most professional job. The Cairngorm Hotel lent us their main dining room for the pre-race briefing. It was a most exciting moment for me when I stood up on the afternoon before the Championships to face a packed room to welcome everyone to Aviemore. I then asked Paddy Hughes to do the detailed briefing on the racing rules, saying, "and I will now ask Flight Lieutenant Hughes to give us one of his inimitable presentations." Paddy jumped to his feet and started, "Yeah, OK, delighted, but hey, Bill, what's inimitable mean?"

The weather, especially the wind, always the wild card in Scotland, was not kind, but we managed to run a Slalom and a Giant Slalom on consecutive days to give some semblance of a proper Combined competition. We made many friends during the week. Very noticeable was the performance of the RAF College team of Flight Cadets, led by Mike Dyer-Ball. Apart from winning the inter-unit competition they quickly distinguished themselves by being willing to take on any boring old job or chore behind the scenes to help with the smooth running of the event. I got accustomed to hearing people saying, "Look. If no-one else will do it ask the cadets, they'll tackle anything!" After the event I wrote to the RAF College Commandant thanking him for allowing his cadets the time to come to Scotland and telling him what a credit to the College the team of Flight Cadets had been. My letter was never acknowledged.

The whole event was enough of a success that when we repeated it the following year in 1967 we attracted 140 entries and although this time we raced more or less over sheet ice everyone seemed to enjoy it. Shortly after that I was posted to the Far East, but we had laid the foundations and over the years the UK Inter-Station Ski Championships event has continued to flourish, and its value has been increasingly appreciated. It now takes place in the Alps, and it is nice to know that

Mike and I founded and pioneered what in terms of numbers of competitors has become the biggest sporting event in the RAF.

All this activity in Scotland was only a diversion from my official job at White Waltham and I had found that a very popular scheme administered in UK by our Headquarters was the International Air Cadet Exchange. This involved Britain, the USA and Canada. During the school summer holidays parties of cadets took part in exchange visits across the Atlantic, cadets from the USA and Canada coming to Britain and the RAF sending parties across the pond in exchange. In early spring we at the Headquarters wrote to all our CCF schools and ATC Squadrons, asking for nominations. We invited them to select cadets whom they felt had made a significant contribution to their units and so deserved to go on this trip as a reward. Each party of cadets going to America was accompanied by an RAFVR officer who was a teacher from one of the participating units or schools and an officer from the Air Cadet Headquarters. Thus Peter Corlett from the Dragon School in Oxford and I set off to accompany the party going to Canada in the summer of 1965.

We assembled at RAF Uxbridge for a couple of days kitting out and to ensure that the cadets were at least competent enough at parade-ground drill and marching not to disgrace themselves. Because they were just leaving school, knew they had been selected as representatives and were off on a well-regarded jolly, they were in high spirits. The object was for everyone to enjoy themselves, but at the same time a standard of smartness was insisted on. The two are not mutually exclusive. In spite of clear instructions to the schools some of the cadets arrived with very unmilitary haircuts or intending to wear the currently fashionable winkle-picker shoes with their uniforms. As our drill sergeant called them, "All curly with 'oles in!" Having arranged some instant and mandatory haircuts, put in a few hours' drill and sorted out such details we climbed aboard an RAF coach to RAF Benson. From there we flew to the Royal Canadian Air Force base at Marville in France where we were to board the RCAF transatlantic flight to Canada.

It had already become apparent to Peter Corlett and me that a happy school-leaver's idea of punctuality and that of the RAF were not at all similar. We realised that once we were in Canada anyone missing flights or even rail and bus connections would have presented us with real problems. We needed to make a point and at Marville we were presented with an ideal opportunity. We had arrived at mid-day and the transatlantic flight departed the following morning. For the afternoon the Canadians offered us a coach trip to see some of the local First World War cemeteries. We told the cadets that the coach would be departing from outside their block at 14.30. I contacted the driver, explained to him that I wanted to impress on the cadets the importance of punctuality and that I needed his co-operation. He duly arrived with his coach at 14.20. At 14.29 and 59 seconds I said "OK, driver, off we go, please." The door slammed and we set off. We completely ignored a loud chorus of, "Hang on a bit, sir,—Fred or Jim or whoever isn't here yet," as well as the half dozen who were running up the road behind us. The point was well made and once we were in Canada we had no further problems.

In alternate years the "Britishers" party went right across Canada to the West Coast and the Rockies, but although I think we would all have liked to see the Rockies we had a splendid time in Eastern Canada. We landed at the RCAF base at Trenton, Ontario and our first outing the next day was quite breath-taking—to the Niagara Falls. In spite of the commercialism of their surroundings they are still one of the scenic wonders of the world. We hung over the parapet at the very edge of the cliff over which the river plunges and watched the Maid of the Mist, the tourist boat, threading its way through the rapids far below at the foot of the falls. We donned all-enclosing rubber suits and went down in a lift to a viewing platform cut out of the rock behind the falling water, which forms a roaring, shimmering green curtain just feet in front of you. We made a quick visit to the site of the forthcoming Expo 67 and then boarded a luxury coach and went off to spend some days camping in Algonquin Park, a wild, unspoilt area of pine forest and lakes. We travelled on the Canadian National Railways, we flew east to Halifax in Nova Scotia and out to Prince Edward Island. We spent a particularly enjoyable day at the mansion of the Canadian millionaire who had originally set up the International Cadet Exchange Scheme. Of more interest to our cadets was that he had assembled a party of stunningly attractive Canadian girls to join us for the day. We seemed to cover vast distances, sometimes by air and sometimes by luxury coach along endless thinly populated motorways. And yet back in England when we looked at a map of where we had been, we had only visited a tiny corner of this enormous country, about the same proportion as is Kent and Sussex to the rest of Britain.

The only aspect of Canada that disappointed the cadets, some of them 18 or even 19, was that they were all deemed by the Canadian drinking laws as being under age for even a glass of beer. Peter Corlett and I promised them that we would have a party at Uxbridge at the end of the trip to compensate. We did and on Uxbridge station the following morning we said goodbye to some wan and temporarily not very fit cadets. But it had been a memorable fortnight, Canadian hospitality had been wonderful and some lasting friendships had been formed.

Back at White Waltham I was asked to undertake a temporary attachment to the small RAF station at Ouston in Northumberland. The Station Commander, a Squadron Leader, had to go into hospital for a minor operation and someone was needed to mind the shop. The station's main role was to accommodate the Newcastle University Air Squadron. It was my first experience of independent command and I was very apprehensive. Of course I need not have been. The rest of the local staff were, not surprisingly, helpful and supportive and by the time the real Station Commander returned from hospital I was thoroughly enjoying myself, not least because I had been able to take advantage of unrestricted access to the Air Squadron's Chipmunks. The station also accommodated a couple of dozen sailors who were working down in the Tyne docks helping to prepare for sea a new destroyer—HMS Glamorgan. The time came for her to be commissioned, formally handed over from the dockyard to the Royal Navy. I was invited to attend a simple but very impressive dockside ceremony, when the ship's White Ensign was raised for the first time. I was greatly impressed by the ability of the Royal Navy to use a purely paper transaction, and by stipulating smart uniforms, a Royal Marine band and a touch of formality, of transforming it into a moving and memorable occasion.

Back at White Waltham I found that there had been a reorganisation. Another squadron leader was temporarily needed across at Shinfield Park, Headquarters of Training Command. For the next couple of months I commuted daily across to Shinfield Park although I was never sure exactly what my job was. I only remember a dull and frustrating time and an extremely unhelpful Air Commodore who seemed to believe that the direction of staff was best done with patronising rudeness.

It only lasted a few weeks before I was summoned to the Personnel Branch to be asked how I would like a year at one of the RAF's unique locations. Britain at that time still retained a large military presence in Singapore. This was maintained by a fleet of VC10s and Britannias which flew regular trooping flights from the UK. One of the staging posts down the route was on the tiny island of Gan in Addu Atoll, the most southerly atoll in the Maldive Islands. I was offered a one-year posting to Gan in the post of Station Administrative Officer and Deputy Station Commander. The setting sounded idyllic, I had had my fill of Berkshire and the Air Cadets and I felt it was high time I went overseas again. I happily got hold of tropical uniforms and started packing.

Just before I left I had a letter from Air Vice-Marshal W. V. Crawford-Compton, CB, CBE, DSO, DFC, RAF who had succeeded AVM Jones as Chairman of the RAF Ski and Winter Sports Association. He wrote, "Dear Bill, ... I would like to say my personal thanks for all that you have done for RAF skiing and for the help and advice you have given me. You will eventually get the rather pompous letter from our committee but I thought I would try to catch you before you leave. Thanks Bill, Yours, Bill C-Compton." Why weren't there more senior officers like that!

## R A F Gan

THE MALDIVE ISLANDS lie to the west and south of Sri Lanka, a string of tiny coral atolls, scattered in an eight-hundred mile necklace down to the equator across the warm, clear waters of the Indian Ocean. They are not in a hurricane area and only the occasional tropical downpour and perhaps an hour of brisk wind interrupts the otherwise endless sunshine and soft ocean breezes. To the north-east of them lie Sri Lanka and India, two thousand miles to the west lies Africa and two thousand miles to the east Indonesia and Australia. To the south the Indian Ocean stretches away to the Antarctic. In recent years they have started to become an exclusive tourist paradise, but in those days they had hardly any contact with the outside world. Each atoll was in effect self contained, an irregular ring of coral and the occasional sand bank just breaking the surface of the ocean and where the waves had happened to throw up some coconuts and other seeds palm-trees and undergrowth flourished and small village communities had developed. Many of the atolls formed irregular circles of islands fringing a central lagoon. While the ocean swell broke continuously with a dull, distant roar on the outer fringing reef, the calm waters of the lagoon within the ring of islands lapped quietly on the dazzling white sand. The villagers subsisted on home-grown crops and fishing.

The most southerly group in the Maldives was Addu Atoll. It might have come straight out of a school geography book. The islands were only the high points of an almost complete ring of coral, eight miles across. The outer edge of the reef dropped abruptly into the depths. The thousand fathom line was only a mile offshore. The islands were, in effect, the top six feet of a six thousand foot mountain because they were only of a height to which the waves could throw sand. There were four deep water channels into the inner lagoon and apart from these one could have waded no more than waist-deep between any of the islands. Everywhere grew the tall graceful palms, some of them leaning far out over the white sand of the beaches. Although the atoll was only 38 miles from the Equator, the heat was kept from becoming too oppressive by the constant ocean breeze. There was not a great abundance of wild life, mainly large snails, crabs, geckos and fruit bats and some most delicate birds, the Fairy Terns, snowy white with large dark eyes and bright blue feet and bills.

There was a time when the route for RAF aircraft to the Far East and Australia was via re-fuelling stops in Libya, Iraq, Pakistan and Sri Lanka before crossing the Bay of Bengal to Singapore. This was the route which we had followed years ago in the Hastings from Lyneham. Since then, as the countries involved had become less willing to grant over-flying rights, the route had been pushed steadily further south. We now flew via Cyprus to Bahrein at the southern end of the Persian Gulf and then out across the Indian Ocean to Addu Atoll. Britain had leased from the Maldivians one of the islands, the island of Gan to act as a staging post, and to provide re-fuelling and servicing to aircraft in transit. In July 1967 I arrived on Gan to relieve Colin Mitchell as Station Admin Officer and Deputy Station Commander.

Gan Island was just two miles long and a mile across. The runway started at the top of the beach at the north-west end of the island and finished at the top of the beach at the south-east end. Between the runway and the lagoon lay all the essential elements of the airfield, from the accommodation blocks and messes at one end, past the admin-istration offices, the Air Traffic Control tower and workshops to the neat rows of silver fuel tanks at the other. On the south side of the island, beyond the runway was the "aerial farm" forming part of the Commonwealth long-wave communication net.

The transport of all British troops and their families between Britain and South East Asia and Australia was by VC10, also at the time flown in its civilian version by BOAC, seating over one hundred passengers.

Our role was much like that of a service station beside a motorway. The VC10 would arrive either east-bound from Britain via Bahrein or west-bound from Singapore or occasionally direct from Hong Kong. As soon as it had taxied in and stopped engines our string of white passenger coaches would have drawn up at the foot of the steps, the passengers would be driven the short distance to a spacious lounge area to relax, change the babies' nappies and perhaps buy picture postcards of our lagoon or painted coconut shells. Almost before the aircraft had come to rest our ground crews would be swarming round it with electrical cables, oxygen trolleys, re-fuelling bowsers and hoses and racks of pre-packed meals for the next leg of the journey. Another coach would take the aircraft crew to our Operations Room for self-briefing. It was our Station Operations Officer's job to keep the room fully up to date, the charts displayed round the walls, the carefully labelled racks of pamphlets, with all the information that would be needed for the next leg—information on radio and navigation aids, landing obstructions, lights under repair, special restrictions or warnings in force at Kai Tak in Hong Kong, at Changi in Singapore or in Bahrein, and of course the latest weather forecasts.

By the time the captain and crew returned to the aeroplane the ground crew would be finishing off their work, the fuel bowsers and cables removed and the heavy duty accumulators plugged in ready to provide external power to start the engines. The crew would call the passenger lounge, "Passengers, please." In the passenger lounge our airmen were ready to play a pre-recorded tape, "May I have your attention, please, ladies and gentlemen. Your flight is now ready to depart. Before boarding the coaches please extinguish all cigarettes ..." It always amused me to hear this announcement on our tiny tropical island, 1,000 miles from the nearest mainland, made in a broad, vigorous Geordie accent. One expected to hear it backed by the strains of "Bladon Races" or "When the Boat Comes In." The last passengers were shepherded up the steps back into the aircraft, the doors closed, the steps were moved away, the engines started and the aeroplane taxied slowly to the down-wind end of the runway. It swung round into wind, the engine note rose to a thunder and just 90 minutes after it had touched down it lifted away over the ocean on its next 2,000-mile leg.

In addition to the VC10s, the less frequent Britannias and the occasional specials flying down the route we also had one more or less resident aircraft. No 208 Squadron, based at Changi in Singapore, flew search and rescue Shackletons and maintained one of these at Gan. Their job was to search for and then to co-ordinate the rescue of anything that went down into the ocean. The Shackleton and its crew spent a fortnight with us, becoming pro-tem honorary members of the island community. They had their own accommodation lines and a well-used sandy netball area. Apart from a couple of short training sorties during their fortnight stay and routine maintenance of the aeroplane there was little for them to do except to enjoy the beach and swim in the lagoon.

Because Gan was so small it was commanded by a Wing Commander and all the other main posts were one rank lower than on a normal station in UK or Germany. We did not have a proper Operations Wing, only Flight Lieutenant "Gillie" Potter in the Ops. Room and the Air Traffic Controllers, so we only had two real branches—Engineering, concerned with everything to do with actually handling the aeroplanes and the electronic navigation aids and Admin. which consisted of everything else. My post as Station Admin. Officer had a range of responsibilities equivalent to a Wing Commander Admin. on a normal UK station. I was known as S.Ad.O. or SADO. I was welcomed to Gan by Wing Commander Ben Fleming who apart from being the boss was to become a very good friend. He was an enthusiastic dinghy sailor and during his previous tour in Singapore he had regularly raced his Sussex Maid, known to his competitors as Sex Mad.

Ben's and my offices were in the small pre-fab Station Headquarters, looking out on the crossroads where the main east-west road down the island intersected the short road going up to the Air Traffic Control tower near the edge of the runway. I found that just by noticing who was going where and who was talking to whom I could keep surprisingly close tabs on what was going on around the place. However I soon found too that my paper-work could get seriously interrupted by Ben, either setting off or returning from a tour round the station, who would stop on the verandah, rest his elbows on my window sill and start, "Good Morning, Bill, did I ever tell you about the time back in Singapore when I was sailing the old Sussex Maid in quite a wind and …" A quarter of an hour later I would have to interrupt, "Sir, that is all so interesting but I really must do some work!"

The Engineering Wing, Commanded by Squadron Leader Charles Churcher, was not my responsibility but naturally as a new-comer to the island, I took an interest, to get a grip on what went on and how things were done here. One evening, shortly after I arrived at Gan, I heard that the VC10 was delayed while some minor unserviceability was fixed. I heard later from various VC10 crews that they would often turn a blind eye to any minor unserviceability or snag which didn't effect aircraft flight safety and carry it until they got to Gan. They said that they knew our lads would fix it quickly and without fuss. On this particular evening I got to the aircraft servicing area to find that many of our airmen, who were swarming in and around the aeroplane, were not in normal khaki uniform but in a colourful selection of tops, shorts—or just swimming trunks—and flip-flops. I sought out Charles Churcher. "Charles, please don't think I'm criticising," I started," but I'm new around here, tell me about our attitude to wearing uniform on duty." Charles grinned. "Oh, they're not on duty." he said, "They're the other shift. Apparently they heard in the Station Cinema that the VC10 was delayed and when the film finished they thought they might as well wander down to see if they could help in some way."

My own responsibilities were largely run by the department heads for Supply, Catering, Accounts and so on. There was an impressive Marine Craft Section, who would have played a vital part in any Air/Sea rescue operation. They also ran a twice-daily boat service to our outlying satellite Radio Unit on the Island of Hittadu. If Gan itself seemed remote, we were regarded as the Big City or the Bright Lights by the elite, as they saw themselves, radio engineers and operators on Hittadu, three miles away up the string of islands. The unit of about 20 was commanded by a Warrant Officer and for someone who liked to be left to their own devices and allowed to get on with their job without interference it must have been the best posting in the Air Force. They maintained another impressive Aerial Farm and a small collection of air-conditioned radio huts. They had an all ranks club and a delightful beach bar right on the water's edge. Opposite this, between the shore and the deep water of the lagoon the shallows of the reef were almost a quarter of a mile wide and a long wooden walkway ran out over the brilliant white sand and blue water to where it was deep enough for the Marine Section Pinnace to come alongside.

On Gan the question of who should have air-conditioning could have become acrimonious but had been solved by a simple answer; in principle no-one did. That is to say you only qualified for air-conditioning if you maintained some piece of equipment, typically electrical or electronic, which needed it. However in spite of the almost constant breeze the mid-day heat was undoubtedly enervating and this problem too was simply resolved. We worked old-fashioned pre-war "tropical hours." Office hours were from 7 am straight through until 1 pm and that was it. After a cold drink and lunch most people slept for an hour before re-appearing to enjoy the relative cool of the afternoon swimming, lazing on the beach, sailing, sub-aqua diving, fishing,—or playing golf. Some enterprising folk had laid out an adequate 9-hole course between the runway and the jungly south shore.

One of the most striking features of Gan was that it was male only. The cost and complications which would have been involved of trying to accommodate families on the island would have been totally impractical. In fact it was not quite male only. Joyce was our resident SSAFA (Soldiers' Sailors' and Airmen's Families Association) lady rep. Her rather vague manner concealed a true professional with a wealth of common sense and the ability to get down to brass tacks. Any man on the island who was experiencing difficulties with his women folk back in UK found it immensely helpful to talk in confidence to Joyce, to hear her offer a woman's perspective and, if asked, to offer advice. She did a great deal of good, which I suspect some of us younger happy go lucky bachelors did not at the time appreciate.

For anyone posted to Gan, if you had a family you left them in your original quarters in UK. We all served on the island for one year. Thus, regardless of rank or position your arrival date would be your date to come home one year later. As with many isolated, self-reliant communities, a number of local customs had grown up. It was suggested to me soon after I arrived that, although I was in fact the deputy station commander, I should not try to introduce too many changes until I had been there a few months. A few months later I realised that this advice had been entirely right.

One pleasant custom was the "flag up." If you had grounds for a celebration, perhaps a promotion, or news of an addition to your family in UK, or you had reached your "hump" (been at Gan six months so now had just six months to go) you announced that this evening you would have your flag up. The mess barman hoisted a small personally designed flag for you at one end of the bar and while it remained hoisted drinks were on you.

I soon heard also the expression "posby" being used as a reference to someone's meanness. A number of people at Gan were sensibly saving money during their tour there, perhaps towards getting a new car, or getting married when they got back to UK. They spent less time than others in the bar, and regularly deposited their pay in the **P**ost **O**ffice **S**avings **B**ank. This was OK but if carried to extremes, so that even when you were in the bar you failed to stand your round, you were branded as mean, in fact a real POSB!

There had originally been a native Maldivian village on the island, as there were on some of other islands in the atoll. As part of the leasing agreement when the British were clearing the island for the airfield, a new village had been built to replace it on the next island in the chain. However, during the day Gan was still a mixed community. We employed Maldivians as waiters, luggage handlers and for many general labouring jobs. The local sailing and rowing boat was the dhoni. They were built of wood from the palm-trees and held together by wooded pegs and raffia bindings, almost flat-bottomed and with a tall curving bow. They carried a short mast and a single square sail held taut by another pole attached to the mid-point of the luff, the leading edge. Each morning about two dozen of these craft would arrive at the lagoon beach, having been rowed, or if the wind was favourable sailed, from Hittadu, Fedu, Midu and the other islands. There they waited throughout the day, moving constantly in the endless swell which kept the lagoon heaving gently like a sleeping sea-monster, minded by the boatmen, until 3pm when they re-embarked all the workers and set off again, rowing or sailing, for their home islands. This mass departure, like a scene from the Arabian Nights, was a unique sight and visitors to the island were always taken to see it.

Much more impressive were the vedis. These occasional visitors to the lagoon from other atolls were much bigger craft, broad-beamed, up to thirty feet in length, with two masts and square sails. I wish I had had a chance to get close up to one, but one of the conditions of our lease of Gan from the Maldivians was that, apart from our RAF doctor, the rest of us were not permitted to visit the other islands in the Atoll.

As well as the "Maldi-men" we employed Pakistani engineers and clerical staff and a dozen or more Sinhalese, hailing from what was once Ceylon, now Sri Lanka, mainly in the NAAFI. To combat the claustrophobic effect of such a small island each community had its own patch of territory, with its living quarter lines and recreational club. The Pakistani camp was like a few acres of distant Pakistan set down among the palm trees on the south shore. Chickens pecked around the huts, providing a welcome supply of fresh eggs and vegetables patches flourished. An invitation to dinner in the Pakistani camp was much sought after. You sat down beneath the green and white flag of Pakistan and a picture of Mr Jinnah to a feast of rice, curried eggs and the rest all seasoned and garnished with authentic aromatic, mouth-watering spices.

Half a mile further along the south shore, in the centre of their lines, was the Sinhalese club—the "Imps," or Imperial Club. Spotlessly clean and freshly painted, there was always a friendly welcome to be had there. Over the bar hung the Union flag and pictures of the Queen and Prince Philip and at the other end of the room of King George VI and the Queen Mum. So much for the hated oppression of British imperialism.

While we, the uniformed RAF, had overlooking the lagoon our standard officers' and sergeants' messes, down the shore beyond the sailing and water sports club the British civilians had their own enclosure, shaded by palm trees and overlooking the lagoon. In this way one could go out for Sunday mid-day drinks or curry or an evening dinner in completely novel surroundings even though the journeys involved were of only a few hundred yards. We younger element reckoned that the best parties on Gan were those in the Corporals' Club. The Sergeants' Mess was welcoming but staid, their main interests being their teenage families back in UK. The corporals were largely a crowd of cheerful young bachelors.

The NAAFI, a popular amenity on all RAF stations, was of course essential on Gan. It did a vigorous trade in flip-flops, beach gear, sun cream and floppy hats as well as in all the usual lines of washing powder, razors, films, socks and the rest. Some of the airman felt that it overcharged, but Geoff Whittle, the NAAFI manager, patiently explained that his supply problems were pretty unique, dependent as they were on our monthly Brocklebank steamer from Singapore and that even Singapore was a long way from Britain. The NAAFI Manager's car was a Morris Mini van and to the delight of the airmen a previous SADO, while arranging vehicle registrations, had allotted Geoff the number plate MR 10 PC (Mister 10 percent.)

The Maldivians we employed, if they spoke English at all, had developed a local patois mainly centred on the verb "having." Depending on the context it could take on a wide variety of meanings. When one was just too hot to bother to speak properly it was a very useful oral shorthand. You would hear, on the day that the VC10 with our mail from UK was due, "Ah, today mail having!" Our waiters in the officers' mess were, like all the Maldis, little men seldom over five feet and a couple of inches. Our Station Medical Officer explained that this was due to many generations of poor diet, mainly coconuts or whatever they could grow in the poor sandy soil and fish from the lagoon. The Doc ran a daily clinic for any Maldivians from the other islands who wanted to visit him. Every morning there would be a queue, mainly of mothers and children, outside his surgery. The Maldivians had a cheerful outlook and a keen sense of humour. When a new officer arrived at Gan straight from UK his lack of tropical tan stood out almost as if he were ill. A widely grinning Maldi would arrive with your bacon and eggs and, glancing toward the newcomer, remark conversationally, "New moonie having!" Moonie being the common name for a white un-tanned face.

Because of the humidity the salt in the salt cellars would get damp and turn into an unusable solid mass. The waiters were instructed to make sure that the salt cellars were always warmed up on the cooking stove to dry them out. One day I came in to dinner and quite failed to notice a sort of happily furtive air of anticipation among the waiters, ranged respectfully by the door. I picked up a salt cellar and then dropped it as if I had been stung and jumped about a foot in the air. It was practically red hot. The Maldis literally fell about laughing. "Oh, please, sir, don't warn other officers ..."

As I have said the Maldivians, male and female, were little people. A delightful limerick circulated round the island.

> There was a young lady from Fedu,
> Who said to her boy friend from Midu
> "Why are white men so tall,
> While we are so small,
> Is it having less often than we do?"

Ben Fleming was to go to Singapore for ten days on some project connected with his previous job there at the Headquarters of the Far East Air Force. That would leave me as temporary Station Commander of Gan and as this would be my first experience of being an overall boss, I was looking forward to it with some apprehension. This probably showed and a couple of days before he left Ben called me into his office. In his low-key, relaxed way he talked about being in command.

The first thing, he said, was although I might be feeling the weight of responsibility quite keenly, probably nobody else would even notice the change of command. "The aeroplanes will arrive, get re-fuelled and go on their way just as they always do, even if you just sit in here and twiddle your thumbs. Being in command is not a matter of having to push the whole thing along all the time," he said. "The most probable thing is that nothing at all will really happen while I'm away. You will have, literally, nothing to do. But say something does happen. Say, for example, a couple of airmen get drunk, have a fight and someone gets badly hurt, or say something gets burned down. Again, quite frankly, whatever you do everyone else will rally round, most of them will do a grand job and eventually the whole thing will have been sorted out."

He grinned. "But then the trouble will start. You see, Bill, once it's all over a number of people will start saying you did it all wrong. You should have done this or you should have done that and so on and so on. But the point is that this will happen whatever you did at the time. That's my experience anyway and so as it always happens there is not much point in worrying about it in advance! You just say to yourself, 'Ah, I was wondering when all this flak was going to appear!' and that's the end of it. If anyone wants to offer advice at the time, you listen, and you just do what seems the sensible thing." I was much re-assured. Over many years I have found that this was such good advice and I have always been grateful to Ben Fleming for taking the trouble to give me some initial insights into the job of the boss. He was a most genial and pleasant boss himself and I was very lucky to have had the benefits of his guidance on the subject of command or leadership.

Ben's tour of duty came to its end, we had a party to see him off and welcomed the new Station Commander, Wing Commander Bob Mullineux. He was a more intense character. I suspect that he had been briefed to smarten Gan up a bit. He decided that for a start we should produce some new road signs. We held a competition to decide a name for the main road down the island, which would be seen by our passengers as the coaches took them from the VC10 to the transit lounge. The best suggestion was Equator Way and smartly painted black and white signs were made in workshops and erected. A path that led off the main road to one of the airmen's accommodation blocks went under a group of casuarina trees, the favourite resting place of a large colony of our resident fruit bats, dozens of whom could usually be found hanging up-side down in the trees. Soon after the Equator Way signs were erected an equally smart new sign appeared on the path—Bat Alley. For the benefit of the bats it was written upside down.

Leading members of the British civilian community on the island were the "works and bricks" department. On UK airfields the Ministry of Public Buildings and Works, MPBW, is often known as the Ministry of Puff-Balls and Wind. On Gan they were good friends. Peter Smith was the electrics man and Douglas Hart the builder—Pete the Power and Doug the Dig. As the admin. man it was my job to prepare the paper-work, the site plans, cost estimates and schedules, for the various building projects which we needed from time to time. Dougie Hart had a great knack of somehow acquiring a few extra bags of cement or planks of wood from some project we were running, so that when we wanted to do a little unofficial building, perhaps a hut for the water-ski boat or a better slip to launch the sailing dinghies, the materials needed were mysteriously instantly available. A bulky brown envelope arrived in my office one day. It contained the paper-work for some building project that was nearing completion and a small covering note. "You can tear all this up. The job is going fine. Doug."

For many of us the wonderfully clear, warm waters of the lagoon provided our main recreation. The fishermen fished from the jetty, the Sub-aqua Club set off every afternoon in their well-maintained motorboat with their air cylinders, snorkels, masks and the rest while we sailors enjoyed the steady breeze. An interesting feature of the sea around Addu Atoll was that the tide, what there was of it, was controlled not by the moon but by the sun. The tide only rose and fell a couple of feet, high tide was at mid-day and mid-night and low tide at 6 am and 6 pm.

Swimming off the lagoon beach was like diving into an aquarium. Under water one could see thirty yards or more, the coral was like a tropical garden and was inhabited by many varieties of brightly coloured fish, angel fish, parrot fish and many others, while sea anemones, clams and other shell fish lurked on the bottom. One day with a friend I was sailing a dinghy a mile or so out in the lagoon. We sailed past what we took, without paying much attention to it, to be a large square cardboard box, water-logged and floating flat in the water. A moment later the "cardboard box" gave a powerful lunge and dived into the depths. It must have been a giant ray, sunning itself on the surface.

One night I discovered what electricians mean by a cascade power failure. At the far end of the island was a building that housed the seven large diesel generators creating all our electric power. This included not just the domestic power for messes and kitchens but also that for all our aircraft navigation and control aids, the beacons, radios and the Ground Controlled Approach radar equipment. One evening one of the generators was off line and had been taken to bits for routine servicing. Some minor hiccup caused one of the working generators to become momentarily overloaded. Its built-in safety cut-out tripped and took it off line. This threw an additional load on the next one, it promptly tripped too... and so on. It took a few minutes for the duty electrical engineers to restore order and to get the power back on, but this was not before there had been a certain amount of stress and excitement in Air Traffic Control who suddenly found themselves with no aids, no airfield lights, no radar and no way of telling the in-bound VC10 to hold on a minute.

After this incident we installed a "no-break" set for the essential ATC services. This consisted of small hut housing an enormous, heavy flywheel which was kept running twenty-four hours a day and which stored enough energy to run all the essential services for the time needed to get the emergency stand-by generators started up and ready to take over the load. With the no-break kit in place, even if the main power had failed when an aeroplane was on the critical final stages of a radar approach, it would not have mattered.

However even with the radars on the top line the weather occasionally caused problems. Because we were practically on the equator there was no cyclonic circulation such as we get up in the latitude of the UK. If a tropical rainstorm, or even a thunderstorm, formed it tended to sit still and to stay where it was. One evening just such a storm formed and positioned itself exactly in line with our runway and about five miles downwind of us. This meant that on its GCA radar approach, at the very stage when the controller wanted to pass his important final corrections to line it up with the runway, the VC10 disappeared into the rain clutter on the radar and became completely invisible.

Our nearest alternate runway was at Negombo, 700 miles to the north of us in Sri Lanka. The drill was that all aircraft approaching Gan had to do so with enough fuel remaining so that if they were unable to land with us they could divert to Negombo. The VC10 had made a couple of approaches but each time had got lost in the rain clutter and had had to overshoot. The captain told the tower that he had enough fuel for one more attempt but after that would have to divert. Our controller then suggested that as in the other direction the radar was as clear as a bell and that the surface wind was very light, about 7 knots, he might like to attempt a downwind approach and landing. Downwind landings are not to be undertaken lightly as even an extra 14 knots of groundspeed at touchdown generates a lot more momentum for the brakes to kill. However the captain agreed to the suggestion and the VC10 landed without incident.

Because at any time decisions might be needed about aircraft operations, it was important that there was at least one General Duties, that is aircrew qualified, officer on the island at all times. The Station Commander was one and I was the other. There was only one occasion during my time at Gan when I got close to having to take decisions about our air operations. The VC10 had been turned round in the normal way, the passengers were back on board, it had started engines and had taxied down to the end of the runway and lined up ready for take-off. The pilot opened up to full power, the aircraft rolled forward and then as it started to gain speed he chopped the power and coasted on down the runway to a halt. The tower asked him what went on and he reported that he had had a cockpit red light, warning of some system malfunction. The crew had no doubt got out their technical manuals and checked the details because a minute or so later the captain radioed the tower again and reported that having carefully checked the implications of the red warning light they had established that it was not a significant problem and it would be quite safe to fly on with it to Changi.

The VC10 taxied slowly back down the runway to the down-wind end, turned into wind and started the take-off run again. What the aircraft captain seemed to have overlooked was the enormous weight of fuel that the VC10 carries when fully loaded. The weight of fuel in the VC10, fully loaded, was in fact more than the total, all-up weight of the Comet. Had he just brought the aircraft to a halt from what was really not much more than a canter at its normal landing weight, with most of the fuel expended, the brakes would have coped without trouble. As it was they had had to kill a far greater momentum and were now just about red hot. What is more in the time he had taken to taxi back to re-start his take off all this heat had soaked through the wheels into the tyres themselves. This time the VC10 gathered speed in the normal way, the nose wheel lifted as the pilot pulled the stick back to rotate and a moment later they were clear of the ground. But just as the aeroplane became airborne we saw a number of the tyres burst, shedding strips of rubber on to the runway as the aircraft climbed away. The pilot had felt the jar of the tyres bursting and guessed roughly what had happened. Without raising the undercarriage he circled and flew slowly past the control tower. Our controller confirmed that through his binoculars he could see that some tyres were still trailing pieces of rubber.

The pilot, the aircraft captain, was now faced with a difficult decision. If he raised the undercarriage the damaged tyres might jam it and prevent it from being lowered again once he reached Singapore and the transport terminal airfield at Changi. This would entail a wheels-up belly landing, not an attractive prospect while carrying a full load of passengers. However if he didn't raise the undercarriage the aircraft's speed was severely limited, he would not have the range to reach Changi, he would have to circle to burn off fuel and eventually land again at Gan. Whereas Changi had the full range of repair facilities Gan's were, to put it mildly, limited. Also if one hundred plus passengers were to be stranded it was clearly better that they should be at Singapore rather than with us. The main point however was that the landing was now in any case going to be a worrying moment. It was not clear how badly damaged the undercarriage already was, or how many tyres were still intact. I had been summoned up to the tower, briefed on the situation and while the captain pondered his decision I was rapidly consulting with our crash crew the best way of laying a foam carpet to minimise the risk of fire if he was going to land again with us.

It was with great, if rather selfish, relief that I heard him announce his decision that he was going to raise the undercarriage, take the chance that it would lower again and go to Singapore. He however now had four hours to contemplate how he was going to manage his landing. If his original decision to take off so soon after his emergency stop had been unwise, we heard later that he played the last part of the drama by the book. It occurred to him that much the best runway in Singapore for an emergency landing was at Tengah. It was both wider and longer than that at Changi. He therefore told Changi that he intended to go instead to Tengah as additional safety insurance. Unfortunately the Duty Operations Officer at FEAF that day, a certain Group Captain, was not as helpful as he might have been. As if the aircraft captain did not already have enough on his plate, this officer started an acrimonious argument with him by radio asking him if he realised all the difficulties he would be causing by asking for the passenger coaches and baggage trucks to be moved right across Singapore during the rush hour. Surely he could land perfectly well at Changi. The captain simply responded by asking quietly, "Are you ordering me to land at Changi?" The story had a happy ending in that the undercarriage lowered properly and they landed safely at Tengah.

As a mere fighter boy I was not really well versed in all the technical details of operating these big aeroplanes. When I did get a trip to Singapore it was only as a passenger and one could not be forever badgering the crew to go up to the cockpit. One interesting element I discovered was the great lengths to which the VC10 crews went for maximum fuel economy. The VC10 even had a fuel tank in its fin. One of the jobs of the Flight Engineer, as the flight progressed, was to transfer fuel to or from the fin tank to preserve the position of the aircraft's centre of gravity. This was to ensure that in level flight the elevator stayed exactly in the neutral position, minimising its drag and so improving the fuel consumption by the last Nth part of a percentage point.

As our main purpose at Gan was to provide re-fuelling for aircraft in transit across the Indian Ocean, to this end we maintained a large store of aviation fuel. Near the eastern end of the island, well way from where we all worked and lived, was an area of many rows of silver tanks, each surrounded by its bund or earth bank. Had a tank ever fractured and leaked, the surrounding bund could have contained the fuel and stopped it spreading to other tanks. About once a month a BP tanker arrived to replenish us and we often went down to the end of the island to watch its arrival. The tanker steamed into the lagoon, slowly skirted our north shore and then turned sharply away toward the centre of the lagoon. It came to a stop and dropped a couple of anchors from its bows. Then the interesting bit started. A motor boat from our Marine Craft Section took a couple of lines from the tanker's stern and attached these to two massive buoys located right on the edge of the reef, opposite the short re-fuelling jetty. With these made fast the tanker then manoeuvred itself delicately backwards, paying out the lines to its bow anchors and hauling in at the stern. It finally positioned itself right up against the reef edge, where the water depth plunged suddenly like a cliff from wading depth down to some thirty fathoms. From here the fuel lines could easily be led across to the jetty and connected. It was a spectacular and highly skilled piece of seamanship, well worth going to watch. The ship's company were welcome visitors. We entertained them and were in turn entertained on board.

My main hobby at Gan was dinghy sailing. We had a small fleets of GP 14s and Ospreys and took full advantage of the tropical warmth and the constant breezes. We therefore had no trouble in raising a team of sailors to go over to Singapore for the FEAF Sailing Championships. It made a very enjoyable break and especially for me as the Air Commander and his lady, Air Marshal Sir Rochford Hughes and Lady Hughes had invited me to stay with them in Singapore at Air House. Although he had the whole of the Far East Air Force to command Air Marshal Hughes always took a special interest in Gan. With our isolation from many of the normal facilities we much appreciated this. Although my racing performance was indifferent, I greatly enjoyed the week of the sailing championships and the Hughes' very kind hospitality. It made a super break.

One day back at Gan I came in to an early breakfast to find the Doc had beaten me to it. I also thought he looked a bit rough. He told me he had been up all night as Marcus, a kind, gentle old man, the Sinhalese NAAFI deputy manager, had suffered a bad heart attack. In spite of all his efforts he had been unable to save him. "I did everything I could for the poor old chap," he said. "But I'm afraid I lost him. So I'm afraid the problem is now over to you. He's in the mortuary and I'm off to get a spot of sleep." I went thoughtfully down to the office wondering where one got advice on running funerals.

Also working in the NAAFI was Marcus' young nephew. He had been told of his uncle's death so I invited him in to the office and asked him if he and the family back in Sri Lanka had any special wishes. They

245

were quite clear, they would like his body taken back to Sri Lanka for burial. I told him I would see what could be arranged. Then the difficulties started to appear. I quickly discovered that there are, not surprisingly, a mass of regulations about carrying cadavers—it was the first time I had come across the word—by air. Skipping some of the details about lead-lined coffins and so on, the main point was that there were no aeroplanes flying between Gan and Sri Lanka and it was not practical to arrange a flight via Singapore. I also soon discovered that a burial on the island was not on either. Marcus had been a Roman Catholic, a Christian, and there was no consecrated land. In addition to this we had wells in the middle of the island. The fresh rain-water which collected in the porous coral sand was our only water supply.

Gently I persuaded Marcus' nephew to accept what was the only practical course of action, burial at sea. In our Marine Craft Section were two very senior Flight Sergeants who knew all about sail making and stitching canvas. I didn't ask where they had acquired this knowledge, surely the RAF hadn't even existed in the days of sail? It was not felt to be appropriate to issue an order on the subject so we let it be known that there would be much gratitude and a couple of bottles of single malt whisky available for those who could make a proper, weighted canvas shroud. In the Baggage Handling Section there was a small, powered truck, like one sees trundling around railway station carrying the luggage, which we used for carrying cases out to the aircraft. Without any prompting the airmen in the Section stayed up all one night, totally re-sprayed its RAF blue paint, with the wheel nuts and rims picked out in red and white. They made a smart linoleum cover for the back and fitted it with small white painted wooden posts loosely linked with white ropes to go round the edge. It was a work of art—and of respect and affection for a popular old gentleman.

On the very day of the funeral we had a real stroke of luck. It was the day of the monthly visit of the Brocklebank supply steamer that brought us all our food and other supplies. Some genius had the thought of radioing to the steamer as she approached the island to ask if by any chance they had with them a Sri Lankan national flag. They did, one of our marine craft boats rushed out to meet her and to collect it and so Marcus' body could be properly covered with the red and gold of his national emblem of the lion carrying the sword. We gave the station photographer half a dozen rolls of film and eventually a smart black album of photographs of the funeral was made up for the nephew to take home with him to Marcus' widow in Sri Lanka. A Roman Catholic padre had flown in from Singapore. In our best uniforms we formed up behind the hearse and walked behind it to down to the jetty. The shrouded body on its bier was carefully lifted by six of our biggest airmen and carried on to the Marine Craft Pinnace. A large crowd of us, some of us in uniform, some in smart civilian dress, off duty airmen and civilians from all parts of the island community, embarked on the other Marine Section craft. In the brilliant sunshine the small flotilla cast off, moved slowly across the lagoon and out through the narrows between Gan and Wilingili and stopped engines. We lay for a time stationary on the vast, gently moving expanse of the Indian Ocean. The padre conducted the short service and we committed Marcus' remains to the deep, throwing the many wreaths of flowers on to the sparkling water as a last mark of respect.

This was not the only sudden death that month. A few weeks later we heard that Mr Holt, the Prime Minister of Australia had died. A VC10 Special was to transport our Prime Minister and the Leader of the Opposition out to the funeral and also the very young Prince Charles. The VC10 did a normal re-fuelling stop with us and while they were on the ground we showed Harold Wilson, Ted Heath and HRH around the island. Our airmen told us afterwards that in their opinion neither of the politicians had made much of an impression at all but that Prince Charles had "seemed to be a good lad."

As the nineteen-sixties passed and the British Empire was dismantled one of the more tricky hot pots from which to disengage was going to be Aden. When the final withdrawal was due it was decided to have a fleet of a commando carrier, a destroyer and a collection of supporting vessels available nearby in case things got difficult. But to avoid raising the political temperature the fleet would remain "below the horizon," that is unseen unless it turned out to be needed. Our calm lagoon sheltered by its ring of islands and coral reefs was the ideal parking place, so it reverted briefly to the role it had often filled during the Second World War. The commando carrier, HMS Bulwark, a destroyer and about twenty smaller ships arrived one afternoon through the deep-water channels and anchored in the lagoon. If all the off-watch members of the ship's companies had come ashore at once Gan would probably have sunk. However the troops of

42 Commando in Bulwark had the worst embarked conditions and did need to get ashore to exercise. So the next morning they landed at the jetty and we welcomed them and told them to feel free to march around the taxi-way and roads as they wished.

The VC10 was due in mid-morning and as I often did I went up to the Air Traffic Control tower to watch it arrive. The duty controller had his binoculars out and was trying to make out what was going on down at the end of the runway at the far end of the island. I guessed what and took off rapidly in my car. I was welcomed cheerfully by 42 Commando. They had had a splendid march and jog-trot round the island and were now taking a break and a rest, sitting about on the clean, warm concrete, on the edge of the water—right on the runway threshold where in about five minutes time the VC10 with wheels and flaps down would have given them a very close hair-cut. Yes, of course they would be delighted to move. Sorry!

In the short time they were in the lagoon the Navy created considerable stress on our limited resources. The different perspectives were interesting. As they arrived the Navy earnestly assured us that they would not cause us any extra work at all. They then went on to say that the force needed really nothing—except, that was, for some eight tons of fresh water daily, 1,500 loaves of bread and flights to UK for about thirty ratings who were due to be repatriated. We explained to them that we had no wish to be unhelpful but that we had no fresh water on the island at all except for our carefully husbanded rain-fall just sufficient for our own needs, a bakery that normally produced nine dozen loaves a day and an entitlement, laid down by HQ FEAF in Singapore, of one seat per flight to UK, and that such flights came through at the rate of about five per week. Could they please re-plan. The task force stayed only a few days and then departed, back to their main base in Singapore, which was no doubt more geared up to their needs.

Wing Commander Mullineux went off on his mid-tour leave and once more I became Station Commander. Two days later a signal arrived from FEAF. "Personal for Acting Station Commander from Air Commander. Do not be alarmed but the Navy is coming back …" I chuckled at the "Do not be alarmed" bit. It was just as if the Air Marshal had laid a fatherly and reassuring hand on my shoulder. I also felt that by now we had learned a bit about how to cope with the Navy. On their first visit we had allowed them to contact various of our sections direct and even if we had eventually to decline most of their requests it had given many people much extra hassle.

I invited the Navy to send ashore one officer as their representative, gave him an office, and asked them to route all their requests through him. It worked like a charm. The poor man initially found himself just about sinking without trace but he soon got the message on what we could and could not do for them. Through the thin office walls we could soon hear him on his ship-to-shore radio explaining this to his friends afloat in suitably salty sea-going terms. He became a firm friend of ours and a most effective filter. On one occasion a passing VC10 dropped off about ten large sacks of Highly Confidential and Secret paper-work for the task force, with clear instructions on the need to store it in secure safes, twenty-four hour guards and so on. The papers covered two whole tables in our naval officer's office about three inches deep. He locked the ordinary office door and we all went off for lunch and a swim. The withdrawal from Aden eventually took place without the task force being needed and they departed again, with grateful thanks and expressions of mutual goodwill.

It had been foreseen that another way we might one day be required to co-operate with the Navy was by letting aeroplanes from an aircraft carrier use the airfield. At that time many RAF airfields were equipped with the "Safeland" barrier. This was like a large tennis net rigged across the end of the runway. It could be lowered at the downwind threshold to allow aircraft to land, and by the touch of a button in Air Traffic Control, raised into position at the windward end. Any aircraft that suffered from brake failure ran across the gravel trap of the over-run, into the net and was brought to rest in a short distance and with the minimum of damage. However Safeland barriers would not have been practical at Gan because in any case they were not designed for anything the size of the VC10 and even the short gravel filled over-run they needed was not available, the runway at each end of the island finished at the top of the beach about ten yards from the water. However Navy aeroplanes are fitted with arrester hooks that the pilot can lower to engage wires stretched across the deck of the carrier. All that was needed was for us at Gan to fit RHAG or Rotary Hydraulic Arrester Gear with its wires rigged across the middle of our runway against the day when a Navy aeroplane might need it. A naval working party arrived, our RHAG was installed and tested.

It was not a couple of months later when we received a signal from HMS Eagle. Having come through the Mediterranean and the Suez Canal and down the Red Sea she was steaming across the Indian Ocean on her way to the Far East. One of the pilots on the embarked Scimitar Squadron had joined just before they left UK and was not yet experienced in deck landings. They proposed that to give him some flying he should fly over to Gan, do some circuits and land there. They would then send over an experienced pilot by helicopter to fly the aeroplane back to the carrier.

The Scimitar duly arrived over the island turned into the circuit, and did three or four circuits and bumps. Turning downwind for his final landing the pilot radioed, "I have some trouble with my hydraulics. Do you have a barrier as I may need it?" Our controller, thinking about our RHAG, called back, "Affirmative. We have the barrier rigged." The Scimitar pilot lowered his wheels, turned finals, touched down and ran the whole length of the runway, across the wires, and at the far end down the beach and into the sea. The Scimitar came to rest in about four feet of water. The pilot and his observer waded wetly ashore and when asked why he had not lowered his arrester hook exclaimed, "Oh, that sort of barrier!" Gan being an RAF airfield he had assumed we had a Safeland. Salt seawater is very corrosive to light alloy aeroplanes and their delicate electrics. I believe they salvaged the clock, although the stripped down carcass of the aeroplane was put on to one of our barges and towed out to go alongside Eagle and to be winched back aboard. Unfortunately our hilarity about the Fleet Air Arm and fish-headed aviators was short lived. It turned out that the pilot was an RAF Flight Lieutenant on exchange with the Royal Navy. The interesting sequel was that shortly afterwards an instruction was issued that in future the Safeland was to be referred to as "Barrier" and the RHAG as "Hook-Wire." It seemed a pity that you had to have the expensive accident before anyone took a serious look at potential communication failures.

The manning policy at Gan was that it was better to have fewer people there working hard rather than more with time on their hands. Even so there had to be adequate facilities for rest and recreation. There was a large and well-equipped Education Section, with two Education Officers, and many of the airmen took advantage of their isolation to work for their City and Guilds and other qualifications. We joked about the time spent in the bars, but much time was sensibly spent either studying or in constructive sports or hobbies. One of the most notable was Radio Gan. It was not unusual to hear a remark such as, "Well, I'll play tennis if you like, but I've got to be back in my room by 6pm, there is a programme on the radio this evening that I especially want to hear." Radio Gan was run entirely by our airmen, both the technical side, which was no problem to our many radio technicians, and the scheduling, programme making, interviewing, announcing and the rest. Radio Gan relayed news and time checks but apart from that generated much its own material for output. In addition to popular music programmes there were more ambitious ventures, one of which was similar to the old BBC's "In Town Tonight." Any VIP who was passing through Gan, relaxing in the VIP passenger lounge, was liable to be accosted by a grinning Radio Gan interviewer, equipped with microphone and tape recorder. Another programme which attracted a large audience was "Greatest on Gan." This was modelled on Brain of Britain. All sections on the island were invited to enter teams of three for a knock-out quiz competition. I was entered as a member of the Officers' Mess Team. It is the only time I have taken part in a live radio programme and in spite of the calmly smooth and reassuring quiz master it was a surprisingly nerve-wracking experience. I think we reached the quarter-finals.

In addition to the VIPs who passed through Gan on a regular flight there were a few who stopped over. We maintained a small (air conditioned) VIP bungalow and were able to offer a complete and in particular a private rest. We were often told that it was the knowledge that they were right away from the prying eyes and telephoto lenses of the press that was the most welcome aspect of Gan for pressurised politicians. I must mention one particular visitor. Coming back from Singapore from some probably difficult and taxing series of meetings, concerning Britain's withdrawal from East of Suez, was the then Secretary of State for Defence, Mr Dennis Healey accompanied by Mrs Healey and another minister and his wife. About four of us, the senior officers at Gan, entertained them to a private dinner. For us at any rate and I hope for our guests, it was a most enjoyable and pleasant evening. Before that Mr Healey had said he would like a swim. We lent him a mask and flippers and showed him where some of the more interesting bits of coral could be seen. He was the easiest possible person to entertain, humbly grateful for our hospitality, charming, amusing and affable. Often since then I have watched him on television and I am not sure that I would agree with all his political views or would challenge his reputation in politics as an old bruiser. But he remains in my memory as the most charming and unassuming guest to entertain.

We sometimes felt that, apart from the Air Commander, few of the officers at HQ FEAF in Singapore really understood Gan and our unique situation and this made them occasionally very tiresome to deal with. A particularly fatuous example was the arrangement they had set up for our mid-tour leave. If you had no family in UK you got a trip to Singapore—no problem. Married men with their family in UK went home to see them, but it was the arrangements for their return flight that caused the trouble. When their leave had expired they reported to Lyneham and then because Gan had no regular entitlement they had to wait for the first available "indulgence" seat. While they waited they were responsible for finding their own local B&B accommodation. They had to check in at Lyneham daily and so could on some occasions spend a week or more hanging about, not enjoying time with their families and equally of no use to us on the island awaiting their return. Not a clever arrangement.

One person at FEAF who certainly did understand us was, perhaps surprisingly, a WRAF officer, Wing Commander Penny Barrett. A tall, slim lady she had a positive beehive of red-blonde hair on which she somehow managed to balance her service hat. A member of some Organisation branch, she was concerned with airmen's accommodation, buildings and the like and was invariably helpful, practical, business-like and shrewd. Perhaps a shade too shrewd. She well understood the advantage we had because, although she was on the staff of our commanding Headquarters, she could not pick up a telephone to talk to us. On one occasion I had from Penny a tiresome signal asking for a number of boring details of some building project. For some days it slipped down and down into the depths of my pending tray. I then got a further signal. Because I had once been a fighter pilot perhaps Penny thought she might prod me into action by some old World War Two wireless jargon. The signal read "TO SADO GAN FROM ORG BRANCH 3, FEAF—ARE YOU RECEIVING ME?—OVER."

Although the normal tour of duty at Gan was for one year I was in no hurry to come back to UK. On a couple of occasions when he was passing through Gan I had taken the trouble to get to know the Group

Captain in the Personnel Branch in FEAF. I had told him I would jump at any posting in FEAF that would allow me to do the full two- and-a-half years in the tropics before going home. But the months sped past and my tour was coming to its end. I had already started packing and had resigned myself to coming back to UK when the signal arrived. "To S.Ad.O. RAF Gan. At this late stage are you still interested in a posting to HQ, FEAF, RAF Changi in the post of …" I didn't bother to read the rest of the text before signalling back an emphatic "Yes." This was definitely a good reason for a flag up. "Posting to Singapore having!"

I would be leaving one small, almost idyllic tropical island for a rather larger and more complicated one. I have often wondered since leaving Gan why so many of us found our time there so enjoyable and satisfying. The climate and the surroundings, the endless sunshine and the beauty of the island and the lagoon were part of the reason, as were the opportunities for the water sports. But I believe more important than these was the awareness of having a straightforward, well-defined job to do and knowing that we were doing it well. We were there on the island for the sole purpose of seeing the VC10 on its way, re-fuelled, re-victualled and in every way prepared for the next stage of its trip across the world. The greatest compliment that the passengers could pay us was really not to notice us. We aspired to be like the welded rails which give such a smooth, comfortable ride to our train journeys. As passengers we only notice the rails at all when we suddenly encounter again the old-fashioned clickety-click. With the British withdrawal from East of Suez the lease on Gan was terminated and the island has slipped back into its former isolation. More recently the Maldives have become a popular but exclusive tourist destination. It had been a rare stroke of good fortune to have spent a year in one of the most beautiful locations on earth.

# *Headquarters*
# *Far East Air Force*

## R A F Changi

S ingapore Island is roughly the same size and shape as the Isle of
Wight, with Singapore City occupying the equivalent position of
Cowes but many times bigger. The island lies off the end of the
Malay peninsular, between the Straits of Sumatra and the South China
Sea and facing Jahore Bahru across the Jahore Straits as the Isle of
Wight faces the New Forest and Hampshire across the Solent and
Spithead. But there the similarity ends. Singapore is only sixty miles
from the equator, it is hot and humid all the year round, with vivid
tropical flowers on all sides and even areas of jungle; it is the home of
orchids and of vividly coloured birds and butterflies. I soon got to
recognise the frangipani, bougainvillea and flame of the forest
blossoms as well as the casuarina trees and over all the tall graceful
coconut palms and the shorter "travellers" palms. The neat branches of
the latter look like an open ladies' fan, and are reputed always to be
lined up north and south. Like so many other travellers' tales—not true.

Although there was plenty of greenery on the island it was most
notably a densely populated city state—an independent Republic and a
member of the Commonwealth. The population was predominantly
Chinese plus Indians, Malays, Tamils and many others including

expatriate British, businessmen, tea planters, the oil company people and a large contingent of the military. For in the late sixties Singapore was also the main South East Asia base for Britain's armed forces. In the late sixties Singapore city occupied about a fifth of the total area of the island with new high-rise office blocks springing up in the central commercial area almost monthly and vast blocks of flats in the numerous suburbs. However, beyond the city there were still unspoilt villages of simple huts, dirt roads and abundant greenery and on every side British military installations, barracks, airfields, workshops and accommodation complete with their garrison churches, sports fields, schools and NAAFIs. There were three large RAF airfields. In the north west was Tengah, the strike base, which a few years earlier during the "confrontation" with Indonesia had operated fourteen squadrons off the one runway; in the north east Seletar, the helicopter base; and on the eastern tip of the island Changi, the Far East terminal of the transport route from Lyneham and Brize Norton in UK. On the north side of the island was the fine Naval Base. A specially revered spot was the Kranji cemetery from the Second World War and the memorial with its moving inscription,

> When you go home, tell them of us and say—
> For your tomorrow we gave our today.

Almost every day as the brilliant giant cumulus clouds towered up around mid-day, there was a violent tropical rainstorm for perhaps half an hour, then the sun re-appeared and the island gleamed fresh and clean again and actually steamed as the moisture dried out. From the city the Bukit Timah Road bisected the island and ran up to the causeway that connected the island to Malaysia across the straits and also carried the railway and the enormous and vital water supply pipe. A notable feature of the streets and gardens around Singapore were the monsoon drains, a metre across and a metre deep. They were definitely needed to carry away the rainwater but were also quite a hazard to night-time revellers coming home with their navigational faculties a bit blurred.

Quite soon after I arrived in Singapore I was challenged by a Singaporean for using the expression Far East. "From our point of view," he said, "you Europeans come from the Far West." "Oh no," I explained, "The Far West is where the cowboys live, Arizona, California and all round there." "That may be so from your European perspective, but for us who live here in South East Asia, that is our Far East, away across the Pacific …" He showed me a map of the world, centred not on the Greenwich Meridian but on Singapore, showing its pivotal position, as the gateway between the Pacific and Indian Oceans and as the hub of all the sea and air routes between, to the west, Europe, Africa and "The Middle East" and to the east, Australia, Hong Kong, Japan, and the USA. And what was that tiny distorted little smudge, falling off the top left hand edge? Gosh, that was Britain! I must try to be less Euro-centred if I was going to understand Singapore and the region. South East Asia—yes. Far East—no.

While the Station Headquarters of RAF Changi was at Temple Hill, the Headquarters of the Far East Air Force (sic) was at Fairy Point. What appropriate names. The Fairy Point officers' mess, a cool, spacious, white, colonial building, rising above the palm-covered slopes to catch the breezes, and overlooking the Johore Straits, was a delightful place to live. With its marble floors, bamboo chairs, the silently turning ceiling fans and white coated Mess servants, as well as the copies of The Straits Times lying around and month-old, well-used copies of The Times, The Tatler and Country Life, it seemed to have come straight out of the pages of W.Somerset Maugham. It was presided over by Ricky Smythe, the Mess Manager. A dapper middle-aged bachelor, Ricky came gliding up to the Mess each morning in his immaculate midnight blue drop-head Rolls Royce. Our normal working dress of open- necked khaki shirts and slacks or shorts gave way when we were off duty to colourful tops worn loose, over shorts and flip-flops. Formal dress in the evenings was "planters rig" which consisted of slacks, long sleeved shirts with ties but no jackets. It was a most practical and comfortable dress. A curiosity of Singapore Island is that there are no mosquitoes. We slept without mosquito nets and with open windows.

There was so much to do living in the present that we took less interest than perhaps we should have in Singapore's past and in particular of the tragic history of the Japanese occupation. We made passing references to Changi Gaol as we drove past on the way into the city, but I suppose anyone who had lived through the occupation preferred not to remember too much, while we youngsters were more concerned with our plans for weekend parties and water skiing.

But there was one character in the officers' mess at Changi that everyone had pointed out to them. I have forgotten his real name so I will call him Mr Tan. Mr Tan was a very elderly mess waiter. He could always be relied on to mix up your order whether it was fried, not poached, eggs for breakfast, tea, not coffee, or lager and lime, not Tiger beer in the evening. He seemed amazingly old, but shuffled about happily muddling along without apparently a care in the world. When I moved into the mess at Changi I had soon decided that he was a complete menace. That was before I had heard his story.

Many officers' messes before the war had acquired a large and very valuable collection of silver, which was lovingly polished and proudly displayed on the dining tables on Dining In Nights. There were cups and other sporting trophies, beautifully crafted model aeroplanes of the old string-bag biplane era perfect in every detail, menu holders, candelabra, models of palm trees and animals presented to the mess suitably inscribed by departing officers before they stepped on to the ship for Britain at the end of their tour of duty. Apart from their monetary value as sterling silver they were often of great sentimental value and so quite irreplaceable. When the Japanese invaded Singapore and everything was in chaos, those British who had not escaped to Australia before the surrender were rounded up into prisoner-of-war camps. No-one had time to do anything much about valuables.

At the end of the war, when things were starting to get back to normal, a dusty figure came trudging up the hill one sunny morning to Fairy Point Mess with a large heavy sack over his shoulder. It was Mr Tan, who had started work at the mess just before the war as an eager teenager. He asked to see one of the returned RAF officers, dumped the sack at his feet and said, "Here is the silver from your mess. I thought someone had better look after it until you came back." As the invading Japanese took over the island, Mr Tan had collected up all the mess silver, taken it away to his home and buried it. Throughout the long years of the occupation, when he could of course have sold it for a king's ransom, he kept a discreet eye on it and kept mum about it. Finally he brought it back to its rightful owners. Mr Tan was promptly told he had a job for life or for as long as he wished. When I left Singapore Mr Tan was still shuffling happily about the RAF Changi officers' mess, an honoured and highly respected figure.

Fairy Point may have been a pleasant location to live and work, but like almost any headquarters in any organisation it was whenever possible "sent up" by the units in the field. The popular name for it when I was at Gan was Wimbledon Court—all balls and rackets. My posting was to the Air Plans department. In normal times the job of the Planners was to dream up any possible future contingency which might arise and then draft the operation orders which would be needed to meet it. What if an anti-terrorist operation had to be mounted half way up Malaysia. How many choppers (helicopters) would be needed? Were they available on the island or would they have to be air freighted from somewhere? From where? How much fuel would they need daily? Where was it to come from? How would it be transported? Where could it be stored? What tented accommodation would be needed? Where was it held? Would it be monsoon proof? All the necessary plans could be sketched out with weights, timings, distances, fuel loads and other details pencilled in. Then the plan, perhaps to be called Operation Clean Sweep, would go into the safe against the day when it or something like it was needed.

But what about a counter-terrorist operation on one of the neighbouring islands? Re-sharpen the pencils, fresh pads of paper and off again. In this case the Navy would obviously be involved so ring up the Naval Base and fix to go up and see Naval Plans. Hopefully they will have thought of this one already and will have done most of the work. At any rate we should get a nice gin-laced lunch out of it.

We spent much of our time sitting around our office speculating on such future possibilities and were consequently regarded by the people in other departments as idle layabouts. They were mostly concerned with the urgency of day-to-day air operations—cargo manifests, dodgy weather forecasts, aircraft serviceability, engine changes, passenger lists, deadlines. Perhaps we would be thinking about a possible need to move some Hunter fighters up to reinforce the squadron in Hong Kong. We would work out the logistic support needed to the best of our ability, mainly by hopefully intelligent guesswork, draft the plans and then go along to show the Hunter boys at Tengah and ask them what they thought about them. "Oh typical planners!" they would say, "Why don't you come and ask the people who live in the real world and know about Hunters. That's all wildly inaccurate, here, let's show you." On the next occasion we would go along to Air Operations or somewhere else at the sharp end and ask them for their facts and figures before we started drafting anything. "Oh typical planners!" they would say, "Always looking for other people to do your job for you. I thought it was your job to do all these sums!" It seemed that either way one couldn't really win.

Another job that came the way of the Planners Department was to give occasional presentations about the aeroplanes and work of FEAF to visiting VIPs—generals, politicians and the rest. Wing Commander Ken Cooke was our regular presenter and he said that he sometimes found himself exasperated by various policy decisions we had to implement. He confessed that he found it increasingly difficult to curb his impatience and sense of humour. His presentation was made using a smart set of 35mm projector slides and he always concluded and signed off by showing the FEAF crest, which was a picture of a traditional Chinese junk heading towards the left side of the picture, above our motto "Eastward." He constantly vowed that one of these days he was going to conclude his show with the comment, "And so as you can see, gentlemen, FEAF largely consists of a load of old junk heading in the wrong direction."

Not long after I got to Singapore two sad items of news arrived from UK. Jimmy Aitken who had been such a good friend at ETPS and had shown me all around Scotland had taken a party of friends up to north Wales for a spot of gentle rock climbing. But however gentle the climbing is intended to be and even using a rope, one of the first rules is that the leader must not fall. Jimmy had been leading up a climb with his less experienced friends and had somehow fallen. He had died within a few hours.

Mike Withey had been my co-student for our initial Flying Training on Prentices at Cranwell with Tug Wilson and later on he had been on 56 Squadron at Waterbeach while I was on 63. Ever since our initial flying training together we had enjoyed a pleasant but, being on the different squadrons, rather casual friendship. At Cranwell Mike had been kidded for his young, baby-faced appearance. At Waterbeach we each had our own circle of more immediate friends and we didn't actually have many interests in common. But I had always realised that Mike, who was a Catholic, was a deep-thinking, serious-minded and quite excellent chap. While we were flying the Prentice together I had got to know him pretty well and for all his fine personal qualities I had sometimes wondered whether he was really cut out to be a fighter pilot. I suspected that he did not have the element of rather brash self-confidence, almost over-confidence that seems to be needed. I was much saddened to hear the news that in bad weather Mike had somehow flown a Mk VII Meteor into a hill in Scotland. Both he and his passenger had been killed.

Singapore, being at the hub of all the South East Asia air routes, was ideally placed as the jumping off point for travelling holidays. At the time I had cousins, Penny and Nigel Brown, who lived in Phnom Penh, Cambodia, where Nigel worked for British Tobacco. This was before the horrors of the Khmer Rouge had been loosed on that beautiful and gentle country. I stayed with Penny and Nigel for a week before going up country to see one of the wonders of the region, the temples of Angkor Wat. There are in fact a whole series of temples, built by successive rulers, each aiming to surpass his predecessor, not necessarily in size or grandeur, sometimes in subtlety and charm. Angkor Wat is undoubtedly the flower of them all—tranquil, spacious and serene. The Bayon, by contrast, is haunting and rather sinister, with its many closely set towers each adorned on each of its four sides with the face of the emperor. Whichever way you turn he gazes silently down on you.

Another memorable holiday was to Australia. I knew that Eddie Edmunds, who had been our boss on 26 Squadron, was now a Group Captain and stationed in Canberra. I had the chance of a ride in a Hercules down to Edinburgh Field, the Royal Australian Air Force airfield outside Adelaide. Once I got there I intended to contact Eddie in Canberra and hopefully arrange to go up to see him and Elizabeth. I walked into the RAAF officer's mess at Edinburgh Field and there was Eddie reading a magazine. "Oh, hullo, boss, I've come to Australia to see you." The familiar chuckle. "Well, how about that then!" The arrangement at the British High Commission was that the High Commissioner's flat in Sydney, overlooking the harbour and the bridge, could be borrowed by senior members of the staff any time it was not being used for official functions. As luck would have it, the next weekend was Eddie's and Elizabeth's turn. We made some quick phone calls around Sydney and spent a splendid evening hearing from Bill Bailey how Qantas airliners full of passengers compared with the old 2TAF days. Eddie fixed me a RAAF lift back to Singapore. The whole holiday cost me about £50.

I managed a brief trip to Hong Kong. With a fellow planner I had persuaded someone who arranged air bookings that we needed to see Hong Kong in connection with the job. By craftily restricting the dates on which we could travel to those when we knew that no RAF scheduled flight was going, we thought that we would be sent in luxury on Cathay Pacific. At the last minute an RAF Special appeared, a rackety old Hastings was flying up to Hong Kong on our dates and it had spare seats. It would be slow, cold and noisy. We suddenly discovered that the dates were not as convenient as we had thought, but the rest of the department, thinking it hilarious, insisted we stuck to them and went. The landing approach into Kai Tak from the south over the sea is slightly less spectacular than that from the north, where you turn hard right past the blocks of high-rise flats. But it is spectacular enough. You know as you come over the threshold that you are definitely going to stop, either gently on the runway, or less gently against the side of the mountain which rises steeply just beyond the far end of the runway. John Canning, an old friend from 63, ran the helicopter squadron in the colony and there is no better way of sightseeing round Hong Kong than by chopper.

It wasn't necessary to leave Singapore Island to enjoy the mass of leisure facilities which mainly depend on warm seas and an endless supply of reliably hot, sunny days. At Gan my favourite pastime had been sailing, but in Singapore this was mainly confined to the regatta season. For three months of the year, the regatta season, there was a reliable breeze ideal for dinghy sailing and all the service units near the coast were equipped with fleets of Snipes, GP14s and Ospreys. We spent splendid Saturday afternoons cruising in the Jahore Straits and among the many jungly islands, which dotted the straits, many of them uninhabited and offering deserted sandy beaches. For the racing enthusiasts, on alternate weekends each sailing club in turn staged a regatta and on the other weekends there was a passage race along the straits or round south through Singapore Harbour to position the fleet at the next club on the circuit. I shared an Osprey with Brian Harris, an old friend from Boscombe Down. The arrangement worked well as Brian enjoyed the cut and thrust racing round the buoys and I preferred the passage races from one club to the next.

Outside these three months the wind dropped to almost nothing and water skiing took over as the main aquatic sport. I found, after I had joined the army Headquarters mess at Tanglin, for reasons I shall come to, that the army had their water-skiing, as so much else, beautifully organised. They simply insisted that you got checked out as a competent ski-boat driver. After that you rang up the booking centre and booked a boat and all equipment for a morning or an afternoon, collected up your friends, picnic and beach gear and jerry cans of fuel at cost price. That is, what it had cost the army and the tax-payer. Pongol was a small Malay village almost hidden by the surrounding jungle on the north-east edge of the island. There the local boatman would have the boat ready for you, complete with tow-ropes, dual and mono-skis, spare plugs etc. for the engine. The best outings for the real enthusiasts were in the early mornings—7 to 9 am—well before the family parties wanted to take the kids skiing. The sun had not long been up and at that hour the water was like glass, the dawn just turning to a brilliantly sunny morning, fish eagles perched on the water-side trees and, it seemed, the world all yours.

But even such a relaxed sport could have its moments. At the end of such one idyllic morning four of us were in the boat coming back to the quay at Pongol from our favourite beach. I was driving the boat with its big 500 cc engine and we were towing Chris Collier, on a mono-ski, to make the most of the journey. Rather than dump Chris way out from the shore for a long boring swim, I kept the boat at full speed until the last moment. At twenty yards from the quay and heading straight for it I snapped the throttle shut ... and nothing happened. Something in the linkage had chosen that moment to break and we had about halved the distance before I realised. I can only remember the fleeting thought that, all being highly vulnerable in swimming trunks or bikinis, we would be less seriously injured if we hit the quay sideways rather than head on. I yanked the wheel hard to one side to achieve this and to my great surprise the boat dug itself neatly into the water and executed a perfectly controlled right angle turn in about its own length. A moment later we were weaving thankfully away among the moored yachts while someone climbed to the back of the boat and switched off the engine. Steely-eyed fighter pilot boat-handling skills had had nothing whatever to do with it. Luck and an excellent design of boat had everything.

Both within Singapore city and in the surrounding districts there was an endless choice of first class local restaurants, Chinese, Indian, Indonesian and many others. I believe, had we chosen to do so, we could have eaten out every night of the year without going to the same place twice. They showed strikingly, as did most of the shops around the island, what standards of service and customer care become the norm in a real buyer's market where you please the customer constantly or you go out of business. There the customer really was king. I hope we didn't abuse the position.

It was while shopping around the city for a Minolta or Pentax or hi-fi system or camphor-wood chest or Noritake china—in Orchard Road, in C K Tang's or in "Cold Storage"—that I first became aware of someone suddenly saying "fifty dollars!" at which every Brit within earshot would burst out laughing. The story then doing the rounds was about this well-dressed young man, sitting at a table in the bar of a very smart hotel, fingering his drink, not really reading his newspaper, glancing occasionally at his watch and then at the door, and sometimes drumming his fingers irritably on the table. Presumably he is waiting for a girl-friend who has got the wrong time, as girls sometimes do, or has gone to the wrong bar, or thinks it's tomorrow or whatever .... At length he notices across the room at the other end of the bar a very pretty girl. He realises that she too is playing with her drink, gazing around in a bored sort of way, glancing at her watch and at the door. Clearly she too is waiting for a friend who has failed to turn up. He makes his way across the room, picking his way between other guests at their tables, slides on to the bar stool next to hers and says, "Hullo. Please forgive me for introducing myself like this but I couldn't help noticing that you seemed to be waiting for a friend, just as I am. I wonder if you would let me buy you a drink?" The girl says at the top of her voice, "Come up to your room with you? Certainly not! Go away and leave me alone."

In the shocked and stunned silence that follows he realises that it would be hopeless to try to explain himself, so he slinks back to his own table and hides himself behind his newspaper, conscious of the muttered remarks all round him of, "What a cad," "Damn fellah," "Dreadful chap." He has just decided to finish his drink and slip away when to his great surprise he feels a hand laid on his arm. It's the girl, who smiles and says, "I'm so sorry about that, please let me explain. I'm doing some post-graduate university research on group psychology. I wanted to see the reactions of all these strait-laced folk to an embarrassing situation. Yes, I'd love to have a drink with you." And the young man says at the top of his voice "Fifty Dollars!"

263

Living on the island we got to know the outlying districts and the best local restaurants much better than any tourist ever could. However all the tourists and we too frequently made for Bugis Street, in one of the older, picturesque parts of Singapore city. No sooner had you settled yourself with your drink at one of the open air bars than tugging at your elbow you would find a bright-eyed eight or ten year old urchin challenging you to play noughts and crosses for a couple of dollars. If you were yourself something of an expert you might occasionally force a draw, but win—never! However the real fame of Bugis Street depended on the large number of incredibly attractive, beautifully dressed and made up girls passing up and down the street. Some were really stunning, with waves of perfectly groomed hair and lovely figures. But the trick was to look carefully at their hands and arms. Invariably these were just a bit too bony—in fact just too masculine—to complete the illusion. The wags would sometimes wait until a particular stunner walked past and murmur, "Good evening, Corporal."

On other evenings it became a game to go out for the evening for a meal in one of the out of town, village restaurants and on the way home to see if we could say we had not seen another white face the whole evening. I was driving home along West Coast Road with a girl friend from such an evening one really dark night when we saw what I would not have believed possible had I not actually seen it. A car had broken down and was being not towed home by a breakdown truck but carried. The truck had the usual crane projecting over the back end, but instead of winching up just the front wheels of the car and towing it, the driver had lifted the broken-down car, horizontally, right off the ground. It was thus being carried but instead of being in line with the truck and the road it was at right angles to them, and so projecting a good three feet out to each side.

The driver was therefore having to keep well out into the road to prevent the car hitting the roadside palm trees but had clearly not foreseen or worked out what was going to happen when he met the inevitable car coming the other way. It had taken a moment for us to see by the light of my headlights what was going on but as soon as we did I stood on the brakes and pulled back a good fifty yards. I was only just in time. A car came the other way and obviously not being able to see anything behind the breakdown truck's headlights hit the projecting part of the carried car fair and square. Squealing metal, sparks, swerving cars, general grief and mayhem occupied the next few seconds and most of the road. When all had become peaceful again there was just room for us to slip past and on our way, still almost wondering if we had dreamed it.

I once saw in broad daylight too an incident which could have come straight out of the Keystone Cops. I was waiting near a roundabout on the Bukit Timah Road, one of the main roads out of the city centre. It must recently have been re-surfaced with a couple of inches of new bitumen but the man-hole covers had not yet been raised up to the same level as the new surface. Along came an old van looking like a direct descendant of the model-T Ford, with narrow wheels, a rickety cab and an open back containing some wicker cages each holding a solitary pig no doubt on their way to market. The driver, an equally ancient Chinese farmer, who was wearing a battered hat, singlet, blue shorts and flip-flops, obviously didn't notice the considerable hole in the road which was the man-hole and drove straight over it. The van bounced into the air and as it landed the chassis split in half. One front wheel took off on its own, the engine skidded into the ditch, the cab toppled over on its side and dissolved into splintered match-wood and the pig crates, the pigs and the driver spread themselves all over the heap of scrap metal which until a few moments earlier had been a reasonably serviceable van.

If these two incidents give the impression that Singapore was ramshackle, that was certainly not the case. As its subsequent story has shown it was rapidly becoming a dynamic, high-tech, high wage powerhouse of the area, well on its way in many respects to rival Hong Kong. Some complained of the autocratic behaviour of Lee Kuan Yew's government. They would have argued, rightly I believe, that the tasks facing the new Republic and the need as quickly as possible to stand on their own feet meant that there was no alternative. This was the time in the late '60s when in permissive Britain apparently anything went. But from our perspective in Singapore it seemed that Britain was giving up and losing much that may perhaps have been square but was also worth-while and of lasting value and has since been greatly missed. It was the time in Britain of shoulder length hair for men. This was one thing not tolerated in Singapore. The story went that male airline passengers from Britain with too much hair were greeted at the bottom of the aircraft steps by a Singaporean policeman who said, "Welcome to Singapore. The barber's shop is to your left, the re-embarkation lounge is to your right. This is a free country so the choice, of course, is yours." Excellent!

Singaporeans were extremely proud of Mr Lee Kuan Yew, their highly effective Prime Minister, about whom stories abounded. Some have wondered why the Malaysian Federation, which merged Singapore and Malaya, never had a chance. Singapore is peopled mainly by thrusting, hard-working, energetic Chinese but Malaya by relaxed, easy going Malays. Two such temperamentally different communities were never gong to become a single political entity.

All the time that I was in Singapore I never once suffered any tummy upsets, once so common in tropical countries. We fell off water-skis and into muddy water around the mangrove swamps, we ate curry at dubious looking local restaurants, such as a not very clean but most popular one at Pongol, where we usually went on returning from a morning's water skiing, and we drank the tap water. Mr Lee went to an international conference in Australia and suffered a really nasty bout of gippy tummy. He is reputed to have muttered, "What can you expect from these third-world countries."

I have described the Air Plans job in normal times, but these were not normal times. A few months previously the Wilson Government had announced the decision that Britain's forces were to withdraw from East of Suez. We were to give up the enormous military arsenal which was Singapore. This would have the most profound effect on the whole population of the island, their economy, employment patterns and the rest. It would also mean that in a few years' time they would have to take responsibility for their own defence in a turbulent and unpredictable part of the world. But for us in Air Plans it rather put us out of a job. The main plans for the future of the RAF in Singapore were now to pack up and go home. For the time being we managed to keep ourselves more or less busy doing odd jobs, but it had all become rather pointless.

One morning my Wing Commander found a routine odd job for me. He asked me to go and talk to P staff (the Personnel Department) and to find out which Squadron Leaders on the island would be tour-ex (tour expired, that is due to come home to UK) between a couple of dates in about eighteen months time. As I myself would be tour-ex at that time my curiosity was aroused. P Staffs are by nature cagey about sharing information with outsiders. They have unhappy memories of self-seeking scroungers aiming to wangle themselves on to the inside track for various plum jobs and then much acrimony and grief when the jobs fail to materialise—or by some extraordinary coincidence are neatly filled by ex-P Staff themselves. However Wing Commander John O'Neill was an old friend so I dropped in on him and asked him if he knew the significance of the errand I had been given.

As we all knew, the announcement of the forthcoming British departure from Singapore had landed the Singaporeans themselves with the fairly urgent matter of creating their own defence forces. To do this they would, at least initially, be heavily dependent on our providing their fledgeling forces with equipment, training, advice and, of course, the real estate which we would soon be abandoning. In Commonwealth countries the High Commission stands in the same position as does the Embassy in foreign countries. Up to now the staff of the British High Commission in Singapore had included one military officer, a Lieutenant Colonel called the Defence Adviser. In fact even that post had once been part-time, but now the present incumbent was rapidly being swamped with an ever-growing flood of correspondence and requests from the new Singaporean Ministry of the Interior and Defence (MID) as they energetically tackled the task of setting up a Singaporean Defence Force, virtually from nothing. The colonel urgently needed an assistant. A new post in the British High Commission was being created for a major or equivalent, an Assistant Defence Adviser. But why the importance of tour-ex dates? It was judged that increasingly the dealings with the Singaporeans would be concerned with air matters, rather than those of the army or Navy. When Lieutenant Colonel Sharland, the present Defence Adviser, finished his tour in January 1970 it was intended that his replacement would be an airman—in fact a Group Captain—and his assistant an army major. Hence he and the Assistant Defence Adviser would need to depart at the same time.

As my Air Plans job had started to fizzle out and that by a stroke of luck my tour-ex date exactly fitted, I asked John if he could set the wheels in motion for me to apply for the job of Assistant Defence Adviser. He was as good as his word and within a week I had been interviewed by the High Commissioner and by Colonel Sharland and was on my way in to the heart of Singapore city and to the High Commission offices in a high rise building on Collier Quay.

267

# The British High Commission

## Singapore

Maritime Building on the seafront of Singapore city was the most exotic location in which I have ever worked. The building overlooked Singapore harbour, constantly thronged with shipping, steamers and freighters at anchor and with hordes of lighters and water taxis threading their way to and fro. Each of these was hung round with old motor tyres as fenders and had two large eyes painted each side of the bows to ward off evil sprits.

A hundred yards along the sea-front, occupying a narrow gap between the buildings, was Change Alley, a thronging hive of oriental food stalls, money-changers, souvenir shops and the rest, running back towards Shenton Way, the banking and commercial district. The modern skyscraper almost next door was the Bank of China and behind that the Singapore River wound back into the city lined with wharves and warehouses, some of the oldest buildings still standing. Across the Singapore River stood the Victoria Memorial Theatre with the statue of Stamford Raffles in front of it, and beyond it the lattice of streets of the city centre and St Andrew's Cathedral. Half a mile to the east was the legendary Raffles Hotel. The streets were crowded with a colourful mixture of races—Chinese, Malay, Indian, Tamil, a sprinkling of European, from smart business men in collars and ties and suits, to tourists hung round with cameras and every variety of local people in graceful sarongs or in battered hats, shorts and flip-flops. The traffic was equally mixed, private cars, pick-up taxis, vans, army trucks and many bicycles.

As Defence Adviser, Colonel Sharland's job was to keep the High Commissioner, and through him the Ministry of Defence in London, informed of what the Singaporean military were doing. In addition, and this was the area in which I was to help, it was to provide a contact point between the Singaporeans and British military, both in UK and here in Singapore, to enable us to provide whatever assistance we could to the Singaporeans as they set up their own new defence forces. On my arrival as his deputy he briefed me that he intended to deal with the broader, policy issues for all three services while I would deal with more routine matters for all three. It was this opportunity to work closely with the army and the Navy as well as with my own service that made the job so interesting. As the weeks passed I got myself acquainted with the functions of a large number of the various British military units and headquarters around the island, not only the RAF units, but also the army's Base Ordnance Depots, Royal Engineer Companies, Signals Units, Cavalry Squadrons and so on and the Navy's many esoterically named Fleet departments. I also spent much time getting to know a wide range of officers and officials in the Singaporean MID. Business visits to MID would often conclude by adjourning to a local restaurant where, of course, their recommendations from the menu were to be taken very seriously. At one favourite restaurant which we often used there were no plates or cutlery. They used large, flat banana leaves as plates and you tore off portions of your chapatti to scoop up the rice and curry.

One part of my job was to arrange for visiting British salesman, anxious to secure orders for all the defence equipment which Singapore was going to need, to meet with the appropriate officer in MID. This sometimes led to a situation which as a westerner I found irritating. The visiting salesman would make a presentation to the Singaporeans about some complicated piece of military equipment, a radio communications net, a new compact mobile radar or whatever. Even with my Boscombe Down experience of such things I would often, not surprisingly, find myself way out of my depth with the technicalities. The presentation finished, the salesman would ask the Singaporeans, "Have you any question?" "No," would be the surprising answer, "No thank you, no questions." Wow, I would think, these guys are really sharp if they took all that in!

The salesman would depart for Australia or Japan or wherever and the following week I would get a phone call asking me to call round at MID. There I would be asked a series of highly technical questions that I had not the slightest hope of answering without long and laborious correspondence with the salesman who was now as likely as not on the other side of the Pacific Ocean. I used to get back to the office tearing my hair out and wondering why on earth these questions had not been put to the man while he was here. Someone with more experience of the East explained it to me. To some eastern senior officers the unforgivable gaffe was to lose face. At the presentation there would have been more junior officers present, so to ask a question would be to admit in front of them that one had not understood something, and so would be to lose face. For some this was a much more important consideration than the weeks of delay and expense that was entailed in asking the questions privately later. As Kipling wrote, "East is East and West is West ... ."

A major part of my job was to act as a post office between, on the one hand the Singaporeans, and on the other both the British forces on the island and the Ministry of Defence in UK. The work entailed much correspondence and I was immediately amazed with the speed with which, having been shown the army's office systems, this could be dealt with. I had never before seen administration so smoothly and efficiently run. The colonel and I shared our office with a clerk, Warrant Officer Dawson. When a letter arrived Miss Dawson put it straight into the appropriate file and this then appeared on my desk, with a pencilled list on the letter of the enclosure numbers of all the earlier relevant papers, which I might want to look at while dealing with it. I simply drafted a reply in longhand and, it seemed before I could blink, back came the file with the typed version ready for signature and the file copy already in place. Perhaps it sounds over lavish and extravagant. In fact it was exactly the opposite. I am not a natural administrator and I worked no faster than usual but, supported by Miss Dawson, I actually got through the work that in the RAF offices which I had experienced would have needed three similar officers, opening their own letters, going to find and fetch their own files, looking up all the previous correspondence and so on. As I was to find later in a number of other ways, by in effect joining the army, I had entered another world.

Having been landed with the responsibility for their own defence, the Singaporeans were now energetically engaged in working out their defence policies and in translating policy decisions into practical steps—into recruitment, training and hardware. One of the items of particular interest to me was that they were basing their air defence on a squadron of Hunters, hardly surprising as the Hunter, one of Britain's most successful export ventures ever, was at the time equipping about half the air forces of the developing world. This led to an incident which, I am glad to say, happened just before I got to the High Commission.

For all types of aeroplane there are strict limits for the physical dimensions for aircrew, especially pilots. Cockpit design is a difficult enough affair anyway, without trying to accommodate 6ft 2ins giants and little guys of 5ft 3ins. The range of adjustments for seat heights and rudder pedal positions just cannot cope. Every pilot who is to fly the aeroplane must be able to fit into the cockpit without encountering either of two possible problems. If he is near the tall limit he must not have a length of upper leg so great that in the case of his having to eject his knees are in danger of striking the wind-screen arch. While if he is small he must still be able to reach and operate all the levers, switches and other controls which a fast jet aeroplane cockpit contains—and this too when tightly strapped in, unable to move his shoulders away from the seat back.

Many of the racially Chinese Singaporeans are small, compact, wiry men, the sort who make devastatingly good Badminton players. Very sensibly it occurred to MID, before despatching them to UK for pilot training, to check whether some of the shorter of their selected potential pilots would be long enough in the arm and leg to fly the Hunter. We had a squadron of Hunters at RAF Tengah, in the north of the island so when Tengah heard of this concern they, in helpful mode, said to the Singaporeans, "Send your guys over here, we will get our station doctor to strap them in a Hunter cockpit and go over them with a tape measure to check that they will be OK." Having got the green light from Tengah, they duly departed for UK.

What the Hunter boys at Tengah had unfortunately overlooked was that the trainers on which the Singaporeans would start their initial pilot training did not have the same cockpit dimensions as the Hunter. At that time initial flying training in the RAF was on the Jet Provost, a delightful aeroplane to fly, docile enough for students, with excellent all-round visibility and, as I had discovered at Boscombe Down, a comfortable, unusually roomy cockpit. Alas, too roomy for some of the Singaporean students. They would indeed have been able to fly the Hunter, had they progressed that far, but once they arrived at their Initial Flying Training School in England it was found that they just couldn't reach some of the essential items in the cockpit of the Jet Provost. The Singaporean Ministry of Defence was extremely nice about it. Having had to pay for the return trip to UK for some of their chaps to no good purpose they still said, "Well, mistakes will happen, and we realise you were just trying to be helpful."

Among the other units at Tengah at the time was a Lightning unit—No 74 Squadron, the well-known Tiger Squadron. Their squadron crest, painted on their aeroplanes, was of a full-face snarling tiger, flanked by black and yellow stripes and their flying suits and helmets were similarly emblazoned. Squadron pride is a good thing but if carried to excess can become offensive and highly irritating to others. Back at Waterbeach we on 63 had sometimes found tiresome the "Albert Ball Syndrome" of 56. This seemed to have happened but rather more so at Tengah where 74 had started to regard themselves as a bit too special and no longer subject to the rules which applied to the rest of the station. If this was so they had reckoned without the Station Commander. Group Captain Phil Largesson was a tough man, a tall, athletic South African who had been brought up on the veld where had had learned to crack an enormous stock-whip. One day the Group Captain telephoned the 74 Squadron Commander. "Ah, Ken, I'd like to have a word with your Squadron pilots tomorrow. Would you have them assembled in your crew-room at nine o'clock, please." At one minute past nine the door crashed open, Group Captain Largesson strode into the room and straight up to the dais at the front. He turned round and without a word lashed his massive whip straight down the centre of the room. Crack! "Just to show you buggers who's the boss around here!" He marched out without another word. 74 got the message.

Having joined the High Commission I was still living in the Officers' Mess at Changi, twelve miles out of the city on the eastern tip of the island. The question arose of how I was to get to work in the city centre. I consulted the Admin. people at HQ FEAF and their answer was simple. I would arrange for a taxi to take me to and fro each day and send in my expenses at the end of the month. In general RAF accounts staff do a fine job and they are, after all, looking after the tax-payers money, but they have been known to be a bit hair-splitting and even parsimonious when it come to paying out on expenses. Someone tipped me off on an even better scheme. I suggested that FEAF themselves should make the arrangements to book the taxi and send it round to pick me up. Would this not be administratively much simpler? Greatly to my surprise they agreed and I enjoyed a few weeks of minor luxury. Finishing breakfast I would stroll down the Mess steps to find my car awaiting me, to settle myself in the back with the Straits Times and to be wafted effortlessly into the city.

One morning a small headline half way down the front page of the Straits Times caught my eye. RAF Jet Buzzes Tower Bridge. I really do claim that I had guessed the name of the pilot before I read the short article. I heard the full story some years later back in UK. The RAF came into existence in 1918 on 1st April, (how appropriate, some say) and so 1968 was our fiftieth birthday. Clearly, at least back in UK, this should have been grounds for celebrations, parades, fly-pasts and the like. But the Air Force was going through one of its periodic money-saving, parsimonious, penny pinching, humourless phases. No parades, no fly-pasts, no nothing. A certain Hunter pilot stationed in East Anglia took a different view that was "Well if no-one else is going to celebrate once in half a century—I am!" He broke away from the training exercise he was meant to be on, dived down over central London and flew through Tower Bridge, underneath the upper footbridge. It is said that the various air marshals looking out of their office windows in Main Building across the Thames were startled to see one of their Hunters flash past—below eye level. It was Alan Pollock—who else!

Part of the interest of working in the centre of Singapore city was to be away from the usual military trappings and surrounded by local sights and the civilian population. While working at the British High Commission on Collier Quay, my lunch breaks were marvellously redolent of the old colonial ways. Colonel Sharland invariably had someone to meet or other business to attend to. So I came out of Maritime Building, walked down past the skyscraper of the Bank of China building and across the footbridge over the Singapore River. Beside it, under the casuarina trees there was always a group of young men playing a simple looking but very skilful game which consisted of kicking to each other around a circle a small, light wicker-work ball, larger than a cricket ball but much smaller than a football. They could keep it airborne for minutes on end with deft flicks from their bare feet or the occasional nudge from shoulder or elbow.

Passing the Victoria Memorial Theatre and the statue of Stamford Raffles I crossed the road and went into the Singapore Cricket Club, white and cool with rush mats on stone floors and with elegant, slow turning ceiling fans. The dining room faced out across the Padang, the cricket ground which stands at the heart of the city, with beyond it the Parliament building and St. Andrew's Cathedral. Many varieties of curry with a lager and lime made up lunch and you signed a chit for "one tiffin." You felt that Somerset Maugham might come round the corner at any minute.

Originally on arrival in Singapore I had bought an Austin Healey Sprite, but it had proved cramped and uncomfortable and had turned out to have a very rust-corroded chassis. I had sold it and acquired from a friend, who was an officer in the Gurkha Engineers, a dark green— British Racing Green—MGA. In that warm, sunny climate the fact that the hood was never waterproof was not a problem as its main purpose was to provide protection from the mid-day sun.

Having acquired a reliable car I planned to use a long weekend to see something of Malaya. With a girl friend I set off one Friday in the MGA across the causeway into Johore Bahru. Once through the city and out into the Malayan countryside the contrast we found there with crowded, bustling Singapore was marvellous.

The roads wound their way among the endless palms and other greenery and were almost deserted except for the occasional slow moving bullock cart. Stretches of jungle were interrupted by paddy fields and rubber plantations. The villages were of wooden huts roofed with woven palm thatch or corrugated iron. We stopped and bought bottles of iced mineral water or lemonade and bargained for batik or big coolie-type straw hats. The sun beamed down out of the brilliant blue sky, chickens pecked around our feet and pie-dogs lazily wagged their tails. The villagers stopped whatever they were doing to watch the car and the grinning children always waved. One might have stepped back a hundred years. We drove gently up towards the west coast where we had arranged to stop for the night in the government rest-house in Malacca.

After dinner we walked along the seafront and among the thriving evening life of the town, the satay and other food stalls, the hardware and bicycle repair shops, and the many groups of cheerful, noisy children. There was little visible interest in tourists. As the last of the brief twilight faded and the stars came out we were among the local community getting on with its own way of life after the heat of the day had abated. It was a magical evening. The next day we wandered on through the plantations and patches of jungle, stopping beside slow moving rivers and listening to the soft, rustling sounds of the insects and the breezes in the grass and the trees. We stopped for a second night at Segamat, enjoyed another lazy day among the jungles and finally on the Sunday evening drove back across the causeway and into bustling, go-getting Singapore.

When I joined the High Commission our offices were at the top of Maritime Building. We could hear constantly the endless thump-clang of pile drivers laying ever more foundations for the growing city. Maritime Building was far from ideal for the High Commission. We were very cramped up on the sixth floor and it was hardly dignified to greet visiting Government Ministers dodging traffic and pedestrians on the edge of the busy street, pushing through the foyer and then conducting them up in the ancient crowded lift. It was decided that we were to move out to spacious, comfortable first- floor offices, part of the Tanglin estate no longer needed by the shrinking Headquarters of Far East Land Forces. We gave up a weekend to shifting furniture, filing cabinets and the rest and although our new home was less colourful it was in every way a move for the better.

My travelling constantly in from Changi was also clearly not a good arrangement, and now that I was on the staff of the High Commission I was entitled to diplomatic allowances, not just military ones. The obvious answer was a flat, and I found just the thing in Leony Hill Road, just a few minutes from Tanglin. I also joined the HQ Far East Land Forces Officers' mess at Tanglin and so had the chance for the first time of getting to know the army socially. At first nothing seemed very different from the many RAF messes to which I had belonged over the years, partly because in Singapore we all wore khaki tropical uniforms only differing in our rank badges—and hats. The army prides itself in its multiplicity of different regimental and corps uniforms, especially hats. My RAF "flat hat" (I have always hated berets) stood out no more that the assorted red, black, green and pale blue (Army Air Corps) berets, forage caps, Glengarrys, Tam o' Shanters and the rest. I was often introduced to others as Major Boult and then quite as an after-thought, "Oh no, you're not really a major are you, something much the same though!" But as I got to know many army friends in the mess, on water-skiing and other outings, and in their houses I found that I had in fact entered another world.

On paper the services are so similar. The equivalent ranks are well-known, the divisions between officers, non-commissioned officers, (NCOs) and other ranks are the same even if given different names, such as the Navy's ward-room and lower deck. I had previously only known the army from the outside and I had always seen them as more formal in their relationships, more rigidly and rather coldly hierarchical, stiffer. Getting to know them better, I found that nothing could have been further from the truth. Unlike the RAF they made a clear and happy distinction between being, as it were, on parade and when they were off duty. In the RAF we never seemed to be quite at ease with how to address other officers of slightly different rank. Plainly if you were driving the water-ski boat it sounded pretty daft to call to the skier in the water getting ready to start, "Come on, for goodness sake get yourself organised—sir." The repeated use of "sir" did not feel comfortable but on the other hand first names often seemed over familiar.

I found that in the army, when Major Smith entered the office of Lieutenant Colonel Brown he would brace himself rigidly to attention and throw up a salute that could have passed muster on Trooping the Colour. "Good Morning, Colonel." An hour later in the mess he would approach the same colonel with, "Morning, Sam, how are you? What did you think of Sally's party last night?" It seemed to me that because when on duty the army's hierarchy of seniority was made so clear cut and formal it meant that when off duty everyone was much more relaxed. As I became accustomed to living in the army Officers' Mess at Tanglin the term "brother officers" took on a real meaning which I began to realise I had never felt in the RAF.

I began to see too that another contrast between the army and the RAF was the very different set of expectations that the two services had of the role of junior officers. For example on both the flying squadrons where I had served it embarrassed me now to remember how little real interest I, and I suspect most of us pilots, took in our ground-crew airmen. If you happened to run a sports team you got to know them but apart from that I doubt if any of the pilots could even have given names to more than a handful of them. The army, by contrast, made no bones about it. The first and over-riding responsibility of junior officers was the command or leadership, and hence the welfare, training and general development of their men.

We aircrew could quote the excuse that our main contribution was our technical knowledge of aircraft operations and our flying skills, which we had to maintain by getting sufficient flying hours each month. This was true, but working with the army forced me to see at once the wider picture of what should have been expected of us. I had to conclude that in fact we had had plenty of time on the ground to undertake these wider and more fundamental duties as officers. For example at Gan, I now realised, I had in fact had endless opportunities to take a closer interest in the welfare of our airmen but had not done so. The main reasons I believe were that these obligations had never been explicitly spelled out and that at the start of our careers we had been given virtually no training in this area. All this provided much to reflect on.

The army also had an attractive way of addressing or referring to very senior officers by using not sir, but by combining rank and first name. General Sir Michael Carver- my old friend from the Shrewsbury School CCF inspection!—when he was not busy being CINCFE— Commander-in-Chief Far East, was an enthusiastic dinghy sailor. He was known around the sailing club and around the island generally as "General Mike." The different atmosphere in the army officers' messes and the more relaxed, genial relationships between the most senior and junior officers was noticeable. It did not really strike me while I was with the army in Singapore, but it did so most forcibly when I got back to UK and back again among my own service. I can best describe it by recalling how perfectly adequate and satisfactory black and white TV seemed to us in the days when we knew nothing else. But one only had to have the briefest glimpse of colour TV to realise suddenly what one had been missing and how inadequate the old version was. Moving back into my familiar surroundings of the RAF was like going back to black and white TV after having seen the alternative.

Although I had driven briefly up into Malaya a friend of mine at Tanglin, an infantry major, pointed out that I had, of course, seen nothing of the actual jungle or of what it was like to trek through it right away from the roads and civilisation. Mike, an experienced jungle soldier, determined to rectify this. He collected three other willing volunteers and arranged for us to spend a weekend out in the Ulu—the jungle. We drew proper kit—bush shirts, trousers and hats, tight, lace up, hopefully leech-proof boots, lightweight sleeping bags, water bottles and rucksacks and heavy jungle knives. We set off one Friday afternoon from Tanglin by Landrover, up the Bukit Timah Road, over the causeway, into Malaya and out to the Jungle Training School, at Ulu Hittam, not far beyond Johore Bahru. The school, with its rows of neat wooden huts and its parade ground outlined with whitewashed stones, stood in a valley, surrounded by low, densely wooded hills. Beyond the school the road became a track, winding up a narrowing valley, with the trees meeting overhead and alongside a stream which gushed down through a series of pools and over small waterfalls. Eventually we stopped and piled out. From here we were on foot. Mike and the driver pored over a large-scale map and agreed on a point some miles away and in another valley where we would be picked up on the Sunday evening.

We picked up our packs, left the road and Mike led the way up a faintly visible path among the trees. He knew this area well and in half an hour we had reached a level patch beside the stream where there was already the remains of a basha—a simple jungle shelter. To sleep comfortably in the jungle, he explained, only two things were needed. Firstly a roof, because it was sure to rain at some time during the night, and secondly some way to keep well up off the jungle floor. A basha was built by first cutting down four strong, straight tree trunks, about three inches in diameter, sharpening their ends and erecting them to form the corners of the shelter. Smaller poles were lashed to them horizontally, two feet from the ground, and on these a floor could be laid. A few more poles formed the framework for the roof which was covered with large, strong banana leaves. As jungle novices we felt justified in using the remains of an old basha to give us a head start and in not much more than half an hour we had our shelter, and dinner was cooking over a fire between some carefully arranged stones.

As always in the tropics the dark came quickly and we were soon relaxing in our sleeping bags listening to the jungle sounds as all the nocturnal creatures came to life. Mike shone his torch down for us to look over the edge of our platform and to show us why it was so important to be up off the jungle floor. The ground beneath us was alive—simply crawling with small beetles, spiders, ants, centipedes and a host of others going about their affairs. They would have been unwelcome company in our sleeping bags.

We awoke with the dawn and spent a not too energetic day trekking over the first ridge and into another similar valley. This particular piece of jungle was much less wet than I had expected and unless the gradient was steep walking was not difficult. One would have needed many years to learn to recognise the great variety of trees and shrubs and the wonderful collection of butterflies and other insects. We found a couple of scorpions. There were many varieties of ants, some of the ant-hills waist or shoulder high. We only saw one snake, a small brilliant green tree snake draped cross the path we were following. However, Mike explained that one of the most dangerous hazards in jungles in this part of the world were hornets. As he put it "Hornets are total fascists. Unlike most jungle animals, they don't get out of your way, you get out of their way." In fact during the war it was said that if you found there was a Japanese patrol to the left and a hornets' nest to the right—if you had any sense you went to the left!

What mainly impressed me was the incredibly detailed accuracy of our maps. Each small hillock and ridge, each depression and side valley, each change in gradient or bend in a stream was faithfully shown, the printed contour lines exactly mimicking the ground. It was possible constantly to pinpoint our position to within a few yards. We spent another comfortable night and on Sunday afternoon crossed a final ridge and walked down into the valley were we expected to find a road and our Landrover. Sure enough a few minutes before the agreed time we could hear it coming up the hill. We had arrived at the rendezvous exactly as planned. Living and I suppose fighting in the jungle was clearly a matter of knowledge, full and comprehensive training, and careful planning. The weekend had provided a most interesting introduction to a special branch of infantry soldiering.

Towards the end of my time in Singapore the Republic celebrated the 150th anniversary of the founding of the colony by Stamford Raffles. One of the most attractive aspects of life in Singapore, especially for those of us who had close and continuous dealings with Singaporeans, was the complete absence of any signs of anti-colonialism. The city theatre was still the Victoria Memorial Theatre and the statue of Raffles still stood in front of it beside the Singapore River. When I commented on this to a Singaporean friend, he said, "But why not? It's all part of our history. Why would we want to sweep it away?" Modern Singapore is a notably and justifiably self-confident society. I suspect that it is only those with a massive inferiority complex who need to keep telling to themselves and others how little they owe to historical events or to outsiders. As ethnic questions and the problems of a multi-cultural society have become more marked in Britain I have often wondered how Singapore retained, as far as I could see, such harmony between its races.

The centrepiece of the celebrations for the anniversary was a dazzling parade and spectacle on the Padang, the cricket ground which forms the central platz or plaza of the city. Someone said to me when I was leaving Singapore, "Any country where the centre of the capital city is a cricket ground can't be too bad." Although there were many smart military elements in the parade and the display it was mainly memorable for the large number of children's teams from many different schools—of dancers, acrobats and the like. They made up swirling masses of little white-clad figures with brilliantly coloured flowers and flags, rows and columns and circles and pyramids of them, greeted by the repeated laughter and loud applause from the watching crowds. I watched the display with a group of friends from the balcony of the Cricket Club. It was a happy and memorable way to celebrate the anniversary of the founding of the Republic.

Someone had suggested that, during the week's celebrations, there should be a display by the massed bands of all the five Commonwealth forces present on the island. It was planned that the Singapore Guards' Band, Australian and New Zealand Regimental Bands, a Malayan Army Band and the Band of The Far East Air Force (RAF) would march and counter-march all under one baton. The Singaporeans were making rapid strides to set up their own armed forces to fill the vacuum which would be left by Britain's precipitous withdrawal from East of Suez, but they would be the first to admit that their recently recruited young officers' organisational skills sometimes failed to keep up with the demands of the situation. As the official guests arrived for the Massed Bands' Display their names had to be found on the seating plan and the guests shown to their seats. The Air Commander arrived. Let us call him Smith. "Ah, Smith, Smith...Name has to be here somewhere … . Please to be waiting one moment, please …" Mutter, mutter. "One short moment, please, what you say name was? …" The Air Commander decided to stand on his dignity, announcing curtly that if his seat were not found immediately he would leave. His Personal Staff Officer told me later that he spent most of the following morning persuading the Air Commander not to write a personal letter of complaint to the Singaporean Minister of Defence.

The Singaporeans had invited as their guest of honour for the week Her Royal Highness Princess Alexandra, accompanied by her husband, Mr Angus Ogilvie. For one evening the Singaporeans had agreed to the British expatriates entertaining the visitors in the pleasant setting of the Singapore Turf Club. Once again the High Commission, and in particular the colonel and I, were much involved in the organisation. On this occasion I was responsible for greeting the Army Commander, General Sir Peter Hunt, introducing him to a few members of the High Commission, seeing that he had a drink and was generally looked after. I was also taking my own guest to the party, a captain in the Women's Royal Army Corps. Lynn and I arrived early, found drinks and some friends of ours and started to enjoy the evening. It seemed no more than a couple of minutes later when someone tapped me on the shoulder and said, "Hey. Weren't you meant to be meeting General Peter? He's been here quite some time you know." Luckily he was a tall man and I quickly spotted his tall figure and white hair where he was already surrounded by a circle of friends. I pushed through the throng and started to mumble my apologies for not meeting him on his arrival. These he brushed aside. "Hello, Bill, how nice to see you. By the way, have you met Mr and Mrs … . Now haven't you got a girl-friend with you this evening? You mustn't neglect her you know. Go and find her and bring her to join us." He, the general, seemed only concerned to entertain me. There are two kinds of senior officer.

On another evening Princess Alexandra and Mr Ogilvie were to dine with the Naval Commander, the Admiral, at Admiralty House. It is perhaps ironical that the naval title for the young officer on the personal staff of an Admiral, the naval equivalent of an ADC, is the Flag Lieutenant, or "Flags." It was one of the Flag Lieutenant's jobs to arrange that as HRH arrived at the Admiral's residence the royal standard was "broken" from the top of the flagpole. Before a flag is broken from the masthead it is first carefully rolled up into a tight ball, secured by looping the flag-halyard round it and hoisting it into position. Then at the appropriate moment a sharp tug on the halyard releases the flag which flutters proudly out for all to see. Unfortunately the Flag Lieutenant had had an extremely busy day with many other details to attend to. The flag was hoisted to the masthead and secured, the Admiral and his lady stood ready to receive and greet their Royal guest. At one minute to seven the gleaming black Rolls Royce turned in to the gates of Admiralty House and glided up the drive. Her Royal Highness alighted and from the masthead broke—the Singaporean national ensign. Flags buried his face in his hands and muttered, "Oh, ****, wrong flag." The Admiral was not amused. Flags was on the very next aeroplane back to England.

One of the more enjoyable occasions in the British High Commission calendar was the annual investiture. The High Commissioner, Sir Arthur de la Mare, acting on behalf of Her Majesty, was to present orders and decorations to locally stationed British servicemen and residents of Singapore in a colourful and dignified ceremony in the garden of the Residence. There were the usual British trappings of the military band, a red carpet across the lawn and a marquee dispensing tea, sandwiches and dainty cakes on the best china. It all reminded me of a well-run school prize giving with the guests, the families of those who were to receive awards and decorations, seated expectantly on rows of chairs across the lawn.

As usual much of the detailed organisation of the day fell to Colonel Geoffrey. In order to balance up the service representation we had recruited to share the chores with me an army major and a naval lieutenant commander. My job was to read out, in best toast-master manner, the decoration to be presented and the rank and name of the recipient. Some of the recipients were likely to be somewhat over-awed by the occasion and would need gently shepherding to get them up to the High Commissioner at the right moment. To achieve this the lieutenant commander had the recipients marshalled, in order, at the far end of the red carpet. When I announced their name, he despatched them, if necessary with a gentle shove, down the red carpet. Rather like launching a torpedo, as he put it. The decorations were laid out in the order in which they were to be presented on a table beside where the High Commissioner would stand. The major would pick up the decoration and present it, on a small red cushion, to Sir Arthur so that he could pick it up and pin it on the recipient's chest, or lower it over his head as appropriate. When all was ready and all the guests were seated, Sir Arthur would emerge from the Residence, walk across the verandah and down a short flight of stone steps.

The first potential problem Col. Geoffrey had foreseen and it was easily overcome. It arose because one of the honours to be presented—the Order of the British Empire—the OBE—involved slipping the ribbon bearing the decoration over the recipient's head so that it rested like a necklace. The recipient was a Merchant Navy Commodore who would, of course, be wearing his naval "flat hat" and no doubt standing smartly and stiffly to attention. We had discovered that the Commodore was a very tall man, while the High Commissioner was a short man. The question was—would Sir Arthur be able to reach?

On this occasion the OBE was the senior award to be presented and so would be presented first. The stone steps were our salvation. Col. Geoffrey carefully briefed Sir Arthur that he should initially stop, standing on the lowest step. The few extra inches made all the difference and he was able to reach over the Commodore's hat without difficulty.

But fate still lay in wait. I had, of course, prepared for my part by carefully reading through the list of names to check if there was any which might prove difficult to pronounce and to see what other pitfalls might be there. No ex-ADC would fail to do so. I would be reading out the names in full and on my list the Commodore's name was typed as "Joe" Lines. Surely this was a mistake by some hasty typist, should it not have been Joseph. There were still a few minutes in hand so I hurried to find the Commodore. "Excuse me, Sir ..." No, there was no mistake, he said, his name actually was Joe Lines, it was good of me to check.

Those who knew London long ago will remember the name "Jo Lyons." Originally in the 1930's this well-known chain of popular, economical and homely cafes were called Lyons Corner Houses. After the war their name had been modernised to "Jo Lyons" and the familiar name seemed to slip so easily off the tongue ... .

All the guests were seated, the band came to the end of God Save the Queen, the High Commissioner arrived at the steps, the ceremony was ready to begin. I cleared my throat and announced loudly and confidently, "Officer of the Most Excellent Order of the British Empire, Commodore Joe Lyons." If looks could have killed. After the ceremony I slunk away and hid behind the tea tent. I couldn't even face the idea of finding him to stammer out an apology. I don't think I could have kept a straight face if I had. If Commodore Lines (he probably retired as an admiral) ever reads this I hope he will accept my very sincere apologies.

My two-and-a-half years in South East Asia were drawing to a close. I sadly sold the MGA and had a final round of buying Noritake china, cutlery, a super hi-fi set and started packing. Everyone who was leaving Singapore soon went to visit Corporal Jones. Cpl. Jones ran the army unit concerned with providing and then dispatching the stout wooden packing cases for the bulk of your kit which would come home by sea. A large, imposing figure, a true professional, Cpl. Jones was renowned across the island as a man who was completely on top of his job. You were sat down and quizzed in considerable detail about the kit you were planning to take home to UK. Where did you want the cases delivered, were you sure you could yourself nail them up properly, when could they be collected, what address in UK were they to be sent to. It sounds straight-forward, in principle it was, but to those of us who have enjoyed the marvels of so much modern air travel—breakfast in London, dinner in Los Angeles, luggage in Moscow—it was a great weight off one's mind to hand over all the details to Cpl. Jones knowing that one need think no more about them.

But in my flat the vultures gathered. This too was a time-honoured routine for those "tour-ex" and packing to depart for UK. As you emptied your cupboards and old, half forgotten treasures appeared "friends" dropped in, sat around and the chorus started. "You're not bothering to take that home are you? It's not worth the bother of packing it. Can't I look after it for you?" Flip-flops, snorkelling masks, beach gear and sun cream were easy game. Then some of your favourite tropical shirts...and wooden elephants ... and tins of Tiger beer and anything else your visitors took a fancy to. It was really quite hard to argue the case that you would have much use for four pairs of swimming trunks in February in Scotland (my next posting) but if you didn't watch it like a hawk pieces of Noritake china, the camphor-wood stools, the Gurkha kukri and other such well-loved souvenirs would start disappearing too.

I started to write down a list of all the good friends I had on the Island whom I should invite to a party to say goodbye. One of the real perks I had enjoyed during my 18 months at the High Commission was my flat. It was a much more personal place to entertain than the officers' mess and clearly this must be the venue. But it was soon clear that the guest list was rapidly outgrowing the available space. The answer was to have two parties. The first was a sedate and I hope dignified affair for the High Commissioner, Lady de la Mare, Colonel Sharland and Marjorie and the considerable number of fairly senior people whom I had got to know through my work including a number of Singaporeans most of whom I was genuinely sorry to say goodbye to.

The second party was for the chaps, male and female. I don't remember a great deal about it except towards the end when only about eight of us remained, perching on the balcony and watching the lights of Singapore city, still finishing off the Tiger beer, dancing bare-foot to a tape of the current hits, or just sitting around talking about nothing in particular—Lynn Hancock, Maggie Tyler and a small crowd of mainly water skiing friends. It was the best sort of party, all of us by then old friends, no-one trying to create an impression, talking shop or about other friends, about recent holiday trips around South East Asia or about others being planned, about what we might do when we eventually met up again in UK. They were the hard core of what had been the best circle of service friends, of all three services, that I ever had.

On my last evening in Singapore I took a girl-friend out to dinner at the Singapore Lady, a floating restaurant in an ornate houseboat in the harbour, decorated with dragons, coloured lanterns and with the gentle scent of joss-sticks wafting across the tables. The evening was still warm, but a welcome relief after the heat of the day. We found a sampan water taxi, Maggie tottered on board coping well with high heels and a tight skirt. We motored across the dark, ever moving water, rocking and swaying in the wash of countless other sampans moving hither and thither about the harbour, the lights of the waterfront and of the anchored shipping, a kaleidoscope of colour. From our restaurant table we looked across the harbour to the Singapore city skyline, from the old green-tiled roofs of the warehouses around the Telok Ayer Basin and behind them to the glittering and ever growing forest of skyscrapers. It was like the stage backdrop of the play we had been enjoying, those two hard-working, fascinating, colourful, sun-filled years. The next day I boarded the VC 10 at Changi and headed for England, or in fact Scotland.

In those days of the early 1970s as each of us in turn came to the end of our tour of duty in South East Asia and came back, probably with nostalgic regrets, to UK, I doubt if it ever occurred to us that we represented the final rear-guard of the British "Far East" Empire. Not many months ahead, as the British garrisons, warships and aeroplanes departed, Singapore would assume responsibility for its own defence, the VC10 trooping flights would end, Gan would be handed back to the Maldivians and Britain's influence would have been withdrawn from East of Suez. I had been lucky to get there just in time and to have been able to enjoy a full tour in the colour and warmth of the tropics and to have seen a glimpse of that fascinating part of the world.

# Headquarters,
# Air Officer, Scotland
## &
# Northern Ireland

### R A F Pitreavie Castle

I ARRIVED BACK in UK in February 1970 in the depths of winter. While preparing to leave Singapore I had investigated the possibility of bringing home my MGA. The Navy ran a scheme of offering deck space on an aircraft carrier if one was due to come back to UK. But the deal was that if there was any whiff of their needing during the passage the deck to do any flying, cars would be unceremoniously bulldozed overboard without compensation. Anyway on reflection it was not a sensible idea. The MGA, with its tatty hood and air conditioning (draughts) was an ideal car in the tropics, it would not have been sensible in the Scottish winter. Looking at car prices in the UK I decided that my sports-car days were over and so bought an undistinguished but very economical Hillman Imp and in it set off for Scotland.

My new posting was to the headquarters of the Air Officer, Scotland and Northern Ireland—AOSNI. This was located in Pitreavie Castle, on the northern edge of the old Scottish town of Dunfermline in Fife. My first mistake was to refer to Fifeshire. It was promptly explained to me by a local Scot that it was "the Kingdom of Fife." The tall old house, Pitreavie Castle, stood on rising ground on the northern side of the Firth of Forth and from the gardens we could see both bridges, the world famous railway bridge and the graceful modern road bridge. Pitreavie housed both AOSNI and the Northern Rescue Co-ordination Centre. Down the road in the Naval Base of Rosyth was our naval equivalent, FOSNI—Flag Officer, Scotland and Northern Ireland. While across the Forth on the way to Edinburgh was the headquarters of the army in Scotland where, I later discovered, the rather autocratic General Henry *****, was known to his staff as Henry the Ninth.

The living-in officers' quarters and the dining room were in single storey wooden huts and all the headquarters offices were in the castle itself. Pitreavie Castle, the house, was of interest. Built of sombre, grey granite, it had tall narrow windows and the rooms were furnished with heavy furniture and dark wooden panelling. There were narrow corridors and steep staircases. Not surprisingly it was said to be haunted.

Stories were told of the cleaning ladies who would on no account go into the castle after dark and who were quite sure that they had actually seen the Green Lady. I am not a psychic sort of person and I like to keep it that way. My office happened to be right at the top of the castle under the eaves, so I made quite sure that I had no occasion either to go into the castle after dark.

When I arrived I discovered that AOSNI was Air Vice-Marshal Desmond Hughes, whom I knew well as the father of the inimitable Paddy Hughes, both old friends from many splendid skiing holidays in Zermatt. Most unfortunately AVM Hughes was leaving on posting that very week and I did not even have a chance to speak to him.

In every way Pitreavie was a marked contrast to my last two-and-a-half years in Gan and Singapore. The first disappointment was the job—Regional Liaison Officer to AOSNI for Civil Defence. It was foreseen that in the event of nuclear war regions of Britain would have to operate independently from central government. I was equipped with an old Air Force blue Morris Minor van, the distinctive half-timbered variety, and a major part of my job was to motor about Scotland checking on disused airfields to see which were actually still usable, at least for light communication aircraft, and which were out even for them, perhaps because a farmer had built a grain silo on the old runway. My predecessor had been on his last tour before retiring, was interested in acquiring antiques and was quite happy to motor gently about Scotland rummaging round second-hand furniture shops and enjoying the scenery. For a couple of months I drove around Scotland, reminding myself what a beautiful country it is and in particular exploring wild, remote parts of the west coast. Had I too been shortly to retire I could have quite enjoyed such an unstressed existence, but it soon palled and I was quite sure that I should be contributing something more worthwhile to the RAF. I hated the prospect of the months that stretched ahead in this backwater. AVM Hughes' successor did nothing at all to provide reassurance. It quickly became apparent that he had as little interest in what I was doing as I did.

I discovered one consolation. Many years previously I had enjoyed the occasional visit to the Rothiemurchus Hut. This simple but delightful refuge was three miles from the ski road near Loch Morlich on the northern edge of the Cairngorm Mountains, the largest upland wilderness in Britain. We had been based there for the memorable mountain survival course when I had been on 63 Squadron. As it was a tri-service outfit the management committee was made up of officers of all three services and I got myself the job of being the RAF member.

The timing was fortuitous. For many years there had been a large sailors' hostel in Edinburgh near the Leith docks and it was realised that this had now outlasted its usefulness. Well-educated modern sailors mostly owning their own transport and with circles of friends around their home ports no longer needed a sheltering hostel maternally offering a meal and a bed and so the Leith hostel was to be wound up and sold. This would release a sizeable sum of money which could be put to new uses. One course could have been to split the sum three ways among the three services in Scotland. However it was not often that a sum of this size became available and so a more imaginative plan was to use it for some big single venture that would be of benefit to all three services.

Rothiemurchus Forest is a few miles out of Aviemore, one of the most popular holiday venues in Scotland offering sailing on Loch Morlich, skiing, walking and mountaineering in the Cairngorm mountains, all among the most beautiful scenery of pine forest, heather moor, open, wind-swept tops and steep crags. Ben Macdhui, the highest peak in the Cairngorms is second only to Nevis as the highest mountain in Britain and is closely followed by Braeriach and Cairn Toul as the third and fourth highest. Incidentally the peak of Ben Macdhui is also said to be haunted and many respected, hard-headed mountaineers believe that they have seen and have recounted in detail their encounter with the Great Grey Man. Funny old place, Scotland.

FOSNI, AOSNI and Henry the Ninth—the admiral, the air marshal and the general—or more probably their staffs, took council and decided to build near the old Rothiemurchus Hut a modern, fully-equipped mountain Lodge. The planned lodge would be available for training or recreational expeditions and when not wanted by service units themselves could be booked for self-catering holidays by service families. It was to have two floors, with corridors of four-berth cabins, showers etc and on each floor two separate kitchen units. In this way four quite independent parties could be accommodated without their getting in each other's way.

The land was owned by a Major Grant, who only charged the services a peppercorn rent but was a stickler for environmental protection. The army's Headquarters, Northern Area, at Perth was to manage the surveying of the site, the detailed planning and the building of the Lodge, and I enjoyed many interesting days out with my army and Navy colleagues, driving up to Rothiemurchus and hiking around the area. We armed ourselves with sandwiches and flasks, and with the architect and the civil engineers worked out exactly where the Lodge could best be sited so that its roof line would not break the sky line and it would merge into the dark hillside behind it. Some years later with friends I enjoyed a Christmas holiday in the Lodge, and it was good to know that I had played some small part in its inception.

In most years once the snow is established in the Cairngorms the skiing season lasts well into the spring and I spent many weekends in and around Aviemore. I often dropped in to see Rudi Prochaska in his flourishing shop in Kingussie. He and Barbara now had a couple of little daughters and I occasionally stayed with them and baby-sat while their parents went out. One weekend I drove up to Aviemore with a friend from Pitreavie, Colin Hind, on the Friday night. In the cottage where we were enjoying bed and breakfast we awoke on the Saturday morning to find to our dismay thick fog. You could not see across the road. In spite of this we decided rather than head lamely back to Pitreavie we would drive up the ski road to see, without much hope, what the weather was like up the hill. Just below the car park we broke out of the cloud into the most glorious sunshine and a completely clear, windless day. The whole of the Spey valley below us was filled with white, glistening cloud like a sea, while the Cairngorm mountains around us and the more distant Grampians across to the north of Strath Spey glowed and shone in the spring sunshine. Just a few other brave souls had come up the hill too and so the few dozen of us had the hills to ourselves. It was one of the best days skiing I ever had.

During the summer the Commonwealth Games were to be held in the Meadowbank Stadium in Edinburgh. The Games were to be opened by the Duke of Edinburgh and it was planned that as HRH arrived in the Stadium he would be greeted by a flypast of nine Lightnings from RAF Leuchars, just up the coast near St Andrews. The interesting question for such events, probably not even appreciated by most of the spectators, is that, as aeroplanes cannot easily gain or lose speed to adjust their timing, how is it arranged that flypasts arrive on time? The management of the flypast was clearly going to be an interesting project more suited to fighter types than to the pre-dominantly Coastal people at Pitreavie and so I took it on and went up to Leuchars to visit Wing Commander Hank Martin, the OC Ops. He explained his plan for the sortie and the limitations he would be bound by. The formation would fly a four-minute oval "race-track" down at the eastern end of the Firth of Forth off Dunbar, near the Bass Rock. Each time they came round on to a westerly heading they would be five minutes flying time from the stadium. Thus on each circuit they could straighten out for Edinburgh or could go round another four-minute circuit. But they could only make a limited number of circuits before the Lightnings, with their high fuel consumption at low level, would be out of fuel.

I went and explained this to the army who were managing the Duke's reception in the stadium. They had to give us a "go/no-go" decision five minutes before the Duke's arrival and if it was no-go they could ask for up to a couple of four-minute delays. In fact the timing of this sort of event is not actually difficult because people such as the Duke of Edinburgh understand full well what has to go on behind the scenes and are quite accustomed to being shepherded along to keep up with the clock. It is the little tin gods who like to throw their weight about and to behave awkwardly who are a menace. On the day I sat in the Control Tower at RAF Turnhouse, linked by telephone to the army in the stadium and in radio contact with Hank, leading the Lightnings. It went pretty well like clockwork. We heard afterwards that as HRH stepped on to the dais in the stadium the flypast was less than three seconds late.

Pitreavie being near the water I was able to spend summer evenings and weekends sailing. On the south side of the Forth, almost underneath the Forth Road Bridge, is the naval base of Port Edgar and here the Navy maintained a small fleet of Bosun sailing dinghies. The Firth is strongly tidal with numerous back eddies and calm patches among the mud and sand banks along its margins so that local knowledge is a great advantage. One evening the race was from Port Edgar to a mark two miles up the Firth to the west and back to a finishing line almost under the bridge. The fleet hugged the south shore and kept out of the tide as we beat slowly against the west wind up to the windward turning mark. I was apparently the only helmsman who had noticed that while we near the bank were in almost slack water, out in mid-stream the ebb tide was running strongly to the east. As we rounded the mark all the other boats set off straight down the Forth back the way we had come. I decided to head due north out into mid stream. We were suddenly out of the shallows and into the tide, there was a clear line on the water surface marking its edge, and we were at once being swept down on our way at high speed. Soon my main concern was to get out of the tide again before we were swept away under the bridges. We managed to do so and crossed the line about ten minutes ahead of the next boat. I think it is the only sailing race I ever won and it was nice to do it so convincingly.

However for my job back at Pitreavie I could generate no enthusiasm at all, time hung heavily and the months passed slowly. In April 1971 a new Group Captain arrived on the staff of AOSNI. He was sociable, energetic and approachable. I only waited long enough for him to get his feet under the table before asking if I might see him on a personal matter. Judging him to be someone in whom one could totally confide, I told him my opinion of my present appointment and of my wish to get back into the mainstream. He heard me out patiently, asked a few questions and told me to leave the matter with him. He came up trumps. Within a month I was joyfully packing my bags and heading south to a new job, a job which turned out to be the most satisfying and holding the most long term interest of any I had in the service. I was going to Henlow in Bedfordshire to relieve one Squadron Leader Harry Roffey as the Officer Commanding one of the training squadrons at the Officer Cadet Training Unit.

# The Officer Cadet Training Unit

## R A F Henlow

THE PURPOSE of the Officer Cadet Training Unit was to start the process of turning civilians into military officers. The course lasted for sixteen weeks and at the end of it the cadets were awarded their commissions and moved on to start their professional training as air traffic controllers, supply, secretarial or other ground branch officers or as aircrew, pilots or navigators. As I drove down from Scotland to Bedfordshire I knew not much more about the OCTU than that. It sounded interesting. I certainly did not realise that my tour at Henlow would turn out to be in many ways the most satisfying in my career and would generate interests that would influence the rest of my working life.

Having driven down from Scotland I turned off the A1 not far south of Sandy and drove through quiet country lanes, following the signposts to Henlow. The RAF station was situated among farmland and pleasant if undistinguished villages in rural Bedfordshire, five miles from Hitchin. Not far to the north the countryside was dominated by the vast hangars of Cardington, home of the R100 and R101 airships. From Henlow village the tree-lined road passed through the Camp and from it avenues ran up between the solid, red-brick buildings housing the squadron offices and lecture rooms of the OCTU. Beyond the drill square stood the modern, attractive Cadets' Mess and beyond that to the left of the cricket ground the Officers' Mess. The station, having been built in the inter-war years, with its mature trees, lawns and flowerbeds, had a pleasant feeling of permanence. On the other side of the main road, beside the disused airfield, were the rows of huts housing the Radio Engineering Unit and we met the REU officers in the Mess.

The Station Commander and Commandant of the OCTU was Group Captain Tony Ringer. The OCTU operated as five Squadrons. Every four weeks a new entry of some sixty cadets would arrive to join Blue, Green, Purple, Red or Yellow Squadron and at the end of sixteen weeks they would march off the square as newly commissioned officers. The Directing Staff then had a four-week break to catch up with their own affairs, perhaps to attend training courses, study for promotion exams or take some leave before the cycle began again. Thus every four weeks one of the squadrons would be graduating and one greeting their new course. I was to be Squadron Commander of Green Squadron. The Chief Instructor and my new boss was none other than my old sailing friend from Singapore, now Wing Commander, Brian Harris. There must be worse ways of starting a new job than sitting in the boss's house, drinking his home brew and laughing ourselves silly over remembered characters and incidents from the past.

In fact when I arrived at Henlow there were not five cadet squadrons but ten. The recruiting needs of the RAF rose and fell and at that time there was a peak in the graph. A squadron of one-hundred plus cadets would have been unwieldy and so each intake was split and the squadrons now worked in pairs having become Blue-Black, Green-Brown, Purple-Grey, Red-Orange and Yellow-White. It was, of course, essential that the bosses of each pair of squadrons worked in complete harmony. I relieved Harry Roffey as OC Green and so would be working with OC Brown, Squadron Leader Vernon Small. Here was another stroke of luck, Rita and Vernon Small were to become very good friends. I am not sure which of them was the more lively and amusing. Vernon had a very quick tongue and a quite devastating sense of humour. Many a potentially difficult policy or planning meeting would be reduced to helpless laughter by one of his quips. When dealing with cadets he could be lethal. At a long-winded cadet presentation, "That's right, McLeod, you just go on arguing among yourself." The cadets collapsed with laughter, they all knew that Mac did tend to go on a bit, and because there was no malice the victims themselves invariably joined in the laughter. We all quickly learned not to cross swords verbally with Vernon Small.

To understand what we were attempting to achieve at the OCTU, it is necessary to consider the question, "What is an officer?" For many of us in the RAF our most visible role was as pilots, navigators or other members of aircrews, but that does not answer the question. Nearer to the answer is that military officers are managers but that still misses the central essence of what holding the Queen's Commission is intended to imply. When an officer is awarded his or her commission they are presented with a document, signed by Her Majesty, which spells out their responsibilities using words like Trust, Loyalty, Courage and Duty. Britain being the place it is, these ideas are not often talked about and some would say that these days they have become unimportant to younger people. I do not believe this. It may be that it has become even more unfashionable than before to talk much about them, but I believe that most members of the younger generation are as idealistic and as ready to tackle the serious business of contributing to society as ever their predecessors were. What may sometimes be lacking during their upbringing is the proper training or even guidance.

The OCTU course challenged the cadets as they had probably never been challenged before. It made them look at themselves, to work out their strengths and weaknesses and to discover what they were capable of. Our approach was that the cadets had elected to join our club and that if they wished to do so they were going to have to conform to the standards which we believed to be important. In some respects society seemed to have moved in the opposite direction. There was at the time, for example, a widespread tendency to challenge and to denigrate authority. A few years earlier while I was with the Air Cadets I had been amazed to discover that even some private schools had abolished prefects, having found that almost nobody wanted to take on the role.

At the practical level the course was similar in many ways to my own training as a cadet at Cranwell back in the early fifties although in some respects the present OCTU course went a good deal further in spelling out the responsibilities of junior officers and in preparing the cadets for them. At Cranwell I do not recall that the subject of leadership had ever been mentioned. At OCTU it made up a major part of the training.

There were other major differences. The most obvious was that our Cranwell course had lasted two-and-a-half years, while the OCTU course was of sixteen weeks. The cadets attended a series of lectures which introduced them to what would be expected of them as junior officers, spent time on the square learning to march and drill as a squad and time in the gymnasium and on the sports field getting fit. Just as it had been for us, many of the real lessons were more subtle, in learning what it meant to work in a disciplined environment, to get themselves to the right place at the right time with the right books and other equipment, to manage their time, their turnout and themselves. If in due course they were going to command others it was important that they experience what it was like to respond to the orders of others. There were some cadets who because of their background and schools took to it all like ducks to water and couldn't see why it was any sort of big deal. Others, the majority, at first floundered and it made us on the Directing Staff wonder what exactly their teachers had believed education was for, and what many years of primary and secondary education had actually taught them about the real world or about how to manage themselves and their lives.

There were times when we deliberately put the cadets under pressure. The fact remains that at the end of the course most cadets were genuinely grateful for the experience and said so, mainly to their Flight Commanders, who had become and remained close personal friends. All the Flight Commanders would agree that we on the staff learned quite as much, at least from our early courses, as did the cadets themselves. It did not take me long, having seen some of the new elements of the OCTU course which my own training had lacked, to begin to understand the reasons for some of the mistakes I believe that I and my contemporaries had made.

To some extent the OCTU's values and beliefs were out of step with at least some parts of the rest of the RAF. During one period between courses I took myself up to RAF Linton-on-Ouse. This was one of the Initial Flying Training Schools in the vale of York, to which those of our cadets destined to become pilots would move after they had graduated with us. I was keen to see how Linton handled the continued development of their students as officers, quite apart from their flying training. I was not impressed by what I found. For one thing there were two officers' messes—one for the staff and the other for students. It seemed to me that this hardly helped to promote the notion of "brother officers" which I had found so novel and helpful while I was serving and living with the army in Singapore. I called on the Wing Commander Flying, the Chief Flying Instructor, to hear his views about our Henlow products and to learn from him how Linton managed and guided their students as new officers. I expressed my concern that perhaps we at the OCTU did not do enough to get them thinking like officers. It quickly became clear that if he had thought about the matter at all he clearly did not find this a major worry and he added proudly, almost vindictively, "Well, here we don't let them answer the telephone!" It seemed not to have occurred to him that his pupils were student officers as well as being student pilots. However at OCTU we persisted in what we believed in, in the hope that eventually our cadets would find opportunities to reap the benefits of our training.

The key to all that the OCTU achieved was the work of the Flight Commanders. The cadets were divided into flights of about ten and in time each cadet formed a close personal relationship with their Flight Commander who became not just their boss but their guide, coach, mentor, counsellor, confidant and friend. At Cranwell, I recalled, there had been no such close supervision or guidance and in fact the post of Flight Commander in the OCTU sense did not even exist. After I had been at the OCTU a little time I concluded that my job was mainly to try to provide the most helpful background and back-up for the Flight Commanders to allow them to concentrate on their cadets. I sometimes envied them the close contact and influence they had on individual cadets and the quite remarkable developments that they often achieved.

Although in the long run they would probably not go as far, the more mature ex-NCOs among our cadets, ex-corporals, sergeants and even the occasional warrant officer usually got more out of the various leadership exercises than the direct-entrant, younger ex-civilians. The latter were inclined to say, "Most of this is so obvious, I can't see what the problem is." Those who already had some managerial experience would retort, "Obvious it may, be but you wait till you try to put it into practice." Another frequent comment from the ex-NCOs was. "My last boss should have done this course." This is a remark which I have frequently heard since in respect to leadership training in many industrial companies.

The dedication of the Flight Commanders to the welfare and progress of their cadets and the hard work they put in to achieve it was remarkable. And these were ordinary run-of-the-mill young officers who had themselves joined the RAF to fly or become engineers or administrators or physical education officers or the rest. It may have been mainly the nature of our job that brought out the best in people but I still believe that I was extremely lucky on Green Squadron in my team of Flight Commanders.

Godfrey Benson, A Flight, was a blunt, no-nonsense Yorkshireman. Whenever necessary he left his cadets, and me too, in no doubt about his views on the error of our ways. I soon found his frank, candid and invariably shrewd advice invaluable.

He would occasionally come into my office, carefully shut the door and start... He had a particularly apt phrase to sum up certain cadets who were clearly out of their depth and should probably never have been selected for officer training in the first place. He would say, "Sir, I'm sorry, but there's just nothing there!" In other walks of life and in other places I have encountered many people who have well merited this entirely accurate description. But Godders did not always get things entirely his own way. We were at camp and we, the Directing Staff, were standing about while the cadets finished off some administrative chores. An attractive, blonde WRAF cadet walked past carrying a broom. "Ah, Ireton, going to sweep the parade ground are you?" said Godders. "Oh no, sir, I'm going to practise my arms drill!" We reckoned that scored about fifteen/thirty.

Shortly after I took over Green Squadron I discover that David Diprose, OC B Flight, the youngest of the Flight Commanders, was not having an easy time. He had only just completed one flying tour and had been pitched into this job without any proper guidance or preparation. The fact that he was not many years older than his cadets, his lack of experience and his own youthful appearance had led to a loss of credibility with his Flight. I was unfortunately away sick for a couple of weeks and when I returned I found that Vernon Small had thought it advisable to take over the Flight temporarily himself and to send Dave on attachment to Red Squadron to be able to make a fresh start. As soon as I could I asked Dave to come and see me. I said that if he opted to stay with Red Squadron I would understand but that I very much hoped that in fact he would chose to return to us. I was delighted when he chose to return to Green Squadron for the start of our next course. In no time he became a highly effective Flight Commander, one of the best. Having gained some experience his youthfulness now worked in his favour and he could get alongside his cadets in a way that we older ones could not. Later on in my tour I once heard him remark that all our formal leadership training probably had less effect on our cadets than having them live and work alongside a group of young officers who demonstrated what was required simply by the way they did their jobs. I don't think I would argue with that.

About a year later he and I had a bit of a stand up row over arrangements for the cadets' recreational sailing, which he managed. It turned out that without my realising it I had created various difficulties for him and he came into my office wearing his No 1 hat requesting a formal interview. It was all most uncomfortable especially as it turned out that in what he was saying he was largely right. It showed me again the value of having a subordinate who was prepared to come and tell the boss that he had got it wrong and also how easy it was to get it wrong, even with quite a small team where informal discussion and keeping in touch with people's feelings should have been no problem. An on-going but much happier disagreement that David and I had was about who, historically, was the greater military leader—Marlborough or Nelson. I supported Nelson, and could quote General Montgomery's views to support me. Dave would have none of it. He knew a great deal more history than I did and nothing would shake his support for Marlborough. I believe he even saddled one of his sons with Marlborough for a middle name. But we drew the line at his wishing to re-name his "B" Flight as Blenheim Flight.

Mike Cole, C Flight, was a gentle giant, a Physical Education Branch officer, a devout, undemonstrative man of complete integrity. He had a rather deliberate manner and would be the first to admit also to a big man's hearty appetite. During a coffee break one day we, the DS, were expressing exasperation about some cadets whom it was said didn't know their left feet from their right when Mike quipped, "Well I always knew which was my right foot, it was the one I scored all my goals with!" Vernon Small's lightning response, "You mean as opposed to the one you eat with?"

The services at that time funded and supported Adventure Training Expeditions and some years after leaving the OCTU Mike Cole found a new vocation by leading a tri-service expedition with a Christian purpose, which was to install a fresh water well and pump for one of the deprived regions of East Africa. This led on to a much bigger expedition to Nepal to pioneer the introduction of the River Rover. This novel and versatile hovercraft was to provide a "hovering doctor" service, analogous to the Australian flying doctors, to remote areas among the mountains. His book about the venture and the subsequent TV programme were called "Journey to the Fourth World." For these and later expeditions to China, Peru and Nicaragua Mike was awarded the OBE.

Roy Malings was the eldest of the Fight Commanders and himself an ex-NCO. He had his own unique way with his cadets and in due course would have his Flight eating out of his hand. One of his techniques was occasionally to issue them an order that seemed utterly pointless such as, "Everybody lying flat on the ground, go!" He would then introduce and discuss with his cadets the topic of what they were going to do when they might not have time to explain the reasons for a perfectly sensible order but one that might on the face of it seem pointless to those affected by it. Roy was also extremely fit. Keen young rugby players and the like would be much disconcerted to find themselves being out-marched by this grey haired, middle-aged man! No-one could pull the wool over Roy's eyes. He had seen it all before.

Dave Clark was a quiet, unassuming Flight Commander but often his F flight seemed to contain some colourful characters. On one course they drove the rest of us mad by insisting on referring to themselves as "F Troop" and by carrying around with them a pennant as displayed in Westerns by the US 7th cavalry.

Underpinning all our training was the notion of a disciplined, hierarchical set-up where orders are regarded not as a basis for discussion but to be obeyed. We taught that there is a right way to do most things, a right or at least an appropriate way on particular occasions to dress, to behave and to speak. The cadets undertook a range of activities all contributing to these aims but the central plank was the regular 1-1 interview they had with their Flight Commander. No punches were pulled in discussing with the cadet their progress or weaknesses. They were effective, I believe, because the cadets could see that their Flight Commander had no personal axe to grind and that their sole purpose was to help and to guide however painful this might sometimes be.

There was one aspect of the OCTU course which, although unavoidable, made our job more difficult. At the end of the course we on the squadron had to recommend to the Chief Instructor whether we believed that a cadet had reached the necessary standard for commissioning. It was therefore possible to fail the course—to be recommended for withdrawal from training. For the clear failures this often came as a welcome relief. Perhaps their initial decision to go for a commission could now be seen as mistaken, it was simply not for them. They left with our best wishes for their success in some other way of life. For the clearly competent there was no trouble either, they well knew they were on their way to a commission and towards the end of the course they would indulge in a little gentle mickey-taking of the Directing Staff. But for the cadets who were going to be marginal there were disadvantages. Sensing that they might be heading for the chop they would wherever possible try to fade into the background, to try to prevent the DS spotting evidence of their progress or lack of it. This was a pity, had we seen more of them they might have found that we rated them more highly than they did themselves, or could at least have provided more focussed guidance for them. Once the commissioning list was published and if they were on it, they would re-emerge but they had often missed out on some experiences and guidance that could have come their way.

The justifiably confident cadets were never afraid to come forward. Some eight to ten weeks into the course, during the mid-morning coffee break, a couple of cadets would approach you. "Good morning, sir, could we ask you, have you written the commissioning list yet?" "Come now, Bloggs, this is much too soon, you know we only write that a week before graduation." "Oh, I see. Well we've already written our list, sir!" The perceptive and alert cadets had already made up their minds about which of their number were going to pass out successfully and which were not. When our official list eventually appeared we sometimes asked them if they thought we had got it right. The answer was invariably, "Yes, almost. But you are commissioning two who we wouldn't have." It was always that way round. They judged their own peers more harshly than we did.

At the start of each course it was most interesting to watch the new intake of cadets, initially just a row of faces, emerge as distinct personalities. It was surprisingly easy, a matter of doing one's homework, to learn the names. As soon as they arrived we had a course photograph taken and we kept a copy, with names printed on it, on our desks and perhaps while waiting for a phone call you would cover the names in the back row and see how many you could remember. I found that within a week of their arriving I could go into a lecture being given by one of the Flight Commanders and respond to any cadet asking a questions using, without hesitation, the cadet's name.

I would drop in regularly to talk to the Flight Commanders in their offices and to hear how their cadets were settling down. Quite quickly the different characters came into focus. Each flight was made up of a mix of younger cadets straight from school and older ex-corporals or sergeants who had been put up for a commission by their previous units. We had a sprinkling of new Commonwealth cadets and some from various African countries. Among the most difficult to help progress were the ex-NCOs who had become set in their ways and who had formed the impression that to be an officer one had to be like an NCO only better. A picture we tried to offer was to say, "Up to now the service has been able to rely on you, as an experienced professional in your trade, to keep the show running reliably along the rails. As an officer it will be your job to work out if the rails are actually going in the right direction. It is not a matter of being better, it is a quite different job." There was a long weekend break at mid-course. If one of our ex-NCO cadets seemed to be stalled his Flight Commander would suggest he find an opportunity to talk about the course to his wife during the break. Often when he returned the cadet would say, "Its quite extraordinary. My wife says that is what she's been telling me for years."

At mid-course there was also a social evening to which cadets were encouraged to invite their wives or girl friends. We on the Directing Staff sometimes got some quiet amusement and satisfaction in noticing that at the end of course ball a different and much more suitable girl friend would appear than the one who had come to the mid-course function.

The cadets from the various overseas Air Forces were a mixed lot. For some although they completed the course we were grateful that we were not required to express an opinion on whether they had passed it. Sometimes their obvious shortcomings began to cause real resentment among the RAF cadets. When this occurred we found a pretext to call just the RAF cadets to a meeting and to point out to them in confidence that we were perfectly aware of the situation and that they could rest assured that none of the visitors in question would be joining our RAF. We never had this confidence betrayed.

The problems did not apply to all. One African cadet Eugene Kilonzo made an immediate and lasting impression on us all. Six foot two, with the physique of a world-class athlete, a voice like Paul Robeson and a sly sense of humour he soon acquired the nickname of Big K. Leading his flight on some strenuous leadership exercise he was heard encouraging them with, "Come on now you whites, let's go. Actually you're not really white at all, more a sort of dirty pink, but LET'S GO anyway!" Big K would have made a popular and highly effective officer in anyone's Air Force.

Another African told us an interesting story from his country. He was already a pilot in their Air Force when a civil war erupted which the tribe of which he was a member lost. The winners insisted that those like him from the losing side should re-train as officers all over again, hence his presence at Henlow. But the most extraordinary element had been during his own pilot training. Their air force had bought Russian two-seat trainers and flew with Russian flying instructors. The snag then was that pupil and instructor did not share a common language, and there was of course no third seat in the aeroplane for an interpreter. The instructor had to transmit his comments, such as "For God's sake watch your air-speed!" to the Air Traffic Control Tower on the ground where, hopefully before it was too late, the interpreter re-transmitted to the pupil.

If a cadet came to the end of the sixteen weeks and had not quite reached the standard for commissioning they could be offered a re-course. This entailed moving to a new squadron and getting an extra four weeks training before hopefully graduating with them. As the boss I interviewed the cadets re-coursed to us and decided which flight they should join. On one course a cadet was re-coursed to us who was an ex-sergeant with an excellent past record and who had in the normal way arranged to leave his family in his married quarters at his previous station for the sixteen weeks of the OCTU course. I read through the report from his previous squadron and called him in. Before I could get a word in edgeways or even ask him to sit down he launched into an indignant outburst about the fact that he was not sure he even wanted to accept a re-course, that he was not clear how long his family could stay in their quarters and about two or three other bees he had in his bonnet.

As he paused for breath I interrupted to say that I was not concerned about his trivial affairs until he answered a question I had for him. Momentarily put out by this unexpected comment he paused and then had another go. Once more I waved him to silence and finally managed to say, "Now, cadet, will you describe to me, please, the impression you have just created for me, your new boss?" Stunned silence. "But before I do, sir, I still want to know …" I interrupted again and finally managed to extract words like self-centred, bombastic, overbearing, insensitive, unconcerned with other people's feelings and the like. I then opened his file and let him read the reasons his previous squadron had given for not passing him for a commission. It was almost word for word! While he read it again and had a little think I went down the corridor to the office of Roy Malings, judging that he would be just right for our new hot-head. "Roy," I said, "I've got just the chap for you. May I bring him along to meet you?" The cadet got the message, learned self-awareness, tact and sensitivity and graduated without further difficulty. In fact he and I went on to share the memory as a private joke. I would say, "Good morning, Bloggs, do you remember the first time we met?" He would chuckle and say, "Oh, Good grief. Don't remind me!"

One of the younger cadets was harder to fathom—until we met his parents. He was tall, athletic, well spoken, clearly intelligent. He seemed to have all the advantages needed to pass out at the top. But whenever he was given the opportunity to shine, to put in a performance that could have been an example to the less able he seemed to freeze. He repeatedly failed to grasp the opportunities that were offered to him to make his mark. He was clearly going to get his commission, but his exasperated Flight Commander knew that really he should have been competing for the Sword of Merit, which was awarded to the best overall cadet. At the end of the course we met his parents. His father was a pleasant, clearly well-to-do businessman, but his mother … . She could only be described as imperious, it was painfully clear who in that family wore the trousers. The cadet, or his father, had only to start to make some remark and, if she felt like it, she would quell them with a look or with some small gesture of her hand which reduced either of them to instant silence. Our poor cadet had lived with that for eighteen years. We heard later that having started pilot training, as that course became more pressurised he eventually dropped out. The burden of his childhood in that home, with that mother, for all its material advantages, had eventually proved too heavy.

Another cadet joined us just a few days before graduation not because he had been re-coursed but because he had been away sick and so had missed graduating with his original squadron. I welcomed him and said I hoped he would enjoy his short time with Green Squadron. I then added that although I was sorry to introduce a sour note I hoped he would get himself a proper haircut before he paraded with my squadron. He looked crestfallen and then explained. After graduation he would be going home on leave—to Northern Ireland. If he arrived in Belfast with an obviously military haircut he could at once have become an obvious target for terrorists. His previous Squadron Commander had given him leave to let his hair grow. I readily agreed to do so too, simply asking him that on the graduation parade he would as far as possible hide it under his hat.

Brian Harris was posted and succeeded by Wing Commander David Leith. Looking back I reckon that he was probably the best boss I ever had in all my time in the RAF. We differed in many respects, but whenever I had a "bright" idea he would listen, genuinely. He would make a clear decision on whether I could go ahead or not, usually I could. He would then stand aside and let me get on with it or would provide whatever support I needed. I was once unaware enough to let him hear me sounding off about a couple of Scottish cadets who had annoyed me and I was making some unflattering remarks about whingeing by the Celtic Fringe. He took great pleasure in reminding me of his own Scottish ancestry and he would subsequently ring me up and point out that my next course contained plenty of Scots—just to keep me interested.

Recalling how valuable I had found the simple training in public speaking we had been given on the Junior Command and Staff Course I introduced on Green Squadron an Inter-Flight public speaking competition. We made a formal social evening of it, inviting the Chief Instructor, the Headquarters officers and their wives as well as all the Flight Commanders and theirs. The flights themselves chose their speakers, there was a short set piece to deliver and a second piece which they also chose themselves.

Various senior officers or their ladies were invited to act as judges and were seated right at the back of the audience so that the speakers could not fail to get the message that they would need to speak up. My idea was that by making the act of getting up and speaking fairly formal, and for some cadets quite stressful, having found that they could do it could not fail to give their self-confidence a valuable boost. The best speaker we ever found was an Arab cadet from a Middle East Air Force who wowed us with his dramatic, eloquent and amusing performance.

When I had arrived at Henlow we were operating with large courses and with the squadrons working in pairs. However six months later the recruiting needs of the RAF declined, the intake numbers dropped and we reverted to single squadrons. Green and Brown merged to become just Green Squadron again and Vernon Small moved reluctantly to Cadet Wing Headquarters. We still invited him and Rita to Green Squadron social events, the place would not have been the same without them. At the same time the OCTU appointed to each squadron a Squadron Training Officer. We welcomed Roger Giles, ex-Brown Squadron Flight Commander.

Roger and Sue Giles also soon became good friends and he looked after a mass of detailed administration for me. We shared an interest in sailing. But we had one problem. Roger tended to start the day not quite at his best until after one or two cups of coffee and at around lunchtime he got himself properly into focus. During the afternoon and even into the evening he was firing on all cylinders and most efficient. I was the opposite. I had found back at school that I am a poor performer pm and have to get the important things up and running after or even before breakfast. I would bounce into the Squadron bright and early and want to talk to Roger about my latest bright idea to be greeted by a blank stare and total incomprehension. The rest of the Squadron used to joke that there was only a narrow window of opportunity of couple of hours around mid-day once the Training Officer had become fully conscious and before the Boss went into his decline, during which we two could sensibly communicate.

For our next entry he caused me a moment of acute embarrassment. On the first morning of the course our Squadron NCO, Flight Sergeant Munday, had assembled the new arrivals in the Squadron lecture room for me formally to welcome them to the Squadron and to the OCTU. He called them to attention as I entered and, followed by the Squadron

Training Officer and the Flight Commanders, walked to the front of the room and stepped on to the dais. I stood at the lectern while Roger and the Flight Commanders seated themselves facing the cadets. "Good morning, ladies and gentlemen, first let me welcome you to the Officer Cadet Training Unit and to Green Squadron. Now let me introduce myself and the staff of the Squadron. First the Squadron Training Officer, Flight Lieutenant … um …" I froze! I stared at Roger, whom I had known for at least six months but all my brain would register that morning was—"Giles, Giles, it can't be Giles, that's a Christian name!" I had a diplomatic coughing fit while my brain unglued itself and I could continue. Roger and the Flight Commanders could hardly contain themselves as they sat there thinking, "Poor boss, he's finally lost the plot!" Lost the plot or not, for every subsequent course I had with me a list of their names printed in block capitals.

It seemed to me that to do the job properly we ought to know something about how the other services ran their officer cadet training. As it was I believe we were guilty of trying to cram too much into the course, especially of academic lecturing, but at the same time there was so much else I believed the cadets ought to see and do. When I passed through Cranwell the course took two-and-a-half years, although that did include learning to fly. The OCTU course should, I believe, have lasted at least six months, but financial pressures were always tending to shorten it even further. I already knew Sandhurst slightly, so during one of our leave periods I arranged to spend a week at the Britannia Royal Naval College, Dartmouth. The setting is superb. The elegant red brick college stands on its hill overlooking the town and the estuary. I was envious and very impressed with their lavish range of equipment and facilities. I commented to one of their directing staff officers that one would expect a naval college to have its own fleet of yachts but he responded by assuring me that there was actually nothing remotely in common between a yacht and a modern warship. Off-shore sailing, in a bit of a wind, was much more a matter of getting their cadets a bit wet and cold, a bit frightened and giving them a bit of an adventure. I was however really jolted to find that Dartmouth had their own flight of Chipmunk aircraft and regularly gave their cadets air experience, week-end trips to France and the like. I came back to Henlow reflecting that our cadets, entering the flying service, never actually saw an aeroplane during their OCTU course.

It was obvious to me that without our policy makers apparently realising it we were indoctrinating our cadets right from the start of their careers to accept that the RAF was the poor relation, was not really on an equal footing with the other services. The pattern that I had first become aware of in Singapore seemed to run right through the RAF. There was so much more that I believe our course should have included. But as we never met the policy makers we never had a chance even to discuss these concerns with them. I am firmly convinced that sadly our course in no way started to compare with those at Sandhurst or Dartmouth.

There was actually one officer at Headquarters, Training Command whom we got to know well. I cannot recall which branch Squadron Leader Paul Miller was in, but having first met him when he visited Green Squadron on some routine matter we struck up a friendship with him and from then on always invited him to our social events. Of course as a mere squadron leader he was hardly among the real policy makers but it was pleasant just to have the chance to air our views to someone from our commanding Headquarters and to hear in return some of their gossip. MOD were at the time considering merging Training Command and Support Command into one single entity. But what to call this vast new set up? Someone suggested Straining Command.

With Wing Commander Leith's support I managed to find one or two opportunities to put a bit of sparkle into our course although finding the time in an already over-crowded programme was always the main problem. During my time at Pitreavie in Scotland I had come across the Highland Pentathlon. This was a weekend of competition, sponsored in fact by one of the tobacco companies, and held in Aviemore. Clubs, colleges and military units were invited to enter teams of three. When the date came round again I got a go-ahead from Wing Commander Leith, sent off an entry for Green Squadron and it was accepted. We selected a squadron team, rushed to King's Cross one Friday evening to get the sleeper up to Aviemore on Speyside, to arrive in time for breakfast.

It had been through the contacts that I had made with the army in Scotland that I had first heard about the Highland Pentathlon. As they were much concerned in its management I was not surprised to discover that the whole event was extremely well organised. For each of the five events competitors competed against a par score to win or lose points. The first event was to swim two lengths in one of the posh hotel swimming pools. The teams then got fitted with boots and skis, climbed into coaches, and were whisked up the ski road on to Cairngorm for a picnic lunch on the hill and to ski down a not too demanding Giant Slalom. In the evening everyone went to the town ice rink for target curling. As there was an excellent bar there this invariably developed into a very social evening and we all stayed up much later than we had intended. After breakfast on Sunday morning the organisers revealed their cunning, as the fourth event was target shooting with .22 rifles, a fiendish trial after a late night! After lunch the last event was a two-mile cross-country race. A quick change, into the hotel lounge for the prize giving and on to the Sunday night sleeper back to the south. Green Squadron did not win a prize but we were the top service unit, beating in particular RAF Kinloss, the big nearby Coastal Command station with its establishment of about twenty times ours. The Highland Pentathlon provided an exhausting but most enjoyable weekend.

I believed that the cadets needed to see during their course a bit more of the Royal Air Force than just a disused airfield in Bedfordshire. We somehow found a spare afternoon for an educational outing. First stop was the RAF museum at Hendon, and then on to the RAF Church of St. Clement Danes. This is always an impressive and moving place to visit. We then retired for a drink to the RAF (officers') club in Piccadilly. The RAF Club was of historical interest too because of the fine collection of oil paintings of many famous aircraft and exploits around the walls. The wonderfully vivid painting of a Lancaster bomber flying low over the Dutch coast, coming straight at you, still always makes me want to duck.

If we were to demand high standards from the cadets it was important that we maintained the same standards in our dealings with them. Their day-to-day wear was airman-style serge battle-dress and about half way through the course the cadets were briefed by David Caldicott, Roger's successor as our Training Officer, on the arrangements for ordering their barathea officer-type uniforms. These would need to be ready for the date of their graduation. On the graduation parade itself they would still wear their white cap bands and lapel flashes as cadets and after the parade simply remove the flashes and replace white hat bands with black to be properly dressed as officers. On the base there was an area of huts rented by three of the well-known military tailors—Alkit, Moss Bros and Gieves. We naturally believed in competition and so the cadets were free to decide for themselves with which of the three to place their order for their officer-type uniform. For one particular course one of these three firms had caused a great deal of trouble in that, although they had known the date for months in advance, the uniforms were not ready on time for the end of the course. It was only by the Directing Staff stepping in and threatening dire consequences that they were finally completed in a rush late on the very evening before the parade. With many other jobs to attend to, such as going into Hitchin to meet their guests, this created totally unfair problems for the cadets. We were determined that it should not happen again and I sent a very stiff letter to the manager in question.

When David Caldicott briefed the next course he made some half humorous remark to the effect that, "as we do not wish to influence your choice of tailor it would be quite wrong of me to warn you, for example, against (a name was mentioned), and therefore I shall not do so." The cadets took the hint unanimously and not one single order was placed with—brand X. When the manager guessed what had happened he hit the roof. The next morning a suitably chastened Dave came and told me the whole story, concluding, "So, I'm very sorry, boss, but this time I'm afraid I blew it. The manager says he is going to the Group Captain about it." I rang up Group Captain Tony Ringer myself and asked if I might go and see him. He listened to the whole story and said, "As a matter of fact the manager has just rung and made an appointment to see me tomorrow. Anyway thank you for putting me in the picture, Bill. I'll let you know what he has to say and what we need to do about it." Late the next afternoon I had a call from the Group Captain. "Oh, Bill, about that tailor. I thought you might like to know—he forgot to keep his appointment. I think that just about takes care of the matter."

Our cadets were destined, after commissioning, to become officers in a wide range of different branches. On a couple of occasions, having compared my views with their Flight Commander, I had concluded that one or two of them were setting their sights too low. One particular cadet was intending to join the Catering Branch. I have nothing against caterers, but they can hardly be rated as the backbone or bedrock of the Royal Air Force. His Flight Commander agreed with me that the cadet in question was one of the best on the course, having ability, enterprise, tact, personality and presence. I called him in, told him that he was doing well, and suggested that he might consider transferring his ambitions to the General Duties (Flying) Branch. He was naturally flattered and pleased with my comments but he would have none of it. His father was a successful figure in the catering world and our cadet was determined in due course to follow him. We went at it hammer and tongs for some time but he was adamant. It seemed to me that he was regarding his time in the RAF as a prolonged apprenticeship and if that was his career choice I could not really blame him for it. He concluded by saying that he hoped to become the best catering officer in the service. This was OK as far as it went, but I was sorry to have lost the battle and I still believe we lost an effective GD officer.

He was confident of his ability in other ways too. I still regularly played squash and I heard afterwards that our budding caterer had asked his Flight Commander, Godfrey Benson, whether it would be tactful to beat the boss at squash. Godders of course said, "Good heavens, yes. Go ahead!" He did, comprehensively, but he was the only cadet who ever did.

The key role for all officers in the services is to provide the leadership. This applies most visibly at the top, in the strategic sense in the way that Air Marshal Dowding led Fighter Command in the Battle of Britain, Admiral Cunningham the Mediterranean Fleet and General Bill Slim the Fourteenth Army in Burma. However leadership is also needed right the way down to the front line—in the fighter squadron armament bay, the warship engine-room and the jungle four-man patrol. Leadership is an enormous subject and many discussions of it are plagued by a Pandora's Box of half-truths, prejudices and mis-understandings. For example, some of the first questions which arise are whether leaders are born or can be trained and whether leaders come from a particular social background. Are schools laying the necessary foundations for leadership, how does leadership fit into increasingly egalitarian British society and into the political spectrum, is the notion of leadership even appropriate in a democracy? These and a host of other questions inform and often misinform the debate. Sociological and political prejudices are not unknown.

The OCTU, however, confined itself to the simple belief that it is a junior officer's job as a leader to get things done, to translate policies and decisions, often from higher up, into actions. This is the job of a junior leader and for this he or she can be trained. One of the key elements of the OCTU course was the training we provided for the cadets in the basic ideas and techniques of "hands on" leadership. The RAF had recently adopted an approach to leadership training which had originated at the Royal Military Academy, Sandhurst.

Dr John Adair had been a lecturer there on military history when he was asked to look into the leadership training of army officers. Having consulted trainers across the world, military and civilian, he had concluded that it was difficult or even impossible to define the personal qualities of successful leaders. Another approach he had studied was that of moving the leadership of a group around to the most experienced person in each new type of situation as circumstances dictated. He had rejected both these approaches in favour of treating leadership simply as a role. He suggested that to be successful a leader has three sets of needs he must work to meet, those of the mission or the task to be achieved, those needed to maintain the cohesion of the working group and to weld it into an effective team and those which meet the needs of the individual team members.

Having been introduced to these ideas the cadets were in turn put in charge of a team of about six others and given a series of command tasks to tackle. At the end of the task the DS would lead a discussion on how it had gone. Using carefully selected questions we would guide the team members and the leader to identify with the benefit of hindsight what had been done well and what could have been improved. We started the cadets' leadership training with simple ten-minute tasks involving, for example, planks, metal drums and "no-go" areas on the floor. From there we moved out on to the airfield for more complicated tasks and to the neighbouring countryside for exercises lasting an hour or more. We ensured that we gave each cadet an exercise to lead that was tailored to their particular current training need. For example if a cadet was suffering a temporary loss of confidence their Flight Commander would ensure that their next lead would be one which brought out their strengths and which allowed them every chance of success.

Outdoor exercises tended naturally to favour physical activity and this could lead to the unhelpful notion that effective leadership depended on muscle power. To balance this the cadets spent a week in an Office Simulator. This provided a training set up analogous to the mock cockpit of the flight simulators used to train aircrews. We used some rows of simple offices equipped with telephones and normal office furniture. The cadets formed teams simulating the Headquarters of a small RAF station and were presented with a series of tasks involving office work, and the management of people within the office environment, communication by paper or telephone or face-to-face, dealing with routine administrative tasks, civilian visitors and so on. The cadets each spent twenty-four hours in a role and so could find themselves Station Commander one day and office cleaner/orderly the next. Effective leadership, the setting of objectives and priorities, good communication, the encouragement of teamwork and so on were soon seen to be just as relevant in the office as they were on the open hillside. We on the Directing Staff had great fun playing the parts of angry farmer, obtuse civil servant, sly cockney trader, indignant retired brigadier, dotty charity flag seller and the rest.

The culmination of the leadership training which also set the seal on most of what the OCTU was about were the two visits the course made to the large army training area near Thetford in Norfolk. For the first camping period we occupied hutted camps and for the second we took with us all the equipment needed to set up tented camps, only relying on permanent kitchens and ablutions. For the final camp all the executive roles were also filled for each twenty-four hour period by cadets, from Camp Commandant downwards. For each leadership role a member of the DS, normally the cadet's Flight Commander, would tag along, keeping an eye on safety and any other aspects of the exercise which called for intervention. A realistic scene was set. The exercise brief explained that we were an RAF detachment sent out into East Anglia to help our friends the West Toftians—West Tofts was one of the permanent camps we used—in their efforts to quell disruptive guerrilla action by the evil Fenlandians. Our exercise brief was to set up camp and then to carry out operations as ordered in support of friendly helicopters in the area. The DS now became friendly partisans who still tagged along and would from time to time pass helpful hints to the cadet leader to make sure that events progressed at least roughly as we had planned and so that subsequent exercises could pick up the threads.

For the DS these camps varied from the pretty unpleasant in mid-winter to the idyllic in high summer. The Stamford Military Training

Area is closed to the public and has become a natural haven for wildlife. This lovely countryside can be glimpsed briefly in television's Dad's Army. The final sequence, as the credits are shown, of Captain Mainwaring and his platoon advancing across the heath was filmed on Frog Hill, the highest point in the area, which consists of wide stretches of unspoiled open heathland, of grass meadows, heather and wild flowers, small copses of oak and beech, stands of pine, narrow lines of woodland and occasional streams and small lakes. A couple of deserted villages of derelict cottages stand beside the few metalled lanes and over it all stretches the wide Norfolk sky. Kestrels, owls and the occasional Marsh Harrier hunt over the ground, it is grazed by a few sheep and you almost have to step over the pheasants, they are so tame.

The exercise situation which we sketched out was that we were working with friendly helicopters. In the past these had been simulated, not very convincingly, by three-ton trucks. However Dave Clarke, Flight Commander of "F" Troop, had been a chopper pilot and still had many friends at RAF Odiham and around the chopper world. He suggested contacting his old boss to ask how his unit would like a few days' jolly around Norfolk. The sequel came a few weeks later while Dave was acting as the friendly partisan for a rather slap-dash member of his flight. Having arrived and set up camp one of our first exercises was to carry out a reconnaissance of the area. The cadet had been ordered to lead his team to make a careful reconnaissance of an area of heathland to check its suitability and safety for a helicopter to land. As the team completed a very superficial survey of the area the leader was overheard by the friendly partisan to remark, "Come on, that'll do, after all it's only a truck really." They set off gratefully back to camp. The friendly partisan told us afterwards that, as they arrived at camp and the unmistakable sound of a real helicopter became audible, the leader's expression of horror and disbelief was a sight to be seen. As the week progressed we arranged the sequence of exercises to ensure that everyone got a ride in a chopper.

The leadership exercises led in progression from the rudimentary to the more challenging and we did our best to extract the maximum training value from each. At camp many of the exercises were necessarily competitive between flights and then in spite of my pleas Flight Commanders would regularly succumb to the temptation to drop broader and broader hints to their cadet leader to help their flight

315

win. At the DS de-briefing and wash-up at the end of the day there was often intense indignation from any Flight Commander who felt that his cadet had been unfairly robbed, while I tried to keep the peace! Many exercises involved building some structure with pine poles. Inevitably from time to time some got broken. At one of David Leith's meetings Squadron Leader Jim Rae, the RAF Regiment officer responsible for their re-supply, was upbraiding us, the users, for our carelessness and extravagance. "You people," he fumed, "seem to think that those things just grow on trees." The meeting collapsed with laughter.

Wing Commander Leith held regularly monthly meetings for the senior members of his headquarters staff and the Squadron Commanders. But the training programme meant that each month one of the squadrons would be away at camp and so the boss missed the meeting. One of the headquarters officers was Peter Mellish. Peter had at one time been OC Yellow Squadron and was a particular friend of mine. For a number of reasons both he and I held a very low opinion of the current Purple Squadron. It so happened that at one such Wing Commander's meeting Purple Squadron was away at camp and so OC Purple was absent. At this meeting Ian Chalmers, the current OC Yellow Squadron, was advocating an idea which I too strongly supported, that of giving the squadrons proper names rather than just identifying them by colours. At Dartmouth, for example, I had found St Vincent Division, Beatty Division and so on. Ian, warming to his theme, continued, "When I first got here I was not impressed either with some of the colours we had chosen. For example I thought— Purple Squadron—Yuk!" Peter Mellish muttered, "I still do."

With about every other course intake we had one flight of Women's Royal Air Force cadets, with a WRAF Flight Commander, always designated G Flight. We were terribly politically incorrect. We never mentioned the phrase "G Flight" except in falsetto. However the female point of view throughout the OCTU was vigorously upheld by a tough, amusing Irishwoman, Squadron Leader Ida McEwan, WRAF. Her post was designated as Senior WRAF Training Officer or SWTO, pronounced most appropriately as Sweeto. Ida often came out to visit us at camp and she was with us one day during an exercise in which a cadet was playing the part of an escaping prisoner. Entering into the spirit of the situation, he decided to hi-jack a Directing Staff Landrover as it drove slowly past his hiding place. He jumped out of the bushes, brandishing a make-believe pistol and climbed in. The passenger in the Landrover happened to be Ida. She said afterwards, "That was terrible. When that young man jumped out of the bushes, to my undying shame, I gave a little scream!"

For some exercises the flights were mixed up and so members of G Flight mingled with the men. On one memorable occasion during a spell of hot summer weather a team trying to make best speed across country, and map reading as they went, reached the edge of the river Wissey. The ineffectual leader was trying to work out with the map which way to go to get to the nearest bridge when a certain enterprising WRAF cadet interrupted, "That's all just a waste of time, come on, let's wade and swim!" She promptly stripped off her outer clothes and led the way. We heard all about it later back at camp when the group turned up with their friendly partisan, the Flight Commander, grinning from ear to ear.

We did make one concession to the girls. Their Flight Commander, Wendy Humphreys, although an excellent officer in every way, found that map reading was not her forte. Many of the exercises took place around a large conifer plantation near Thetford. The trees were intersected by rides or fire-breaks and we discovered that the corner tree of each of the blocks so formed had a unique number painted on it. In great secrecy we wrote to the Forestry Commission and obtained from them a map showing these numbers, which we presented to Wendy. While her cadets struggled with compass, distances and "distinguishing features" their Flight Commander strolled over and took a quick look at the "Wendy Number" on the nearby corner tree.

One young man just hadn't got it. He was already a doubtful and his Flight Commander asked me, the boss, to go with him on an exercise to see how he got on. His brief was to lead his team across country for about a mile to one of the old flint quarrying pits that are common in that part of Norfolk and to rescue an injured man who had unfortunately parachuted into it. We had already taken another cadet and left him in the pit, briefing him that he had a simulated broken ankle and was to wait there to be rescued by the stretcher party.

Cadet "Jones" let us call him, selected a second-in-command, briefed him to follow along with the stretcher party and first aid kit while he, Jones, would run on ahead, survey the situation and form a plan. I didn't feel like running so I followed on with the stretcher party.

We arrived at the pit to find that our gallant leader had climbed out on to the branch of an overhanging beech tree to see and talk to the casualty, the branch had broken and we now had at the bottom of the pit two cadets, one with a simulated broken ankle—and one with a real one. The original casualty was told that the exercise had changed. Like it or not, although he had been looking forward to a nice restful morning, he was now one of the real stretcher party.

One of the more interesting exercises raised the question of how to deal with issues of confidentiality and secrecy. The cadet leader was briefed to take his team across country, map-reading the way, to a rendezvous with another team and then to co-operate with them. He was then warned that one of his own team was a traitor who could be expected to try to thwart and disrupt his plans. The day before the DS had selected the "traitor," given him his own map and briefed him to prevent the leader from succeeding in his task. The cadet leader, not knowing who was the traitor, was then faced with the problem of how to alert his team to the threat. Some decided to risk taking one other team member into his confidence, and explaining the situation to them. When he did so, we found that the team member he chose to trust was almost invariably the traitor! On reflection the reason why this was so became clear. We had selected as the traitor the most enterprising member of the team whom we could rely on to act cleverly and independently. Not surprisingly the leader unwittingly selected the same cadet as his trusted No 2.

On one such exercise I joined a team as the friendly partisan and I thought that on this occasion the leader had found a novel way of thwarting the traitor and of preventing him from breaking away, as I knew he was planning to do. As he briefed the team on the task he explained to them the possibility of a traitor and invited suggestions. One of the team suggested that he should order them all to tie on to a length of rope as mountaineers do. This seemed to me a very shrewd move, and I tagged along wondering how the traitor would react now or whether this time he would be thwarted. Each team was required to carry with them a heavy rucksack containing first aid kit, a thermal blanket and various other safety items. It came to the traitor's turn to carry the rucksack. As he tied on again, nobody noticed, I certainly never noticed, that he tied the rope to the frame of the rucksack, not to his own belt. As they set off again he simply dropped the rucksack and ran, leaving the rest of the team still attached to the rucksack like a ball and chain. He deservedly got clean away.

The country-wide exercises and the minor stress they generated brought out the best and the failings in cadets in ways one could not possibly have foreseen in less demanding situations. Camp was a popular diversion for the OCTU Headquarters officers and they would often come over to Norfolk to join us for a few days. We planned the programme so that as many as possible members of the DS got to see each cadet in the lead and in supporting roles and in this way a fair, rounded picture was built up. At the end of the day we, the DS, held a wash up. Over a welcome cup of tea we would each in turn relate the main events of the exercises and of the team of cadets we had been with. This was for the benefit of each cadet's own Flight Commander who listened carefully, noted what was said and in this way built up a comprehensive picture which took account of the observations of many other people in addition to his, or in the case of G Flight her, own and of the cadet's behaviour in different situations.

Vernon Small still frequently joined Green Squadron at camp and after a clearly trying day trudging around in the wind and rain, he paused in his narrative to phrase carefully and accurately his considered opinion of a particular cadet. "That young man is just … is just … a whingeing little git!" I'm afraid those of us who knew the cadet in question had to agree. On another occasion, "Ah yes, him. Well, I'm afraid he didn't actually contribute all that much to the day. He carried the rucksack, he tripped over a tree-stump and he asked if it was time for lunch." Actually we all took this part of the job very seriously and even if some of the descriptions were sometimes phrased in colourful terms this did not detract from the fairness and objectivity of our assessments. None of us, aircrew in particular, had ever found any merit in pulling our punches.

The airmen of our supporting staff entered into the spirit of the exercises too. A cadet leader was carefully briefing our coach driver on the rendezvous he had planned. "Right, Corporal Williams," he said briskly, "I want you to meet me here at this point at 15.00 hours. Is that quite clear?" "Yes, sir." The cadet moved away to collect his team. The corporal called after him. "Excuse me sir, do you want me to bring my coach?"

No account of the Green Squadron training camps during my time can be complete without mention of our Squadron RAF Regiment

Officer. Flight Lieutenant David Felwick, blunt, outspoken, no sufferer of fools, was about the most insensitive handler of machinery I have ever known. One only had to get into a Landrover with him, to watch him grinding the gearbox, abusing the clutch and moving off like a kangaroo, muttering, "Bloody machine!" to understand why in the past he had failed to become a pilot. But having said that, his running of the camps, the meticulous planning, the prompt supply of the maps, pine-poles, vehicles, camping and cooking equipment, his direction of all our supporting staff and a host of other details was exemplary. Although he worked for us in Green Squadron, his nominal boss was Squadron Leader Jim Rae the Senior RAF Regiment Officer. When it came to annual report time Jim came to see me and to hear my views on David's work. Jim started the conversation by saying, "I am inclined to write that David is the best junior RAF Regiment officer I have ever met …" I told him I agreed entirely and would not want to modify that in any way.

David eventually left the RAF and embarked on a very successful career in commerce, initially as a management trainee with Peter Jones, the well-known outfitters in Sloane Square. Another RAF officer, a friend of David's who had not heard about his retirement, was shopping there one day and was astonished to see David at the top of a ladder, struggling with some large awkward boxes on the top shelf. "Hi, David," he called out, "what are you doing, man? Why don't you get hold of some berk who works here?" David screwed his head round and managed to gasp out, "I am the berk who works here!"

Wendy Humphreys left us on promotion and was succeeded as OC G Flight by Anne Worthy. Neat, elegant and demure Anne was always ready to take a stand whenever she thought that the special requirements and welfare of her young ladies was not being properly looked after. On the first camp that Anne attended she of course made a tour round the various exercises to see what would be involved for her Flight. One of the exercises was a fairly strenuous assault course, designed to prod the more diffident cadets into the need sometimes to lead physically from the front, to raise their voices and to raise a sweat. It consisted of normal assault course stuff, walking over narrow planks six foot up over a swamp, swinging across a ditch on a rope, climbing over an eight-foot wall, not difficult if tackled as a team, crawling through a muddy pipe and so on. The event was known as Exercise Earl's Court. Anne was most disturbed by the look of the Earl's Court course; she came to find me and told me quite firmly that in no way would she agree to her Flight taking part in such a strenuous, dangerous, un-ladylike caper.

David Felwick caught my eye. "Quite right," he agreed loudly. How would Anne like to go round the course again with him and work out a much gentler and more suitable exercise for G Flight. David reappeared at tea-time. "It's OK, sir, it's all fixed. As we got to each element of the course I launched into an eloquent defence of the delicate nature of her girls and how it would be quite beyond their puny stamina and muscle power. And each time Anne contradicted me and said that this particular item would be just about acceptable." For Anne's peace of mind during Earl's Court we called the girls' almost identical version exercise Girl's Vault.

We might tease the girls but often many of the G Flight cadets emerged as among the best, the leading members of the course. Penny Parker had a pleasantly regal manner which earned her the nickname of The Duchess. Lynn Morley as Cadet Camp Commandant checked almost every other cadet for the poor standard of tying of their puttees. She became known as the Puttee Queen or the Chief Puttee Officer. At the Final Dinner Night the course presented her, mimicking the Sash of Merit for the best WRAF cadet, with the Puttee Sash. Its gold badge centrepiece was the brass-coloured lid of a corned beef tin and the sash itself was made of a khaki puttee trimmed with brilliant emerald green ribbon. At the Graduation Ball Lynn wore it proudly over her white evening dress and the emerald ribbon was exactly right with her striking gold-red hair.

On more than one occasion I told Wing Commander Leith that we on the Squadron had decided that we really wanted to present the Sword of Merit to a member of G Flight instead of to one of the men. The truth was that the girls were generally of a higher calibre both educationally and in terms of personal qualities. Whether it was a matter of supply and demand I cannot say. Perhaps I was now not alone in believing that in terms of a man's career the RAF was becoming seen as the poor relation among the three services. It had by this time become a rather sick joke that any air marshal's son who wanted to join the services invariably went to Sandhurst and into the army.

The subject of personal reports brought up again an issue that I had first met as a Flight Commander completing annual reports for members of 26 Squadron. Throughout their career all officers are reported on annually by their immediate boss on such items as performance in their current job, suitability for promotion and so on. Naturally the report also included the reporting officer's comments on perceived weaknesses as well as strengths. The reports were of course confidential, that is they were only seen by those in the chain of command and the personnel staff. For many years a brisk controversy had existed as to whether the subject of the report, the officer being reported on, should have been entitled to see the report too. It is a question which I was to meet again many times in industry, long after I left the RAF, but my views have never changed.

The report is, I believe, in the nature of a private conversation between whoever is writing the report, and their own boss. It is thus not appropriate for it to be seen by the person being reported on. Alongside the job of writing the report is the equally important one of the reporting officer talking privately and in confidence to the person being reported on. This gives them the opportunity to compliment them whenever possible on their strengths and to point out to them any perceived weaknesses or performance shortcomings that they can improve on. The two jobs are equally important but quite separate. Say, for example, my boss calls me in and asks for my views on the progress of young Bloggs. He wants my full, frank assessment and the question is whether I would be able to give that as well if Bloggs himself were in the room. The same applies to confidential reports. If I know that Bloggs is going to be able to read what I write, I am going to be inhibited and inclined to water down some of my comments.

The point is well illustrated by taking the case, for example, of two young, inexperienced pilots. One may be making just about adequate but rather shaky progress, partly due to lack of confidence. I must tell my boss frankly of my concerns about him, but I will try to conceal these from the man himself and I will be looking for every available opportunity to compliment him and to boost his self-confidence. The second young man may have excellent potential but may suffer at the moment from over-confidence and the tendency to take silly risks. Here I want to tell my boss that we may have a star in the making, but I shall find every opportunity to cut the tearaway down to size, to point out to him every slip and in short to try to prevent him from killing himself! I have frequently had to defend these views from the left who invariably raise the question of whether you can trust bosses to be fair and impartial. The answer to that is very simple. If you can't trust the boss to be fair and impartial you sack him and get one whom you can trust, but that is a job for his own boss, not for his subordinates.

At our OCTU camps, the field exercises were deliberately designed to put cadets under pressure. This was not out of vindictiveness but for very good reasons. Say a cadet had been commissioned and perhaps a few years later had found himself in command of a detachment in the Gulf, in Kosovo or wherever happened to be the current trouble spot. That would be no time to discover that he could not cope with stress and collapsed under pressure. In that case lives could well be put at risk. It was far better for all concerned for us to discover it under controlled, safe conditions in the middle of Norfolk. Out on exercises the cadets felt themselves to be in strange, unfamiliar countryside. We on the Directing Staff knew the area intimately, nowhere was more than fifty yards from a track giving access to a Landrover and no cadet was ever in fact more than ten minutes from a thermal blanket and a hot drink if he or she had really needed it.

The second camping period came right towards the end of the OCTU course. The big day was when we broke camp, collapsed all the tents, loaded everything into our articulated trucks and came back to Henlow. The starring role of the whole camping week was to be Cadet Camp Commandant for that day. The cadet selected for this role was in effect being told, you are being offered the Sword of Merit, show us if you are up to it.

Once we got back from the final camping period we, the DS, went into a huddle to make our decisions on whom we were recommending for passing out and being awarded the Queen's Commission. Most of the Commissioning List wrote itself. As the cadets themselves well knew, the majority had either clearly passed or equally clearly failed. It was those who were marginal that we agonised over. This was where we got the pay-off for the trouble we had taken to ensure that as many members of the DS as possible had seen and commented on a cadet. By this stage in the course the Flight Commander's file on each of their cadets contained comments on their showing in a range of activities and from many different people. What was remarkable was the similarity and consistency of what had been written.

The final decision rested with the Commissioning Review Panel. This consisted of the Wing Commander, me, as the cadet's Squadron Commander and one other Squadron Commander who did not know the cadet and had only read the paperwork. The cadet was invited in to be interviewed by the Panel and given a chance to justify why they should not be withdrawn from training. Often I was initially inclined to give the cadet the benefit of the doubt, but had put him up for review at the insistence of his Flight Commander. However in these cases more often than not the cadet in effect dug his own grave. Not unusually it would be an ex-NCO who could not grasp the wider vision and responsibilities that as an officer he now needed to embrace. Often his line of defence would be, "On this course I have done everything I have been asked to do." What he sadly could not see was that this was all he had done. He had just waited to be given instructions but had been quite oblivious of the opportunities that had been presented to him to use his own initiative or of the need for enterprise without waiting to be guided on what to do. The more he talked the more I would realise that his Flight Commander had been right. The other typical category of failures was of cadets who had emerged as simply too young and immature. If they were failed they would be told, "Go and get some broadening experience and then come back to OCTU in a couple of years."

It was during one such Commissioning Review week that I discovered what I regarded as a disgraceful practice in the MOD system for selecting the candidates to be sent for officer training at OCTU. Those running the selection process rightly acknowledged that they were not infallible. I discovered however that they had introduced a certain system to try to verify their judgements and to validate their procedures. They occasionally deliberately sent to us a cadet which their selectors had predicted was not just marginal but who could confidently be expected to fail. We would give all the cadets the best we could, but although we were quite unaware of the special reasons for their selection, it did not take long for these particular "guinea-pigs" to emerge.

Before I had found out about this system I had on one or two occasions gone to Wing Commander Leith, told him about a cadet whom we reckoned had not got a hope of a commission and was consequently having a thoroughly miserable time. However this "experimental" system put the Wing Commander in a difficult position. He would normally, I believe, have accepted my plea to offer the cadet an opportunity to withdraw from training but in these cases he then risked the accusation that we had not given the cadet time for a fair chance. So we soldiered on. The cadet in question feeling themselves more and more out of their depth would become withdrawn and, the rest of the course not being complete fools, would become the butt of derision and contempt. I believe this trial system showed a complete disregard for the welfare of those exposed to it. To have to persist for the whole OCTU course and then to fail so comprehensively must have severely damaged their self-confidence and their chances of success in whatever else they went on to do. I believe this system was quite indefensible and that some air marshal's head should have rolled for having condoned it and allowed it to be introduced.

Just after I had left the OCTU I heard about one more example of a misguided, ill-informed decision made at Training Command Headquarters without any attempt having been made to find out the views of us at the OCTU who were doing the actual training. The OCTU headquarters had always taken care to ensure that each flight of cadets consisted of a mix of experienced, older ex-NCOs and younger direct entrants, mainly school leavers. This, as we on the Squadrons well knew, was entirely right. The older cadets could offer much wisdom and guidance to the new entrants on a mass of service matters, just as I so well remembered the ex-airmen had for us new-boys at Cranwell. And equally the new comers, by challenging many of the assumptions and perhaps stick-in-the-mud ways of their seniors, could get them thinking afresh and jolt them into new ways. Just after I had left the OCTU I heard that an edict was issued from Headquarters Training Command that henceforth all flights were to consist either of new entrants or ex-NCOs but not a mix. How the battle was fought and what was the eventual outcome I do not know. I know very well that the edict was entirely misguided and could have only been made by someone completely ignorant of the way the OCTU worked.

Often during my tour at Henlow I found it helpful to try to remember my time at Cranwell, and to try to recall how things had looked, all that time ago, from a cadet's point of view. I remembered that there had been one item that we had reckoned was an omission from the programme for our last term. Knowing that we were to be commissioned in just a matter of weeks we believed that some occasion could have been found to invite us into the Officers' Mess, to let us have a glimpse however briefly of the new world we would shortly be entering. With this in mind for my last couple of courses I arranged to entertain the Green Squadron cadets, one flight at a time, for dinner in the Officer's Mess. I hope the cadets enjoyed those evenings—I certainly did. With hindsight I would have taken longer over it, had smaller groups, and mixed up cadets from different flights.

Towards the end of one course I invited down to a dinner party with some of the cadets an old skiing friend, now Squadron Leader Ian Dick, leader of the Red Arrows. We were enjoying a splendid, rather liquid dinner when a further inspired thought struck me. I said, "Ian, what will the Arrows happen to be doing on …"—I named a date a few weeks ahead which the cadets well knew would be the date of their graduation parade. Ian, sharp officer, replied, "Ah, ask me that again will you when I'm not half pissed!" I rang him up the next day and he agreed to arrange a normal training sortie for the Red Arrows which would be timed, to the huge delight of the graduating course, to allow a fly past over the parade ground at the climax of the parade. By another happy co-incidence on this occasion the Reviewing Officer was none other than my old aerodynamics tutor (and amateur dramatics director!) now Air Vice-Marshal "Flash" Button.

During the final weeks of one course two cadets presented themselves in my office one morning and requested an interview. "Sir, please get out your diary for the next course. We would like to agree with you a date when we can come back for an evening and make a presentation to your next Green Squadron. We believe it would be helpful for them to hear from us of our experiences during the first couple of months after we have graduated, and of how what we have learned here has fitted in to our new role as officers." I was delighted to agree to this helpful and enterprising suggestion and in due course they reappeared with a couple of other friends and gave us a most interesting evening.

Graduation Day was the climax of the course. The squadrons, commanded by cadets themselves, marched on to the square, accompanied by the station band. I had selected as our Squadron March the stirring and excellent marching tune Sousa's "Liberty Bell."

Quite co-incidentally it was also the signature tune of Monty Python's Flying Circus. The parade was inspected by some invited air marshal who presented the prizes and made a short speech. The Graduating Squadron then marched off in slow time and as they left the square they were deemed now to be officers. Throughout their course they had been drilled, sometimes mercilessly, by the Senior Drill Instructor, Warrant Officer Jordan. As they marched off the square for the last time Mr Jordan always positioned himself at the corner of the square and stood at the salute as they passed. As he said, "I have sometimes given you a tough time, ladies and gentlemen, so I reserve for myself the privilege of being the first to salute you as officers." The slow march was accompanied by "Old Lang Syne" and as they left the square and changed to a normal quick march the band played the old Gracie Fields favourite "Wish Me Luck As You Wave Me Goodbye."

After a short Inter-Denominational Service of Dedication the new officers were free to mingle with their families and other invited guests as they strolled towards their Mess for the formal luncheon. However on one occasion they told us they intended to vary this. In spite of the stress and pressures of the course, or perhaps because of them, they realised that they had now reached the end of what had been a unique and important experience in their lives and in their personal development. When they came out of chapel they intended to march to their Mess together as a squad, as Green Squadron, for the very last time. Cadet, or rather after the parade Pilot Officer, Andy Johnson was a Scot and a piper. As new officers they formed up as a squad and with Pilot Officer Johnson's pipes at their head they marched away from the OCTU and into their new careers. They told us later that by the time they reached the Cadets' Mess there was hardly a dry eye to be found.

At and after lunch we, the Directing Staff, had an opportunity to meet the families. Often mums and dads could hardly conceal their amazement in the changes that had come over their sons and daughters, now smart, happy, confident and articulate. What have you done... Had we been uncharitable we could have answered that we believed we had done in four months what some of their schools had failed to do in a dozen years. We had stretched them, physically and mentally, as they had never been stretched before, we had shown them a new way of life, of discipline, of self- discipline, of the fun of hard work and of relying and being relied on by colleagues, of worrying less about their rights than about their obligations—to others, to the service they were entering, to society at large and ultimately to their own potential. We believed that we had shown them what life was all about and that we had given them the pride and confidence in themselves to tackle it.

For simple fun nothing would ever equal flying, but at a deeper level my time at the Officer Cadet Training Unit was by a long way the best and most satisfying of my career. We all acknowledged that we on the DS learned on every course much more than the cadets. What we were doing was so very worthwhile. The more I have seen of civilian life since leaving the RAF the more I am convinced of it. I have been lucky enough during a second career to find some opportunities to go on promoting these ideas but never at the intensity we were able to generate at Henlow.

At the end of the course the young officers were entitled to a few weeks' leave before starting their professional training. However my Flight Commanders and I believed that something a bit more exciting might appeal to at least some of them. Wing Commander Leith, supportive as ever, had let me sidestep a much less interesting duty in charge of the Cadets' Mess so that I could revive Adventure Training for the OCTU. With Britain withdrawing from so many overseas bases the forces had lost many opportunities for trekking across deserts, canoeing down jungle rapids and the like. To offer some alternatives and to help put back some of the sparkle into service life the Nuffield Trust had generously provided valuable hardware such as ocean-going yachts and would fund enterprising expeditions.

For our first venture we offered our ex-Green Squadron graduates an outing in cross-country skiing and mountain survival in Norway. On the day after they graduated we flew to Kinloss and then to Bergen and took the train up through the fiords and mountains to Geilo and we had a ball. We skied, we danced with Norwegian blondes, we even spent a night, and slept quite snugly, in snow holes we dug into a glacier, to show that arctic survival like so much else is about knowledge and know-how. We came home by sea from Bergen to Newcastle and played at being Hornblower all the way across. Soon after that Red Squadron, following our lead, went to the French Massif Central to canoe down the gorges and later Green Squadron expeditions went to Cyprus to climb on Mount Troodos, to Malta to see the services working in the Mediterranean, to Oxfordshire for sport parachuting and to the Hamble to sail one of the RAF yachts to Cherbourg and back.

My tour at Henlow came to an end and I was posted to Chivenor in North Devon. I felt that at the OCTU I had been exactly a round peg in a round hole. I had been doubly lucky in a fine crowd of Flight Commanders and in David Leith as a boss. As I have already said, he was always prepared to listen patiently, he gave me clear boundaries on what he considered was acceptable and then let me get on with it. You can hardly ask for more than that.

I was due to leave Henlow when the current course ended at the end of April 1974. However in mid March Geoff O'Brien who was to relieve me as OC Green Squadron arrived and moved into his married quarter. No-one could blame him, he had been at the Ministry of Defence in London and escaped at the first opportunity. He was naturally keen to find out what went on around the OCTU, to prepare himself to pick up the reins, and he was soon a familiar figure around the squadron. He came to camp with us. As the course entered its final weeks, some of the Flight Commanders' time was directed towards preparations for the next course when Geoff would be the boss. Whom then should they consult on future plans, Geoff or me? Although I had no wish to leave, I discussed this with Geoff and came to the conclusion that this was not a helpful situation. Reluctantly I went to David Leith and told him that on balance I thought it would be better if I handed over the Squadron to Geoff sooner rather than later. This would achieve a clean break and allow the Flight Commanders and others to get on with their planning without distraction.

As usual he listened to my reasoning and accepted my suggestion. I handed over to Geoff but stuck around long enough to enjoy being memorably Dined Out with the course during their final week. I believed that another aspect of our officer training which was deficient was the lack of opportunities we provided for the cadets to meet senior officers. I had therefore invited to the Dining In Night a friend I had known briefly in Singapore through sailing when he was Station Commander at RAF Tengah. Peter Latham was now an Air Commodore and just the sort of ebullient, charming, unaffected senior officer we could all admire and whom I believed that the cadets should meet as a role model. He did not disappoint us. As the party games after dinner

329

started to warm up he came into the ante-room brandishing a broom stick, with his broad Air Commodore's stripe gleaming on his sleeve, and called out to the cadets, "Right, come on, its us one-ringers against the rest!"

I had a month to spare before my next appointment and I was summoned to the MOD Sales Executive to be given an interesting job of running a Defence Sales exhibition at Bedford airfield. This provided an opportunity to try putting into practice the management and leadership techniques we had been teaching cadets for the last two years. I think it was reasonably successful. The display stands and all their associated electrical wiring and power points were being supplied, constructed and erected by the well-known firm of Beck and Pollitzer. This gave me the novel experience of working with civilians, they were a good crowd and I enjoyed it. On the opening day a VIP came down to do the honours. The VIP turned out to be Air Marshal Sir Michael Giddings, my old Wing Commander Flying from Waterbeach. Small world!

Shortly after I arrived at Chivenor I received three letters. The first was from a Group Captain in the Ministry of Defence which said, "It is a pleasure for me to have this opportunity to write to you concerning your recent attachment as Liaison Officer at the Surveillance and Reconnaissance Exhibition which was held at the Royal Aircraft Establishment, Bedford, in March. Air Vice-Marshal C W Coulthard, the Head of Defence Sales, has written to the Department and asked that we pass on his appreciation for the enthusiasm, efficiency and tact you showed in your liaison duties during the period of your attachment to Bedford. Undoubtedly, your efforts contributed to the great success of the Exhibition and were invaluable to the Defence Sales Organisation."

The second letter was from Paul Miller in HQ Training Command, who wrote, "I've very much enjoyed our close association with the great Green Squadron, I wish we'd forged the link earlier. I was interested to note the other evening several of your Hobby Horses being gently ridden by your Flight Commanders, so I'm sure that much of your enthusiasm for better things and better ways of doing them will live on at the OCTU after you've gone. We will have that Shakespeare thing re-written about the evil that men do living after them!"

The third, which meant the most to me, was from David Diprose. He wrote, "Dear Boss, I know that Green Squadron is annoyed at the way the service has kept you hanging about, though this has been difficult to demonstrate without possibly offending the new boss. You have achieved a great deal for Green Squadron and OCTU. While our present is not large it carries with it many thoughts of these achievements and firm good wishes for your health and happiness in the future.

Dave Dip."

# No 229 Operational Conversion Unit

## R A F Chivenor

# The Tactical Weapons Unit

## R A F Brawdy

# Directorate of Flying Training

## Ministry of Defence (Air)

I LEFT HENLOW and the Officer Cadet Training Unit most regretfully as I had greatly enjoyed my tour there. I felt that I had been able to make some original contributions and had introduced a number of changes that would live on after I had left. I drove down to RAF Chivenor in North Devon realising however that I was coming to a very attractive part of England. Chivenor enjoyed a most popular location, just west of Barnstaple town and near the sandy north Devon holiday beaches. The Taw and Torridge rivers meet as they flow into the Bristol Channel and the wide, shallow estuary as it curves round between the villages of Appledore and Westward Ho! and the sand dunes of Braunton Burrows formed the southern boundary of the airfield. Chivenor's weather factor was excellent too. Lying almost at sea level between the estuary and the hills running up to Ilfracombe, it was sheltered behind more high ground to the south-west and so we often had a high enough cloud base for us to fly when practically nobody else could. The buildings were mainly ancient pre-fabs held together by bitumastic paint but altogether the station suited its role well and fitted like an old, shabby but comfortable pair of shoes.

Once pilots had completed their initial training they were divided into three streams to go on to advanced flying training for fast jets, heavies or helicopters. The fast-jet stream, having learned to fly the aeroplane pure and simple then moved to the Operational Conversion Unit at Chivenor to learn to use it as a weapon, the same stage of training as we had done at Stradishall back in '53. The aircraft used now was the Hunter, cheaper and simpler than the Harriers, Tornados, Phantoms and Jaguars on the front-line squadrons but perfectly satisfactory to learn techniques. I was to be Squadron Leader, Operations reporting to Wing Commander "Moose" David, OC Ops. Wing. I had got to know Moose long ago when we were both at White Waltham. He was a kind, considerate, unassuming man whom I had always liked.

For the first few months the job was pleasant enough but undemanding. I tried not to be nostalgic for the constant activity, challenge and interest of the OCTU and got used to being general assistant for the Wing Commander Ops. When I got to Chiv the summer holiday season was just about to get into its stride and being right on the edge of the water it seemed sensible to get a boat. I bought a Drascombe Lugger. It needed a mooring and as it turned out nothing could have been simpler. A local garage gave me a large lump of concrete with an iron ring fitted to it. I waited for a low spring tide and buried it in the sand as far out as I could get. A length of chain and a buoy produced a most satisfactory mooring. The Drascombe was very mediocre as a proper sailing boat, poor at getting to windward, but as a fun boat for children and for picnics it was ideal. For one thing it had no boom for the mainsail and so there was nothing to whack people on the head even if they were not paying attention when the sail swung across. Ted Wood ran one of the squadrons, he and Muriel were old friends from No 26 Squadron at Gütersloh where they had been newly-weds. They now had three delightful daughters—and a motorboat. We had some splendid joint outings.

Just as there had been at Henlow, the O.C.U.'s students included some from foreign air forces training with the RAF. One story which had passed into legend concerned a certain Middle East pilot some years previously who had been briefed one morning to go off on some exercise, signed the Flight Authorisation Book, signed out a Hunter and took off into the wide blue yonder. At the end of his sortie he re-entered the circuit, turned downwind, came round finals and landed, but much too hot and fast. He had no chance of stopping before the end of the runway and, it being before the days of Safeland barriers, shot across the over-run and disappeared into the hedge sending pheasants, blackbirds and the rest scattering in alarm. As soon as they saw what was happening the crash truck raced after him, skidded to a halt, and the crash crew plunged into the hedge. The Hunter's cockpit canopy was open, the straps were thrown back—and there was no-one there. Perhaps he had concussion, perhaps he was in the hedge somewhere ... . The crash crew searched all around but the pilot was nowhere to be found, so the aeroplane was rescued out of the hedge and towed back to dispersal.

Someone, acting on intuition, went up to his room and there was the pilot, in bed in his pyjamas. "Oh, what has happened, have I overslept? My goodness, so sorry!" He tried to brazen it out. He had not been down at the airfield this morning, he had not flown, his signature in the authorisation book was a forgery—and it was all an outrageous lie and victimisation. In the end they had to ring up the embassy and suggest he be collected as not really a suitable candidate for aircrew training.

Although so well suited to its role and so popular with all those stationed there Chivenor was undeniably showing its age. As the Station Engineer put it, he was running out of bitumastic paint to hold the place together. At the same time the Navy had a well-built Royal Naval Air Station at Brawdy, beyond Haverfordwest and only a few miles short of St David's Head in the far west of Wales. They wanted to hand it over. It was decided that to renovate Chivenor properly would have been uneconomical so the station would close and we would move the unit to Brawdy. Before the move could take place a large amount of detailed planning had to be done.

I spent much time trundling back and forth between Chivenor and Brawdy in a Chipmunk looking at accommodation plans, the new works that would be needed and many other details.

Brawdy's location on the craggy western tip of Pembrokeshire was certainly picturesque in the extreme. The Pembrokeshire Coastal Path wound past the airfield along the edge of the jagged cliffs and past the sandy coves of St Bride's Bay. The cliffs and the off-lying islands were the homes of vast flocks of sea-birds. We calculated that we were so far west that we were nearer to Ireland than we were to Cardiff. Although the brick-built station buildings may in themselves have been a great improvement on the pre-fabs of Chivenor, as a flying station Brawdy had major drawbacks. Where Chiv had nestled at sea level with its outstanding weather factor, Brawdy was on the top of a three-hundred foot headland exposed to the westerly Atlantic gales. We were often actually in cloud when down on Newgale beach it was clear. We all agreed that we had never before encountered gale-force fog. The single runway was orientated north-south, so that with the strong prevailing south-west winds the cross-winds could be fierce and were often well outside the limits for flying. To add to the problems the airfield was surrounded by army gunnery ranges and the air traffic procedures for recovery in poor weather were the most complicated I have ever seen. It seemed a strange place to send student pilots. Rumour had it that we were going there in order to provide employment in this corner of Wales rather than for any good operational reasons. However the decision had been taken and so sadly Chivenor was going to have to close.

An RAF airfield, especially one flying jets, is unavoidably noisy and so never the most popular neighbour for the local populace especially in a holiday area. Throughout its history successive generations at Chivenor, realising that the noise of our aeroplanes must have been a constant trial to the inhabitants and holiday-makers in Barnstaple, had taken great care to keep on good terms with the townspeople. Now that we were closing down our Station Commander came up with the excellent idea that we should hold a formal luncheon for the mayor and mayoress of Barnstaple, the aldermen and their ladies, to say goodbye and to thank them for their forbearance over the years. Although in all the services we rather take for granted our facilities in an Officers' Mess for laying on a smart formal luncheon or dinner, with silver on the table and smart, white-coated stewards, this is not readily available in civilian circles. This was therefore clearly a good way of entertaining the dignitaries from the town and at the same time would provide a pleasant and welcome break for us in the middle of our hard work preparing for the move. On the day therefore, promptly at a quarter to one, about seven or eight of us, the senior officers of the station, in our best uniforms, were standing about the ante-room, sherries in hand, ready to welcome and to entertain our guests.

The Air Officer Commanding the Group of which Chivenor was a part, an Air Vice-Marshal, had decided that he too would attend the luncheon. Most of us had never met him but as our overall boss he would perhaps take the opportunity to wish us well with the move and even to say a word about all the disruption that was inevitably going to be caused for the families and, for example, to the children's schooling. As we waited for our civilian guests to arrive the Station Commander ushered the Air Marshal into the room. The Mess Steward moved forward with his silver tray and the Air Marshal accepted a sherry. He then turned round and for the next five minutes stood with his back to us, chatting casually to the Station Commander. He totally ignored us. We might have been so many pieces of furniture. He did not even say, "Good morning, gentlemen."

Chivenor finally closed on a happier note. Someone suggested that we should invite for the final week-end party some representatives of the front line squadrons flying all the types of more advanced aircraft that our graduates went to after leaving us. We thus welcomed old friends arriving in Phantoms, Tornadoes, Lightnings and the rest. Naturally the guests of honour were the Red Arrows. Punctually on the Saturday afternoon they zoomed into the circuit, landed and taxied in. Ian Dick, leading the Arrows, (when not busy leading the RAF Ski Team) came up into the Control Tower and quietly asked our Station Commander who was the senior officer at Chivenor that afternoon. The Group Captain was able to say, "Relax, I am." The Arrows took off again and then proceeded to give us the most spectacular, low, fast exhibition of super display flying that any of us had ever seen, or is ever likely to. On the Monday morning we started packing up and preparing to move.

There was much work to do to move the unit into Brawdy. The major items were the setting up of all the engineering departments while the flying squadrons set to with saws and hammers to construct their operation rooms with Hadley Box communication links to the Control Tower, the Met office and the rest. Part of my empire which had to be set up anew at Brawdy was the Station Operations Room. We unpacked all the gear, the charts, the secret documents etc. and prepared to get ourselves up and running. We banged a nail into the wall and hung up the electric clock. It functioned immediately—and went—backwards.

Since the departure of the Navy, Brawdy had been looked after by a skeleton care and maintenance staff commanded by a Wing Commander. On our arrival he would revert to Wing Commander, Administration and report to our Station Commander—a much younger man. Perhaps he resented his loss of status but for some reason which I never discovered he and Wing Commander David did not hit it off. On a number of occasions Moose actually called me into his office and said to me, "Bill, as you know Wingco Admin and I are not actually on speaking terms, will you go and see him, please, about … ." I wondered whether the Station Commander knew that this situation existed. Whether he did or not it hardly reflected much credit on him when two of his three wing commanders were literally not speaking to each other. Having spent the previous two years impressing on cadets the importance of leadership, of human relationships and of creating effective teams I found the situation quite extraordinary and deeply depressing. Not surprisingly the pattern of poor relationships soon extended all through the station and many people seemed to live in a constant state of irritability and stress.

While at Brawdy I did get a memorable and most enjoyable Christmas break. I suggested to the Wood family that we should take the girls up to Scotland and introduce them to a spot of skiing. We booked a week in the Rothiemurchus Lodge, on the edge of the Cairngorm Mountains above Aviemore. Muriel valiantly resigned herself to getting no real Christmas break from cooking and general Mum's chores. We drove up in two cars staying one night on the way at a friend's house in Inverkeithing almost overlooking the Forth Bridge. On the way up we had told the girls about all the splendid wildlife there would be in the Cairngorms. Sure enough just as we started breakfast on our first day in the Lodge, there outside the windows was the famous herd of Rothiemurchus reindeer. As is always the case in Scotland the actual skiing was not quite what one would get in the alps, but the whole Highland scene, the vast scale of the mountains, the heather, the lochs, the unspoilt relaxed way of life was as appealing as ever.

For many months rumours had abounded that the RAF was soon to announce a redundancy programme for middle ranking officers. A bulge had been allowed to grow up of Squadron Leaders and Wing

Commanders. Even allowing for natural wastage there were now far too many for a proper percentage of them ever to be promoted and they (we) were in turn blocking promotion for junior officers. Having allowed the situation to develop there was now only one way to cure it and that was to declare redundant some four hundred officers. Many of us were on what were designated as "permanent commissions." However tough as it was this was not going to be allowed to stand in the way. It was therefore no real surprise when one morning I had a call asking me to go to see the Group Captain. He was sorry to tell me that my name was on the list of those declared redundant. The redundancy programme was particularly unpleasant news for officers with dependant children whose education would now be completely disrupted, and some of those concerned had a bare four month's notice of the date when they would be required to leave the service. I had no dependants and as my date happened to be right at the end of the programme, almost two years hence, I was rather better off than most.

I managed one final jolly. A naval de Havilland Heron dropped in, a bigger and more powerful development of the Devon and with four engines instead of the Devon's two. I persuaded the pilot I had flown lots of hours on Devons, casually forgetting to mention that this had been about fifteen years ago. With the Navy's typical good nature he let me sit in the left hand seat to take off and fly one circuit and landing, and so I notched up my twenty-eighth, and first four-engine type.

For those retiring normally at the end of their careers, the RAF tries to arrange that they spend their last tour in an area of the country of their choice. Friends suggested to me that if I wanted to get into a meaningful second career I should get to the London area. Britain being Britain it is London where it all happens. I had never wanted to be a townie but I had to admit that this seemed sound advice. I discovered that Roy Bowie, who had once been Squadron Commander of No 20 Sqn at Ahlhorn all those years ago was at the Ministry of Defence and, being a keen rugby follower, he wanted to get to Wales. We arranged an exchange posting. I left Brawdy without regret and started my last tour in the Directorate of Flying Training located in Lacon House, two blocks along from Adastral, in Theobald's Road. I lived at RAF Uxbridge and commuted daily.

Also living at Uxbridge was Tom Shepperd, younger brother of Bill Shepperd of No 63 Sqn at Waterbeach. Tom, a most effective and enterprising chap, had recently distinguished himself by leading a tri-service expedition across the Sahara Desert. He was invited to address the Royal Geographical Society to show the photographs and to tell the tale of the adventure. It was a fascinating evening and when he had finished speaking he was approached by the guest of honour, Field Marshal Sir Michael Carver, now Chief of the Defence Staff. The Field Marshal said to Tom how encouraging it was to find that young officers were spending their time on such worthwhile exploits. He then asked, "Where is the Air Force sending you next, Shepperd?" Tom replied, "Well actually nowhere, sir, I've been made redundant."

Before I finally left the service I was keen to record my views on the officer training that we had been providing at Henlow and how I thought it fell short of what was needed. One possible medium for this was a magazine—The Royal Air Forces Quarterly where Air Vice-Marshal Button was the current editor. In the Winter 1976 edition, the magazine published my article "Officer Training in the RAF." In it I wrote:—

> "It has been said that the price of freedom is eternal vigilance. It may equally be said that the price of maintaining the highest standards in such a volatile resource as manpower is constant alertness to the special needs and problems of the times. For a small, voluntary service such as the Royal Air Force, operating such vastly expensive equipment, one of its prime assets is the quality and dedication of its personnel, and especially its officers. But the very fact that our equipment is so costly and complex poses a special problem when the balance is being struck between our technical needs and those of our human resources. If we in the service have been slow to recognise this problem, there are those outside it who have not. In September 1971 the Duke of Edinburgh, comparing the Royal Air Force with the Royal Navy, said, "Aboard ship you learn to live with people, this is the important thing … . The Royal Air Force has probably an even more highly developed professional qualification but I think probably at the expense of personal relationships." Some would say that the expense has been too high. In any organisation personal relationships, learning to live with and get results through the work of other people is the special responsibility of that organisation's leaders and any shortcomings in these areas are a direct reflection on their performance and almost certainly on the training that they are being given."

I went on to list the changes which I believed were needed, and concluded by writing,

"Concentrating all our officer training and associated expertise at Cranwell and ensuring that it attains the eminence of Sandhurst and Dartmouth would do more for the long term good of the Royal Air Force than any other single measure."

After I had left the service the OCTU was in fact closed and all the officer training in the RAF was re-located at Cranwell. Whether the second part of my plea has been met it is for others to judge.

The other item of advice I got while considering my future as a civilian was from an old friend, Derek Parry. He and I had not quite overlapped at Boscombe Down and since his voluntary retirement he had set himself up as a financial adviser. He had advised me, as he still does, on financial matters. His advice was quite clear—buy a house or some property on the biggest mortgage you can arrange. This at first sounded to me crazy. I was soon to leave the RAF, I had no idea how I was going to earn a living and to saddle myself with a mortgage sounded most unwise. However Derek brushed aside my misgivings and so in May 1976 I went ahead and bought a third floor flat at 66 Gloucester Street, Pimlico. It was probably the best advice I ever had.

Having always lived in RAF accommodation I had never owned any furniture. While negotiating to buy the flat I discovered in High Wycombe a regular monthly auction and spent a series of amusing Saturdays there acquiring at least some of the items that I needed. The auctioneer was a born entertainer and his banter with prospective customers was delightful. I found a local craftsman to make me a small kit trailer to tow behind the car and would drive back to Uxbridge with it piled high with my latest haul of loot. Before I left Uxbridge my sitting room was so congested you could hardly open the door, but I had found some very good bargains. Finally I hired a van and a friend helped me cart all the furniture up the three floors to the Pimlico flat. I moved out of the Officers' Mess at Uxbridge, moved into the flat and now caught the No 24 bus up to Trafalgar Square on my way to Lacon House.

While at Henlow we on the Directing Staff had speculated on how interesting it was going to be to watch the future careers of our cadets. This I was not now going to be able to do, but some years after leaving the service I happened to be watching a television news item about some aircraft incident and a young RAF officer was being interviewed. I do not recall the details of the incident but the officer was Flight Lieutenant Alan Bone, who had been one of the stars of a Green

Squadron not that long before. What was particularly gratifying was that on his pullover Alan was already wearing the red and white ribbon of the AFC—the Air Force Cross. I hope that his time on Green Squadron had contributed something to what had clearly been a most satisfactory start to his career.

I was due to leave the RAF in July 1977 and I had to make up my mind what I was going to do. Another old friend I had tracked down for advice was George Cannon. He had stayed on at Boscombe Down to see the arrival of the Harrier, also picked up a well deserved AFC in the process and had then commanded a Harrier squadron in Germany. Leaving the RAF he had decided to become a schoolteacher and had trained at the Roehampton Institute of Higher Education in Wimbledon. As I had found so much satisfaction in training cadets, this direction seemed worth investigating so in August I went out to Wimbledon to have a look at the place and to form some impressions. I got a most friendly welcome and the unexpected offer of a place for the start of the next academic year in October. If I left the RAF at once I would by next July, my planned retirement date, be well on the way to qualifying as a maths teacher. I had already said to myself that after so many years of the apparent security of service life I had better get used to the idea of sticking my neck out and "taking the plunge" when an offer came along. I told Roehampton to put my name down for October, went back to MOD and simply informed my boss that I would be leaving shortly.

Before I retired I had time to reflect on my time in the RAF. For a start all had gone well. Although I had not shone at Cranwell I had passed out satisfyingly high in the flying order of merit. After some early difficulties on fast jets, especially in instrument flying, I had enjoyed two front line squadron tours, the second as a flight commander and during which I had captained the 2 TAF Gunnery Team. I had got into ETPS at the first attempt and had enjoyed three years of the cream of fast jet flying as a test pilot, being one of the first dozen or so members of the RAF to fly the Lightning. During that tour I had narrowly missed getting into the RAF Ski Team and had also been short-listed for the job of equerry to the Queen. My year at Staff College had not been a success and I had as a result got some backwater postings to follow. Gan was better and Singapore extremely interesting but I finally fell on my feet at Henlow.

By that time I had the experience and some insights to see the relevance and importance of the training we attempted to provide there. I could also see that the principles of service and leadership which I was beginning to understand had applications far beyond the RAF. I did not know at the time what my future held or how I would be able to use these insights as a basis for a very satisfying second career. That is what happened and in due course I enjoyed a second career as interesting and, I believe, as worthwhile as the first.

Nothing, of course, was ever going to compare with the sheer fun of being a jet jockey. My mind went back to the early days of my flying career at Waterbeach. For Pilot Officers and Flying Officers there were few responsibilities other than flying. I had by then flown enough hours on Meteors to be completely confident in them but everything else on the Squadron was novel and exciting. Our whole attention was directed towards improving our performance in the air—more deft handling of the controls and use of the radio, smoother formation flying, more precise flying on instruments, better air gunnery scores. In due course we were entrusted to lead sections, making more competent and shrewder decisions as the sortie progressed, and giving better and more helpful guidance to the newcomers. The weekends had become just those two boring days when you couldn't fly! It was hardly surprising that during the 1930s so many young men of generations before ours had wanted nothing better than to spend their weekends flying the fighter aeroplanes of their time in the Royal Auxiliary Air Force. A bit later they had contributed massively to the defence of this country in the Battle of Britain. For my generation the Berlin airlift and the Korean War had been before our time and mercifully the Cold War never got hot. We had enjoyed all the fun without, as they had, having later to pay the price.

After those splendid early years nothing else was ever going to be like that clear-cut, uncomplicated job. So often we had had the fun of getting up with the dawn, to find the dew still thick on the grass and the mist still hiding the meadows as we walked down to the hangar while the only sound was the clatter of the tractor as our airmen towed the aeroplanes out on to the line. A quick look at the weather chart and then the feeling that, as the dawn started to break, one was stealing a march on everyone else by getting airborne while they were still in bed. Nothing would equal the satisfaction of being a member of a slick, well-drilled formation, operating the splendid piece of precision machinery which is a modern jet fighter aeroplane, of knowing that you had the skills to use it in the way that the designer had intended, of belonging to the close-knit team which is a front-line fighter squadron, with its complete inter-dependence in the air and its firm friendships on the ground. As I have said, at the time we took it all so much for granted, it was just the job we did, and there seemed no reason why the fun and the friendships need ever end. But all that is the stuff of youth. No matter what career you follow the fleeting, golden years soon pass and that land of lost content can't be revisited.

What had been the purpose of it all? Our predecessors had confronted the evil of Nazism and eventually with our allies had won over it a complete and decisive victory. I believe that the evil of Communism was more subtle and much more powerful. Nazism only lasted some twelve years and directly polluted mainly just the continent of Europe. Communism endured for seventy years and in that time blighted or destroyed many more millions of innocent lives. Communism too had to be confronted and stopped in its tracks whatever the cost, until it finally collapsed under the weight of its own inconsistencies and lies. My generation of fliers had no spectacular battles to fight or victories to record to compare with the Battle of Britain, North Africa and the Battle of the Atlantic, the Bomber Offensive or the Second Front in Europe, but we had played our part in what became the great bloodless victory of 1989. As part of NATO, the North Atlantic Treaty Organisation, we had made our contribution to holding the ring against Communism and had helped to prevent in Europe the advance that the Communists enjoyed in many other parts of the world. Our individual contributions could be compared to those of the little coral insects, each on its own insignificant, but together forming a vast, enduring structure. The structure which we helped to build is the continuing survival of the free world with its opportunities to move ahead and to try to do a bit better than in the past. I believe that we confirmed again the truth of the old Roman saying, which was neglected throughout the twenties and thirties, with such tragic consequences, "If you wish for peace—prepare for war."

For my final year of service at the Ministry of Defence I was living in my flat in Pimlico and travelling by bus up to Lacon House, but I was still being administered, dealt with as the army puts it for "pay and rations," by RAF Uxbridge. As the date drew near for my departure from the RAF I went out to Uxbridge to "clear." The system which we followed on every posting from one station to another was to collect a form from the Station Headquarters which listed the sections where you might have unfinished business. For example you might have been responsible for an inventory, at the end of a flying tour you would need to hand in to stores many valuable items such as your "g" suit, flying helmet, possibly a stop-watch. The medical section may have needed to know where you were going in order to send your medical records on to your next unit. The Accounts Section always had their own forms they wanted you to complete.

At each section you obtained a signature to confirm that you had cleared with them and when the list was complete you took it back to Station Headquarters. It was a good system—rather like completing your Pre-Take Off Checks—and it ensured that nothing got overlooked. One of my last calls was at the personnel department. They reminded me that I had not used up my entitlement of free leave travel warrants for the year. Actually I seldom did but it now seemed a pity not to take a final advantage of a spot of free travel. I have always loved Scotland and so I asked for a railway pass from London to Mallaig.

I awarded myself a long weekend and early one Friday took the Inter-City to Glasgow, changed trains there and so travelled up the length of Loch Lomond to Crainlarich, over Rannoch Moor to Fort William for a late dinner and bed & breakfast. Mallaig is at the western end of the romantic Road to the Isles and is linked to Fort William by what was once the independent Caledonian Railway, threading its way among the mountains, past the head of Loch Shiel and so, as the song says, "… by Shiel water the track is to the west, by Ailort and by Morar to the sea." The trip onwards from Fort William was memorable, through some of the most spectacular scenery in Scotland and although I had driven this way in the past, it was good for a change to let the train take the strain and just to watch the views. Even the weather was kind, I spent a day tramping over the hills and stayed two nights in Mallaig. Waiting on the platform for the train back to Fort William I strolled up to the engine and started chatting to the driver. Right on cue, just as I had hoped he would, he asked me if I would like to ride down with him in the cab. The views were even more spectacular and it was a fitting final free jolly.

My last week arrived. The office kindly told me to get myself a leaving present and to give them the bill. I found a smart black briefcase and they said, "Fine, we'll hide it and then present it to you at your leaving party." After quite a long career I had, I suppose, visualised eventually leaving the Royal Air Force by being "Dined Out" one evening in some Officers' Mess, in mess kit, with candles on the tables and with all the trimmings. It wasn't quite like that. Just down the road from Lacon House, the Bung Hole in Holborn is no doubt perfectly adequate as a pub but it was not quite the same. I noticed it was No 57 Holborn, so having entered the service at Cranwell with No 57 Entry it was quite appropriate. One Friday, my last day in the Royal Air Force, the whole department gathered there for a lunchtime ham sandwich and a pint. The Group Captain tried to overcome the general hubbub and the canned pop music to say a few kind words.

He then confessed that they would have to present the briefcase later because they had temporarily lost it. Back in the office I looked around various cupboards and found it. Someone sent out for a couple of bottles of wine and at half past four we had a small second party for the presentation and final farewells. That really was the end of the road. I went down in the lift and in the foyer handed in my MOD security pass and my F1250, my personal identity card, to the Reception Desk. I walked out of the building, across Theobald's Road and through Red Lion Square, past Holborn Underground Station and down the length of Kingsway. A Kardomah cafe used to stand on the corner of the Aldwych, and I turned in to it for a cup of tea. It occurred to me that since arriving at Cranwell I had served twenty-six years, twenty-six weeks and a couple of days. Viva 26! I finished my tea and, now as a civilian, caught the bus down to Pimlico.

# Second Career

## Southlands College

TWO WEEKS AFTER I left the RAF I started the autumn term as a student at Southlands College, part of the Roehampton Institute of Higher Education, in Wimbledon. I found that I had entered a very different world. The pace of life was unbelievably slow. Three of us had been designated as "mature students" and we were joining a course of mainly teenagers who had already spent a year at the college, so we were actually joining in at the start of the second year of the syllabus. In no time we were wondering what on earth the others had been doing for the whole of the previous year. It seemed to take us all of a fortnight to catch up!

I was planning to become a maths teacher and I found that the staff in the maths department were probably the best in the college. Even so by the end of the first year I had begun to realise that I was going to suffer from two main obstacles. In my mid-forties I was too set in my ways to adapt to the role of school-teacher rather than school-master and all which that implied. Added to that was so many years becoming accustomed to the service way of life, of respect—even if sometimes grudging—for authority, of punctuality, self-discipline, a certain standard of dress and so many other factors which I had been able to take for granted until they no longer applied. However I had set out to qualify as a maths teacher, I could for the present see no other way ahead and so I continued with the course.

During my second year we started teaching practices. This at least was a most interesting and educational experience. The college made arrangements for us to get in touch with the appropriate departments of local schools and to go over to take two or three periods a week. I did my first term of teaching practices at a school in Hounslow and my second at Rutlish School in Wimbledon. Teaching practice brought home to me most vividly the nature of the world I was heading for. I had decided on teaching as a second career mainly having found my time at Henlow so satisfying but it did not now take me long to realise the great difference between the cadets whom I had been dealing with and teenage school children. The former were, of course, at the OCTU because they wanted to come into RAF as officers and so were there of their own volition. Although they no doubt found many elements of our course irksome and even stressful it was matter of like it or lump it. It was in effect our club that they had elected to join and so if they wanted to succeed they were going to have to conform to our standards. None of this applied to the school children I was now confronting and I soon discovered that it was me that was going to have to change a great deal if I was going to be any sort of success as a teacher.

One small incident clinched the matter. I was holding forth to some fifteen year olds about some aspect of maths when I noticed a piece of paper being passed along the back row with suppressed giggles. I walked down the room, pocketed the paper and continued with what I was saying. At the end of the lesson I looked at the paper. It read, "We haven't got him next week." I realised that we had all got the message—I so wish I had kept the paper as a souvenir.

At about this time a notice was put up announcing a weekend visit to Luton Industrial College. The purpose of the visit was to introduce us putative teachers to the world of industry, the world to where many of our pupils would be going when they started work. There would be speakers from both management and the trade unions, it all sounded moderately interesting and so I put my name down for it, not realising that the week-end and the many subsequent visits I made to Luton would open the door to a very enjoyable second career. The Industrial College was a Methodist foundation and at the time the Director was the Revd. Bill Gowland, a very human, most amusing and enthusiastic individual. He had the previous year been the President of the Methodist Council and so now referred to himself as the Methodist Pope.

I quickly discovered that many aspects of industry, the relations between management and the "shop floor" and between management and the unions provided many echoes of the leadership training we had offered at the OCTU. But the industrial situations were much more complicated. In the services, in the last resort, officers issued orders and there were sanctions available to ensure that they were obeyed. Industrial relations were more complex and here in the last resort anyone had the right if they wished to withdraw their labour. To some extent the boot was on the other foot. However it seemed to me that industrial management was clearly a field where the ideas about leadership which I had learned at Henlow were clearly relevant and that this might be a field where I could make some sort of contribution.

At Luton I met someone who mentioned that he was on the council of an organisation called The Industrial Society and he promised to send me details about it. Within a few months I had contacted them, arranged an interview and so for the first time met John Garnett. I couldn't have been luckier; John eventually became a much loved friend, a marvellous boss and a most inspiring exemplar of all that is best in industrial leadership as well as a charismatic speaker in putting the message across. John introduced me to one of his heads of a department and we agreed a date for me to join. At the end of our course at Southlands I obtained my Cert Ed, my Certificate in Education and I was invited by the college to stay on for a further year to get a B. Ed. I thanked them but told them that I already had a job lined up as I had decided that I was more suited to industrial management training than teaching.

# The Industrial Society

It is hard to believe that I stayed at The Industrial Society for eighteen years. I had totally fallen on my feet and found myself an ideal second career. Once again I found that I was exactly a round peg in a round hole. It was a delightful place to work and I soon discovered that the whole ambience of friendship, co-operation and fun was most appealing. In those far off days before political correctness had soured so many institutions it was not unusual to come into the office after an absence of a few days and before I could even take off my coat or check my in-tray to be greeted by my secretary, Val Hudson, with, "Hey, don't I get a motivational cuddle then?"

The main department offices and training rooms were in elegant Carlton House Terrace, at the bottom of Lower Regent Street and overlooking St James' Park. The rooms for our training courses were organised, the right number of tables and chairs arranged, film projectors and OHPs placed and adjusted and everything meticulously prepared by Bill Gordon. "The Baron" was one of the pillars of the Society, he and John Garnett had enormous mutual regard and affection for each other, which the Baron sometimes tried unsuccessfully to disguise by stumping around the corridors muttering to himself, "Now what on earth does that man Garnett want ...."

My first Head of Department, Reg Penson, in view of my almost non-existent knowledge of the world of industry, initially sent me to learn something about the workings and justification for trade unions. I spent a week with the South West Regional Secretary of the Transport & General Workers Union in Bristol. I sat in his office while Ron Nethercott dealt with a stream of visitors, some of whom had truly dreadful stories to tell of unjust treatment by their companies which would have had anyone, however right wing their views, reaching for a red flag and fighting for justice. But almost as many he dismissed as time-wasting whingers, telling them that from what he could see they were lucky to have a job at all and to stop wasting everyone's time. I quickly learned to understand something of the legitimate place of unions in the work place and I later realised the rightness of the fact that the Executive Council of The Industrial Society was made up of distinguished managers and directors of companies and equally distinguished general secretaries of the trade unions and other prominent union figures. In spite of this we were sometimes accused of bias but, as John remarked, just so long as the flak continued to come about equally from both sides we were probably getting it about right. One of the obstacles to harmonious industrial relations is that we talk about "the two sides of industry." One aspect of our campaign was to try to persuade people that it would be more helpful, while we tackled our foreign competitors, if everyone was on the same side.

Reg then sent me to sit in on the standard leadership course conducted by experienced advisers to learn the message and the techniques of running the training. Although I had been teaching the same ideas at Henlow, I came to realise that I was now seeing it done far more professionally and taken into far greater detail. The difference too was that here our course members were practising managers of various levels of experience.

Our standard leadership course at that time was a three-day package based on exactly the principles suggested by John Adair that we had used at Henlow, also using the film "Twelve O'clock High." But familiar as I was with the film, I soon found that I was now noticing many more incidents and scenes that could be highlighted in discussion to make important points about effective leadership. The fact that the film was about a military leader could sometimes be seen as an obstacle. But the more I used it and discussed it with fellow trainers and our industrial clients the more I came to see that the principles of military and civilian leadership were identical and that the differences were merely in style, idiom, custom and the like. An interesting aspect of running the training for industry, commerce, the public sector and others was in the wide variety of backgrounds of the course members, the points of view which they had developed and the need for us to appreciate the different starting points that they were coming from.

For me the new element in the training was the use of a number of table-top leadership exercises which allowed each course member in turn to have an opportunity to put into practice the notions we were discussing. These replaced the outdoor exercises which at Henlow we had used at camp and allowed many of the same points to be made but much more quickly and simply. Naturally I discussed my earlier experience with my new colleagues and subsequently I heard of an instance of one of them during the summer running an exercise which involved counting the number of ducks on the St James' Park lake. I subsequently had opportunities to use some of the outdoor exercise with which I was familiar, both for a college in Clifton and in particular for the Police Staff College at Bramshill.

The most crucial part of any exercise was the debriefing and I was constantly reminded of the similarity with running a debrief after a training sortie in Meteors or Hunters. We attempted to draw out what had gone well and what had not gone so well. For any course member who, in leading the exercise, had struggled, perhaps even floundered, running the debriefing presented the need to achieve a delicate balance. It had to be incisive enough for the necessary lessons to emerge but positive enough not to damage too much the person's ego and self-confidence. We constantly tried to send our customers away with the overall thoughts: Leadership is important. It is fairly straightforward and is largely common sense. I am not too bad at it already, although I can now probably do better.

We called our courses Action Centred Leadership, not an ideal title but at least better than the RAF's convoluted FALA—The Functional Approach to Leadership Analysis. We wanted to indicate that rather than talking about what qualities they need, we were mainly concerned with what effective leaders do, as we believed this was a more useful approach. Our simple, down-to-earth concern was: So what are you going to do about the leadership you are providing in your department—on Monday?

We all enjoyed running training courses, but often rather less so the busy programme of visits we all had to make to sell the work of the Society. We were a self-financing charity. It was important that we were self-financing, as if any course member was inclined to accuse us of being detached from harsh reality we were able to say, "Not so, we have to balance the books just as you do." John Garnett constantly reminded us that without visiting and explaining and selling our wares and bringing in the work there would soon be no work and so no salaries. One of his favourite sayings was, "There is no celestial slush fund!" We were each allotted an area of the country in which to build up a network of clients whom we got to know, and if all went well would on occasions ring us up to ask us to call to discuss new training needs or simply to book some work.

In addition to the public courses run on our own premises we took our training out to industrial companies, government departments and other organisations around the country. I particularly enjoyed this in-company work. It got me out of London and gave me the opportunity to increase my understanding of the world of industry and to visit many parts of Britain that I did not already know. I found that quite by chance my Pimlico flat was ideally located. I could get off a train from the

351

midlands or the north of England at Euston or King's Cross, nip down on to the Victoria Line and be home in less than 25 minutes.

One clear measure of your success as a trainer was how much repeat work you attracted from a particular client. I ran series of courses for Devonport Dockyard, for the Police Staff College, for Brown and Root, a world-wide engineering company and for the Ford Motor Company in Dagenham. At Fords I spent a fascinating day "walking the job" and being shown round their foundry. I also became very friendly with their Senior Training Manager. One day I pointed out to him that he had a number of able and effective trainers on his staff whom we could train and equip to run courses instead of his continuing to spend fairly large sums on employing us. He explained why he did not plan to do so. "If my chaps stand up and run this training," he said, "people say, 'Its just the old company party line', but if you, as a stranger, come to us they say, 'Do you know what the interesting chap from The Industrial Society was saying …'" It was a classic case of the prophet not being without honour save in his own country.

Each adviser had to develop their own style and techniques, how they behaved "on platform." One colleague of mine, Ian Barker, had come to The Industrial Society with extensive experience in the tough world of transport and the T&G Union and of managing long-distance lorry drivers. He was able to get straight on the wavelength of the toughest, most outspoken delegates. Within an hour of the course starting Ian would be standing at the lectern with his jacket off, his tie at half-mast and would be trading genial insults with course members, without either side taking offence. "Look at you, call yourself a proper manager? God, if you had any brains you'd be dangerous!" The rest of the course would be sitting there convulsed with laughter. I found that if I tried to be too serious I seemed to come across as stuffy and pompous. I eventually found that my best approach was to indulge in a certain amount of fooling about. "I saw this story last week in the Tory-graph, sorry, the Telegraph … ." I wanted to put across that although I was taking the training seriously I was not taking myself too seriously. A technique we all learned was of how to deal with a delegate who seemed determined to nitpick, to challenge anything you said and to be generally negative and offensive. Rather than challenge them yourself the answer was to get them to make a statement or to express a view and then to invite the rest of the course to comment. In no time at all you would probably then have to intervene to rescue for them some shreds of dignity and plausibility.

Thanks to Bill Simpson, a very experienced and able adviser, I was lucky enough to be involved in one particularly interesting series of courses for the Royal Ulster Constabulary in Belfast. This was back in the time of regular and frequent IRA bomb attacks and it was both educational and very humbling to work with the RUC and to learn from them something about their way of life. Having never been in a shooting war situation during all my time with the RAF I suddenly discovered what it was like when good friends and colleagues were suddenly no longer around and arrangements were being made to look after their children and widows. At the end of the planned series my last course kindly presented me with an RUC tie. But they added, "Don't ever wear it here in the Province—not if you want to keep your knee-caps."

One of the difficulties with our management/leadership training was to evaluate its effectiveness. If we were booked for repeat work the company clearly thought it had been worth-while and sometimes confirmation came back in a roundabout and particularly satisfying manner. One course I ran was for two dozen middle-aged and very set-in-their-ways machine-shop supervisors. The whole notion of working to promote the motivation of their men, of visiting them regularly at the bench, of talking to them about their families, of consulting them about decisions, of explaining to them how the company was progressing they rejected out of hand as simply a waste of time. They repeatedly insisted that all their employees were interested in was the money. All my arguments and pleas fell on deaf ears. I just didn't know what I was talking about. I tried to remain at least courteous, and it became a matter of being determined to keep smiling till tea-time even if it killed me. About a year later a colleague, Chris Garrett, rang me up to say he had just returned from running another quite different course at the same company. A machine-shop supervisor, hearing that he was from The Industrial Society had approached him and asked him if he knew me. The message was, "Would you please just tell Richard that it works …."

One day I had a phone call from one of the most lively, energetic and engaging personalities in the Society. Julia Cleverdon headed the department who dealt among other things with schools. They ran a regular package for sixth formers on 'The Challenge of Industry'. Julia told me that she had recently been at a head teacher's conference where she had overheard two heads in discussion and had heard one say, "What's all this about something called management. Should we have some of that?" "Now," she continued, "I know you are trained teacher. So even if you never actually taught full time, at least you've had chalk under your finger-nails! So, darling man, why don't you come and join my department and we will put together some leadership training packages for heads and senior staff in schools." I felt that I needed a change of scene and so I was happy to agree to move over to the Education Department in Robert Hyde House at 48 Bryanston Square.

Julia's department was housed in an older building, rather a rabbit warren, at the top of Great Cumberland Place, a few minutes from Marble Arch. Julia was among the best bosses I ever worked for. She was far quicker then me to see helpful connections and opportunities, she was unfailingly supportive and encouraging but equally hard hitting with her criticisms and guidance. We put our heads together and sketched out a two-day programme for heads and senior staff in schools calling it simply Leadership in Schools. It was virtually identical to the two-day version of the normal ACL course. We printed and sent off a mailing of the brochure and almost at once bookings started to come in. Within a few months we were struggling to keep up with demand. One early course member was Tony Millard, at that time Deputy Head of Wells Cathedral School. We immediately hit it off well and I persuaded him to take the occasional days off from his school and to come to run courses for us as an Associate when I was otherwise double booked. The Industrial Society had at that time regional offices in Leeds, Manchester and Glasgow and they all became the regular venues for courses. Perhaps the most distinguished of the early courses was when I had as course members the Headmasters of Charterhouse and Gordonstoun and the Deputy Head of Harrow. Quite soon schools were inviting us to take our training to them for senior members of their common rooms, Local Educational Authorities were organising courses for the schools in their area and I started another most enjoyable series of journeys all over UK.

I was tiring of living in central London. My move to Bryanston Square pointed to Marylebone as the obvious station if I was going to commute out to greener surroundings. I sold my flat and moved out to

Denham, just off the A 40, near the pleasant towns of Gerrards Cross and Beaconsfield and on the eastern edge of the Chiltern Hills. I bought a small, convenient bungalow in a quiet country lane. Denham station was only 25 minutes from Marylebone and it was a very pleasant spot in which to live while working in central London.

Admiral Sir Peter White, a four-star officer until his retirement from the Royal Navy, was a long-standing friend of John's and Julia's and worked for The Industrial Society mainly behind the scenes, often helping to restrain Julia when her constant flow of enthusiastic "eyes on the hills" ideas needed to be tempered with some "feet on the ground" considerations of what, in the light of the latest cash-flow figures, was financially possible. Policy planning meetings were said to include exchanges such as: "Well I think it would be marvellous if we started ..." "Julia, before we take on extra commitments may I point out that last month's figures show ..." "Oh, Peter you really are such an Eeyore!" However really Julia greatly valued Pedro Blanco's advice and guidance. He had a dry, throw-away turn of phrase, a wealth of nautical wisdom and memorable sayings. "He's quite new to his job, you know, only been there about half a dog watch." "Sloping shoulders."—a refusal to accept responsibility. "Steering by the wake."—self explanatory.

For our school teachers' London courses we introduced at the end of day one, after a pleasant buffet dinner, an additional session. Peter related his experiences and views on Leadership at the Top, what it really is like when there is no-one else to pass problems up to, when the buck really does stop here. He offered some items of direct and hard-hitting advice. "Showing Consideration for others. We must care for our staff and be seen to care. We must learn to listen. We must show appreciation and thanks. Otherwise our leadership will be seen as purely selfish." But also, "Acquiring a Hard Streak. In this country this is not regarded as an attractive trait and so is often in very short supply. Are we prepared to get rid of those who are not up to the demands of their jobs?" He had some delightful stories to tell against himself. One was of when he was a newly promoted junior admiral during the war and had encountered a threatening and dangerous situation at a certain shore establishment. He had concluded his report to the Admiralty with the comment, "I feel as if I am sitting on an active volcano." It received the somewhat brusque reply, "As you very well know, White,

355

none of the resources you request is available—and admirals are paid to sit on active volcanoes." He would sometimes start his talk with, "As it is fairly late in the day you may have tendency to drop off and doze. My only advice is—don't fight it—I have plenty of experience of talking in other people's sleep." In fact his wise, apt and pithy comments held our course members' attention riveted.

The success of our courses for schools encouraged us to produce another variation as Leadership in Voluntary Organisations. Clients included the National Council for Voluntary Organisations, the Citizens Advice Bureau and the Commission for Racial Equality. All these successful versions of essentially the same package confirmed our belief that the basic principles of leadership are identical wherever people work together to attain common objectives. The language and idiom may have to be modified and I sometimes teased teachers that they usually insisted on developing strategies where everyone else made plans! But particularly for me, with my military background, it was especially satisfying to find that I could influence these typically "liberal" organisations. It is disappointing that the importance of effective leadership is still generally so poorly recognised. I used to refer to myself as merely a primary school teacher of the simple basics of leadership, but added the rider that so many people never seem even to have been to primary school. I wrote a short book trying to distil the essentials. In it I called leadership the invisible craft and suggested that while other craftsmen make things, leaders make things happen.

With experience we introduced some minor changes that we discovered the course needed for teachers. In most industrial and commercial companies at least the place of management is well understood and accepted even if its performance is sometimes not very good. For many in education this was not so and we had to start by establishing the very legitimacy of management. One of the most controversial aspects of the organisation of many schools was that individual teachers are responsible to more than one "boss." For example a French teacher would be responsible to the Head of Languages, but also as a house tutor to the House-master or -mistress and possibly as hockey coach to the Head of Physical Education. Who, then, to go to for help in sorting out conflicting demands and priorities? We consulted many of the best heads around the country and they confirmed our belief that it is necessary for everyone to have

ONE person to act as the overall boss, guide, mentor, etc. But it was always a hard battle to get the principle of clear, single accountability accepted.

We tried to distil our message into simple, sometimes obvious, suggestions such as the advantages to be gained from dividing up large schools, or any organisations, into manageable departments of about ten. Even so some teachers accused us of advocating novel, unproven drills and techniques, and kept asking, "Where is the literature or evidence that any of this is useful or effective?" For this particular point it was fun to refer them (and in particular RE teachers!) to the Book of Exodus, Chapter 18, verses 13–26.*

In Pontefract the King's High School suggested that they would like to invite a few middle managers from local industrial companies to join the course with their staff. The course was a great success and we tried to spread this format around. The teachers discovered the importance of being a bit more direct and tough than they were used to, and the managers realised some of the benefits of being more sensitive to people's feelings.

On this and other courses we sometimes found that to achieve such helpful exchanges we needed to put our planned programme on hold and to let the discussions run on. We had also discovered already that the best courses were those with a mix, where people came from both private and state schools.

Gordonstoun School invited me up to their delightful site on the banks of the Moray Firth to run a course to which they had invited a number of members of staff from Fettes College in Edinburgh. The following year Fettes ran a sort of return fixture to which they invited teachers from Gordonstoun. They both involved most enjoyable outings for me, but perhaps the best of all was a trip to the annual conference of the European Council of Independent Schools in Vienna. Sheffield University was the first where I ran 'Leading a University Department' for professors. Soon they were followed by the Universities of Liverpool, Surrey, St Andrew's, Edinburgh and Heriot

* The suggestion for "rulers of fifties" is a red herring. It makes no managerial sense. It seems to have been introduced by the author in order to preserve the swinging pendulum or balanced pairs rhythm characteristic of much Hebrew literature. ("The sheep and the goats," "… the sun shall not burn thee by day neither the moon by night." Who ever heard of Moon-burn?)

Watt. Cheltenham College was the first to let me run a day on The Principles of Leadership for their sixth form. This idea also spread and even since I have retired from The Industrial Society I still visit every year some half a dozen schools to talk to the new generation of Prefects.

It was at Wells Cathedral School that some prefects pointed out to me a simple principle which, up to then, I had not noticed applies in schools just as in other organisations. I had originally regarded the school as being commendably progressive in that they let the pupils elect their own team of prefects. However during my discussions with them we got on to a topic which can often cause difficulties with adult courses, whether in schools, industrial companies or wherever. This is the question of a leader's responsibility for passing on and supporting decisions from further up in an organisation, perhaps from his own boss, with which he may not himself agree. I asked them how, for example, they would deal with passing on and supporting rules about the playing of loud radios, or keeping shirts tucked neatly into trousers—even in hot weather! As the discussion proceeded one of then remarked, "But, sir, that's not what the school elected me for." He was on reflection, of course, entirely right. The pupils when invited to elect their prefects had in effect chosen their representative, their shop stewards. The principle was, in fact, quite clear. If we require people to represent views and opinions upwards to senior management they must be elected; if we require them to represent management's views and instructions downwards they must be appointed. I suggested to the school that perhaps they should re-think their policy of electing prefects.

One of the most satisfying aspects of working with the world of education was that we continued to get many letters of appreciation and thanks, possibly because we were among the first to take into education our campaign and our belief in the universal relevance of the simple ideas of leadership. Very seldom did we encounter remarks such as that from the deputy headmaster of a leading public school, whom I was trying to persuade to let me run some training for his sixth form, who said with a smirk, "Surely you are not suggesting that we start to indoctrinate our boys with führer-prinzips!" More typical was a letter from the Head of School at Repton, "I would like to thank you on behalf of all the school prefects for a most useful and enjoyable day on

Friday. You introduced aspects of our new role that we had never even considered before and your stories illustrating each example gave us real insight into the problems lying ahead. I feel that I will constantly be referring back to Friday not only this year but in my career ahead of me." A professor of Ecclesiastical History at Edinburgh University wrote, "I wish to thank you again for the superb course 'Leading a University Department'. You had a rather difficult group of academics, many of us sceptical about the need for improved management techniques at the university … . From my conversations with other course participants, I can say that everyone was favourably impressed with your presentation and had benefited in some way from the course. I certainly learned a great deal, and have started applying some of the techniques in my department with considerable profit."

However some courses were an uphill struggle from the start. It was apparent that in some schools the whole concept of vigorous, proactive management or leadership by senior staff was a totally foreign idea and that many of them would much prefer to let sleeping dogs lie. On one of my courses during a discussion it was suggested, very sensibly, by one course member that before he introduced some change he would want to find out the views of at least his senior pupils. Another head commented, "Oh I couldn't possibly do that, the unions wouldn't let me!" We wondered whether such schools were being run for the benefit of the children or of the staff.

More encouraging were instances where the majority of course members responded to our suggestions positively and constructively even if one or two were proving resistant. On one course we were discussing the subject of staff motivation and I had recounted the well-known ideas proposed by the psychologist Douglas McGregor. He had described one of the two alternative approaches to managing staff as Theory X—making all the negative assumptions such as that staff are intrinsically work-shy, uncooperative and need constantly driving. He had contrasted this to Theory Y—the more positive assumptions that most staff are eager to give of their best, and mainly enjoy their work just so long as we bosses stop interfering and creating obstacles! He had pointed out that whichever set of assumptions we adopt usually become self fulfilling prophesies. One head teacher would have none of it. He was adamant that he had found by long experience that none of his staff could be left to their own devices and initiatives. We broke off

359

the discussion for our coffee break. When we re-assembled we found that someone else on the course had slipped back into the room and had amended his name card. It now read "Big X"

At about this time the government introduced into state schools the requirement for them to conduct teacher appraisals. From the uproar that initially greeted this one would have thought that the Gestapo had reappeared. We designed a quite separate new course specifically on the subject of Teacher Appraisal, inviting a number of practising heads to join us as visiting speakers, and as the furore died down it also became greatly in demand.

John Garnett retired from The Industrial Society in 1986. To help preserve the memory of all that he campaigned for I wrote a short booklet of all the memorable parables and stories he had used to add colour and interest to the principles of effective leadership. It seemed to many of us that after he had left an initially gradual but steady decline soon set in, the good fellowship and much of the fun started to disappear and it became just another training organisation instead of the campaigning one that it had been. Having Julia as our director in Bryanston Square shielded us for a time from many of the changes but she too left a couple of years later. A serious blow for me was that the Education Department was moved to Birmingham. As the M40 was still being built, reaching the office now entailed a two-hour cross-country drive. I started the habit of staying many nights at Maxstoke Priory near Coleshill for bed & breakfast to reduce the travelling. Penny and Richard Tyacke became very good friends to the extent that one year they invited me to stay with them for the Christmas holiday.

In the months before I retired it seemed to me that The Industrial Society was abandoning much of its clear, simple stance on leadership. It had started to advocate such vague, ill-defined notions as "Self Managed Teams." I started to wonder if actually the problem was that I was failing to keep up with valid new ideas. In our library I found a magazine article on this topic that explained that a certain well-known retailer was opening a new branch in Oxford Street, with specially recruited staff, which was going to be run specifically as a Self Managed Team. Here was my chance to get myself up to date. I jumped on a bus and in Oxford Street found the new branch concerned. I showed the magazine article to an assistant and asked for her comments. "Ah," she said, "you had better talk to the manger ..." The manager told me, "Oh yes, I was here at the time. We've moved on a bit since then you know." So now I was going to hear about the real state-of-the-art situation, and these were his exact next words, "Its like communism. It looks great on paper. It just doesn't work." Perhaps I was not quite so out of touch after all.

I reached my retirement age of 65 in 1996. John and Julia insisted on coming back to my leaving party and saying some very nice things. Tony Millard even travelled all the way down from North Yorkshire where he was by now Headmaster of Giggleswick School. The party was organised by Philippa Caris, my last and probably my best secretary. She had tracked down a large number of old friends and colleagues to come to the party and so made it a moving and memorable evening. She and her husband now live in Australia, we exchange Christmas cards and they regularly press me to go out to visit them.

# *British Executive Service Overseas*

I was reluctant to retire properly. At a leadership conference not long before I left the Society I had met the Director of British Executive Service Overseas who suggested that I join them. BESO maintains a database of some 3,000 mainly retired people who can offer some special skill or expertise. They also maintain networks of promoters in both the third world and the ex-communist world to accept requests for volunteer advisers to visit briefly and to work with local organisations. The intention is to provide expertise and advice to those who cannot afford to pay commercial rates. For four years I enjoyed working in BESO's London office, dealing with tracking down the most suitable advisers to meet incoming requests, and the associated paper work for their assignments. BESO was at that time another delightful place to work. We "recruiters" were all pretty elderly and from a wide range of backgrounds and I made some very good friends. The high spot of the day was when we all retired to a local cafe or pub for lunch and much gossip.

However the main interest for me was provided by the chance to read other people's in-trays and so to spot assignments which I felt that I could do. In this way I undertook three fascinating visits to Eastern

Europe to run training events on aspects of leadership. In Ternopil in the Ukraine I stayed with Bohdan Pelykh and his family. He was the Managing Director of the company I was working for. I enjoyed their kind hospitality and some memorable outings around that potentially rich but utterly bankrupt country. It was heartbreaking to see the devastation and poverty that was the legacy of all those years of communism. If there is still a widespread need for better leadership in UK, the need is vastly greater in the ex-communist world still trying to emerge from the suffocating effects of the commissar culture. In Romania, the local BESO rep persuaded me to stay on after the end of my assignment and we took a memorable weekend trip up to the Carpathian mountains. The legendary home of Dracula!—is actually a delightful land of picturesque old towns, pine covered mountains with, above the trees, wide open meadows already equipped with gondola lifts, all just waiting to become a flourishing area of ski resorts. Also in Bucharest my clients liked the book I had written on The Craft of Leadership and they have had it translated into Romanian.

The most exciting visit was to Russia itself. Our rep met me off the aeroplane at Moscow Airport and I stayed the night with him before catching another flight the next morning on to Rostov-on-Don. On our way to dine at a pleasant restaurant he suggested a special spot of sight seeing. We parked and walked across Red Square. Around us were other tourists and family groups enjoying the evening with children laughing and playing tag, with the onion domes of St Basil's Cathedral on one side of us and the high castellated wall of the Kremlin on the other. Spot-lighted on top of the Kremlin now flew not the hammer and sickle but the red, white and blue flag of the new Russia. It was a memorable moment and illustrated so vividly that the long years of the Cold War are now consigned to history, as Russia works to overcome all her problems and to rejoin the family of nations.

When I left the RAF in 1976 I made a resolution that I was not going to surround myself with pictures of aeroplanes or wear an RAF blazer and tie for the rest of my life or live on nostalgia. I wanted to look forwards rather than backwards and to this end I rather cut myself off from the RAF and was then so lucky to find the Industrial Society, in those days at the pinnacle of its influence and campaigning fun. But more recently having left there and with more time available it has been interesting to catch up with old RAF friends. Last summer, fortuitously, an ETPS Association was started and there have been a couple of most enjoyable re-unions back at Boscombe Down—where ETPS now lives. At one of these I met again John Harper and Robbie Robinson, both fellow cadets of No 57 Entry. I hadn't seen John for just on fifty years and it occurred to the three of us that the coming December would be the fiftieth anniversary of our graduation from Cranwell. Clearly an excuse for another party.

With much help from RAF Innsworth we eventually tracked down fourteen of the Entry although, especially sadly for us on "C" Squadron, not our old resident comedian Chris Doggett. Ron Humpherson wrote from Australia to say that unfortunately he would not be able to make it but Dave Hinton flew over from Spain where he now lives. The College provided us with accommodation, was most hospitable and we enjoyed a buffet dinner in the Cadets' Mess on 17th December, the actual anniversary of our graduation. It was extra-ordinary how one could pick up the threads again and rediscover the same traits and characteristics in old friends that one had known half a century before. We discovered that our two stars had turned out to be Brian Huxley, "A" Squadron and Les Davis, "C" Squadron, both of whom had retired as Air Vice Marshals.

Due to a reorganisation and together with most of my old colleagues, I have now left BESO, but last summer and through a contact I made there I ran a course for the Oxford University Polish Society, and this may lead to my getting back to Eastern Europe. A few schools still invite me each year to talk to their new generation of prefects, but the main obstacle in state schools continues to be the ignorance and prejudices of left-wing teachers—they are the ones who need training before one could have any hope of influencing their pupils. While still at The Industrial Society I was invited by the Headmaster of a prep school near Hertford to become one of his school governors, and I have enjoyed a long innings there. I worked for a time for The Prince's Trust and after some work I did for the Centre for Tomorrow's Company I was invited to become a Fellow of the Royal Society for the Arts, so I have not been entirely idle.

Now that I no longer need to travel into London, I shall move away from Denham before long, probably back to the wide open spaces of Salisbury Plain and not too far from Boscombe Down and Upavon. There are still so many in all walks of life who cannot see the relevance of effective leadership and it makes you weep to see headlines such as that recently in The Times which read "Cathedral staff call Dean 'bully and tyrant' ," and he is meant to be a *Christian* leader! So the battle goes on. I was very fortunate to find such a satisfying second career, I am still so convinced of the value and importance of what we try to do and I hope to play a part for a few more years yet.

*    *    *

*Appendices*

## Aircraft types flown as 1st Pilot

| Piston-engined | Jet-engined |
|---|---|
| Tiger Moth | Jet Provost |
| Chipmunk | Vampire F5, T11 |
| Provost | Venom F2 |
| Prentice | Hunter F4, F6, T7, F10 |
| Harvard | Swift F5, F7 |
| Auster | Gnat T1, F1 |
| Auster Airedale | *Meteor F4, T7, F8, NF11, NF12, NF14 |
| Tipsy Bee | *Javelin NF2, NF3, NF5, NF7, NF9 |
| Beaver | *Lightning F1, F2, F3, T4, T5 |
| Balliol | *Canberra B2, T4 |
| Spitfire F16 | |
| *Oxford | |
| *Anson | |
| *Devon | |
| *Sea Prince | |
| *Varsity | |
| *Freighter | * Twin-engined aircraft |
| **Heron | **Four-engined aircraft |

## Record of Service

| | |
|---|---|
| Royal Air Force College, Cranwell | April 1950–December 1952 |
| No 209 Advanced Flying School RAF Weston Zoyland | January 1953–May 1953 |
| No 226 Operational Conversion Unit RAF Stradishall | June–August 1953 |
| No 63 Squadron (Meteor Mk VIII) RAF Waterbeach | August 1953–February 1956 |
| ADC to Air Officer Commanding, Transport Command, RAF Upavon | February 1956–May 1957 |
| No 63 Squadron (Hunter Mk 6) RAF Waterbeach | June 1957–May 1958 |
| OC "A" Flight, No 26 Squadron (Hunter Mk 6) RAF Ahlhorn & Gütersloh | May 1958–January 1960 |
| Empire Test Pilots' School RAE Farnborough | February 1960–December 1960 |
| "A" Squadron, Aeroplane and Armament Experimental Establishment, Boscombe Down | December 1960–December 1963 |
| RAF Staff College, Bracknell | January–December 1964 |
| HQ Air Cadets, RAF White Waltham | January 1965–June 1967 |
| Stn. Admin. Officer & Deputy Station Commander, RAF Gan, Maldive Islands | July 1967–July 1968 |
| HQ Far East Air Force, RAF Changi | July–August 1968 |
| Assistant Defence Adviser, British High Commission, Singapore | September 1968–January 1970 |
| HQ, Air Officer, Scotland & Northern Ireland RAF Pitreavie Castle | January 1970–April 1971 |
| OC Green Squadron, Officer Cadet Training Unit, RAF Henlow | June 1971–March 1974 |
| No 229 Operational Conversion Unit/Tactical Weapons Unit RAF Chivenor and Brawdy | April 1974–July 1975 |
| Ministry of Defence, Lacon House | July 1975–October 1976 |

## Maps

MALLAIG

AVIEMORE
ROTHIEMURCHUS
CAIRNGORMS

DYCE
ABERDEEN

United Kingdom

LEUCHARS

PITREAVIE CASTLE

EDINBURGH

ACKLINGTON

OUSTON

VALLEY

WADDINGTON
CRANWELL
BARKSTON HEATH
SPITALGATE

WEST RAYNHAM

COLTISHALL

LONG MYND

WATERBEACH

STRADISHALL

BRAWDY

HENLOW

KNOCK
DEEP

LYNEHAM

PEMBROKE DOCK

UPAVON
BOSCOMBE DOWN

WHITE WALTHAM

BRACKNELL

SALISBURY

CHIVENOR
WESTON ZOYLAND

TANGMERE

CULDROSE

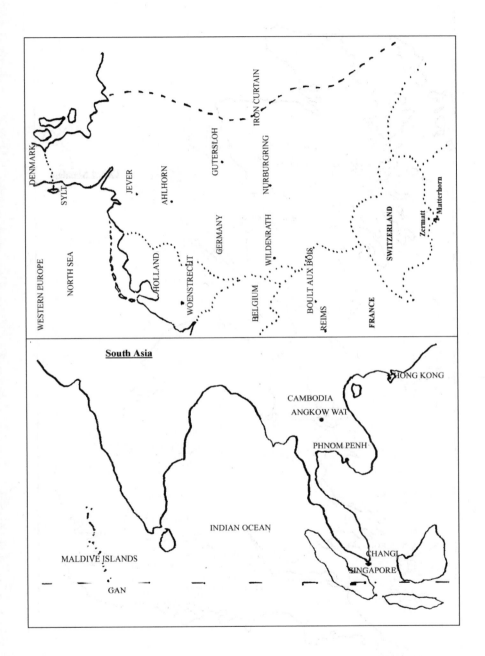

WESTERN EUROPE

NORTH SEA

DENMARK

SYLT

JEVER

AHLHORN

HOLLAND

WOENSTRECHT

BELGIUM

GERMANY

WILDENRATH

GUTERSLOH

NURBURGRING

IRON CURTAIN

BOULT AUX BOIS

REIMS

FRANCE

SWITZERLAND

Zermatt

Matterhorn

**South Asia**

MALDIVE ISLANDS

GAN

INDIAN OCEAN

CAMBODIA

ANGKOW WAT

PHNOM PENH

HONG KONG

CHANGI

SINGAPORE

371

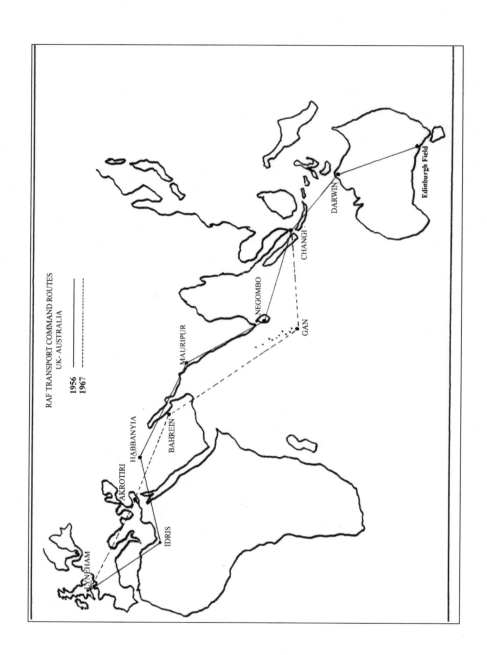

RAF TRANSPORT COMMAND ROUTES
UK–AUSTRALIA

1956
1967

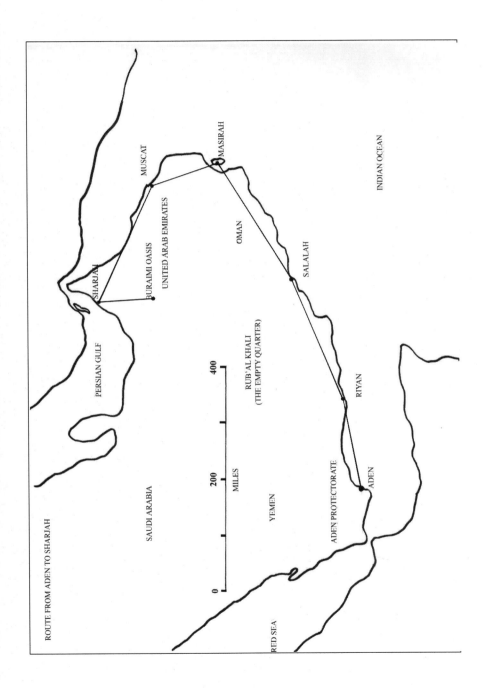

ROUTE FROM ADEN TO SHARJAH

373

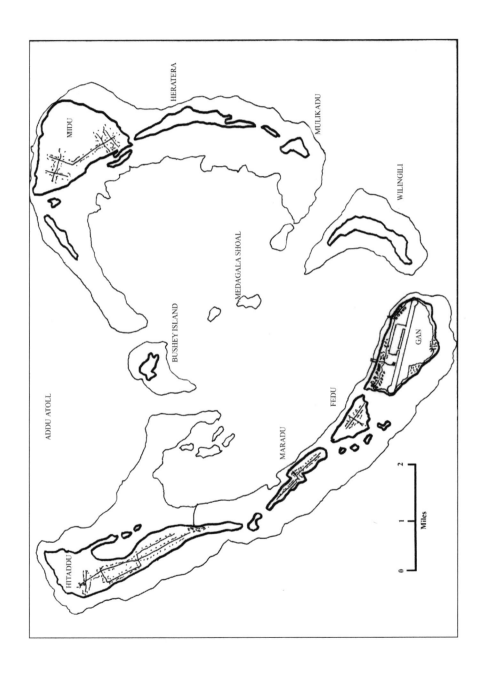

ADDU ATOLL

HITADDU

MARADU

FEDU

GAN

BUSHEY ISLAND

MEDAGALA SHOAL

MIDU

HERATERA

MULIKADU

WILINGILI

Miles
0    1    2

374

*Some Flying Technicalities*

In the body of the book I have tried as far as possible to avoid technicalities. However some people may be interested in them so while this is not aiming to be a text book an account of some of the technicalities, as they affect the pilot, are added here. Personally I believe that aeroplanes and their operation become much more interesting if one knows something of the science and the principles of how they work.

## Isaac Newton and the Mechanics of Flight

To understand aeroplanes one must start with Isaac Newton. It was he who first understood how things move in the way that they do and identified the three basic rules that explain it all. The first law or rule is that any body, a car, a bullet, a swimmer, a space-ship or an aeroplane stays still *or moves at a steady speed in a straight line* unless a force (a push) acts on it. It is sometimes thought that a force such as the power of the engine is needed to make something move along at a constant speed.

Not so. The force exerted by the power of the engine balances exactly the forces of friction and air resistance which are tending to slow it down, so that *the sum* of these forces is zero. The misunderstanding arises because friction and the other forces which resist movement are so universal that we tend to forget about them. For an aeroplane the power of the engine produces *Thrust* which exactly balances friction

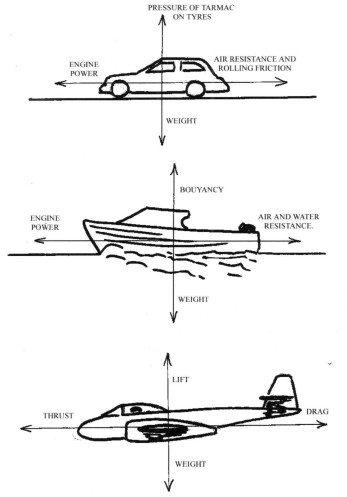

PRESSURE OF TARMAC
ON TYRES

ENGINE
POWER

AIR RESISTANCE AND
ROLLING FRICTION

WEIGHT

BOUYANCY

ENGINE
POWER

AIR AND WATER
RESISTANCE.

WEIGHT

LIFT

THRUST

DRAG

WEIGHT

EXAMPLES OF BODIES IN EQUILLIBRIUM MOVING AT CONSTANT SPEEDS

and the rest which produce *Drag*. In normal level flight there are two other forces, the *Weight* of the aeroplane which must be exactly balanced by the *Lift* produced by the wings. When a body is in this state with all the forces balanced it is said to be in equilibrium, it stays at rest or moves at a constant speed. We will come back to the question of how the wings produce the force of lift after looking at Newton's second and third laws.

The second law is that when a force acts on a body it *produces an acceleration in the direction of the force*. Notice it is acceleration but not necessarily a velocity in that direction. Imagine a bullet fired straight up into the air. From the moment the bullet leaves the gun barrel it will, under the force of gravity or its weight, start to accelerate downwards. However we are more likely to describe this as saying it starts to slow down in its flight upwards. In this case the force of gravity, obeying Newton's second law, is causing it to *lose* speed and this is also defined as acceleration. In some cases a force will not alter the speed of a body

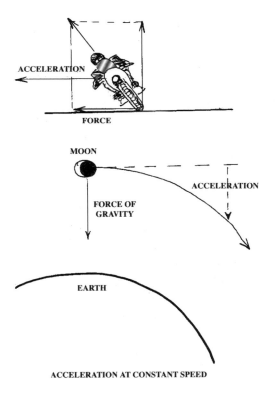

ACCELERATION AT CONSTANT SPEED

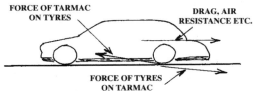

EQUAL AND OPPOSITE REACTION.

but only its direction. There are many familiar examples of this, a car or motor-bike cornering on a road, a train rounding a corner on its track, or a space-ship or the moon circling the earth or the earth circling the sun. In all these cases the speed stays the same but the body is not in equilibrium, it is being acted on by *an unbalanced force* and, while travelling at constant speed, is *accelerating towards the centre of the circle*. This is the type of acceleration with which pilots are most familiar. In straight and level flight, as when standing still on the ground, you and the aeroplane are subject to the gravitation of the earth (your weight). This is measured as 1 "g." When you are in a tight turn or are pulling out of a dive you may be subject to 2, 3 or even more "g." Excessive amounts of "g" can cause blacking out, as the blood is prevented from getting up to the brain. Various means are employed to counteract the effects of "g."

The third law is that for every action (by a force) there is an equal and opposite reaction. The tyres of a car, driven by the power of the engine, push the tarmac of the road backwards, the tarmac pushes the car forwards with a force which, if the speed is constant, balances the friction and air resistance. (If the force exerted by the tyres on the tarmac—and vice versa—is greater than the total resistance the car will accelerate.) The swimmer kicks and scoops the water backwards with his hands and feet and the water pushes him forward. (The space-ship or satellite, once it is in orbit, is in a vacuum, there is no drag and so there is no need for any thrust.) The propeller or the jet of the aeroplane pushes the air backwards and the air pushes the aeroplane forwards against the retarding effect of the drag.

So to the wings. Consider first a convergent and then divergent nozzle, or if you like a bottle-neck with air flowing through it. In order to get past the narrow neck the air has to accelerate to do so. In accordance with Newton's Laws this acceleration is caused because the neck becomes a region of low pressure. The air moving towards it is moving from normal pressure to low pressure and so experiences a force accelerating it forwards while the air leaving it is leaving the region of low pressure and so experiences a force retarding it back again to its original speed. The curved surface of the top of an aircraft's wing creates a similar effect. There is therefore a region of low pressure on the top surface of the wing, centred about the point of maximum camber. Taking the pressure under the wing as not much different from

378

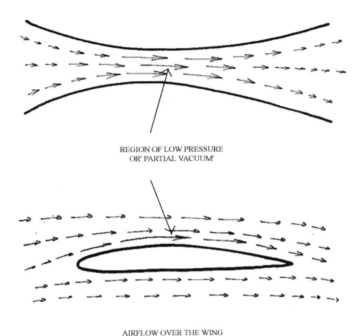

REGION OF LOW PRESSURE
OR' PARTIAL VACUUM'

AIRFLOW OVER THE WING

normal, there is then a net force on the wing upwards. This is the force of lift. In accordance with Newton's third law there is an equal and opposite force exerted by the wing on the air flowing over it deflecting it downwards in what is called the downwash. In deflecting the air downwards to produce lift it is impossible, however well the wings are designed, to avoid deflecting the air slightly forwards as well. This produces another small amount of drag called Induced Drag to distinguish it from the ordinary Form Drag suffered by bullets, cars and the rest.

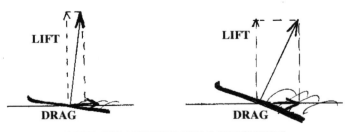

**WATER SKI AT HIGH AND LOW SPEEDS.**

379

An instructive example of induced drag is provided by a water skier. The skis deflecting the water downwards produce the lift which holds the skier up but also produce plenty of induced drag. Note that *the slower* the skier goes the greater the angle of the skis needed to produce enough lift and *the greater* the induced drag. The same applies to induced drag for aeroplanes. In most aeroplanes before the induced drag becomes excessive the wings stall. This is described below. But for some highly swept wings it is possible to get to the point where as the speed is reduced the induced drag gets so great that an increase in engine power may be needed just to maintain speed. This is called getting behind the drag curve and is dangerous because the engine may not have enough power available to cope.

If an aeroplane is flying straight and level the lift produced by the wings must remain equal to its weight. Just as with the water skier, as

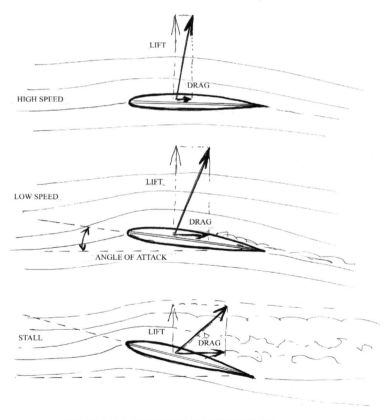

LIFT AND DRAG AT INCREASING "ANGLES OF ATTACK"

an aeroplane's speed is reduced the angle at which the wings meet the air— the Angle of Attack—must increase. But there is a limit to how much the air can be deflected downwards along the wing surface toward the trailing edge. If the

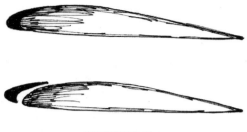

AUTOMATIC SLAT

angle of attack at which the wing is meeting the air becomes too great, the air suddenly breaks away from the surface and instead of being deflected downwards it becomes turbulent and simply flows straight back. There is a sudden loss of lift and the wing is said to have stalled. Many devices have been used to delay the stall or to make it occur gradually rather than abruptly. One which was for a time widely used was the Handley Page slat. A small slat, like a thin airfoil normally rested flush on top of the leading edge of the wing. As speed was reduced and the angle of attack increased the lift force on the slat became inclined forwards as well as upwards and the slat then automatically opened, to form a slot for the air to flow through.

The effect was similar to that of the jib on a sailing boat. Just as the jib leads the air to flow smoothly round the mast and on to lee side of the sail, the slat smoothed the air flowing over the leading edge helping it to flow on across the top surface of the wing and delaying the stall. Ideally an aeroplane approaching to land is flying not far above the stalling speed. As it levels out just above the runway it is allowed to stall and settles gently on to the ground.

Before the stall was properly understood many accidents were caused, particularly during the approach to landing, by letting the speed become too low and the angle of attack too great. At the stall the aeroplane would pitch violently downwards and there was too often not enough height in which to recover. An even more dangerous condition occurs when, perhaps because an aeroplane is turning, one wing stalls before the other. The sudden loss of lift on one side throws the aeroplane into a diving spiral—the spin. Pilots would try to raise the nose be pulling back on the control column but this in fact kept the stalled wing at a high angle of attack and kept the aeroplane in the spin. Eventually it was learned that to recover from a spin it was necessary to put the stick forward to

381

'unstall' the wings, before easing out of the dive. This presents no problem, just so long as there is sufficient height to do so.*

To understand any manoeuvre by an aeroplane it is only necessary to consider its speed and direction and especially any change of speed or direction and then apply Newton's three laws. For example if it is flying in a turn, something must be supplying a force directed towards the centre of the turning circle. The only force available to do this is the lift from the wings. Hence the aeroplane must bank over into the turn so that some of the lift is doing this. At the same time the lift still has to hold the aeroplane up, balancing the weight, therefore the total lift must be increased while the aeroplane turns. In the turn the increased lift will

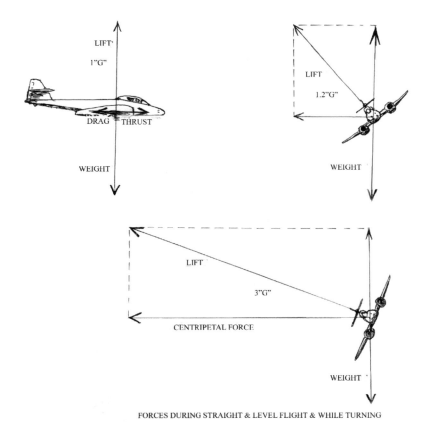

FORCES DURING STRAIGHT & LEVEL FLIGHT & WHILE TURNING

* There is a vivid account of a spinning accident, due to ignorance in the early days of flying, in Neville Shute's novel "So Disdained."

also mean that the induced drag will increase and so unless the pilot increases power the aeroplane will lose speed.

In most aeroplanes the limit to how tightly they can turn is reached when the engine is at full power overcoming the induced drag. The aeroplane cannot generate any more lift directed towards the centre of the circle and so cannot turn any more tightly. If an aeroplane is turning tightly or pulling out of a dive it needs more lift than if it were flying straight and level, and the stalling speed will therefore be higher. The term the stalling speed is usually taken to refer to the stall in straight and level flight. If "g" is being pulled we will encounter a *High Speed Stall*. This occurs at a higher speed than the normal stalling speed and is often quite violent. It can take an unwary pilot by surprise.

## The Flying Controls

The driver of a train has control in only one dimension: fast-slow, (or go-stop). The driver of a car has control in two dimensions: fast-slow and left-right. The pilot of an aeroplane has control in three dimensions: fast-slow, left-right and up-down. The three flying controls are the elevators, controlling pitch, the rudder controlling yaw and the ailerons controlling roll. The control surfaces are formed by having a small portion of the tail-plane and the vertical fin and for the ailerons a pair of surfaces at each wing tip hinged and able to move relative to the fixed surface to which they are attached.

When describing the manoeuvres of an aeroplane in three dimensions it is important to be absolutely clear about what is going on. Thus the three possible rotational movements are given precise definitions. These are:—

a. Movement about the fore-and-aft axis     –    –     Roll
b.       ”          ”       lateral axis     –    –     Pitch
c.       ”          ”       vertical axis     –    –     Yaw

To move the control surfaces and so to manoeuvre the aeroplane the pilot has a control column, in the old-fashioned parlance a joystick, and rudder pedals. These are connected to the control surfaces so that the movements needed are entirely instinctive. For example, to cause the aeroplane to pitch nose up (to raise the nose) the stick is pulled back, to pitch nose down it is pushed forward.

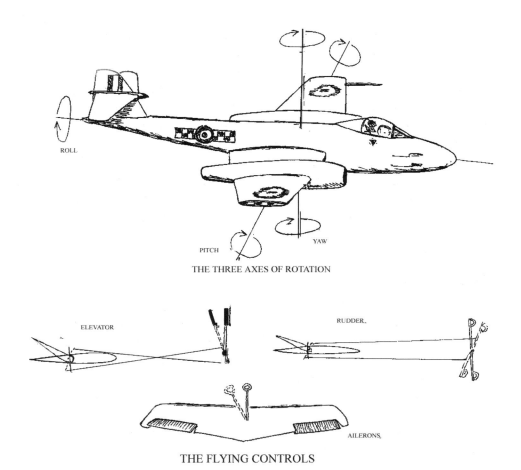

THE THREE AXES OF ROTATION

ROLL

PITCH

YAW

ELEVATOR

RUDDER

AILERONS

THE FLYING CONTROLS

Moving the stick to the right causes the aeroplane to roll to the right and moving it to the left causes a roll to the left. With the rudder, pushing forward on the left pedal causes the aeroplane to yaw to the left and vice versa.

The control column is usually managed with the right hand while the left rests on the throttle and also operates many other controls such as the flaps, airbrakes, undercarriage selector, radio channel selector and so on. To minimise the hand movements needed some of these are incorporated into the main controls. Typically the radio press-to-transmit button, airbrake selector and gun-sight ranging (working like a motor-bike throttle twist grip) may be incorporated in the throttle with the trim switches, brake lever and its lock (for parking) and gun firing trigger (with safety catch!) located on the top of the stick. Larger aeroplanes may have a "pair of spectacles" on the top of the stick to allow both hands to be used and more force exerted on the ailerons.

To move these controls against the force of the airflow may require considerable effort by the pilot and so they are designed to have a small part of their area in front of the hinge line. The air acting on these portions assists the movement and reduces the effort needed from the pilot. This is called Aerodynamic Balancing.

In addition to this there is the need for Mass Balancing, particularly for the ailerons. The wing-tips to which they are attached are relatively flexible. If a disturbance makes a wing-tip flex momentarily upwards, an unbalanced aileron, with its centre of gravity behind the hinge line,

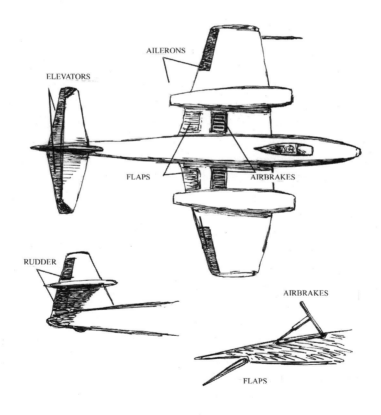

THE FLYING CONTROLS

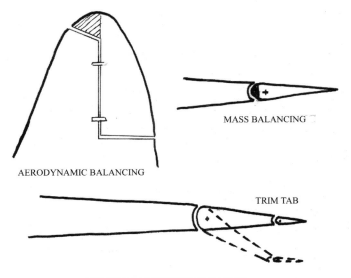

MASS BALANCING

AERODYNAMIC BALANCING

TRIM TAB

CONTROL BALANCING & TRIM TABS.

would lag slightly and so be deflected momentarily downwards as it followed the wing-tip upwards. As the wing-tip reached its elastic limit and started to flex downwards the aileron would again lag slightly and be deflected upwards. These movements would thus produce forces tending to augment and increase the flexing movements of the wing-tip. This sequence can produce the phenomenon of Flutter, and until its cause was understood aeroplanes have had their wings torn off when the flexing oscillations built up to the point when they exceeded the structural limits.

The cure is to incorporate a heavy mass in the nose of the aileron so that its centre of gravity is in front of its hinge line. This is Mass Balancing. With fully hydraulically powered controls aerodynamic balancing is no longer needed, but mass balancing still is.

The control in most continuous use is the elevator. This works exactly like a ship's rudder turned on its side through 90°. The pilot pushes the control column forward, the elevators, hinged to the back of the tail-plane, move down, the air flowing over them produces an upward force on the tail of the aeroplane, tilting the nose down.

If while flying straight and level a slight disturbance causes the nose to drop slightly the resulting dive causes the speed to increase. It is important that without intervention by the pilot the aeroplane now pitches slightly nose-up automatically restoring the original conditions. When this occurs the aeroplane is said to be longitudinally stable. This is achieved by careful design of the tail-plane and elevators. The aeroplane will also have been designed to be directionally and laterally stable. Stability is a very complex subject as introducing stability on one plane can bring with it other undesirable characteristics.

The odd configuration of the Phantom, with the marked negative dihedral of its tail-plane and its cranked wings is the result of a long, complicated story which eventually arrived at satisfactory stability.

The Centre of Lift from the wings and the Centre of Gravity of the aeroplane are very close together. However as fuel is used up, passengers and crew members move around, the centre of gravity moves. In addition, at different speeds and hence different angles of attack the centre of lift moves too. To keep the aeroplane in trim and to

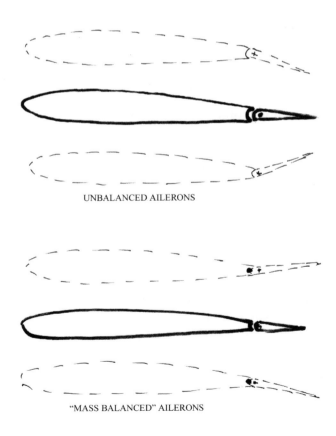

UNBALANCED AILERONS

"MASS BALANCED" AILERONS

maintain level flight the elevators have to be almost continuously adjusted. If the pilot had to keep consciously doing this it would become immensely tiring and irksome, and so small trim tabs are attached to the elevators which can be adjusted to hold the elevators automatically in the new desired position. One of the secrets of smooth flying is frequent use of the trimmers which allows the aeroplane to be flown virtually hands off. Similar tabs are also fitted to the rudder and ailerons.

All modern high performance aeroplanes have hydraulically powered controls at least for the elevator and ailerons. (The Hunter's and Lighting's rudders are "manual" or rather foot operated.) Hydraulic oil pressure is provided by the engine and the pilot's controls move valves in the hydraulic jacks which in turn move the elevator and ailerons. The question then arises of what is to be done if engine power is lost. The aeroplane may be able to glide perfectly well, and for long distances, if it can be controlled. On single-engine types the loss of hydraulic power causes the valves in the jacks to freeze, effectively locking the jack body to the control rods. The pilot is then able to move the jacks and hence the controls by manual effort. The controls are heavy, but perfectly manageable and allow a safe recovery and landing. On multi-engine types each engine is able to provide hydraulic power and so the loss of one engine is no problem.

An interesting problem with the powered elevator controls occurred during the development of the Folland Gnat. It was found that lowering the wheels and flaps each produced nose down trim changes. Due to its short fuselage length the elevators did not have much leverage or turning moment about the centre of gravity to control this and hence large up-elevator movements were needed for the approach and landing. Had the elevators had a one-to-one link to the control column throughout their movement, this would have resulted in serious over-sensitivity at high speed, with the wheels and flaps raised and the stick at the forward end of its travel. The link was therefore fitted with a cam, which gave reduced elevator/stick gearing at high speed, to prevent over-sensitivity, and much greater gearing at low speed and at the rearward end of its travel.

But now a further problem was encountered. On the final approach to land and perhaps meeting turbulence and wind gusts a pilot instinctively makes fairly large, coarse stick movements. On the final approach the engine will of course be throttled back to idling and hence the output from the hydraulic pump will be at a minimum. In the Gnat it was found that the large elevator movements being demanded during the final approach could outstrip the hydraulic oil supply from the engine-driven pump giving a most alarming feeling that the elevators had momentarily frozen. The first pilot to encounter this condition said that he at first thought that something had got jammed between his seat and the stick preventing its backwards movement. The problem was overcome by fitting a spring-loaded resistance to the stick which still allowed but discouraged its full backwards movement.

In transonic and supersonic types the changes in longitudinal trim around Mach 1, for reasons explained below, may be very large. Even with hydraulically powered controls they may be more than a conventional elevator can cope with. To solve this, the "fully flying" tail-plane was introduced. Here the trimmer moves not a tab but the whole tail-plane to a new angle of incidence.

## The Cockpit

Anyone peering for the first time into an aeroplane cockpit, especially a high performance type, is usually appalled by the mass of instruments and dials facing the pilot. It is hard to persuade them that with familiarity these become no more daunting than those on the family car. In a well-designed cockpit the instruments are grouped into logical clusters, each dealing with some specific aspect of the aeroplane, its engine, its flying controls, navigation aids and so on. The most important group of instruments is the set of six in the centre, often surrounded by a white line to help them stand out, known as the Blind Flying panel.

In the earliest days of aviation some reckoned that with experience pilots would be able to learn to fly blind, at night or in cloud when they couldn't see the ground or the horizon, by a natural sense of balance. It took some time to show that flying "by the seat of the pants," alert to the wind in your face and the changing direction and strength of the force of gravity was not only risky but could be shown scientifically to be impossible. All student pilots have to learn to disregard physical sensations of rolling or accelerating, which although dangerously misleading can be extremely powerful, and to rely instead on the instruments of the blind flying panel. We have all from time to time suffered from "the leans."

The blind flying panel consists of the Altimeter, the Airspeed Indicator, the Climb and Descent Indicator, the Compass, the Turn and Slip and the Artificial Horizon. Some are in principle simplicity itself. Inside the altimeter is a flexible box containing almost a vacuum, linked very sensitively to a set of hands on the dial, like those on a clock. On the ground the pressure of the atmosphere holds the flexible box squashed almost flat and the hands point to zero. As you climb up, the air pressure gets less, the box starts to expand and the hands move round the dial. There is a knob on the instrument so that you can set it for the existing air pressure and to show either your height above an airfield or above sea level, whichever you wish.

The airspeed indicator is only slightly more complicated. In this case the flexible box, or capsule, is connected to a small tube, the Pitot Tube, pointing out the front of the aeroplane facing straight into the air-stream. The faster you go, the harder the air blows into the tube and the further round the dial goes the pointer. Another tube from the case of the instrument is connected to a side opening to allow for the change of pressure as you climb.

In the climb and descent indicator an otherwise airtight capsule has a small hole in it and a gadget to sense if the air is going in or coming out. As you climb, the air pressure around you is reduced, the air blows out of the hole in the capsule and the dial shows a climb, as you descend the air blows into the hole and the dial shows a descent.

The compass is often quite complicated. The actual unit sensing the earth's magnetic field is put, perhaps in a wing tip, but somewhere well away from all the electrical and magnetic influences of the aeroplane itself. The dial on the blind flying panel itself is just a repeater.

The turn and slip, otherwise known as the needle and ball, is in two parts. The needle of the turn and slip is connected to a gyroscope. We have all been shown in fifth- form science lessons that a gyroscope tends to point always in the same direction and resists any attempt to turn it. The harder you turn the aeroplane the more the gyro resists and the further the needle moves across the scale showing the rate of turn. The ball is just a curved and inverted spirit level. The ball should always stay in the middle of the tube and will only stray if you do not have your wings level or if in a turn you are allowing the aeroplane to slip in (too much bank) or to skid out (not enough bank). In an aeroplane, just as on a motor-bike, for any radius of turn there is an appropriate angle of bank. None of these instruments can exactly be regarded as rocket science.

The last instrument of these six, the most complicated and the most useful, is the artificial horizon. It functions exactly as its name suggests. In the centre of the glass, attached to the case of the instrument, is a small silhouette of an aeroplane seen from behind, as if it were flying along in front of you. Beyond it is a white bar which is cleverly kept parallel to the real horizon. If you now bank the aeroplane over to the left, the instrument panel, the instrument and the little silhouette all bank to the left too. But the white horizon bar stays level, really level, parallel with the actual ground, so that you can see, even in thick cloud, exactly what is happening. Equally if you raise the nose the bar goes down below the silhouette and again you can see what is happening just as well as if you could actually see the ground. The artificial horizon is in fact so realistic that you come to rely on it too much. What are you going to do on the day it develops some fault? To prepare for that it is essential that you periodically practise some "limited panel," that is you put a cover over the artificial horizon and fly blind on just the primary instruments. It is much more difficult.

A limitation of the artificial horizon is that it can be toppled. The core if the instrument is a gyro and some delicately balanced pendulums controlling small air jets which kept the gyro always upright. At large angles of pitch or roll the mechanism reached the limits of its travel and hit the stops. To overcome this, a very sophisticated replacement was designed the core of which was a large Master Reference Gyro (the MRG) in gimbals with freedom to move through 360° in any direction. On the instrument panel in place of the original

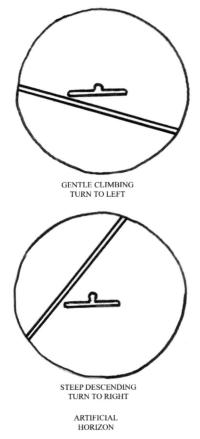

GENTLE CLIMBING
TURN TO LEFT

STEEP DESCENDING
TURN TO RIGHT

ARTIFICIAL
HORIZON

391

self-contained artificial horizon was a roller-blind, coloured black to represent the ground and white the sky, which was also able to rotate through 360° and which sensed the movements of the MRG. Instead of just the simple horizon bar which during a loop got to the bottom of the display and them toppled, the instrument blind scrolled on down. When you were pointing vertically upwards the zenith star appeared and eventually when you were pointing vertically down the nadir star.

This was all a great advance, but for some reason the original small aeroplane silhouette against which you could assess the movements of the horizon was replaced by just a round blob. When flying on instruments you need to keep your eyes moving around a continuous scan of the whole blind flying panel. To assess angles of bank on the new roller-blind horizon you now needed to scan not just the central blob but also a pointer which moved against a scale at the bottom of the instrument. Someone complained soon after we first saw it, "How on earth can you decide which way up is a full stop?" The solution was simple if crude. On climbing into the aeroplane you got out a wax pencil and drew in the missing silhouette! It seemed a strange omission on an instrument system which must have cost millions to design and develop and was sadly one of many examples of poor communications between instrument designers and boffins in general and the pilots who were actually going to use the kit.

For jets, due to their high performance, especially at height, there is one more flight instrument, the Machmeter. Instead of reading in miles or kilometres per hour or knots this instrument displays the speed as a decimal part of the local speed of sound, for example .65 or .9 if you are sub-sonic or 1.2 or 1.6 if you are super-sonic. The speed of sound is significant because it profoundly affects the way in which the air flows past the aeroplane and hence how the aeroplane behaves. It is therefore important to know the flight Mach Number. The speed of sound in air depends on the air temperature, so the local speed of sound means the speed of sound at the height and at the air temperature where you happen to be. In fact the speed of sound at sea level and at, say 40,000 ft does not vary all that much and there is also a rather lucky co-incidence in that speed of sound—Mach 1—at any height is roughly 10 miles a minute. This is very handy for navigational calculations, as Mach .8 is roughly 8 miles a minute and so on.

Why can't the normal airspeed indicator also be used for navigational purposes? As we climb the air gets thinner and for any given true speed the pressure of the air blowing into the front of the Pitot tube gets progressively less. Thus the indicated air speed (IAS) will only be equivalent to the true airspeed (TAS) at sea level. At height the IAS may be reduced to less that half the TAS, but in spite of this it is still a useful thing to know. Apart from the effects of compressibility, which become significant as you approach the speed of sound, the aeroplane behaves in the same way at the same IAS at any height. For example, if the stalling speed is 150 kts at sea level it will also be 150 kts IAS at height, even though the actual speed over the ground may be more than 300 kts.

The next group of instruments is for the engine and are similar to those in any well-instrumented car. There is a tachometer or rev counter, an oil pressure and possibly an oil temperature gauge. As any driver knows, loss of oil is soon going to be catastrophic and the sooner you know about it the better. Because aero engines are often operating at very high power, depending on whether it is a piston engine or a jet, there is a cylinder head or jet-pipe temperature gauge. High performance engines must not be allowed to overheat so it is important to keep an eye on these temperatures too. On a multi-engine aeroplane there will be this set of instruments for each engine, which is one thing which makes the cockpit display look more complicated than it really is.

The rest of the indicators and dials tell the pilot about various systems around the aeroplane such as the fuel contents, the electrical system, navigation kit, the weapons, the oxygen supply and, important when you are about to land, whether the undercarriage is up or down.

If you think of the average car and house and add up all the indicators for the central heating, the oven, the washing machine and the video recorder on the television, to say nothing these days of the PC and the mobile phone, then the aeroplane begins to seem quite simple by comparison. The difference is that the pilot needs to have all the information brought to him in one place, and this is what makes the initial impression so daunting.

The aircraft controls—the tits and knobs and levers and switches—also at first sight seem complicated. That is until you remember that you are not going to have to operate them all at once, just as you are hardly likely to be trying to change gear in the car at the same time as you dial up a number on your telephone, select the wash cycle on the washing machine and set the TV video recorder.

The throttle is the equivalent of the car's accelerator. In a car the engine can be kept operating at around its most efficient revs by changing gear. In most piston-engine aeroplanes the same effect is achieved by altering the pitch of the propeller blades, except in the simplest which have fixed pitch propellers. The aeroplane has the advantage in that instead of needing a heavy complicated gearbox, it has a Constant Speed Unit. This consists of a couple of small weights attached to the propeller which work like the old-fashioned governor on a primitive steam engine. You select the revs you want and the CSU automatically adjusts the pitch of the propeller to maintain these regardless of throttle movements or changes in the aeroplane's forward speed.

Among the other cockpit controls the purpose of the undercarriage selector is obvious and an indicator shows whether the wheels are locked down—green lights, unlocked (moving up or down)—red lights, or locked up—all lights out. Because this is such a vital indicator the lights are all duplicated. Near the undercarriage lever is the flap selector. Sometimes too near, as instances have occurred of the wheels being raised after landing instead of the flaps. The flaps, not to be confused with the ailerons which control the aeroplane in roll, serve three purposes. They increase the camber, and sometimes the area too, of the wings, allowing a slower approach to landing to be made, as the new wing shape generates more lift for a given speed. The flaps also increase the drag allowing a higher power setting on the approach and so a quicker engine response. And thirdly they increase the effective angle of attack of the wings allowing a more nose down, or at least less nose up, attitude and improving the forward view from the cockpit.

When the throttle of a piston engine is closed the propeller creates much drag and the speed falls off immediately. An idling jet engine creates very little drag and some other means is needed to reduce speed. Airbrakes consist of some drag-creating device which can be extended into the air-stream. On most jets of my era such as the Hunter, Meteor and Vampire the air-brakes were either in or out but on the Javelin they could be inched out progressively.

## Aero-engines

The simplest aero engine during my era was the four-stroke piston engine driving a two-bladed fixed-pitch propeller on the Tiger Moth, Oxford and Chipmunk. A fixed- pitch propeller has a relatively limited speed range. The blades must be set at a sufficiently fine angle so that they are not stalled when the aeroplane is stationary. This then limits the top speed because at speed their angle of attack soon approaches zero. Variable pitch propellers allow them to operate effectively over a wide range of speeds. Fine pitch was selected for take-off and power at slow speed, and coarse pitch for low revs and economy at cruising speed.

In some special cases fixed-pitch propellers had the blades set at a much coarser angle in order to obtain the highest possible top speed. The propellers of the seaplanes which won the Schneider Trophy outright for Britain were one example of this. It was accepted that at the start of their take-off run the propeller blades were fully stalled. The propeller turned clockwise and as the seaplane initially slowly gathered speed, the torque produced by the engine tended to dig the left float into the water (Newton's equal and opposite reaction) and to make the aeroplane turn to the left. To make matters worse the wash from the propeller, spiralling back clockwise round the fuselage struck the fin on the left side also tending to turn the aeroplane to the left. The take-off was started at right angles to the wind direction and the pilot held on full right rudder. Even so the aeroplane turned relentlessly left against the rudder until as the speed built up, the propeller blades unstalled, the floats started to plane, the rudder became more effective and proper control was achieved by the time that the seaplane was heading into wind for the actual take-off. Just for good measure, to achieve minimum drag the pilot was seated right behind the engine and had no forward facing windscreen and so no forward view, only to each side and above.

Radial engines could be air cooled but in-line engines, allowing a more streamlined profile, soon had to be liquid cooled. Engine power steadily increased with more cylinders and supercharging and propellers had to be developed to absorb the extra power. Three-, four-, and five- bladed propellers were produced, but this proved to be the limit as each blade was now following closely in the wake of the preceding one. Finally the engines of aircraft such as the Shackleton each had two three-bladed contra-rotating propellers, with all the necessary complications involved. The propeller engine had reached the limit of its potential.

A jet engine has in principle just one moving part, a central shaft carrying the impellor at the front and, to drive it, the turbine at the back to extract power from the jet. Actually there are many other moving parts, to drive fuel and hydraulic pumps, electrical generators and so on but they do not affect the basic principle. The revs and power output are controlled by metering the amount of fuel fed into the flame tubes. The power can be greatly increased by using re-heat or afterburning. Here extra fuel is fed into the jet pipe and burned there, dramatically raising the temperature of the jet and hence its velocity. Re-heat is effective but very expensive in fuel and can only be used for short periods.

The early jet engines such as the Rolls Royce Derwent and the de Havilland Goblin and Ghost had centrifugal-flow compressors. They

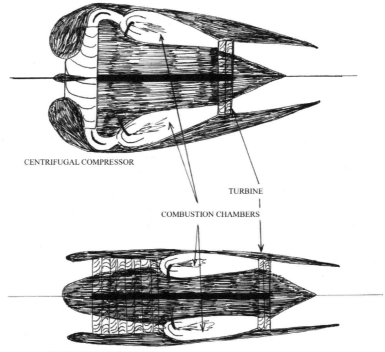

CENTRIFUGAL COMPRESSOR

TURBINE

COMBUSTION CHAMBERS

4 STAGE AXIAL COMPPRESSOR

operated rather like a hair-drier in that a flat disk fitted with flanges flung the air out radially by centrifugal force and the air had then to be turned back parallel to the engine's axis into the flame tubes. While the centrifugal compressor was simple and robust, a large, flat disk mounted at right angles to the airflow was not the ideal shape around which to design an engine while the compression ratios which could be achieved were strictly limited. The axial-flow compressor is now universal. It consists of many stages of alternate fixed and rotating blades, it has an ideal profile and much higher compression ratios can be achieved.

One major challenge in aircraft design is to obtain adequate flexibility. For example, for very high speed flight only very small wings are needed. But how, then, are you going to land? The swing-wing is one answer and some sort of compromise is invariably needed. The Hunter's engine air intakes are small, of optimum forward area for high speed and in order to let the engine breathe adequately at low speed there are above and below the normal intakes a pair of "letter boxes," whose covers are spring loaded to remain shut but which are able to open inwards when needed. The Harrier, which needs to develop full power in the hover with zero forward speed, is an extreme example and around each intake is a whole row of letter-boxes.

## Aerobatics

Aerobatics are fun but their actual purpose is to provide experience in handling the aeroplane to its limits and in any unusual attitude that it may get into. The loop is the simplest. It is effected by diving to gain speed if necessary and then by pulling steadily back on the stick, checking all the way round that the wings are level, up past the vertical, over the top, out of the dive and back to level flight. Left to itself the aeroplane, as it loses speed over the top, will fly round a tall, narrow shape instead of a proper circle, so it is necessary to ease off the backward pressure on the stick over the top and it is usually desirable to close the throttle over the top too, to prevent excessive speed building up on the way down. If the loop is done accurately there is a slight bump on the way down as you fly through the turbulent wake you have just created on the way up.

The barrel roll is started by diving down and then as you pull up starting to roll steadily to one side so that you fly round a spiral like one

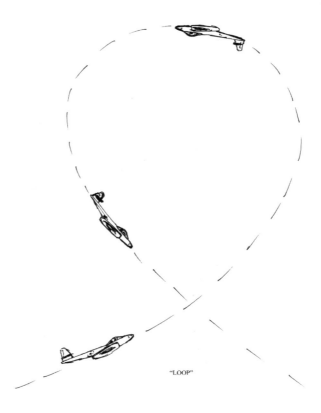

"LOOP"

turn of a corkscrew. As the nose is pointing up at its steepest angle the wings should be vertical and as the nose passes down through the horizon the aeroplane should be exactly inverted with the wings level. The wings should be vertical once more as the nose is pointing most steeply down and as the nose comes back to the horizon the aeroplane should be straight and level. The barrel roll is a comfortable manoeuvre as it entails much less positive "g" than the loop—and no negative "g."

The slow roll is more challenging. As there is going to be negative "g" during the manoeuvre it is important to have your straps tight, no loose objects around the cockpit and to be wearing goggles as all the dust and bits are going to float up off the cockpit floor. In the slow roll the intention is to keep flying along in a straight line while rolling through 360°. A completely accurate slow roll is not possible as when the wings are vertical there is nothing to counter the weight and the flight-path will inevitably start to curve downwards. The technique is to raise the nose slightly and then to start rolling in the desired direction.

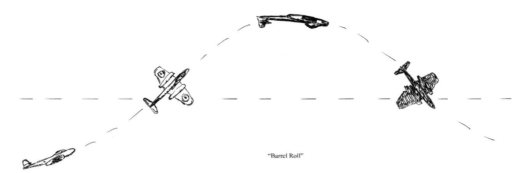

"Barrel Roll"

As the bank comes on you apply progressive amounts of top rudder to hold the nose up, to a maximum when the wings are vertical and then decreasing as you roll inverted.

As the wings pass the vertical you move the stick forward as for the next 180° of the roll the wings are acting in reverse and producing lift from what is usually their bottom surface. This is the uncomfortable bit, you are hanging in your straps, and in a piston engine aeroplane unless the carburettor has been modified the engine will cut. You close the throttle so that it does not restart with a bang, keep the stick forward, keep on a steady rate of roll and feed on the new top rudder for the second half of the roll. As the wings pass the vertical you bring the stick back and as the wings come level take off the top rudder. It is a manoeuvre which requires smooth co-ordination of the stick, the rudder pedals and the throttle and takes much practice.

The stall turn is not stressful and very satisfying when you get it right. From straight and level flight, at a moderate speed and power setting, you pull up into the first stage of loop but only as far as the vertical. You check at the vertical pushing the stick forward to give the wings zero angle of attack and to ensure that they are producing neither positive nor negative lift. The critical moment to judge is when to feed on

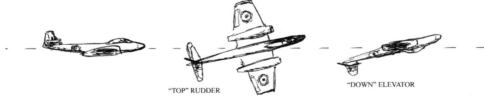

"TOP" RUDDER                    "DOWN" ELEVATOR

"SLOW" ROLL

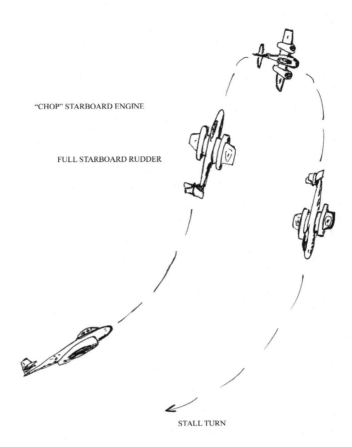

"CHOP" STARBOARD ENGINE

FULL STARBOARD RUDDER

STALL TURN

rudder in the direction in which you want to turn. Feed it on too soon and the aeroplane skids awkwardly upwards, probably starting to pitch nose up or nose down. Leave it too late and it has no effect leaving you still pointing skywards but fresh out of airspeed and ideas and the aeroplane flops over in any direction it chooses. However if you get it right the aeroplane, just as it stops moving upwards, cartwheels over through 180° and points vertically downwards. You catch the yaw with rudder and ease out of the dive.

The stall turn was a favourite manoeuvre in the twin engine Meteor. Although it is not possible to apply instant power from idling with a jet, it is possible instantly to cut the power. You went into the manoeuvre with a fair amount of power from the engines and then at the crucial instant you closed one throttle, allowing the suddenly asymmetric thrust to get the yaw started, closing the other throttle as you cartwheeled round. One or two famous aerobatic pilots perfected the technique of getting the Meteor yawing round so well that they could complete another full 360° before diving way.

Aerobatic displays are made up by linking together a series of the basic manoeuvres and variations of them. Some of the variations are, for example, a half-roll off the top of a loop, or a hesitation roll where you pause after each 90° or even each 45° of the roll. This was easiest with powered ailerons as very positive control inputs are needed if the manoeuvre is going to look crisp.

## Ejection Seats

In the Spitfires and Hurricanes of the Second World War, pilots who had to abandon their aeroplane often met considerable difficulty in doing so. As speeds increased this problem could only get worse and some mechanical means was needed to help. The Martin Baker Company soon became and remain the world leaders in designing an ever more sophisticated series of ejection seats. The seat is mounted on vertical rails and incorporates in its back what is in effect the barrel of a gun in which the piston is fixed to the floor of the cockpit. When a cartridge is fired, the locks holding the seat in position are released, the barrel is driven up it taking the seat with it and throwing it clear of the aircraft. A small drogue is streamed to stabilise the seat and to prevent it tumbling. In the first "manual" seats the pilot had, once clear of the aircraft, to release his seat harness, push himself clear of the seat and then pull his rip-cord to open his parachute.

At low level he might not have sufficient height to do this and so Martin Baker immediately went on to design the "fully automatic" seat. The seat was again thrown clear of the aeroplane but then the seat harness was automatically released, the pilot was tipped out of the seat and the parachute operated without requiring any further action on his part. By carrying out many tests with dummies it was found that a number of safety devices needed to be incorporated. The pilot operates the seat by reaching up over his head with both hands and pulling down a stout canvas blind. By having to do this it is ensured that the blind covers his face and his forearms cover his torso providing good protection when he clears the cockpit and meets the air-stream. When the seat is fired the first immediate effect is that the transparent but very

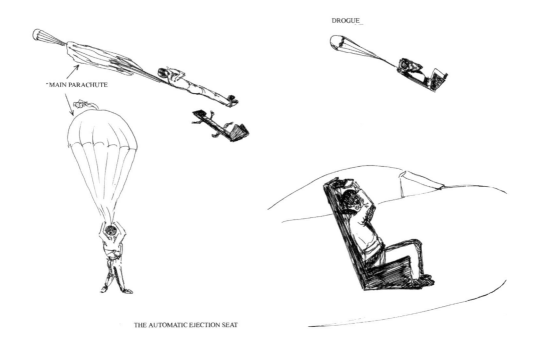

DROGUE

MAIN PARACHUTE

THE AUTOMATIC EJECTION SEAT

strong cockpit canopy is jettisoned so that the seat does not have to punch through it. One second later the seat fires.

The seat has to be shot high enough for it to clear the aircraft's tail even at high speed and if the aeroplane is pulling "g." On the other hand when the cartridge fires the initial acceleration up the rails inevitably imposes considerable compression stress on the pilot's spine and there is a limit to how much acceleration can be tolerated. To accommodate these two requirements later seats had a series of cartridges. Only one fired initially and then, as the barrel moved up, further cartridges were exposed and fired in succession. Also a second sleeve was fitted around the piston which moved up with the barrel, like an opening telescope and allowing the acceleration to be carried further on up. The automatic seats then had to be prevented from tipping the pilot out and opening his parachute prematurely, for example at high altitude or at such a high speed that the parachute would have been ripped apart by the air-stream. A barometric capsule was fitted which only allowed the seat to operate below a certain altitude, and above this the pilot would have ridden the seat, with its own small oxygen supply, rapidly down through the freezing, oxygen-lacking higher altitudes to a more benign height. An accelerometer also ensured that the seat, decelerated by its drogue, had slowed enough before it operated the parachute. In high-speed ejections it was found that injuries could be sustained by the pilot's legs being flailed in the air-stream. Garters were worn and leg restraint chords threaded through them while strapping in.

A continuous series of improvements allowed the seats to be used safely at lower and lower altitudes and a later development was produced for the Harrier which could even be used at zero forward speed, that is in the hover. This utilised rockets to throw the seat out and up and to give it enough height to allow the parachute to open.

## Contrails and Streamers

The vivid white contrails created by high-flying aeroplanes are a familiar sight. At all altitudes the atmosphere contains water vapour. When the relative humidity reaches 100% this vapour condenses out into water droplets and forms visible clouds. At some high altitudes the air may be very close to 100% humidity. One of the normal waste products of any internal combustion engine is water vapour and on occasions this extra amount left behind in the exhaust gasses from the engines is enough to raise the local relative humidity to 100% and so form the condensation trail or contrail. Depending on the ambient conditions the trails may soon evaporate and disappear or may remain for long periods.

Streamers are a much smaller-scale effect. As has been described, an aeroplane's wings, in the process of creating lift, have an area of marked low pressure over their top surface and a less marked area of high pressure under the bottom surface. Naturally the air will tend to escape round the wing tip, moving from the high pressure area to the low pressure area. Thus viewed from behind there will be at the left-hand wing tip a clockwise vortex and at the right-hand wing tip an anti-clockwise vortex. A characteristic of any vortex (such as a weather cyclone or, as an extreme case, a tornado) is that its core is a region of extremely low pressure. The low pressure core of a wing-tip vortex may be intense enough to lower the ambient pressure and hence the temperature of the air in it to the point where the water vapour condenses out and forms a visible filament or streamer. The effect is particularly marked when the aeroplane has sharply pointed wing tips and is pulling "g." Similar streamers can also occasionally fleetingly be seen, especially on wet days, forming at the end of the "wings" of Grand Prix racing cars.

## Helicopters

The first successful rotary-wing aircraft were autogyros. As the name implies the rotating blades which provide the lift are driven round automatically by the airflow, generated by the autogyro's forward speed, and the energy for this is provided by a conventional horizontally-facing engine and propeller. An example of a small, modern autogyro is provided by "Little Nelly" as used by James Bond in the film "You Only Live Twice." It may be recalled that Bond needed to reach up to start the rotor spinning by hand and required a short run to gain speed before he could take off.

In a true helicopter the lift-generating rotor disk is driven directly by the engine and thus the lift is not dependent on forward speed. It is this ability to hover stationary that gives the helicopter its unique usefulness in so many roles. Compared to a conventional fixed-wing aeroplane the helicopter's control system is more complicated and, although some automation has been developed, fixed-wing pilots still need considerable extra training to master it.

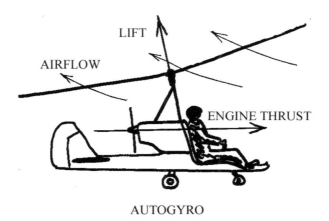

AUTOGYRO

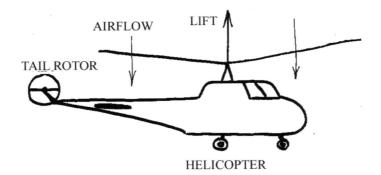

AIRFLOW    LIFT

TAIL ROTOR

HELICOPTER

The helicopter engine powers the rotor blades, its torque maintaining their rotational speed against the aerodynamic drag on them. But in doing so the engine also imparts a torque in the opposite direction (Newton's equal and opposite reaction) on the helicopter's body. This has to be counterbalanced by the thrust force from the small tail rotor.

The tail rotor is geared to the main rotor shaft so that any changes in main rotor speed are matched by the tail rotor, thus minimising the need for alterations in it pitch setting.

In the hover the rotor generates lift vertically upwards exactly balancing the weight. The helicopter is manoeuvred by tilting the rotor disk. To move forward the disk is tilted forward and some of the lift force is directed horizontally. As the total lift has increased the throttle must be opened to generate more power. The increased torque then has to be balanced by altering the pitch (the angle of attack of the blades) of the tail rotor.

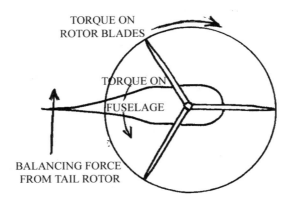

TORQUE ON
ROTOR BLADES

TORQUE ON
FUSELAGE

BALANCING FORCE
FROM TAIL ROTOR

The pilot's flying controls consist of firstly, for his right hand, the Cyclic control. This is equivalent to the fixed-wing aeroplane's control column and works in the same sense. Moving the cyclic control forward operates through a linkage in the rotor head to reduce the angle of attack of the forward-going blade and increase that of the retreating blade. The forward-going blade therefore flies slightly downward, the retreating blade flies slightly upward and hence the disk is tilted forwards. The cyclic stick operates laterally as well and so it can therefore be thought of as controlling the direction of the lift force, tilting it fore or aft, left or right as required.

For the pilot's left hand is the Collective lever. This is positioned beside the pilot's seat rather like the hand-brake in many cars. It is used to alter the angle of attack of the whole rotor and also incorporates the throttle control. To increase the lift produced by the rotor the lever is raised and simultaneously, to open the throttle, as more power is going to be needed, the hand-grip is rotated, like on a motor-bike but in the opposite sense. As the collective lever is raised it is a natural movement to roll the wrist outwards. Finally the pilot's rudder pedals control the angle of attack of the tail rotor, allowing the helicopter to be yawed (steered) by increasing or reducing its thrust.

It may be noted that the rotor blades are kept out close to the horizontal plane simply by their centrifugal force and if revs are lost too far there is nothing stopping them from collapsing upwards into a cone. In early helicopters a very close watch had to be kept on maintaining the engine and rotor revs within a very narrow range. Too few revs invited the danger of coning and too many revs imposed too much tensile stress on the rotor head. Most modern helicopters dispense with a pilot's throttle control, the engine power setting being adjusted automatically to maintain the right revs.

For the equivalent of the circuits and bumps phase of a fixed-wing pilot's training the novice helicopter pilot practises spot turns. The aim of the exercise is to maintain a hover at constant height over a chosen spot on the ground while turning at a steady rate through 360°. If there is any wind this is not as simple as it might appear. The exercise may be started by heading straight into wind and so flying slowly forwards through the air to counter the wind speed and to remain stationary over the ground. As the helicopter is turned out of wind the forward speed must be reduced, eventually to zero. As the wind starts to come from one side the helicopter must be flown to the side, and eventually as it turns its back to the wind it must be flown backward and so on to complete the circle. To achieve this while maintaining a smooth rate of turn and constant height requires very close concentration.

Whereas a fixed-wing aeroplane, losing engine power, is able to glide quite satisfactorily down to a forced landing, the loss of power in a helicopter presents a more demanding problem. While the helicopter cannot glide in the normal sense, it can descend under control if, when power is lost, the angle of attack of the rotor blades is very promptly reduced, by lowering the collective lever, to allow the rotor to act as an autogyro. Considerable height is lost in achieving this but then the helicopter can continue to descend, using the potential energy of its height to maintain the rotor revs. As the ground is approached the kinetic energy now stored in the rotor may be used to affect a flare and to reduce the rate of descent and allow a safe landing to be made. The kinetic energy of the rotor can only be used like this once, and the rotor energy having been used up in this way there is no second chance. Very precise judgment is needed to carry out a successful engine-off helicopter landing.

## The Speed of Sound

The significance of the speed of sound is that this is the speed at which any disturbance or pressure wave travels through the air. Sound itself is, of course, a succession of such small pressure waves and being the most familiar manifestation of them has given its name to the whole phenomenon. At or near this speed the pattern of the air flowing over the aeroplane changes radically. The most significant of these changes is the way the air flows over the wings.

As we have seen, the air flowing over the top surface of an aeroplane wing accelerates. When the actual speed of the aeroplane is Mach 0.9 or even Mach 0.85 it may locally, over the wings, reach the speed of sound or Mach 1.

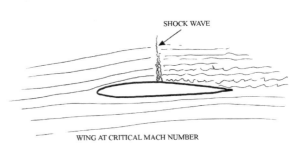

SHOCK WAVE

WING AT CRITICAL MACH NUMBER

The point at which this happens is known as the Critical Mach Number, 'Mcrit'. Once Mcrit has been reached a shock wave forms perpendicular to the wing surface causing the air no longer to follow the curved surface of the wing but to separate from the surface and to become turbulent. The ailerons and the elevators can loose their effectiveness, there may be large movements of the centre of pressure while the turbulence causes buffeting and vibration. As the shock wave builds up there is a steep rise in drag and this is what causes the "Sound Barrier." A straight-wing type such as a Meteor even under full power and in a steep dive will never, because of the drag, exceed about Mach 0.88.

The appearance of much more powerful axial-flow jet engines led to the development of transonic types like the Hunter and Swift and eventually to truly supersonic ones such as the Lightning and Concorde. These incorporated much thinner wings and sweep-back. Thinner wings reduce the acceleration of the air over the top surface, so delaying Mcrit and sweep-back also raises Mcrit because it is the component of the air-stream perpendicular to the line of maximum camber of the wings which is important. The Hunter's wings are swept back at about 35°, those of the Lightning at 60°.

As the speed of sound—Mach 1—is reached the shock waves have built up, not so much like the waves of a ship but more like the wall of snow in front of a snowplough. Given the power to do so and very thin, usually highly swept, wings the aeroplane breaks through this into truly supersonic flight. The shock waves are now no longer perpendicular but slope back like the waves created by a speed-boat or as can be seen in the flash photographs of speeding bullets. The buffeting and

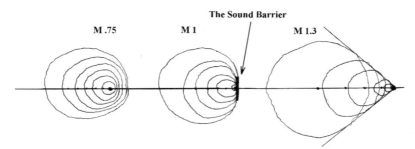

PRESSURE WAVES AT INCREASING MACH NUMBERS

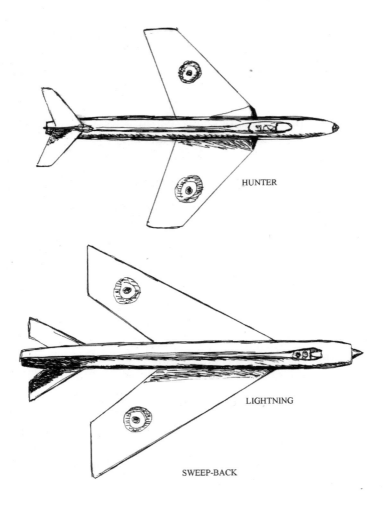

HUNTER

LIGHTNING

SWEEP-BACK

vibration of transonic flight are left behind and the main aerodynamic problem now is thermal heating, caused by the friction of the air on the aircraft's skin.

To reach such speeds the aircraft's design must have ensured that drag has been reduced to the very minimum, for example by the Concorde's extreme sweep-back and needle nose. These features, however, raise their own problems.

When the aeroplane slows down to land the marked sweep-back allows the Concorde's wings to reach a very large angle of attack without stalling but this then entails the complications of the drooping nose to provide adequate forward vision.

## The Way Ahead

Advances in aircraft design now seem to appear almost monthly. Their performance, in terms of their range, load-carrying ability, versatility, safety and relative cheapness have brought passenger flying almost to all. The fields of aeronautics and astronautics seem to be merging together. This makes it hard to remember that it is just over a hundred years since Orville and Wilbur, the bicycle engineers, first wobbled into the air that windy day at the sand dunes of Kitty Hawk for their memorable twelve-second flight, the first ever for a powered, heavier than air machine. By the time that I started flying less than fifty years after that, it was already a different world. Wing warping, rotary engines and Hucks starters had come and gone as had the great years of the biplane. I just experienced fabric covered airframes, Handle Page slats, open cockpits, swinging the prop to start the engine, and flying without radios. By my time the piston engine and the propeller had reached the peak of their development. The great excitement in my era was the leap forward in performance offered by the jet engine, hydraulically powered controls, pressurised cockpits and the first sorties into the stratosphere and beyond the speed of sound. Now however, many of the characteristics of aeroplanes and operating practices which are described above have also been superseded and in their turn have vanished from the scene.

The basic science and mechanics of aeroplanes does not change, but the way they are applied has moved on by the appearance of new more detailed knowledge, new materials but in particular by the enormous advances in electronics, the growing use of computers and all the other electronic gear such as that in head-up cockpit displays, satellite navigation systems and 'smart' weaponry. What has not changed is the care and dedication needed from all those concerned with flying and the special fascination and fun it affords them. But others must bring the story up to date and chart it on the way ahead.

\*     \*     \*

# Index

415

# *Index for Second Career*